FPCC
JAN 1 1 2000

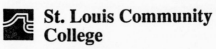

Jews and the American Slave Trade

Saul S. Friedman

Jews and the American Slave Trade

Transaction Publishers

New Brunswick (U.S.A.) and London (U.K.)

Library of Congress Catalog Number: 97-32532
ISBN: 1-56000-337-5
Printed in the United States of America

Library of Congress Cataloging-in-Publication Data

Friedman, Saul S., 1937–
    Jews and the American slave trade / Saul S. Friedman.
        p. cm.
    Includes bibliographical references and index.
    ISBN 1-56000-337-5 (alk. paper)
    1. Secret relationship between Blacks and Jews. 2. Slavery—History. 3. Jews—Social conditions. 4. Jewish slave traders—History. 5. Jewish slave traders—United States—History. I. Title.
E185.S44F75   1998
306.3'62'0973—dc21
                                                                97-32532
                                                                    CIP

For my sisters, Phyllis Friedman, Jeanne Friedman Young,
Raquelle Friedman Ross and Rosalind Friedman Black who have brought
wisdom, art, humor and compassion into this world.

"I've heard it said that the hottest lie's the best to tell."

—Plautus, *The Ghost*

Contents

Preface

This is not a text in American history, Jewish history, nor, for that matter, the history of slavery. Neither is it intended as an update of Robert Weisbord and Arthur Stern's excellent study of black-Jewish relations, *Bittersweet Encounter.* Rather it is intended as a response to a series of charges which have been widely circulated in the last several years. To wit: (a) that the shipment of millions of Africans to the New World was a black Holocaust; (b) the number of victims and suffering in American death marches and ghettos measured over a 400-year period dwarfs anything experienced by European Jews under Hitler; (c) chief among the villains responsible for these degradations throughout the colonial world and well into the antebellum period were Jews who have successfully managed to paint themselves as chronic victims; (d) Jews not only masterminded the slave trade, they continue to exploit American blacks to the present day. In its simplest form, the charge is that Jews were responsible for the slave trade to and in America. As Louis Farrakhan noted, while trying to explain away the rants of his lieutenant Khalid Abdul Muhammad in February 1994, Jews owned 75 percent of the slaves in the South on the eve of the Civil War.[1]

Such rhetoric has generated distress in the Jewish community as far afield as Youngstown, Atlanta and Boca Raton, especially since the publication of *The Secret Relationship between Blacks and Jews* by the Nation of Islam in 1992. Since then, two sources have responded to the charges: Harold Brackman, *Jew on the Brain: A Public Refutation of the Nation of Islam's Secret Relationship between Blacks and Jews,* and the Anti-Defamation League, *Jew-Hatred as History: An Analysis of the Nation of Islam's "The Secret Relationship between Blacks and Jews"* (1993). With a few exceptions, notably David Brion Davis of Yale, Seymour Drescher, and Eli Faber of John Jay College, most academics, aware that the accusations are baseless, have declined to make comment. Any response might dignify the charges, create a debate where none exists. It is a position similar to that taken by most academics who refuse to share a podium with Holocaust revisionists, the coterie of anti-Semites and anti-Zionists who deny that six million Jews were murdered by the Nazis. No rational person questions that fact. But as the last survivors die off and people's memories fail, there may be a greater tendency to dismiss the Holocaust as exaggeration. Reputable historians have no obigation to debate the Revisionists, but they must refute them, to remind the public that the extermination camps were real.

It is the same motivation that has prompted me to address the charge that Jews dominated the slave trade. I have been lecturing against this notion in history classes at Kent State and Youngstown State University for more than nine years. The incendiary appearances of Khalid Abdul Muhammad at Kean State, New Jersey in November 1993, at Howard University and the Holocaust Museum in Washington in March 1994, and the repeated jibes of Louis Farrakhan added the final impetus. Assisted by a Youngstown State University research grant, I made my first trip to the Deep South in the summer of 1993. In Charleston I worked in the records of the South Carolina Historical Society, the City Library of Charleston, and Temple Beth Elohim, the oldest Reform synagogue in America. I interviewed local historian Sol Breibart, Professor James Hagy of the University of Charleston (author of the major text on Jewish life in the city), an old colleague and expert on the South, Dr. Alvin Skardon, and Attorney Robert Rosen (author of an excellent general history of Charleston.) In Savannah I worked through documents in the Georgia Historical Society, interviewed Rabbi Sol Rubin (editor of the definitive history of Temple Mickvah Israel), attorney Warren Swartz and two authorities on black history, W.W. Law and Carroll Greene. Back in Columbia, I worked through materials in the South Carolina State Archives and the University of South Carolina library, and interviewed several local Jewish historians including Hyman Rubin. In Atlanta, I spent several days in the Georgia Historical Archives and the Archives of the Jewish Community Center. My research there was also assisted by Marc and Laura Connelly. In the summer of 1994, I was fortunate enough to be designated a Lowenstein-Weiner Fellow at Hebrew University College in Cincinnati where, with the assistance of Dr. Abraham Peck, I scrutinized documents, particularly the Rabbi Bertram Korn Archives, in the American Jewish Archives. During the summer of 1995, I made a third research trip to the East Coast. In New York City, I was aided by Susan Tolan, archivist of Shearith Israel, Steven Siegel of the New York Jewish Historical Society, John Celardo and Greg Plunges of the National Archives/Northeast Division, and librarians at the New York Historical Society, New

York University, and the Jewish and Manuscripts Divisions of the New York Public Library. I am also indebted to Laurie Alfieri of the Rhode Island Historical Society, as well as librarians at the Library of Congress in Washington, the Virginia Historical Society in Richmond, and the Maryland Historical Society in Baltimore, as well as research assistants from Youngstown State: Jim Guy, Carol Litty, Dirk Hermance, Mike Beverly, and Anne Heutsche. Laurence Mintz of Transaction Publishers did a superb job of editing the final manuscript. Special mention must be made of my wife Nancy and our son Jason who worked long hours alongside me in dusty archives, as well as editing this final manuscript.

Not surprisingly the research outlined in this book sustained what I had always suspected and what most people intuitively knew—Jews, whether on the continent of Europe, in West Indian and South American colonies, in the Old South played a small role in the slave trade. In the course of my research, however, I was troubled by two considerations. The first was the revelation that some of the most important heroes in American Jewish History—Francis Salvador, Judah Touro, Haym Salomon—had at one time either dabbled in the slave trade or owned slaves. How was I to treat this and other data detailing the slaving activities of Rhode Island merchant Aaron Lopez or the Davis family of Petersburg, Virginia? To publish such accounts might reinforce accusations of Jew-baiters. To withhold information would be disreputable. I have decided to publish whatever I have found, relying upon the good judgment of the reader to conclude whether a few exceptions prove the rule.

There is a second problem in dealing with a world more than a century removed from the slave marts of Charleston or Atlanta. Attitudes and behavior change over the course of time. What was acceptable, even desirable, in one era may later be scorned. Abortion once was unthinkable in most societies. Now it is part of U.N. recommended programs for population control. Capital punishment was once an accepted way of dealing with homicide. Today, it is rejected in many civilized areas. So, too, throughout history, and certainly in America, was slavery an accepted, if not approved, institution. Even in ancient times, people were troubled by the taking of another person's freedom. But it was done. As someone who has been criticized for applying current standards in judging the actions of people in the past, I now find myself asking how far do we go in applying contemporary morality in the reconstruction of history? In 1997 we say, of course slavery is wrong.

In 1997, we say of course it has always been wrong. But how can we judge the behavior of free blacks, as well as Jews, who yielded to the societal pressure and the lucrative lure of the "peculiar institution" more than a century ago?

I do not claim to have answers for all these questions. I anticipate criticism, even misrepresentation, of what I have written. Some may feel that I have given the editors of *Secret Relationship* an unwarranted platform for their views by devoting six pages in the opening chapter to a recitation and refutation of the contents of their book. I did so believing this may be the only opportunity for readers, who will never purchase or read *Secret Relationship*, to assess such arguments. Some may deem the chapters dealing with slavery in the ancient and medieval worlds superfluous. I believe them to be essential to an understanding of the institution, just as I believe it important to review traditional Jewish positions on slavery and the historic powerlessness of Jews. The choice of title (*Jews and the American Slave Trade*) and extent of coverage (French, Spanish, Portuguese, Dutch, Danish and English colonies in the Western Hemisphere) is deliberate since the authors of the *Secret Relationship* attack Jewish slave ownership not only in the United States, but also in the West Indies and South America. The astute reader will readily note the reasons for the popularity of this canard in the last three chapters of this book. I take responsibility for opinions and errors contained in this volume. It is my hope that other academics will publish their own responses. We shall only reinforce one another. The reader of this volume will note a repetition in my own arguments. For good reason. The repetition of a lie creates the illusion of truth. Yet the plain truth, sustained by fact, not myth, is that Jews did not dominate the slave trade in the European colonies of South America and the Caribbean or the ante-bellum South.

1

Handbook of Hate:
The Secret Relationship between Blacks and Jews

Teaching Anti-History

On July 20, 1991, Leonard Jeffries, professor of African-American studies at City University of New York, provoked angry responses from both Italians and Jews with a two-hour speech he delivered before the state-subsidized Black Arts and Cultural Festival in Albany. In his remarks, subsequently broadcast over cable television in New York, Jeffries charged (a) there was a conspiracy on the part of Hollywood producers to denigrate African people; (b) this conspiracy was a product of cooperation between the Mafia and Russian Jews bent on "the destruction of black people"; and (c) Jews were no strangers to domination and control of blacks since they had financed the slave trade. Jeffries was especially exercised about this last point, taunting that Jewish grandees and court favorites had done the handiwork of slaving for the Spanish, Portuguese, Dutch, Germans, and English. They were allegedly assisted in this enterprise by "their Jewish community brothers" who established the slave trade next to synagogues in Recife, Curaçao, and New Amsterdam, The partisan audience at Albany gave Jeffries a standing ovation.[1]

This was not the first time a black nationalist had come forward to heap the woes of his people at the doorstep of Jews. Marcus Garvey, the celebrated founder of the "back to Africa" movement, regularly used the editorial columns of his newspaper *Negro World* to flog "powerful" Jewish financiers whose goal was to submerge and destroy the black population of America. Whatever problems Jews experienced, said Garvey, had been brought upon themselves for…"Jews like money. They have always been after money. They want nothing else but money.

1

A Jew is always a Jew. His history has been one of selfishness. His greed has clouded his judgment."[2]

At least Garvey had the decency to denounce Adolf Hitler. Not so, some of his contemporaries. Visiting Harlem in the 1940s, Stephen Derounian (aka John Roy Carlson) listened as Arthur Reid, director of the African Progressive Business League, declared: "I like Hitler...Yeah, I like Hitler.... Let the White Man kill his brother white man. It'll leave fewer whites to bother with later—when the black man can step in and get justice for himself." When would that be? Two black youths volunteered: "Inside of five years you'll see the fighting goin' on in this country, man. I'll fight like I never fought before. There'll be race riots like they never was."

A crowd, gathered at the corner of 131st St. and Lennox Avenue, listened as a black woman shouted: "Do as Japan does. Copy like she does. She don't preach no social equality stuff. There ain't no such thing. She just walks in and takes what she wants. Be like her. Step up and take your freedom. Don't you believe all them things about brotherhood. There ain't no brotherhood for the colored man, except in his own kind. The white man can never do you no good." There was a more familiar refrain to the harangue offered by one Carlos Cook to a group at the corner of 116th Street: "Jews are all Communists and Communism wants to exploit the Negro just like the white man. I wouldn't lift my finger to save a Jew. We came here against our will. *They brought us here as slaves and they've treated us as slaves* [italics mine]. We owe nothing to America. America owes everything to us. This isn't my home and my culture and my name are in Africa." These were voices of despair, voices of anger, voices of hate. Astonishingly, these statements were uttered by young blacks in Harlem, not in 1968 or 1991, but in 1942, at a time when every Jew in the world was threatened with extermination by Adolf Hitler and the Nazis.[3]

What is especially distressing among the accusations of Professor Jeffries today and street radicals in Harlem in 1942 is the claim that Jews controlled the chattel slave trade in and about the Western Hemisphere. This hoary canard, repeated in the respectable chambers of black churches in Cleveland and Youngstown as well as on the stage of the Apollo Theater when Morton Downey, Jr. brought his travelling video circus to Harlem a few years ago, owes its revival to Nation of Islam spokesman Louis Farrakhan. Farrakhan, the former Louis Eugene Wolcott, a onetime calpyso singer from Bermuda, joined Elijah Muhammad's Nation of Islam in the early 1960s. Displaying a bent for oratory, Farrakhan denounced Malcolm X when the latter questioned the direction of the movement shortly before Malcolm's assassination in 1965. Thirteen years later, following the death of Elijah Muhammad, Farrakhan assumed a greater leadership role in the Nation of Islam and proceeded to outrage many Americans with his rhetoric that helped rupture the civil rights alliance between blacks and Jews. For Farrakhan, Adolf Hitler was a "great man," albeit a destructive one. Far worse were the Zionists who had conquered and persecuted the Palestinians. Or American Jews, who were admonished not to criticize Jesse Jackson after the onetime presidential candidate had referred to New York as "Hymietown." Jews in general followed a corrupt, "gutter religion." In 1984, Farrakhan gave an interview to the *Washington Post* in which he declared "a small clique of Jews" were responsible for "the ships that brought our fathers into slavery." For Farrakhan, his disciples and allies, the transatlantic slave trade was a human tragedy far outstripping the Jewish Holocaust. From Jeffries, Tony Martin of Wellesley and Farrakhan's lieutenant, the self-proclaimed "Doctor" Khalid Abdul Muhammad, came figures of 60, 100, even 600 million Africans slain in the overall operations of African slavery. And much of it could be blamed upon Jews.

To validate these charges, the Nation of Islam assigned its "Historical Research Department" to document Jewish involvement in the slave trade. Actually a group of graduate students from the Boston area, the Research Department published volume one of *The Secret Relationship between Blacks and Jews* in 1991 (suggesting that further volumes were to follow). A slick paper publication, laced with tables and charts appealling to a mass audience, *The Secret Relationship* contains citations from prominent American Jewish academics (e.g., Jacob Marcus, Salo Baron, Leonard Fein, Leonard Dinnerstein, Bertram Korn, Marc Raphael, Henry Feingold, and Jonathan Sarna). Readers who desired more information were invited to call a toll-free number—1-800-48 Truth.

Far from serving as a useful tool of research, *The Secret Relationship* violates the basic canons of historical methodology. Designed to capitalize on the victimization of two peoples, it may properly be termed a handbook of anti-history. Instead of attempting a thoughtful study of black-Jewish relations, the editors have indulged in (a) distortion; (b) exaggeration; (c) emendation; (d) use of ben trovato (made-up tales); (e) prevarication; (d) misquoting sources; (d) citing shaky sources; and (e) citing no sources.[4]

A common (and obvious) failing of pseudo-scholarship is to take the words of an author out of context. Thus, in the *Secret Relationship* the name of Jonathan Sarna is invoked to suggest "there is 'much evidence' to show that many Jews decided to remain loyal to the crown in the American Revolution" (p. 17), that of Marc Raphael to suggest that the slave trade was "a major feature of Jewish economic life" in Surinam (p. 36), that of Judith Elkin cited to prove thirteen Portuguese Jews managed to build up the trade of Buenos Aires through the illegal import of West African slaves (p. 83) and that of Henry Feingold, utilized in a section dealing with Jews and the rape of black women, to suggest that the number of mulattos counted to Jewish parents was only "the tip of an iceberg" (pp. 196–201).

Frequently, the editors of *Secret Relationship* stretch their sources or even turn them on their heads to prove a point. Arnold Wiznitzer, perhaps the foremost scholar of Brazilian Jewry, is cited as claiming that Jews held economic dominance over colonial Brazil, especially in the slave trade (p. 31–32). The evidence: a twelve-line quotation pasted together from four separate references in Wiznitzer to read: "Portuguese merchants, many of them [Jews] had controlled most of the slave trade between Africa and America until the Portuguese rebellion of 1640" (p. 28) Unsophisticated readers would not suspect that the word Jews does not appear in the original quotation. The actual term was "New Christian," applied to Portuguese whose ancestors once had been Jews. According to Wiznitzer, many of these individuals never practiced Judaism and "there is no reason or basis to call them Jews."[5] Moreover, he writes, "It cannot be said that the Jews played a dominant role in Dutch Brazil as *señhores de engeñho* (operators of sugar mills)."[6] As for their role in the slave trade, Wiznitzer says that between 1636 and 1645 23,163 African slaves were brought to Brazil through its four functioning ports. There were approximately 1,000 to 1,400 Jews in Brazil at the time. Using Wiznitzer's own formula of one adult male for every four women and children, we may estimate 250 adult Jewish males in the land. Most were merchants or small farmers, only a handful (20–30) were brokers. Yet Jews, everywhere, bear responsibility for the slave population of Brazil which reached more than four million when the institution of slavery was abolished in the nineteenth century

Equally sloppy scholarship is evident in the misuse of Rabbi Max Kohler and Elizabeth Donnan who are cited in support of the claim that Jews of Curaçao were forbidden by the Dutch West Indies Company to purchase more slaves because they were "notorious for their perceived ability to control trade" and "flout established rules of trade" on the island in the seventeenth century (p. 66). A search of Donnan's writings reveals very much the opposite, for the Amsterdam Directory instructed Peter Stuveysant to foster agriculture with the import of African slaves "by any means," including barring anyone from leaving the country.[7] Such topsy-turvy methodology is evident also in the attempted manipulation of Jacob Marcus, dean of American-Jewish historians. Marcus is quoted as saying that Jews in the Caribbean secured domination in sugar production, when he clearly states "there is no evidence that Jews or persons of Jewish ancestry ever dominated the industry."[8] Even the venerable Simon Wolf is abused. Using his *American Jew as Patriot, Soldier and Citizen*, the editors of *Secret Relationship* conclude that Jewish enrollment in the Confederate forces (1,324 men) demonstrates the pro-slavery sentiment of the 150,000 Jews who lived in the United States at the time of the Civil War (pp. 157–59). Such a conclusion, of course, overlooks Wolf's figure of 6,611 Jews who fought for the Union, including six young Jewish men who won the Congressional Medal of Honor while participating in the conflict.[9]

The editors of *the Secret Relationship* do not distinguish between legitimate scholars and people who simply have managed to publish a book. Thus George Cohen, Rabbi Harold Scharfman, Philip Birnbaum, and the radical Lenni Brenner are cited as authorities on Judaism and the Jewish way of life when they support the editors' position. Brenner is even a victim of emendation. He is quoted denouncing "Sephardic merchants" and cotton factors who brought thousands of Africans to America. Brenner goes on to remind his readers that 7,000 Jews fought for the Union, that many were committed to abolitionism in part because they had been oppressed in tsarist Russia or because being German "48ers" (the liberals who tried to revolutionize Central Europe in 1848) they were "light years ahead of most Northern whites in this regard."[10] Readers are not told that. Nor are they offered sources for charts listing slave owners in Surinam (48) or Jamaica (77) or the fifty New York Jews simply listed as prominent slave owners (97).

Occasionally, the editors of *Secret Relationship* bend their own facts to fit their prescribed goals. On one page (22) the reader is told that Jews contributed less than 0.5 percent of funds that originally capitalized the Dutch *West* Indies Company in 1623. On the very next page, however, we read that within a century as many as one-fourth of the directors of the Dutch *East* Indies Company were Jews. The confusion of one stock venture which focused primarily upon Indonesia with another dealing with fading Dutch ventures in the Caribbean could only be deliberate.

If there are no facts, the editors of *Secret Relationship* just make them up. Thus we learn that Jean Lafitte, the pirate who fought alongside Andrew Jackson in the battle of New Orleans, was actually a Jew more interested in smuggling slaves past the British (86–87). Without providing a shred of genealogical evidence, the research staff devotes two pages in their chronicle of "Jews responsible for the Black Holocaust" to the DeWolf family of Rhode Island. John C. Femont, son of a ne'er-do-well Catholic from Lyons and a Norfolk, Virginia Protestant woman, is also transmuted into a Jew. So, too, was Joseph Ottolenghe, referred to on three pages (133–36) as "A Jew Teaches Slave Religion." Ottolenghe, an eighteenth-century immigrant to Georgia from England did teach the catechism to slaves—after he converted to Anglicanism at the age of twenty-eight and remained a devout Christian for the rest of his life.[11]

The editors are not above repeating legends and applying new spins to them. Thus we have conjecture about the ancestry of Christopher Columbus definitely resolved. Columbus is presented as a Jew and slave trader (14–17), a brutal warlord who enslaved natives in the New World. Those fluent in Spanish will delight in learning that the admiral managed to set sail not through the presentation of jewels (*joyas*) to Isabella. Rather, he used the influence of Jews (*judios*). An even more bizarre twist of an old wives' tale concerns Lord Jeffrey Amherst (1717–1797), victor at Ticonderoga, Crown Point, and Montreal in the French and Indian Wars. This vaunted British commander is accused of deliberately spreading smallpox among Indians through the gift of infected blankets. It is a vicious, unsubstantiated canard which pops up from time to time in badly written American history books, infuriating legitimate colonial historians. The tale is revived and refined in *The Secret Relationship*. In this telling, Amherst was assisted by eight Jewish contractors who also exploited the "hapless Indians" by selling them liquor and the diseased blankets. "It was only a matter of time before the pogrom reduced the once mighty Indian nation to but a few holocaust survivors." (105–13).

The widespread deaths of Native Americans, through disease and brutality is well-chronicled. It makes no sense to impute these deaths to a deliberate scheme on the part of Amherst and his Jewish commissariat.[12] According to John Long, Amherst's principal biographer, the Baron was very supportive of Indian agent William Johnson. Writes

Long, Amherst solicited the support of the Six Nations (e.g., Oneidas, Onondagas, Senecas, Cayugas, Mohawk, Tuscarora), tried to mediate differences among the tribes, and disapproved of scalping or mutilations. In an effort to "solidify good feeling," Amherst created an Indian flag.[13] As for Jewish co-conspirators, it is true that the Philadelphia trading firm of Moses and David Franks (and their Christian partner William Plumsted) did supply Amherst's troops between 1761 and 1763. The available documents refer to barrels of salt, beef, and pork, wagons loaded with flour, bread, peas, butter, rice, and broadcloths. There is no mention of blankets for anyone.[14]

The Secret Relationship offers howler after howler in the name of scholarship, beginning with a preface which claims to offer understanding for Jewish suffering throughout history, then indicts Jews for economic exploitation of Gentiles (sharp practices, usury, etc. vii, 10, 73). Jewish law supposedly permits "exploitation and oppression of the Gentile" (202). If Jews were barred from British colonies in the seventeenth and nineteenth centuries, it was not because of religious bias, but because they were feared as lawbreakers who exercised inordinate economic influence (26). Whatever temporary adversities they faced, the "majority" of Jews who reached North America in the seventeenth century were not "destitute, huddled masses" but "savvy businessmen with wealth that far surpassed most of the other immigrants" (89). Despite their avowed sympathy for the British crown (115–19), after the Revolutionary War, "the Jews were accorded equal rights and freed of all legal restrictions, and then continued to finance the enslavement, shipment, and murder of Black Africans"(99). Before the Civil War, no Jewish congregation, North or South, denounced chattel slavery (144). American Jews not only supported the rebels, northern Jewish merchants sent gold to the South to help prolong the conlfict and make more profits (161). This, not some fancied anti-Semitism, was the basis of General U.S. Grant's Order no. 11 barring Jewish merchants from border districts of Tennesee (165–66). Whatever post-Reconstruction rapport existed between Jews and blacks was "feigned friendship" on the part of the Jewish merchant designed to bankrupt the black farmer (169–175).

Consistently, though, the editors return to the principal sin of the Jews—their commitment to and success in various forms of slavery—sanctioned in the Bible (202), manifest in medieval trade (9), evidenced in international prostitution (73).[15] Farrakhan's aides suggest that the Spanish Inquisition came about because "slave dealing and slavery and its connection with Judaism and Jews was offensive to the Spanish reformers." (33–34). The research department maintains that Puritan America's "Blue Laws" resulted from Jews taking unfair advantage over Christians by trading in blacks on the Sunday sabbath (205). The Nation of Islam also offers "irrefutable evidence that the most prominent of Jewish pilgrim fathers used kidnapped Black Africans disproportionately more than any other ethnic or religious group in New World History" (vii). Jews supposedly dominated the transatlantic slave trade. Jews dominated the slave trade and plantation industries in New Spain, Brazil, and the Caribbean. Jewish merchants brought "countless thousands of Africans" to North America in the colonial period (90), served as slave traders (121) and "entered the planter class in substantial numbers." (121) Jews massacred the freedom fighters of Surinam and Guyana in the seventeenth century (36–54). They served as jailers, marshals, militia, and detectives in the Old South, helping to squelch the 1831 rebellion of "the Great" Nat Turner. The editors of *Secret Relationship* conclude: "Much like the Nazis at the concentration camps of Auschwitz, Treblinka, or Buchenwald, Jews served as constables, jailers, and sheriffs, part of whose duties were to issue warrants against and track down black freedom seekers"(p.207). The charges are endless. They are also untrue.

A Conspiracy of Silence

The number, exact or approximate, of Africans transported to the New World is open to debate. Following a tour of the Holocaust Museum in Washington in the spring of 1994, later when he spoke before a special convocation at Howard University (where he shared the podium with Leonard Jeffries and Tony Martin) Khalid Abdul Muhammad shrilled about the millions of slaves forcibly uprooted from their homes in Africa. Six million "so-called" Jews suffering in ghettos for six years could not compare to the agony endured by Africans at the hands of "white crackers" and "honkeys" over six centuries. "Doctor" Muhammad reminded a cheering audience at Howard that more than 100 million of his people had perished in the worst Holocaust in history.[16]

The figure 100 million black deaths in the slave trade has been bandied about so often in recent years that it has gained acceptance among some members of America's black communities. Though no reputable historian has posited such a figure, 100 million deaths is accepted by many as fact. In *From Plantation to Ghetto,* a work deemed seminal to black studies, August Meier and Elliott Rudwick do refer to "one author" who suggested that counting the wars and raids in Africa and the horrors of the Middle Passsage, "the transatlantic slave trade might easily have cost Africa as many as 50,000,000 people."[17] The unnamed author (he is never cited in Meier/Rudwick's text) may be Basil Davidson who speaks of the removal of one-quarter of the African population in his *Black Mother: The Years of the African Slave Trade*.[18] F.George Kay uses the figure of 50 million as casualties in *The Shameful Trade*. Kay dips into reckless rhetoric when he compares inmates of Nazi concentration camps with slaves on plantations in the Old South and concludes that the crimes of World War II "pale into a brief and minor aberration of a civilised people."[19]

It seems unlikely that sub-Saharan Africa maintained a population in excess of 300 millions in the fifteenth through eighteenth centuries. Because of war, famine, disease, the region barely sustains that many today. Tribal conflicts, still evident in Zaire, Rwanda, South Africa, Angola, and Somalia, cannot be ascribed solely to European interlopers. For 50 million Africans to have perished aboard sloops and schooners making the Atlantic crossing, slave traders bent on making a profit would have had to drag off more than 75 million people, hoping that a minimum one in three might survive. Records show this kind of death rate was unacceptable to slavers. In *Black Southerners, 1619–1869*, John Boles dismisses "wild estimates" of 50 or 100 million and instead offers the "consensus" view that between 1451 and 1870 a total of 10–12 million Africans were brought to the New World.[20] That is a figure accepted by Herbert Klein (*The Middle Passage: Comparative Studies in the Atlantic Slave Trade*), Philip Curtin (*The Atlantic Slave Trade: A Census*), and James A. Rawley (*The Transatlantic Slave Trade*) all of whom reckon shipboard mortality at between the norm of 10 percent and the rare 20–30 percent.[21]

Assuming the worst (30 percent mortality), the transatlantic slave trade would have cost the lives of perhaps three to five million Africans. That is horrible enough without anyone having to enter into a contest of comparative pain. There is no excuse for one group that has endured persecution to deprecate the suffering of others. Shortly before her death in 1989, the Holocaust historian Nora Levin urged people to be sensitive to the horrors of Armenian, American Indian, Baha'i, and black history: "Each genocide has its own etiology, the characteristic environment that fuels it, the kind of society that sanctions it."[22] Each tragedy has its own configuration and merits study.

Unfortunately, black nationalist historians do not seem so charitably disposed.They not only see the Jews playing the predominant role in the dehumanization of their people, they also believe Jews have manipulated the world of scholarship, successfully concealing the facts from the public—until now. That the Jews who endured ghettos, pogroms, expulsions, and mass murder, could have wielded such power is patently absurd. Still, over the course of centuries, this vulnerable people has also been accused of the most outlandish conspiracies. Beginning with the Middle Ages, Jews were blamed for ritual murder, host desecration, well poisoning. In the sixteenth century, those who converted under force to Christianity were accused of secretly working with Polish and Dutch Jews to undermine the church in what was termed "La Complicidad Grande."[23] Not until the publication of *Nostra Aetate* in 1965 were Jews generally relieved of the crime of deicide, carrying with it the implication of eternal hatred of the Christian church. Christians still prayed for their "perfidious" souls. The success of the Rothschilds in the nineteenth century, Napoleon's call for a Sanhedrin in 1808, Herzl's convocation of a World Zionist Congress in 1897, the creation of the Jewish Socialist Bund in the same year, all lent credence to the notion of a Jewish plot to seize control of the world, outlined by 1903 in the *Protocols of the Elders of Zion*, a spurious document subsequently debunked as a forgery.[24]

For a people that supposedly masterminded the slave trade, the Jews are remarkably absent from major texts on the subject. There are several references to the activities of Arabs in James Rawley's *Transatlantic Slave Trade* (telling of contacts in West Africa before the time of Henry the Navigator and their abuse of Senegalese in the 1780s)[25] but no mention of Jews. Roger Anstey speaks of "the considerable Arab slave trade in Central Africa' in *The Atlantic Slave Trade and British Abolition* but says nothing of Jews.[26] F. George Kay devotes thirteen pages to what he terms "disgusting" trafficking in slaves by Arabs in Malawi, Zambia, Mozambique, Guinea, Madagascar, Zanzibar, Botswana, Oman, and Khartoum,[27] but does not even include Jews in his index. In like manner, Curtin and Klein omit Jews from their comprehensive indictment of Danes, Frenchmen, English, Portuguese, and Spaniards who dominated the slave trade. David Eltis blames British, French, and Hispanic families (especially the latter who enjoyed a monopoly to the West Indies, Cuba, and Brazil) but also says nothing of Jews in his *Economic Growth and the Ending of of the Transatlantic Slave Trade*.[28] There is a reference to Jews in Colin Palmer's *Human*

Cargoes: The British Slave Trade to Spanish America 1700–1739 , but it is as victims. For Palmer writes that "blacks comprised only one category in a slave population that included Jews, Arabs, Berbers and Moors."[29] The single mention of Jews in Patrick Manning's *Slavery and African Life: Occidental, Oriental and African Slave Trades*[30] offers the suffering of the Jews in the Holocaust as a parallel for Africans in the transatlantic slave trade.

It is possible to find passing reference to Jewish slave traders in ancient Arabia or working alongside Gypsies and other exiles in the Portuguese trade to the Caribbean and South America[31] and we shall look at these in future chapters. Most texts that deal with slavery, however, yield little on Jewish involvement. There is no mention of Jewish slave merchants or ownership in J.R.Ward, *British West Indian Slavery 1750–1834* (1988); Rollando Mellafe, *Negro Slavery in Latin America* (1925); Hubert Aimes, *A History of Slavery in Cuba 1511–1608* (1907); Robin Blackburn, *The Overthrow of Colonial Slavery* (1988); Danniel Mannix, *Black Cargoes: Translantic Slave Trade 1518–1865* (1962); Robert Toplin, *Slavery and Race Relations in Latin America* (1974) and *The Abolition of Slavery in Brazil* (1972); Leslie Bethel, *Abolition of the Brazilian Slave Trade: Britain, Brazil and the Slave Trade Question 1807–1869* (1970); Eugene Genovese, *The World the Slaveholders Made* (1965). Oliver Ransford makes a single mention of Jews in the Maghreb in *The Slave Trade* (1971). Herbert Klein devotes one paragraph in 300 pages to Jews in *African Slavery in Latin America* (1986). And Johannes Postma mentions the Belmonte family and David Nassy (pp. 8–10) in his *Dutch in the Atlantic Slave Trade 1600–1815* (1990).

If Jews were such a dominant force in the domestic/American slave trade, how explain their virtual absence from texts which are considered standard? In *The Peculiar Institution: Slavery in the Ante-Bellum South* (1956), Kenneth Stampp speaks of Muslims and Christians finding victims among "the Negroes of Africa," of the Spanish, Portuguese, Dutch, French, and English bringing human cargoes to the New World (pp. 16–17). Stampp lists some of the most prominent slaveholders in the Old South and even refers to slavetraders as "Southern Shylocks" (256–68), yet there are no references to Jews in his book. Nor are there any in U.B. Phillips' *American Negro Slavery* (1918) or Robert Fogel's *Without Consent or Contract: The Rise and Fall of American Slavery* (1989), Fogel and Engerman's *Time on the Cross*, William Van Deburg's *Slavery and Race in American Popular Culture* (1984); James Roark's *Masters without Slaves: Southern Planters in the Civil War and Recon-*

struction (1977); Richard America, *The Wealth of Races; The Present Value of Benefits from Past Injustices* (Greenwood 1990); Eric Foner, *Free Soil, Free Labor, Free Men* (1970); Merton Dillon, *Slavery Attacked: Southern Slaves and Their Allies 1619–1865* (1990); Paul Finkleman (ed.) *Articles on American Slavery* (1989); Edgar Thompson, *Plantation Societies, Race Relations and the South* (1975); or Willie Rose (ed.), *A Documentary History of Slavery in North America* (1926). Harry Ploski and Ernest Kaiser's massive (1,000-page) edition, *The Negro Almanac* (1971) contains one reference (p. 441) to black hostility toward Jewish shopkeepers and service workers in the inner city.

Searches in regional studies yield similar results. Not a word on Jews in Ronald Lewis' *Coal, Iron and Slaves: Industrial Slavery in Marylnand and Virginia, 1715–1865* (1979); Bernard Steiner's *History of Slavery in Connecticut* (1893); Boles' *Black Southerners*; William Jenkins' *Pro-Slavery Thought in the Old South* (1960); J. Winston Coleman's *Slavery Times in Kentucky* (1940); Orville Taylor's *Negro Slavery in Arkansas* (1958); Charles Sydnor's *Slavery in Mississippi* (1965); Peter Wood's *Black Majority: Negroes in Colonial South Carolina from 1670 to the Stono Rebellion* (1974); Betty Wood's *Slavery in Colonial Georgia, 1730–1775* (1984); Randolph Campbell's *An Empire for Slavery: The Peculiar Institution in Texas, 1821–1865* (1989); Barbara Fields' *Slavery and Freedom on the Middle Ground: Maryland during the Nineteenth Century* (1985); R.Douglas Hurt's *Agriculture and Slavery in Missouri's Little Dixie* (1992); James Johnston's *Race Relations in Virginia and Miscegenation in the South, 1776–1860* (1970); Charles Davis' *The Cotton Kingdom in Alabama* (1974) or the collection titled *Slavery in the States* (1969) which reprints turn of the century essays on slavery in New Jersey, Rhode Island, New York, Connecticut, North Carolina and Missouri. Joseph Karl Menn's multivolume, *Large Slaveholders of the Deep South 1860,* may be the most comprehensive list available, detailing major slaveholders in Alabama, Georgia, Louisiana, Mississippi, and Texas. None of the sixty women cited were Jewish. (pp. 205–8) None of the seventeen railroad contractors were Jewish (213). None of the fifteen individuals listed in building construction, brickyards and sawmills were Jewish (213). None of the fifteen largest producers of cotton, or of rice, or of sugar were Jewish (244–56). None of the sixteen largest slaveholders in the entire South were Jewish (233–34). In fact, not one of the 6,000 persons owning fifty or more slaves in the states examined by Menn were Jewish.[32]

American Jews were, for the most part, merchants and traders clustered in cities like New York, Philadelphia and Newport in the North,

Charleston, Savannah, Richmond and New Orleans in the South.[33] Because they were concentratred in urban areas, one might expect to find something in Richard Wade's *Slavery in the Cities: The South 1820–1860* (1964). Wade discusses the active role of specific religious groups (Catholics, Episcopalians, Baptists, and Methodists) among blacks (pp. 167–68). He quotes black abolitionist spokesman Frederick Douglass on slavery in the cities and highlights the relative decline of the black urban population after 1820. At no time in his discussion of living conditions, trades and employment, shopping, clothes, food, and health, patrols in pursuit of runaways, even the suppression of the Denmark Vesey insurrection of 1822, does Wade make reference to Jews. Jews are mentioned in a few places in Frederic Bancroft's classic *Slave Trading in the Old South* , the product of an exhaustive search of thousands of Southern newspapers, city directories, and business listings. Their numbers were, in the words of Rabbi Bertram Korn, amazingly small— 3 of 70 slave brokers in Richmond, 4 of 44 in Charleston, 1 of 12 in Memphis.[34] According to Rabbi Korn, "probably all of the Jewish slave-trades in all of the Southern cities and towns combined did not buy and sell as many slaves as did the firm of Franklin and Armfield, the largest Negro traders in the South."[35] As an example, Jacob Cohen, the most prosperous Jewish slave trader mentioned by Bancroft, earned commissions totalling $2,500, less than nine other Gentile slave traders in Charleston, less than one-fourth of that obtained by Louis DeSaussure in 1860. Adds Rabbi Korn, none of the major slave-traders were Jewish, "nor did Jews constitute a large proportion of traders in any particular community."[36]

The last half-century has witnessed a veritable explosion of black studies programs at colleges and universities in the United States, with commensurate publications in black history. Yet here, too, writers have been remarkably silent about Jewish activity in the slave trade. The lone mention of Jews in Eugene Genovese' 800-page study *Roll Jordan Roll: The World the Slaves Made* comes in the context of slaves identifying with Jewish Biblical history and "the persuasive theme of deliverance" that Moses presents as redeemer.[37] Meier and Rudwick mention Jews only in connection with Bayard Rustin's 1963 call for a march on Washington.[38] W.E.B.Dubois, the first and foremost black American scholar of this century, wrote extensively on the slave experience. Dubois chronicled the extent of slavery in various colonial empires at the start of the nineteenth century.[39] He described the rivalry between the Dutch and British in the West Indies, the temporary successes of Napoleon, the prominence of Newport, Rhode Island as a slave depot; he even listed the foremost slave spokesmen in Southern commercial conventions between 1855 and 1859. DuBois, the Harvard-educated socialist, makes no reference to Jews. Booker T. Washington and William Hannibal Thomas both allude to hostile, unscrupulous Arab slave traders but say nothing about Jews in their studies of the American Negro at the turn of the century.[40] *White over Black* author Winthrop Jordan quotes a seventeenth-century source telling of "Jues" on the island of Barbados. But that is the extent of Jordan's reference to Jews as slave traders in a volume strident in its assault against the Puritan oppressors of his people.[41] As a group, Jews are mentioned in John Hope Franklin's and Alfred Moss' *From Slavery to Freedom: A History of Negro Americans* within the context of the civil rights struggle of the 1960s.[42] The only individual Jew to be mentioned more than once (and this in a favorable light) is George Gershwin.[43] Morgan State historian Benjamin Quarles mentions only one Jew in *The Negro in the Making of America* and that is the philanthropist Julius Rosenwald who devoted more than $4,000,000 to black education in the South before his death in 1932.[44]

There are no references to Jewish slaveholders or traders in *From Slavery to Freedom* , in James Horton's *Free People of Color: Inside the African American Community* (1993), Lerone Bennett's *Before the Mayflower: A History of the Negro in America, 1619–1964* (1962–66),[45] Leslie Owens' *This Species of Property: Slave Life and Culture in the Old South* (1976), Alphonso Pinkney's *Black Americans* (1975), Nathan Hughes' *Black Odyssey: The Afro-American Ordeal in Slavery* (1977),[46] John Blasingame's *The Slave Community: Plantation Life in the Antebellum South* (1979),[47] Vincent Harding's *There is a River: The Black Struggle for Freedom in America* (1981), Charles Davis and Henry Louis Gates' *The Slave's Narrative* (1985), Donald Wright's *African Americans in the Early Republic* (1993), or in any of the data-filled works of Carter Woodson.[48] Extensive scrutiny of the *Journal of Negro History* dating back more than sixty years also yields few references to Jews in the slave trade. Search of the multivolume Slave Bills of Sale Project developed by the African-American Family History Association in Atlanta, Georgia is equally fruitless. The collection lists 2,539 slaves and 1,368 buyers and sellers dating back to 1796. The names that crop up repeatedly are James Grubbs, Zachariah Lamar, Elijah Smead, Allen Inman, the McAlpin family. No Jews are cited.

There is a good reason for such lacunae. Much as the editors of *Secret Relationship* would have it otherwise, the charge of domination of the slave trade simply is not born out by the facts. My onetime colleague Dr. Amos Beyan, now of West Virginia University and the author of a volume on the Liberian slave trade, like most legitimate historians, dismisses the notion that Jews dominated the slave trade as crank history: "It's just not a serious debate among scholars. It's popular history. No one like John Hope Franklin or Genovese would take it seriously. There was no control of the slave trade on this side by common Americans. The power was concentrated in the hands of the aristocracy, kings, and bankers in Europe. England controlled it after 1713, but even as far back as the Armada in 1588. Were there Jews close to the monarchs? Even if there were, they were not as groups, but individuals. It had nothing to do with being Jewish or the Jewish religion."[49]

2

Slavery in Antiquity

A Universal Human Fault

From recorded time, slavery has been an accepted part of society. It was, as Fustel de Coulanges declared "a primordial fact, contemporaneous with the origin of society; it had its roots in an age of the human species when all inequalities had their raison d'etre."[1] In northern China in the third century, unfree masses constructed the 1,500-mile-long Great Wall designed to protect the Chin empire from Mongol raiders. The Old Kingdom pyramids of Egypt may have been raised by slaves. In Mesopotamia, much of the wealth of Assyrian and Babylonian warlords derived from slave labor. As Sumerologist Samuel Noah Kramer has written: "Slavery was a recognized institution and temples, palaces, and rich estates owned slaves and exploited them for their own benefit."[2] In sub-Saharan Africa, along the Amazon, on outriggers in Polynesia, aboard *dhows* bound for Muslim lords in Persia and Arabia, in the Yucatan Peninsula, among American Indian tribes, men warred with their fellow men and degraded the survivors.

Plato assumed the institution of slavery would serve the needs of his elite Greek "guardians" in the *Republic*.[3] According to Aristotle, nature dictated that certain creatures were superior, others inferior. Just as there were differences between men and women, so there were different abilities among men. ("He who is by nature not his own, but another's, and yet a man, is by nature a slave.") Just as there were animate and inanimate "instruments" helpful in navigating the seas (a rudder and a human lookout), so the slave was nothing but an animate "instrument," a possession, useful to the management of a houshold. Some men, warned Aristotle, are slaves everywhere, and some (meaning his fellow Greeks) are slaves nowhere.[4] In his *Utopia,* Thomas More called for "fetters of gold" appropriate for the "hardworking, penniless drudges" who would perform tasks unworthy of free men (i.e., hunting, cooking, oxcart driving, butchering).[5] John Locke included a provision on slavery for the charter of Carolina, holding that slavery was "entirely outside the social contract." The Englishman who provided the inspiration for Jefferson's Declaration of Independence, suggested that slaves who did not accept their condition might opt to commit suicide.[6]

The persistence of slavery demonstrates a basic flaw in human character. Scholars suggest that none of its previous incarnations can compare with the insidiousness of the transatlantic trade and slavery as practiced in the Western Hemisphere over the past five centuries. As Bernard Lewis wrote in 1971: "At no time did the Islamic world ever practice the kind of racial exclusivism which we find in the republic of South Africa at the present time or which has existed until very recently in the United States."[7] According to Claude Meillassoux, chattel slavery left Africans in a state of desocialization (aliens uprooted from their homes), depersonalization (stripped of their humanity) desexualization (the destruction of love and family), and decivilization (devoid of legal guarantees and freedom.).[8] Philip Curtin, who traces the origins of slavery in the west to the medieval world, would agree. The brand of slavery practised in the ante-bellum South was unique, says Curtin, for "never before in world history had agricultural enterprises on such a large scale depended so heavily on an export market." In such a system, slaves were dehumanized as nothing more than labor units.[9]

Judging another society by contemporary standards always presents problems. As M.I. Finley has written: "Slavery is a great evil: there is no reason why a historian should not say that, but to say only that, no matter with how much factual backing, is a cheap way to score a point on a dead society to the advantage of our own; retrospective indignation is also a way to justify the present."[10] Self-justification is what some Afrocentrist writers like those who composed *Secret Relationship* seem to be about. They argue that chattel slavery is a recent invention, unique to Western society. There is something inherently corrupt in modern, industrial Europe which made of the slave a deracinated outsider, stripped of homeland culture, family, and identity. By way of contrast, traditional African tribal societies are presented as pristine, untainted by class structure. Technically all people were *dewoa*, possessions of the tribal chief. There were "house servants," to be sure, but master and servant lived together, working, sharing food, celebrations, and a sense of common purpose. Slaves intermarried with their masters, adopted the Islamic faith, and even ran away without consequence. Africans may have taken other Africans away from their homes, but never in the inhuman fashion of the West. Skin color was never a factor in slavery until the Europeans combined racism with economic exploitation after the fifteenth century. Ultimately, responsibility may be traced back to Jews and their holy books. Such Manichaean images, while comforting, are overdrawn. The lamentable fact is that wherever the institution of slavery existed, it corrupted the slaveowner and degraded the slave, and to some degree race, tribe or national identity were part of the process.

Slavery in Ancient Egypt

According to one Afrocentrist view, civilization originated along the banks of the Nile more than 5,000 years ago. "Black" African clans were then united by an heroic generalissimo (Menes) and from this society came the principal inventions (art, philosophy, writing, metallurgy, science, mathematics, organized religion) that make for the amelioration of life. The greatest construction projects known to ancient man (pyramids, granaries, irrigation canals) supposedly were raised not by slaves but by a combination of volunteer free workers and alien "guest laborers." The serenity of this society is reflected in Egyptian art which remained static, unchanged, for centuries because this idyllic land bounded by sea, desert, cataracts (Nile rapids), and mountains was relatively secure from invasion. In this telling, every Egyptian hero is identified as a black African. Years ago, Langston Hughes started the process by claiming that Ikhnaton (the fourteenth-century pharaoh who antedated Moses with ideas of monolatry), even Cleopatra, a descendant of Alexander's Greek general Ptolemy, were black Africans.

While most ancient historians privately reject such contentions, only a handful, led by Mary Lefkowitz, Andrew Mellon Professor of Humanities at Wellesley College, have had the courage to say so publicly.[11] Egyptians understand that anthropological evidence suggests different racial types existed side by side in the many nomes of ancient Egypt.[12] Unquestionably, there were contacts with blacks beyond the Upper Nile. Sudanese trackers (*medjai*) were employed by pharaohs of the Middle Kingdom (2000–1800 B.C.) and volunteered to assist the beleaguered Egyptians in the time of turmoil known as the second interregnum (1750–1580). In 945 B.C., the African monarch Sheshonk swept through the Delta on his way to conquests in ancient Judaea. Three hundred years later, Taharka, another Ethiopian, established his own dynasty in Egypt.[13]

Black Africans were not always welcome in Egypt. Fear and loathing of southerners was such that lords in the Middle Kingdom erected a string of fortresses below the first cataract as protection against the *Nehsiu*, a derogatory Egyptian word for Hamites and Nubians. Boundary steles also warned blacks against setting foot on Egyptian soil without permission. From Senusert III (1878–1840 B.C.) came two admonitions at Senmeh—the first politely warning against any Nubian ship or herds passing north, the second employing insulting phraseology about blacks (the Nehsiu "fall down at a word," "they run from battle," "they are not worthy of respect," "they are poor and broken of spirit.")[14] But it was not just Nilotic blacks who were unwelcome in the lush Nile valley. A host of early dynastic inscriptions (a rock carving of Sekhemkhet at Wadi Mashara, an ivory label of King Den, the Two Gazelles Palette, the Bull Palette) show Egyptians battling with Libyans of the western desert. The Palette of Narmer, the first artifact to portray a single king wearing the *deshret* (red crown of the delta) and *hedjet* (white crown of Upper Egypt), also shows the pharaoh clubbing desert dwellers and dragging survivors off in a snare.[15]

Despite its natural insularity, Egypt could be a violent land, its peace disturbed by invaders from Crete and Semites from Upper Retenu (the name for ancient Palestine). Occasionally, the invaders were rebuffed (as in the reign of Rameses III, c.1190 B.C. when the sea peoples were defeated). There were times, however, when an influx of migrant traders might be succeeded by armed hosts. That was precisely the scenario with the Hyksos (shepherd kings), Semitic hordes that conquered Egypt in the eighteenth century. Historians see harbingers of this invasion in wall inscriptions of nobles at Beni Hasan where colorfully garbed foreign merchants known as Apiru or Habiru are displayed.Some historians (beginning with Flavius Josephus) made the mistake of equating the Hyksos with the pastoral Israelites.[16] The Egyptian priest-historian Manetho suggests that they were 240,000 Semites who eventually fled back to their ancestral lands.[17] The probability is that some of the interlopers remained in Egypt and were enslaved.[18] Included in the multitude were the Israelites, the ancient forebears of the Jews. Which presents a dilemma for the Afrocentrists. Essential to their arguments of victimization is the claim that blacks historically have been powerless, unable to enslave. But if the Egyptians were black, how justify their use of slavery? And if, as some Pan-Africanists have argued, the Israelites themselves were black,[19] how explain the additional paradox of the black Egyptians enslaving black Israelites?

The answer may, unwittingly, come from historians who downplay the extent of slavery in ancient Egypt. Jon Manchip White, for example, believes this noble society employed few slaves. The image of the taskmaster lashing slave gangs, he argues, is "almost certainly false." The 100,000 men required to raise the pyramids were, wrote White, "not helots but skilled men who rejoiced in their abilities" and who were motivated by love and respect toward their monarch.[20] Similar views were expressed by Henri Frankfort and Sir Leonard Woolley. The former offered the novel suggestion that there were not many slaves in Egypt before the New Kingdom (1500 B.C.) because "the successful growing of grain requires a personal interest on the part of the cultivator which slave labour lacks."[21] For his part, Woolley maintained that the thick Delta population available for corvee, made slavery unnecessary.[22] For Frankfort and Woolley, the mass of Egyptians were "small men," energetic serfs who owned homes and property, yet still found time to work the royal fields, clear canals, strengthen dikes, and raise monuments for pharaoh.

A distinction between free serfs and slaves was also attempted by the dean of American Egyptologists James Henry Breasted in his *History of Egypt*.[23] Serfs, he noted, paid taxes, while slaves were generally aliens. But even Breasted found it difficult to distinguish between the two groups. Both lived in low, mud-brick thatched-roof huts whose walls were contiguous with their neighbors. Both faced the constant threat of starvation. Both literally were the property of the priests and temples at Memphis, Heliopolis, Medinet Habu, and Karnak. By the time Julius Caesar and his Roman legions arrived in Egypt, "slaves or serfs formed the bulk of the population." An estimated seven million, they belonged to the ground and were bequeathed with it."[24]

If Breasted sometimes used the terms serf and slave interchangeably, there was no confusion in his description of the degrading process by which defeated peoples were brought into bondage by the Egyptians. Writing of the booty won by Thutmose III as a result of his annual sallies into Syria in the fifteenth century, Breasted says:

The Asiatics themselves, bound one to another in long lines, were led down the gang planks to begin a life of slave-labour for the Pharaoh. They wore long matted beards, an abomination to the Egyptians; their hair hung in heavy black masses upon their shoulders, and they were clad in gaily coloured woolen stuffs, such as the Egyptian, spotless in his white linen robe, would never put on his body. Their arms were pinioned behind them at or crossed over their heads and lashed together; or, again, their hands were thrust through odd pointed ovals of wood, which served as hand-cuffs. The women carried their children slung in a fold of the mantle over their shoulders. With their strange speech and uncouth postures, the poor wretches were the subject of jibe and merriment on the part of the multitude; while the artists of the time could never forbear caricaturing them.[25]

This image of press gangs, not enthusiastic volunteers, working at pharaoh's monuments or on temple estates is consistent with the folk-lore of captive peoples, epigraphic evidence, and the written testimony of Egyptians themselves. The Book of Exodus relates that a pharaoh arose in Egypt "who knew not Joseph." (Exod. 1:8) To punish the Isra-elites, the Egptians "set over them taskmasters to afflict them with their burdens" (Exod. 1:11). Among these forced labors was the construc-tion of Pithom and Per-Rameses, arsenals and granaries built as safe-guards against further incursions of Semites. "They made their lives bitter with hard service in mortar and brick and in all manner of service in the field" (Exod. 1:14). The Egyptians hoped by this manner to re-duce the number of foreigners. They obviously failed because the Isra-elites multiplied in number, which prompted the decree for all newborn males to be slain; females were to be bred as slaves (Exod. 1:15–22).

Such tales of Egyptian jealousy and oppression prefacing the mis-sion of Moses impressed Josephus who recounted them in detail in his *Antiquities* (II:9). According to the ancient Jewish historian, the Israel-ites were forced to cut a number of channels to restrain the overflow of Nile waters during the flood season, build walls and ramparts and even raise smaller pyramids for the pharaohs. For Josephus, the aim of the Egyptians was clear: "to destroy the Israelites by these labours." Be-cause of the miraculous delivery which followed, Jews in every age since have celebrated the Passover holiday. Their dinner plates have been laden with matzos (the bread of affliction baked in haste during the Exodus), bitter herbs (symbolic of the Egyptian bondage), haroseth (a mix of apples, almonds, raisins, and wine representing the mortar used to make bricks). The Passover Haggadah intones: *Ovdim hayinu l'faro b'mitzraim* (we were pharaoh's slaves in Egypt...had God not brought our forefathers out of Egypt, then we and our children and our children's children might still been slave to Pharaoh.) Black slaves in America drew hope and inspiration from the tale of deliverance and incorporated it into their spirituals.

Whether the ancient Egyptians intended genocide against a particu-lar set of slaves may be debated, but not their practice of slavery. The Leyden Papyrus, a lengthy chronicle of social upheaval from the reign of Pepi II, offers a series of laments related to slavery. In this age when "strangers have become Egyptians" (the Hyksos interregnum) "nay, but men's slaves, their hearts are sad." The social structure is upset , for gold and lapis adorn the necks of slave girls, "ladies are like slave girls," serfs have become lords of serfs, and children of nobles are forced into prostitution."[26] The tomb of Djehutihotep, a noble of the twelfth dynasty, at El Berseh shows 172 men dragging a sixty-ton alabaster statue on a sledge. Accompanying them are several taskmasters armed with sticks.[27] Another inscription from the tomb of Rekhmire (vizier for Thutmose III) at Thebes shows a number of Syrians and Nubians, their hands and feet clotted with wet clay, fabricating bricks much like the Israelites. Standing nearby, wielding rods, are Egyptian taskmasters.[28] Thutmose III himself strikes a virtually identical pose vis-a-vis Asiatics in an inscription from the temple of Amon at Karnak.

According to John Wilson, by the end of the New Kingdom (1200 B.C.) perhaps 20 percent of the Egyptian population was slave. They included not just Hyksos and Nubians, but Libyans, bedouin, Syrians and Apiru. Employed as drones by the army, on government public works projects, in the temple workshops, in the mines of Sinai and on the estates of pharaoh and his nobles, theirs was a particularly "heavy yoke."[29] Flogging, even of a freeman, was commonplace in ancient Egypt. Among popular sayings was one that a young man has a back and listens to a man who strikes it and another telling of someone "beaten like papyrus."[30] A series of manuscripts from the New Kingdom (nineteenth dynasty) refer to the plight of runaway slaves who, once recaptured, were chained and beaten with a hippo-hide whip and warn how a husbandman may be beaten, his children fettered.[31]

Perhaps the most chilling evidence in support of the tale in Exodus comes from what Ian Wilson terms the "surprising number of graves" uncovered with bodies whose left forearms were broken. It was as if people in their last agonies were trying to protect themselves from the lash of the Egyptian overseer.[32] Far from being the picture of serenity painted by Afrocentrists, Egypt could be as brutal as any society. House or body slaves may have enjoyed a tolerable existence, but as John Wilson notes, the typical Egyptian peasant/slave was "a chattel, a beast of burden, a draught animal" whose life was "closely akin to the lives of the animals who were beside him night and day."[33]

Slavery in the Fertile Crescent

Slavery proved to be just as oppressive in the Fertile Crescent. The earliest known legal documents from Mesopotamia contain references to the sale of slaves. As Leonard Woolley has noted, "The institution of slavery was traditional, universal and essential to social life and progress, nor was any man's conscience (not even the slave's) hurt by it."[34] People in the Fertile Crescent became slaves in the usual ways: capture in warfare, through debt forfeiture, the sale of infants, minors and wives, even self-sale in societies where farmers and craftsmen were charged as much as 80 percent interest per year on loans. The slave had no human personality. He was, as George Contenau writes, merely an item of real property, a "slave unit."[35] Unlike a freeman whose parentage was recited in legal documents, the slave had no genealogy. Rather, he appeared as "A ardusha B" (A the son of nobody, slave of B).[36]

Simple chattels, labor units, slaves could be bought or sold in an open market place for twenty-five shekels of silver, the price of five jars of wine or an ass. They might be hired out, exchanged, given in gift or inheritance. Just as in Egypt, bas-reliefs show lines of pathetic prisoners, men, women and children, driven like cattle to accompanying blows of soldiers.[37] Evidence suggests that the Phoenicians may have introduced the sale of black African slaves to the Mediterranean world.[38] Owners were entitled to the bodies of their female slaves and could arrange unions for the purpose of breeding.[39] Some slaves wore a distinctive hairdo. Others were branded with a red-hot iron or marked with a star on their hands. In some regions, slaves wore an identity disk about their necks. Elsewhere, they were forced to wear fetters.[40] No laws protected slaves from beatings and mutilations. Only common sense restrained masters from destroying their own property. Of Hittite society, James Gurney writes: "It is clear that the master was assumed to have unlimited right, even the power of life and death to deal with his servant as he thought fit."[41] A public insult to the master, any attempt at running away, might result in mutilation of eyes, ears or nose, even death not only for the slave responsible for such infraction, but his entire family as well.[42] In Babylonia, such offenses also merited mutilation, in Sumeria merely the application of shackles.[43]

We can only guess at the number of people degraded as slaves in this region. Georges Roux claims they were not numerous until the Assyrian domination. He does, however, mention that in the early dynastic city-states where populations ran to 20–30,000, thousands of men, women, and children were associated with temple workshops, serving as gardeners, cooks, servants, weavers.[44] This latter statement seems to accord with Samuel Kramer's interpretation of ancient Sumeria where "slavery was a recognized institution and temples, palaces, and rich estates owned slaves and exploited them for their own benefit."[45]

The laws of Amoritic Babylon (2000–1500 B.C.), the most detailed codes we have from ancient Mesopotamia, show how slavery figured prominently in society. More than a dozen of sixty precedents in the law code from Eshnunna relate to claims on slave girls, the marking of slaves, return of fugitive slaves, and punishment for an ox goring a slave. There are even more references, six outlining punishment (death) for assisting a runaway, in the celebrated code of Hammurabi (c.1600 B.C.) What makes this last code so notable is the *lex talionis,* familiar to Western readers as the "eye for an eye"principle. The law of retaliation operated a little differently in Babylonian society. The Babylonians were a class conscious people who divided into three specific groups—*awilum* (aristocracy), *mushkenum* (free masses), and *wardum* (slaves)—and who applied the law differentially according to one's station. Thus "if a freeman has destroyed the eye of a member of the aristocracy, they shall destroy his eye." But "if he has destroyed the eye of a commoner or broken the bone of a commoner, he shall pay one mina of silver." And "if he has destroyed the eye of a freeman's slave or broken the bone of a freeman's slave, he shall pay one-half this value."[46]

Slavery remained widespread a thousand years later when the Chaldaeans ruled Babylon. As A.T. Olmstead writes, "Slave sales form the largest single group of our documents and testify to an enormous increase in the slave population."[47] Armed struggles among peoples attempting to prove which of them was the fittest provided a continuous supply of slaves. Victorious warlords showed little mercy to the vanquished. Monumental steles and orthostats of Assyrian monarchs reveal a general policy of annihilation and deportation. Tukulti-Ninurta I (1242–1206), for example, boasted how he deported 10,000 captives from Syria and dragged the king of Babylon to Ashur in chains. Ashurnasirpal II (884–89) celebrated his victory at the town of Kinabu by burning 3000 prisoners and taking the king back to his own capital to be skinned alive. Shalmaneser III (858–824) proudly told how he slaughtered more than 14,000 of the men of Karkar, filing up the streams with their bodies and causing "their blood to flow in the furrows."[48] Ancient Jews also felt the wrath of these ancient conquerors. Assyrian records, supported by II Kings: 17, tell how Sargon II (721–705) carried out the destruction of Samaria/Israel obliterating all traces of the people, their 800-year-old culture, cities, and religious institutions.[49] Apparently the twin policies of genocide and enslavement worked, for this northern Jewish population, known as the Ten Lost Tribes, vanished from history. Babylonians under Nebuchadnezzar tried to replicate the feat in a series of attacks against Judaea between 597 and 586.

Second Kings: 24 and the Book of Jeremiah tell how the people, deported from their homeland, languished in slavery. Deracinated foreigners, they farmed the estates and tunnelled mines of their new masters. Bred, bought and sold, they functioned very much like chattels in the ante-bellum South until the Persians under Cyrus and Darius brought them some relief at the end of the fifth century.[50]

Slavery in Ancient Greece

For the Greeks, slavery was *"the* form of labour"[51]—not only for agriculture, but in industry, on public buildings, in silver mines, and as oarsmen for seafaring vessels. Once again, the only restraint imposed upon owners was common sense: masters were commanded to treat their slaves kindly. In practice, Greeks cared little about the condition of their human chattels. "The attitude of the Athenians toward slavery was unreflective," writes John Fine. "They accepted the institution as a fact of life, as their ancestors had done."[52] Slaves had a different view, reflected in constant threats of escape or rebellion. Thucydides tells of 20,000 artisans who fled during the Peloponnesian War to Decelea in 413, misguidedly exchanging Athenian bondage for that of Thebes. Large numbers of slaves also deserted Sparta during the invasion of Pylos a decade later.

Race played a definite role in the creation and treatment of slaves in Greece. When Dorian tribes swept through the peninsula after the tenth century B.C., they reduced native ethnic groups to slavery. The best example were the Messenians who became helots of the Spartans as a result of two wars fought in the eighth century. There is some question over whether the helots were slaves or enjoyed a higher status as state serfs. The matter seems moot to me. Helots possessed no political rights, no freedom of movement. They were not uprooted from their ancestral lands, but were barred from land ownership and were confined to hovels in marshy swamps. There was no process of manumission and they could only intermarry with superior castes with special permission. The deracinated helots were compelled to wear distinctive dress (a dogskin cap and leather jerkin) which distinguished them from the elite Spartiates. Feared and abused,the helots outnumbered their masters by more than ten to one. Each year, therefore, the Spartiates unleashed a band of secret police, the *Krypteia*, whose task it was to purge with blood potential rebels from the serfs.[53]

Sparta has never been the favorite of those who teach Hellenic history. At the peak of its power in the fourth century, this reactionary oligarchy possessed 300,000 helots. Its democratic contemporaries were little better. Athenaus of Naucratis (a second century Egyptian Greek) quotes a census taken in 310 B.C. which lists 460,000 slaves in Corinth, another 470,000 in Aegina. Even Athens, with its spendid reputation counted 31,000 citizens and 400,000 slaves.[54] Many had been uprooted from their ancestral homes. Some were purchased on the island of Chios which, in the Lyric Age, became "the first specialized Greek 'slave state'" and which specialized in trading eunuchs.[55] Others were descendants of *hektemoroi* , ancient sharecroppers entitled to even less produce (one-sixth) than the Spartan helots (who kept one-half of what they farmed.) Many were assigned to military biremes. 30,000 worked in the silver mines of Laurium. Concludes A.R.Burn, "Slaves, like corn were a typical export from an undeveloped to a developed area."[56]

Slavery in Ancient Rome

The Romans, too, were hardly troubled by the institution of slavery which became especially widespread after the Second Punic War. According to Keith Bradley of the University of Victoria, Rome was one of five genuine slave societies in history. Ancient Athens, Brazil in the nineteenth century, the colonial Caribbean and America before the Civil War were the others where more than 20 percent of the total population played a vital role in production. By the first century A.D. perhaps three million people (30–40 percent of Italy's population) were slaves, a percentage virtually identical with Brazil in 1800 and the U.S. in 1820.[57] The figures were even higher in the eastern part of an empire which counted 20 million slaves.[58] There were 400,000 slaves in Trajan's Rome, a city of 1.2 million people.[59] Simply to keep pace with the demand between 65 B.C. and 30 B.C. Italy required an annual supply of 100,000 slaves. Between 50 B.C. and 150 A.D. the empire required 500,000 per year, a figure reminiscent of the average of 60,000–80,000 Africans taken to the Western Hemisphere at the height of the transatlantic slave trade.

Carthaginians, Egyptians, Alpines, blacks from Somalia, Macedonian Greeks, Germans, these slaves were obtained as prisoners of war, through kidnapping or piracy,by will and gift, via debt slavery or abandonment. They were dragged away from home to market by *mangones* (wholesalers) and sold in lots or as individuals, not once, but several times during their lives. The process was, wrote J.P.V.D. Balsdon, "a hideously traumatic experience." Balsdon's description of a market should ring familiar to anyone who has studied American slavery: "the bawling voice of the auctioneer (in a language which most of them could not understand), the indignity of standing on a platform (*catasta* or *lapis*) with bare white-chalked feet, of being slapped, punched, pinched, even made to jump by a potential purchaser who wanted to make sure of the quality of the human flesh that he was buying. Burnt jet might be thrust under their noses to find if they epileptic. They might be made to strip for a medical inspection."[60]

Such slave auctions were held in the Roman forum near the Temple of Castor, in Septa, at Tithorea in Phocis at the time of the Isis festival. Slaves, who cost between 1200 and 8000 sesterces, were sought for the internal and external needs of city households, to assist in shops and industry, as water carriers and night attendants, to work on landed estates, to tote their masters in sedan chairs to the circus, as gladiatorial trainees, for hard labor in mines, quarries, and ships, and as objects of sex (particularly good-looking boys and prostitutes.) Just as in the antebellum South, a slave in the Roman world could not testify in a court of law, had no rights of marriage or kinship. His very name (an allusion to the place of purchase and often ending with the suffix *-por* Latin for boy) might be arbitrarily assigned to him by his master. Regarded as moral inferiors given to theft, lying, and gluttony, slaves could be whipped, branded or chained with metal collars.[61] They lived, quite simply, in a state of absolute subjection.[62] As Professor Bradley notes, "The rightlessness and degradation of the slave were made manifest in countless ways, but particularly through sexual exploitation and physical abuse." [63]

Those who were skilled, urban, household slaves were relatively well-treated (excepting women who experienced "the degradation of harem sex."[64]) But the consensus of historians is that most were "production slaves...ordinary laborers who lived under miserable conditions."[65] Those who worked in the fields, forests, and mines were treated as little better than animals. The accepted standard of conduct was outlined by Cato the Elder in *De Agricultura*. The vindictive censor who preached the obliteration of Carthage recommended that slaves be treated like cattle. On large estates, they should be bred like other stock, denied family life, and chained in underground prisons at night. The only food and clothing given them, was that which deemed necessary to sustain life. During inclement weather, masters were urged by Cato to find work indoors for their charges. Offspring could be separated from parents and sold. Once an elderly or sick slave was no longer productive (Cato compared such an individual to worn-out oxen, blemished cattle or sheep, an old wagon, anything which was superfluous), he was to be turned out to starve. Protests were answered with a rod or whip or by banishment to a more miserable working venue.[66]

A disobedient slave might be assigned to a living death in the mills or mines. Plautus tells of the plight of pathetic millhands whose ribs were covered with bloody welts. Their owners cursed and beat them, treating them "more like donkeys than human beings."[67] Such gloomy impressions are confirmed by Lucius Apuleius who wrote of slaves in the mills: "Ye gods, what a pack of runts the poor creatures were!... Their skins were seamed all over with the marks of old floggings, as you could easily see through the holes in their ragged shirts that shaded rather than covered their scarred backs; but some wore only loin-cloths. They had letters branded on their foreheads, and half-shaved heads, and irons on their legs. Their complexions were frightfully yellow, their eyelids caked with the smoke of the baking ovens, their eyes so bleary and inflamed that they could hardly see out of them, and they were powdered like athletes in the arena, but with dirty flour, not dust."[68]

The situation was equally deplorable in the mines where slaves starved and suffered under the lash of overseers. Commenting on the high mortality rate, Diodorus Siculus wrote: "They are not allowed to give up working or have a rest, but are forced by the beatings of their supervisors to stay at their places and throw away their wrteched lives as a result of these horrible hardships. Some of them survive to endure their misery for a long time because of their physical or sheer will-power; but because of the extent of their suffering, they prefer dying to surviving."[69]

Not surprisingly, slaves hated their masters and plotted rebellion, knowing the probable outcome would be death. Between 138 and 132 B.C. 70,000 slaves from Pergamum, Delos, Athens and Sicily waged a futile struggle for freedom. A second Sicilian slave war (104–99 B.C.) resulted in the deaths of 100,000 people. Thirty years later, Spartacus directed the most celebrated uprising in Roman history. A band of 70,000 fugitive and slaves bedeviled the armies of Rome before the Thracian gladiator and 6000 of his followers were crucified in 72 B.C.[70] Despite the knowledge that an entire household of slaves might be punished for the wrongdoing of an individual, slaves continued to conspire against their masters to the end of the first century A.D. when the ex-praetor Larcius Macedo, one of Pliny the Youngers colleagues, was assassinated by a group of his house slaves.

Dreading such attacks,[71] the lords of imperial Rome modified some of Cato's rules. Under the *lex Petronia,* masters no longer could deliver slaves to beasts in the ampitheater. An edict of Claudius forbade the abandonment of sick slaves. Domitian outlawed castration. Nero ordered inquiries into the mistreatment of slaves. And two centuries after Spartacus was martyred, he won a posthumous victory when Hadrian forbade the training of slaves as *lanistae* (gladiators).[72] There were also some efforts at manumission. Balsdon estimates that first-century Rome counted 100,000 freed males, 10 percent of its population.[73] Tenney Frank suggests that as many as 80 percent of the people living in imperial Rome traced their lineage to onetime slaves.[74] If either surmise is true, it did not translate into a general policy of manumission or generosity toward ex-slaves. Three laws, the *Lex Fufia Caninia* (2 B.C.), *Lex Aelia Sentia* (4 A.D.) and *Lex Junia Norbana* (17 B.C.) were designed to limit the number of slaves that might be emancipated by a single owner at any given time. For example, the *Lex Fufia Caninia* forbade anyone who owned 2–109 slaves from freeing more than half of his possessions. If the individual owned 10–30, he was limited to freeing one-third. If he owned 30–100, he could free one-fourth. And if the number of slaves was 100–500, the limit of freed men was one-fifth.[75] The purpose of such laws was to prevent mass emancipation of alien slaves who might swamp Roman citizens in numbers and, in the words of Professors Fritz Heichelheim, Cedric Yeo and Alexander Ward, thereby "defile" or "pollute" the racial purity of Italian stock through intermarriage.[76]

Slavery Unchecked

A society every bit as corrupt as Brazil in 1800 or the ante-bellum South of 1820, ancient Rome bequeathed another legacy to the medieval world—the concept of chattel slavery where men were referred to as boys and regarded as things to be disposed of when they were used up, where their women could be sexually exploited and children sold off into bondage, where whole families labored at gruelling tasks under the constant threat of collective and corporal punishment, where foreign cultures were deemed worthless and had to be eradicated. Whether in the form of the *colonus,* the poor tenant farmer who was reduced to serfdom at the hands of a great lord, or as the *servus,* the individual whose being and offspring belonged to a master, even to the point of life and death, Rome gave new dimension to the brutal notion of men dominating men.

Not even the spiritual revolution presented by Christianity could challenge the institution of slavery. Justification for slavery might be found in Holy Writ. In his epistle to the Colossians, St. Paul instructs, "Slaves, obey in all things your masters according to the flesh" (Colossians 3:22). In his first epistle to Timothy, Paul writes,"Let slaves who are under the yoke account their masters deserving of all honor." (I Timothy 6:l). Again, in his letter to St.Titus, Paul distinguishes among the classes of men, and says,"exhort slaves to obey their masters, pleasing them in all things and not opposing them" (Titus, 2:9–10). Masters were advised to be just and fair to their slaves. Few, if any, of the early church fathers felt "the horror of slavery" or entertained an "embryonic vision" of a slaveless society.[77] The greatest Christian sages of the Middle Ages and early modern times (St.Augustine, Ambrose, Thomas Aquinas, and Martin Luther) merely attributed the existence of the institution to the fall of man.[78]

Throughout the Middle Ages, the Church became a great proprietor of slaves—imported to Europe from Scandinavia, North Africa, and Slavonic lands of the East. Slaves were so common among Christians that one Visigothic council decreed that parish churches had to own at least 100 to merit assignment of a priest. Pope Gregory the Great suggested that slaves purchased in Marseilles be trained as missionaries. Charlemagne went so far as to tax his subjects for the maintenance of slaves in Saxony. Church councils delineated rights of slaves, ostensibly prohibiting the enslavement of fellow Christians (while at the same time offering the sacraments to Christian slaves and sanctuary to runaways.) Not until Pius II (1462), Paul III (1537), Urban VIII (1639), Benedict XIV (1741), Pius VII (1814) and Leo XIII (1888) did the Papacy issue formal denunciations of slavery. As James Fox noted, writing in the *Catholic Encyclopedia* more than eighty years ago, "Christianity found slavery in possession throughout the Roman world and when Christianity obtained power it could not and did not attempt summarily to abolish the institution."[78] Neither, apparently, did the Muslims who rivalled Christians in world power and in the trade of Africans (see chapter 17). One group, however, that definitely lacked the resources or influence to have much impact upon the operations of slavery were the Jews.

3

Jews and Slavery

The Biblical Dilemma

The Secret Relationship is replete with references to the Newport "Jewish merchant" Aaron Lopez, the "Jewish Confederate" Judah Benjamin, "Jewish Senator" David Yulee, the "Jewish family" Monsanto, Judah Hays,"a Jew from New York", "a Jew" named Salzburger, "Jews" who funded Columbus, "Jews" and international prostitution, "Jews" as smugglers, "Jews" and the rape of black women, "Jewish loyalists" during the American Revolution, "Jews" in the planter class, "Jews" in the medieval slave trade, "Jewish shipowners" in London, "Jewish slave traders" who predominated in the Caribbean. The "Jews" of Jamaica, Brazil, South Carolina, Charleston. "A Jew," "some Jews", become the Jews, all Jews, without benefit of definition. Any trace of Jewish ancestry is sufficient for an individual to be identified as a Jew and an oppressor. It is a familiar and illegitimate practice of anti-Semites. For centuries the Spanish utilized a *limpieza de sangre* (certificate of blood) tracking lineage seven generations to determine if someone bore the taint of Jewish blood. The Nazis did the same after the passage of the Nuremberg Laws in 1935.

That any Jew would have engaged in slaveholding, let alone slavetrading, seems incredible today. For those who sought justification for the institution of slavery, however, the Old Testament offered ample evidence of slaves in ancient times. In Genesis 9:25, Noah pronounces a curse upon Canaan the youngest son of Ham saying that he would be *eved avadim* (a servant of servants) to his brothers.[1] Later (Gen. 14:14), 318 men born in Abraham's house accompany that patriarch in his mission to rescue Lot at the Battle of Slime Pits. All of the males who were "part of the household" and their sons must be circumcised (Gen. 17:12). The slave/servant Eliezer of Damascus is promised inheritance if Abraham fails to have a legitimate heir. (Gen.15:2). Subsequently, Eliezer is entrusted with the important task of finding a bride for Isaac in the city of Nahor (Gen. 24:1–56). In turn, Isaac blesses his own faithful servants. (Gen. 26:29).

Scholars continue to debate whether the decalogue implicitly sanctions slavery. The Fourth Commandment (Exod. 20:10, Deut. 5:14) proclaims the sanctity of the sabbath and forbids work not only by any freeman or his family, but also on the part of his "man servant or maid servant" or "bondsman or bondsmaid." Biblical scholars point out that "the system of slavery which is tolerated by the Torah was fundamentally different from the cruel systems of the ancient world and even of Western countries down to the middle of the last century."[2] In the first place, Hebrews could only become slaves in one of two fashions: by being sold by a *Bet Din* (rabbinical court) in payment of a debt (Exodus 21) or by selling oneself into slavery on account of poverty (Lev. 25:39). No person, Jew or Gentile, could be whisked away from his homeland and sold into bondage for "he that stealeth a man and selleth him—he shall surely be put to death" (Exod. 21:16).

Biblical slaves, like the armed retainers of Abraham, were regarded not as inferior chattels, but brethren entitled to all rights of members of the household in terms of residence, food, clothing, duties, and inheritance. *Evedim* for Yale scholar David Brion Davis was a noble word for hired servant or worker.[3] They could not be assigned menial or degrading work (Lev. 25:40) nor might they be abused (Lev. 25:43). The *mishpatim* (legal codes) remind how bitter was the experience of bondage in Egypt (Exod. 1:11–16) and warn that if a heathen slave suffers damage to any of twenty-four organs or limbs, he is to be set free (Exod. 21:26–27). No concubine might be degraded (Exod. 21:7) nor could any female slave be sold to a foreign people (Exod. 21:8). The punishment for chastizing a slave too severely is not clearly defined (Exod. 21:21), although some judges considered the killing of a slave a capital offense.

Unique among ancient systems, Biblical slavery provided for the release of all Hebrew bondservants after seven years (Exod. 21:2, Lev. 25:1–4, Deut. 15:12–18 where masters are required to supply freedmen with flocks, grain, and wine to begin life anew) and especially in the fiftieth or Jubilee year ("and ye shall hallow the fiftieth year and proclaim liberty throughout the land unto all the inhabitants thereof" [Lev. 25:10]). Unfortunately, the provision does not apply to non-Hebrews who are to be an inheritance forever (Lev. 25:46). Those who seize upon the distinction as evidence of Jewish perfidy toward non-Jews should note that slaves unhappy with their lot enjoyed yet another protection. According to Deuteronomy 23:16: "Thou shalt not deliver unto his master's bondman that is escaped from his master unto thee." There were no fugitive slave laws in ancient Judaea where the number of slaves was relatively small, where we have no mention of slave markets, and where in fifteen centuries of existence as a nation torn by war, revolution, civil strife and catastrophe, there is not a single reference to a slave uprising.

Neither the Quran nor the New Testament formally condemns the institution of slavery. Jewish canonical texts, however, offer a litany of rebuke of what, for enlightened souls, was a violation of natural law. Micah (2:1–7) denounces those who covet and seize fields and houses, oppressing and casting out their fellow men. Among the transgressions of Israel cited by Amos (2:6) are the selling of the righteous for silver and the needy for a pair of shoes. Isaiah instructs all to seek justice and relieve the oppressed (1:17) and asks "what mean ye that ye crush my people and grind the face of the poor?" (3:17). Isaiah is also invoked on Yom Kippur: "Is not this the fast that I have chosen? To loose the bands of wickedness, to undo the heavy burdens, and to let the oppressed go free, and that ye break every yoke" (Isaiah 58:6).

In ancient Israel (particularly in the age of David and Solomon) slaves were imported from Phoenicia for use in building palaces, royal stables, and the temple precincts. The practice began to wane long before the intertestamental period for a variety of reasons. Apart from competition with and opposition from free hired workers, a host of religious decrees restricted slavery. Before the fall of Jerusalem to the Romans in 70 A.D. it was forbidden to expose oneself or children to bondage through indebtedness. In the Talmud, rabbis admonished "whoso acquires a slave to himself acquires a master to himself" (Kidd. 20a) as well as "he who multiplies female slaves, increases licentiousness." Masters were encouraged to manumit slaves who converted following either ritual ablution or circumcision (Yebamoth 4b–48a). Such proselytes were deemed to be human beings, not complete equals, but certainly above the ranks of pagans and others (Yeb. 37a). Wrote Salo Baron: "A whole system of laws was evolved to eliminate every conceivable abuse and, finally, to abolish the entire institution."[4]

The Jews offered no general emancipation proclamation in the ancient world, but they were unique in their loathing of the slave system and sympathy for its victims. Shunted about and despised when they were a formless tribal confederacy in Canaan, attacked and conquered when they tried to mold a state, Jews knew only too well the realities of chattel slavery. They suffered firsthand the deracinated homesickness of people uprooted from their ancestral lands when they toiled for Pharaoh in the fourteenth century and again when Nebuchadnezzar forced the Babylonian Captivity upon them 800 years later. They witnessed the pillaging of their shrines by Philistines, Moabites and the Ethiopian Sheshonk. Thousands were massacred by the Assyrian kings Tigleth Pileser III and Sargon II who succeeded in exterminating the ten northern tribes of Israel in the eighth century. Inspired by a similar racial hatred, the Syrian Greek monarch Antiochus IV massacred thousands more between 168 and 164 B.C. Over the course of two centuries, the Romans killed an estimated two million Jews and enslaved tens of thousands more as they tried, unsuccessfully, to obliterate the Jewish state and religion.[5]

Jewish Slave Traders in the Middle Ages

Roman legal codes (Theodosian 438, Justinian 565) grudgingly accorded Jews minimal protection in a hostile society as long as they practised their religion quietly and continued paying a special state tax (*fiscus judaicus*). Once Christianity became the established religion of the Roman world, it was only a matter of time before the rights of Jews would be circumscribed.[6] Intermarriage between Christians and Jews was forbidden throughout the Christian world. Social interaction (including dining together) was banned. Jews could not practice law or medicine, could not hold public office (save in the dubious case of the decurionate). Their word was inadmissable in a court of law. Jews could not interfere with the conversion of individuals to Christianity, nor were they permitted to engage proselytizing themseslves. Rituals deemed essential to the observance of Judaism (circumcision, kosher butchering) were either banned or severely limited. Jews were not supposed to be out in public during Holy Week or Christmas and were not supposed to celebrate Passover before Easter. Sunday became the mandatory day of rest and Jews were forbidden to work on the Christian sabbath. Under constant scrutiny from church and secular officials, Jews were forced to swear degrading oaths, subjected to conversionary sermons, and further stigmatized after the Fourth Lateran Council in 1215 decreed the wearing of a badge.

Their social and economic opportunities progressively restricted, some Jews in the Middle Ages, did own some slaves, but by no means on a grand scale. A host of traditional strictures operated against engaging in the practice. Jews were not permitted to enslave their fellow Jews, and were enjoined to ransom any member of their community who became a slave. Church assemblies (the Council of Elvira in 313, the First Council of Macon 583, Tenth Council of Toledo 656, Second Council of Meaux 845) forbade purchase or possession of a practicing Christian or circumcision of a pagan. Jews could only hold a noncircumcised heathen for two months, then had to dispose of him to a non-Jewish master. Jews were forbidden to brand (by their own biblical laws against mutilation) or circumcize (which the church deemed castration). Jewish women could not hold male slaves. Nor by the same token could Jewish men indulge in concubinage.[7] Should masters take advantage of their female slaves or should the female attend a mikveh, the woman was to be liberated and married. Slaves might also be freed by demanding to be taken to Palestine or by running off to the Holy Land.[8]

Moses Maimonides, the greatest Jewish sage of the twelfth century, elaborated at great length on the institution of slavery in the code known as the *Mishneh Torah* (mirror of the Torah). According to Maimonides, men who owned large numbers of slaves "added daily to the sum of their sins." Those who possessed slaves were bound not to humiliate or abuse them ("for one's slave is regarded as his own person").[9] God commanded his people to be merciful and pursue justice, therefore the slave was to eat and drink the same food as his master.[10] Maimonides stressed the many ways by which a slave might achieve his freedom. Manumission was commanded whenever slaves were sold to heathens, a king's servant or noble out of fear. A slave sold outside the land of Israel, one that was abandoned, or one who married a free woman and learned Torah also automatically were awarded freedom.[11] For Maimonides there was no stigma attached to pedigree. Manumission cancelled all previous rights and obligations and the onetime slave was to be regarded as "an Israelite in every respect."[12] Instead of buying slaves, he advised wealthy individuals to give emploment to orphans and the poor who roamed the streets.

In the sixteenth century, the *Shulchan Aruch* (the code of Orthodox Jews) recognized that Jews did own slaves, but advised that masters be merciful lest they lose them. "Mercy is the mark of piety and no man may load his slave with a grievous yoke. No non-Jewish slave may be oppressed; he must receive a portion from every dainty that his master eats; he must be degraded neither by word nor act, he must not be bullied nor scornfully entreated; but he must be addressed gently, and his reply heard with courtesy."[13] According to Israel Abrahams,"The Jewish owners of slaves were mild and affectionate masters." They would educate young slaves as their own, marry them off, and never sell a slave to a harsh master. For these reasons, many of their slaves beseeched their masters to convert them to Judaism since they knew they would not be traded from Jewish hands.[14]

There is a great deal of confusion about Jewish possession of slaves (which provoked outcries from Agobard and church councils) and their trading in slaves (which was encouraged by Gregory of Tours, Charlemagne, Louis the Pious, and other medieval lords). The notion of Jewish slave domination gained popularity among nationalistic writers like Houston Stewart Chamberlain (who lamented that "even in the earliest Western Gothic times, they [Jews] understood how to acquire influence and power as slave-dealers and financial agents")[15] and Henri Pirenne (who offered that "many were slave merchants, for example at Narbonne.")[16] According to Robert Reynolds, what trade existed in slaves between 500 and 700 was "thin" and shared among Frisians, Syrians and Jews.[17] Robert Latouche, on the other hand, maintains Jews not only were importing pagan slaves into markets of Mainz and Verdun by the ninth century, they were also trading in Christians as well.[18] Pierre Dockes suggests European magnates turned to Jewish brokers only after the church bungled its control of the slave trade. Thereafter, with the approval of Christian lords, Jews secured "a virtual monopoly over the slave traffic."

Jewish historians offer a different point of view. Bernard Bachrach chronicles the adversities of Jewish slave traders in sixth century Naples, Visigothic Spain, and Merovingian France. A few Jewish merchants who lived in the Rhone Valley (known as Radanites) did benefit from the *capitula* (beneficial decrees of Charlemagne and Louis the Pius), but Bachrach concedes it is "impossible, however, to develop a quantitative estimate" of such activity.[19] According to T. Oelsner and Bertram Korn, "The role of the Jews in the slave trade was also vastly exaggerated. This was done either to overemphasize the importance of Jews in early medieval trade or to put the odium of this trade onto the Jews (according to modern views—in disregard of the acceptability of slavery during the period of Jewish participation in it.) This tendency was reinforced by anti-Semitic prejudices."[20] Heinrich Graetz, the father of modern Jewish historiography, maintains that barbarian invasions of the fifth and sixth centuries left West European cities depopulated, their fields in desolation. The numerous wars and conquests also increased the numbers of prisoners. Supply encouraged demand.[21]

Not only Justinian and Charlemagne, but Pope Gelasius and the Muslim caliphs of Cordova actively recruited slaves.[22] According to Salo Baron, Jews served a useful function in this regard. Barred from land ownership and the crafts, they filled "peripheral occupations like slave trading." Dispersed in many lands, they maintained contact with their brethren, seeking quick profits before possible expulsion.[23] *The Secret Relationship* cites Baron in support of the notion that Jews controlled the medieval slave trade.In fact, Baron states the exact opposite. Of the Byzantine East, he writes,"Obviously only a small minority of Jewish merchants traded in slaves"[24] and "the small Jewish share was almost entirely limited to the Empire's periphery."[25] Others did engage in the lucrative trade in Central and Western Europe. There were Jewish merchants at Raffelstetten on the Danube in 906, in Franconia (Bavaria) at the end of the tenth century, at Coblenz in 1004, Meissen in 1009, and Silesia in 1085. But these were anomalies, in no way reflective of a consistent pattern. Jews were not exclusive traders in any of these markets.[26] Nor were the slaves Africans, as Farrakhan's scholars imply.

Most of the slaves in the Merovingian-Carolingian period came from lands beyond the Elbe, east of Bohemia.[27] Because so many human chattels came from Slavonic peoples, what the Romans once dubbed *servi* were now called "slaves." Jews did not participate in the conquest or roundup of these pagans. Some were merchants, dispensing White Europeans, not Africans, to various lords. They rationalized that the Slavs were descendants of Canaan and thus subject to the ancient curse of Noah that they were to be servants of servants to the end of time.[28] The exploitation of Slavs ended with their subsequent conversion at the hands of saints Methodius and Cyril and the concurrent development of feudalism (and serfdom) in Western Europe.

With the exception of Majorca (where a few Jews owned large plantations in the thirteenth century), there is, write Oelsner and Korn, "no evidence of a slave trade carried on by Jews in Christian Spain."[29] Baron agrees. The rare mention of Jewish slaveholders in documents cited by A.Gonzalez Palencia, J. M. Milas Vallicrosa, C.Verlinden, and Ahmad al-Albadi prompt Baron to conclude: "Even in Christian Spain where the shortcomings of slave ownership were to be so gravely deplored by later moralists, practically no sources relating to Jewish merchants in this human commodity during the eleventh and twelfth centuries appear in the voluminous documentation assembled by Baer."[30]

A search of documents from Muslim lands would prove equally unproductive. Islamic rulers adopted many of the discriminatory decrees first promulgated by their Christian counterparts. While some Middle East historians have it otherwise, just as in Europe Jews were confined to *mellahs* or *haras,* filthy ghettos where they were forced to wear garments which distinguished them from the Islamic faithful. Under the so-called Rule of Umar, they could practice their religion only in so far as it did not upset Muslims in their own meditations. Jews were subjected to insults, physical assaults, and expulsions. Labelled *dhimmi* (protected peoples), they were forced to pay discriminatory taxes to protect them from attacks from the very Muslim people among whom they lived. Jews were barred from specific vocations, among which were law, medicine, and slave trading.[31] According to S.D. Goitein, study of the numerous documents from the classical *Genizah* period indicates Jews had "no share" of the Egyptian slave trade between the llth and 13th centuries.[32] Jewish participation in the slave trade was officially opposed throughout the 600-year history of the Ottoman Empire.[33]

Whether in the East, the Mediterranean or northern Europe, it is highly unlikely that Jews could have dominated the medieval slave trade. According to David Davis, Christians "greatly exaggerated" Jewish control over trade and "became obssessed with alleged Jewish plots to enslave, convert or sell non-Jews," all of which were impossible because most European Jews lived on the margin of Christian society and "continued to suffer most of the legal disabilities associated with slavery."[34] The final word on this canard belongs to Salo Baron who wrote: "Neither slave trade, therefore, nor slaveholding seems ever to have been so important a factor in Jewish economic life as it long appeared to students familiar only with the fulminations of churchmen against them. As a commercial branch, in particular, it doubtless was insignificant and dwindled to very minor proportions after the Christianization of the Slavonic peoples in the tenth century."[35]

Jews and Capitalism

If we are to believe *The Secret Relationship,* somehow Jews who were outcasts in both medieval Christian and Muslim societies magically became the progenitors of the great commercial revolution in the age of discovery. In this regard, the editors of *Secret Relationship* owe much to Werner Sombart's *Jews and Modern Capitalism ,* originally published in 1908. Sombart (Adolf Hitler's favorite economic historian) preaches that actions of Jews, not the discovery of America or new trade routes to the Indies, revitalized Europe in the sixteenth and seventeenth centuries. Jews, wrote Sombart, were "atoms of molten money which flow and are scattered but which at the least inclination reunite into one principal stream."[36] Judaism, with its alleged emphasis upon rationality, its rejection of physical labor, its contractual nature with God, its special treament of strangers, rather than the evolution of Protestant ethics was responsible for modern capitalism and its illegitimate offspring—African slavery.

Looking back, Sombart asks,"Cannot we bring into connection the shifting of the economic centre from southern to northern Europe with the wanderings of the Jews?"[37] He cites the interlocking relationships of wealthy Jewish families like the Costas, Coneglianos, Sassoons, Carceres, and Gradises, and then, without noting the host of expulsions that drove Jews from one spot to another, he concludes,"It is well known that Jews turned away the flow of trade from the lands that expelled them tothose that gave them a hospitable reception."[38]

Sombart wrote at a time when a single Jewish family did possess phenomenal wealth and influence throughout Europe. The Rothschilds maintained fabulous mansions in London, Paris, Frankfurt, and Vienna. They helped underwrite the takeover of the Suez Canal, sustained British colonial efforts from Cairo to Capetown, financed Zionist ventures in Palestine, and despatched personal couriers to forestall armed clashes between their host nations. But the Rothschild phenomenon was of relatively recent vintage. The founder of this banking clan,Mayer Rothschild, only made his fortune through investments for Frederick William of Hesse-Kassel during the wars against Napoleon, two hundred years after the Commercial Revolution. With all their marbled salons, rare vases and tapestries, the Rothschilds hardly represented the Jews of their own age, let alone those who endured hatred throughout the modern period. The entire Jewish population of Europe in the sixteenth century has been estimated at less than two million.[39] Among these were mendicants, scholars, teachers, rabbis, beadles, itinerant preachers , common laborers, servants and artisans, some independent craftsmen, the aged and infirm, women and children. Above them were a pathetic handful of moderately well-to-do merchants who acted as intercessors in lands where Jews were none too welcome.

There were no formally practicing Jews in Spain or Portugal after expulsion decrees in 1492 and 1495. None in England between 1290 and 1648. A handful in Amsterdam during the seventeenth century. No more than 8,000 Danish Jews when the Nazis attempted to purge that nation in 1943. In the sixteenth century, a small number of Sephardic refugees made their way to Italy where they lived in fear and squalor in the ghettos of Rome, Venice and Genoa. Periodically, they were subjected to conversionary sermons, forced to run gantlets on Christian holidays, and were even asked annually to pay the weight of their fattest congregant in candy and paper. Perhaps 2,000 of the 200,000 who fled Iberia nestled in towns along the Bay of Biscay and the Riviera in France, from which their co-religionists had been expelled in the previous century. By the time of the French Revolution, there were fewer than 40,000 Jews in France. Most of these were Ashkenazim from the disputed Rhenish provinces of Alsace-Lorraine. Regarded as less cultured, the German/Polish Jews were accorded civil rights in 1791, two years after their Mediterranean cousins. The Ashkenazim were typified as "ravens," ragmen, hawkers, and small-time moneylenders who preyed upon Gentile peasants. For this reason, in 1808 Napoleon (a) barred the entry of any more Jews from foreign lands; (b) stopped Alsatian Jews from moving to other French departments; (c) required Jewish merchants to secure patents from the prefect of police; and (d) placed the entire sect under government control.

The Napoleonic Code was no more severe than laws imposed upon Jews in Germany by Frederick the Great. For more than a millennium, since their first ancestors tagged after the Roman legions, through the massacres of the crusader period, Jews flocked into the hodgepodge of Teutonic principalities in Central Europe. Once maligned as *vogel-frei* (masterless men), *fidei inimici* (enemies of the true faith), until the middle of the nineteenth century they were regarded as *fremder* (aliens.) Neither lord nor master, they were simply *Kammerknecht* (servants of the Imperial treasury) or *Schützjude* (protected Jews) whose existence was, at best, tenuous. They lived in dark, overcrowded *Judengassen* where their activities could be monitored. Each year they were required to pay the *Leibzoll* (a version of the Roman poll tax) as well as the degrading *Gulden Opferpfennig*, golden penny due at Easter. They found employment where Germans permitted—in textiles, clothing, tobacco, cattle raising. By 1784, their numbers had grown to 200,000, 10 percent of whom were domestics, two-thirds tradesmen and peddlers. The legend of the Rothschilds notwithstanding, 84 percent were poor.[40]

When Christians in Switzerland, Bavaria, and Tyrol reacted to the Great Plague of the fourteenth century by slaughtering Jews, survivors fled eastward seeking, but not finding, sanctuary in Poland. There was a glimmer of hope in this rich agricultural land. After all, in 1264 Duke Boleslaw issued the Statute of Kalisz investing all Polish subjects, including Jews, with the protection of the king and according Jews freedom of movement, religion and trade. A century later, Casimir III, hoping to expand trade, formally welcomed Jews to Poland. By 1551, Jews living in Greater Poland (West), Little Poland (Crakow), Podolia (Galicia) and Volhynia (the region about Pinsk) were granted a degree of autonomy by the government which formally sanctioned the creation of the Council of Four Lands.[41] There were also portents of disaster in this supposed idyllic land. Already in 1266 the first ghetto was created in Breslau. While Casimir was attempting to entice Jews eastward, San Juan Capistrano was urging the introduction of the Inquisition into Poland. The first charge of host desecration occured at Poznan in the fourteenth century, a ritual murder accusation in Crakow about the same time. In 1447 an Assembly of Notables revoked the pledges of Boleslaw and Casimir. In 1495 Jews were expelled from the Lithuanian towns of Grodno and Brest. Then in the middle of the seventeenth century, Jewish merchants and stewards were caught in the middle of a bloody civil war between Poles and Ukrainians. Poland's Jews suffered the worst persecution until the time of the Holocaust. Tens of thousands were slaughtered in what were supposedly impregnable towns like Tulczyn where Jews were massacred after surrendering on promise of safe conduct out of the city; in Nemirov on the Bug where the 6,000 Jewish victims included young girls who had been raped; in Moghilev where fathers were forced to dig the graves of their own families; in Zaslav where Jews were burned to death alongside Catholic priests. Tens of thousands died in Kherson, Zaslav, Minsk, Smolensk, Lemberg, and Brody as pogromchiks dubbed one method of killing (dragging Jews through the streets) "presenting the red ribbon." Perhaps 250,000 Jews died in what some historians label the *Gezerah* (Catastrophe).[42]

Small wonder that some Jews may have welcomed the Russians as deliverers from chaos. Whatever sense of relief they felt was not reciprocated as the Tsarist state expanded into Eastern Europe. Master of 250,000 Jews at the start of the eighteenth century, Peter the Great declared: "I prefer to see in our midst nations professing Islam and paganism rather than Jews. They are all rogues and cheats. It is my endeavor to eradicate evil, not multiply it."[43] When Poland was subsequently partitioned (1772, 1793,1795), Catherine the Great reluctantly assumed control of another million Jews. Alexander I "inherited" another 200,000 as a result of the victory over Napoleon. Both Catherine and Alexander hoped to restrict Jewish activities—confining them to the conquered Polish territories known as the Pale of the Settlement or by sending their children to military camps (cantons) where they might be forcibly converted to Orthodox Christianity. While *khappers* (child snatchers) seized 40,000 Jewish children and police censored writings of the despised *zhidy* (kikes), Jews multiplied. By 1881 there were more than five million in tsarist Russia, given false hope by the moderate regime of Alexander II. His assassination in St. Petersburg on March 13, 1881 prompted a wave of nationalist, fundamentalist brutality that surpassed anything Russia had known since the reign of Ivan the Terrible in the sixteenth century. With the blessing of government reactionaries who hoped to deflect reform, anti-Semitic mobs attacked Jews in 167 locales from Kiev to Warsaw. Damages mounted to $80 millions. 100,000 famlies were reduced to beggary. 50,000 persons lost their lives. And when a Russian commission investigated in 1882, it concluded that the disturbances stemmed from legitimate grievances of the Russian-Polish-Ukrainian peasants. In short, the Jews by their devious buisiness practices, had brought the massacres upon themselves.[44]

Promises of a better life offered by Alexander II were now withdrawn in a series of imperial decrees known as the May Laws. Jews were physically uprooted and sent packing back to the Pale. Jews were expelled from border regions. Those who enjoyed privileged status as artisans were declassed. The few that could vote in local zemstvo elections lost that right. Jews were barred from using certain names reserved for Christians. Jews were subjected to the *numerus clausus,* quotas designed to limit their numbers in educational institutions and the professions. According to John W. Foster, the American ambassador to St.Petersburg, the acts which were perpetrated against Jews were worthy of the Dark Ages. After viewing 1800 homeless Jews who had taken up residence in a barn, Foster declared,"All of these sufferers are in rags, most are barefoot, many bear marks of mutilation upon their faces, their heads bound up, their expressions blanched and glazed."[45]

What Foster described was not an isolated incident. When President Benjamin Harrison sent a commission to the Pale in 1891, it reported finding masses of terrified people, forbidden to work at any but the most demeaning jobs, unable to emigrate and wary of impending starvation. J.B. Weber, U.S. commissioner of immigration, and neurologist Dr. W.Kempter visited a stocking factory in Vilna where girls with "glassy eyes" and "emaciated limbs" worked fourteen hours a day for forty kopeks (less than fifty cents.) In that same city, an anti-Semitic journal reported that some of these "poor white slaves" had only three hours sleep each day. "They lived in miserable hovels, dirty and badly ventilated. Filth is everywhere, inside and outside. In the same dwelling may be found four, five or even six famlies, each of them having a number of children of tender age. To add to the misery, neither beds nor chairs, nor tables are to be seen in the wretched hovels, but every one has to lie on the damp and infected ground."[46] Even before the May Laws, a fifth of the Jewish population in the Pale subsisted on the dole. Many more were on the verge of starvation. Said the *Wilna Journal:* "The poverty amongst the Jewish laborers and artisans has attained considerable proportion. One Jew who was a bootmaker kept himself alive during many weeks on raw potatoes until at last he became dangerously ill; another, a weaver, fell down dead whilst engaged at his loom; he had died of starvation.... Few labourers can boast that they are able to earn the daily bread for their families. Meat is an unknown luxury, even on Sabbath. Today, bread and water, tomorrow, water and bread, and so on day after day."According to the *Fortnightly Review* and *Journal du Nord*, conditions were much the same in Berdichev, Grodno, Kovno, and Odessa where "cadaverous" Jews, subsisting on a farina paste, crowded dilapidated huts. There, said one observer, they died off "like flies."[47]

This was the situation facing the majority of Jews in the world one generation after the end of the American Civil War, three hundred years after the age of discovery and the commercial revolution. Hardly a pack of conniving plutocrats laden with sacks of gold shuttling about in quest of lands to conquer and slaves to control. Jewish historians like Salo Baron, Julius Guttmann, Itzhak Schipper and Gordon Zahn likened the Jews to a pariah people who could not have dominated any aspect of European trade. Dismissing the thesis of Werner Sombart and bigots who think like him, Max Weber noted there was little *commercium*, little *connubium* between Jewish and Gentile communities.[48] Joseph ha-Cohen, the historian who chronicled the seventeenth-century catastrophe in Ukraine, painted a simpler picture. No band of turbaned Sephards thriving at the cities of the Hanse or in Salonika, historically Europe's Jews were a frightened band "counted as sheep for the slaughter."[49]

4

Marranos and New Christians:
Jews as Traders in the Hispanic World

Europe Rediscovers Africa

Through much of the Middle Ages, Africans were regarded by Europeans more as a curiosity than a necessary source of manpower. Drone labor required for manorial estates was supplied by serfs. There were times, during the Black Plague and prolonged wars, when manpower needs became exceptional and Africans were peddled in the slave marts of Europe.[1] The number of blacks employed at court as bodyguards, executioners or entertainers was small and limited, for the most part, to lands surrounding the Mediterranean. Few Africans could be found in the northern regions of Italy. Records indicate that only four of the 58 slaves sold in Genoa between 1186 and 1226 were black.[2] A handful were traded in the early medieval markets of Marseille. When, during the Crusades, Europeans acquired a passion for sugar, they purchased thousands of slaves from Arabs to help farm the cane plantations of Cyprus, Crete and Sicily.[3] A few merchants from Genoa, Venice and France tried to establish *fondachi* (forts) on the West Coast of Africa in the thirteenth and fourteenth centuries, but none of these ventures was long-lived.

There was one European land where, from the Middle Ages, black Africans were present and reduced to bondage. In Iberia, the Portuguese and kings of Aragon and Castille had been on a crusade since the eighth century when a Muslim army commanded by the freedman Tarik conquered virtually all of the peninsula. A desire to avenge this national humiliation along with a sense of religious superiority, sparked this holy war against "Moors." All dark-skinned inhabitants of Africa, whether Berbers from the coastal rim or tribesmen from the Sahel were lumped together as the enemy. Enslavement was a fit punishment for such "godless inferiors."[4]

Raiding parties moved both ways across the straits of Gibraltar. The Almohades and Almoravids, Muslim holy warriors from Morocco, devastated much of Spain in the twelfth and thirteenth centuries. Christians dragged several thousand Moors off to market following a victory at Las Navas de Tolosa in 1212. It was not until King John I of Portugal captured Ceuta opposite Gibraltar in 1415, however, that any European could send his vessels out into the Atlantic with impunity.

The third of John's five sons, Prince Henry, known as the Navigator, was largely responsible for the seizure of Ceuta. Prompted by legends of sub-Saharan empires rich in ivory and gold, Henry sent out maritime expeditions as early as 1418. These resulted in the discovery by 1430 of the Azores, Madeira, and the Canary Islands. In 1434, one of Henry's captains, Gil Eanes, rounded the coastal bulge of Morocco. Seven years later, Antonio Gonzales (aka Antana Goncalvez) was sent beyond Cape Bojador in search of the skins of "seawolves" (i.e., sealskins.) Clashes ensued with rival North African merchants. Taken captive by the Portuguese, two Moors negotiated their own release in exchange for ten Africans. This action, rationalized by Henry who believed he could never save the souls of devout Muslims, was the beginning of Europe's massive intrusion into the African slave trade.[5]

In 1444, Henry chartered the Company of Lagos which explored the Senegal River and Cape Verde Islands. Within one year of his death (1460) the Portuguese had established a permanent base at Arguin and penetrated as far south as Sierra Leone. Initially, Henry intended to bring back 200–500 slaves per year from Africa. Such commerce proved too lucrative. Africans were desired for work in mines, as house slaves, on public projects, as fieldhands in agriculture, for warships and galleys. Some historians reckon that as many as 150,000 blacks were taken to the slave markets of Lisbon and Seville during the sixteenth century. A more reasonable estimate is that of Philip Curtin who maintains that there were approximately 49,000 Africans imported into all of Europe between 1451 and 1600.[6] The disparity in numbers might be attributed to the enslavement of defeated Moors in Spain.

Slave trading prompted concern on the part of the Catholic church. Henry was able to secure the blessing of Martin V for his enterprises, but not his successors. Despite expressions from Catholic sages that blacks were eminently adapted for slavery, in 1462 Pope Pius II declared the institution to be "a great crime." By the end of the century, however, the church itself was in possession of thousands of African menials. When Alexander VI issued his famous bull in June 1494 dividing the world for exploratory purposes between the Portuguese and Spanish (the treaty of Tordesillas), he made no mention of slavery. For good reason: by the end of the century the Spanish were already exporting hundreds of Indians back to Europe and arguing for replacement labor as they killed off the remnants of natives in Hispaniola, Mexico, and Peru.[7]

While the Portuguese were ensconced in Guinea and Angola, it was Spanish ventures in the new world that gave impetus to the slave trade in the sixteenth century. Following the explorations of Columbus to the Caribbean, Hernan Cortes subdued Mexico in 1519–21 and Francisco Pizarro followed up with the conquest of Peru between 1531 and 1533. When efforts to enslave the indigenous peoples of America proved disastrous (millions of Indians perished as a result of brutality and disease), a few Africans were imported in 1501. Elizabeth Donnan writes: "When or how the first Negro came to the Western World, we shall probably never know."[8] In 1502, however, Queen Isabella, acting upon the advice of Cardinal Ximenes, temporarily suspended the trade. This most Catholic monarch of Spain remained under great pressure to replace the decimated population of the Americas. Courtiers in the Queen's Council, colonists seeking labor for mines and a burgeoning sugar industry, Jeronimite friars and Dominicans like the priest Batholomeo de las Casas, all urged the import of Africans to supplant Indians. Isabella's death in 1504 removed one barrier and her husband Ferdinand issued a license to Nicolás de Ovando (the non-Jewish governor of Hispaniola) to bring in fifteen blacks.Before the end of the century, a number of merchants would be competing with one another to expand the number to more than 4000 each year. Most were Spanish Christians like Lorenzo de Gamenot, Fernando Ochoa, and Guzman de Silva. There were others like Laurent de Gouvenot, a Flemish nobleman who was governor of Breza, and Messrs. Eynger and Sayller, German courtiers at Seville. One who dabbled in the trade during the year 1576 was a Portuguese Jew—Miguel Nuñez.[9]

The first formal *asiento* (slaving monopoly) was not issued by Phillip II until January 1595. Under terms of this patent, Pedro Gomez Reynal was granted an exclusive charter to import 4250 slaves per year for nine years. In the next century, the number increased to as many as 29,000 as the monopoly was successively issued to Juan Rodriquez Coutinho (1601–9), Antonio Rodriquez de Rivas (1609–22), Manuel Rodriquez Lamego (1622–30), Melchior Gomez Angel and Cristobal Mendez de Sosa (1631), Domingo Grillo and Ambrosio Lomelin (1663–

74), Antonio Garcia and Don Sebastian de Silice (1674), Don Nicolas Porcio (1682–87) and Don Balthazar Caymans—none of them Jews.[10] In the spring of 1713 the asiento was transferred to the British under terms of the treaty of Utrecht. Despite this formal cession, the Spanish still managed to import a half-million Africans to Cuba before 1865, through the efforts of men like Jose Villanueva, Pere Labat, the Marques de Casa-Enrile, and Luis de las Casas.[11]

The Destruction of Spanish Jewry

Few of these slaving magnates were Jews because Jews had been expelled from Spain and Portugal by the end of the fifteenth century. The saga is familiar. The first Jewish merchants may have trickled into Iberia on the heels of Carthaginian and Roman warriors as far back as the second century B.C.E. They were followed by emigrants fleeing the destruction of the Jewish state three hundred years later. More came from Mesopotamia in the medieval period, despite persecution at the hands of Visigoths.[12] Jews flourished in what they called "the Golden Land," building synagogues and seminaries. Spain produced some of the greatest luminaries in Jewish history—Solomon ibn Gabirol (an eleventh century poet and philosopher who influenced Duns Scotus and Albertus Magnus), Moses and Abraham Ezra (responsible for hundreds of odes), Judah ha-Levi (an impassioned Zionist from Toledo in the twelfth century) Moses de Leon (credited as the source of the cabbalistic Zohar), Moses ben Nachman (Nachmanides, who engaged in a spirited public defense of his faith in Barcelona in 1263) and the greatest Moses since Moses—Moses ben Maimonides (author of the *Mishneh Torah* and the *Guide for the Perplexed*, two works which sustained Jews through times of doubt and massacre).[13]

Just as elsewhere in Europe and the Middle East, there were difficult times for Jews on the Iberian peninsula. Confined to *Juderias* (Jew streets or ghettos), where they were forced to wear the *Rouelle* (the circular Jewish badge), Jews also were subjected to compulsory sermons. Whenever one of their minions became too presumptuous, he might be assassinated, as in the case of Joseph ibn Nagrela, vizir of Granada, who was crucified on the door of his villa in 1066. Both ibn Gabirol and Judah ha-Levi were murdered by Saracens, and Maimonides had to practice his Judaism in secret to survive. Jews endured wholesale massacres at the hands of the Almoravids and Almohades in the twelfth century. The fabled benevolence of Muslims toward Jews was just that—a fable—in Spain.

Christians had never ceased their attacks since the seventh century. Envious of the wealth and influence of Jews who accounted for 5 percent of the population of Spain and Portugal, Christian mobs massacred 12,000 Jews in Toledo in 1355, 5,000 in Lisbon in 1373. Persecution became especially acute in the spring of 1391 as a result of a series of incendiary sermons offered by Ferran Martinez, an archdeacon from Seville. Pogroms erupted in 70 towns of Castille. Synagogues were burned, perhaps 50,000 people slain, and unknown thousands were forcibly converted to Christianity. Incited anew by the preachments of St.Vincent Ferrer and sanctioned by riots past which went unpunished, in 1411 Christian zealots dragged 35,000 Jews to priests to be baptized.[14]

These *Conversos* (converts as they called themselves) were not favored by their co-religionists who remained true to Judaism. Openly practising Jews pitied them as *Anusim* (forced ones). Christians used a more derogatory term, *Marranos* (swine) and, as we have noted, demanded proof of purity of blood dating back seven generations before permitting marriage to someone whose lineage was questioned.[15]

For the remainder of the fifteenth century, there were two Jewish populations in Spain, one openly, the other secretly professing Judaism. Overt Jews, physicians, lawyers, inventors were tolerated as long as Christians battled the more important enemy—the Moors. Not so, the Marranos. Unimpeded by traditional strictures against Jews, some of these Crypto-Christians became *hidalgos* (nobles), members of the *Cortes* (parliament). and the king's inner council, even bishops and archbishops of the Catholic church. That was the problem. As Cecil Roth wrote: "Had the Marranos been insincere but not successful, it is doubtful whether the problem would have become so acute. Had they been successful, but not insincere, on the other hand, the jealousy and the consequent difficulties would have been much the same."[16]

Mainly as a result of the efforts of Tomas de Torquemada, the Dominican monk who had served as Isabella's father confessor, an episcopal inquisition was introduced in Spain in 1478. Its purpose was to root out heresies and it was directed primarily against the Marranos. In February 1481, six men and women, including Diego de Susan, onetime confidant of King Ferdinand, were burned to death in the public square of Seville. Thereafter a wave of bigotry swept over this beautiful land. Denounced to the authorities for the most trivial of offenses, Marranos and their innocent neighbors would be dragged off to a *casa santa* (jail). There, the accused would be subjected to a variety of tortures—the *strappado* (a system of pulleys which yanked an individual's arms from their sockets), the *aselli* (where jars of water forced down the prisoner's throat until his stomach ruptured), the rack (the device which broke backs), the vise (where leather throngs applied excruciating pressure to a person's hands) or fire (which burned the prisoner's feet to the bone.[17] The church did not sully its hands, preferring instead to turn backsliders over to secular authorities for questioning. In the next 400 years more than 300,000 people in Spain and the New World would be "reconciled" to the faith, meaning they were scourged, sent to galleys, shamed (in the case of women paraded in the streets stripped to the waist), or forced to wear the *sambenito* (the costume marked with St.Andrew's cross and mitre stigmatizing the wearer as a penitent), their families permanently degraded. Thirty-thousand were burned at the stake or garroted.[18]

Jews who never converted were spared this hysteria for twenty years. In November 1491, though, the forces of Isabella and Ferdinand subdued Boabdil, the last Muslim outpost in Spain. The *Reconquista* achieved at last, the two Christian monarchs proclaimed the expulsion of Muslims from Spain. As an afterthought prompted by a ritual murder accusation in La Guardia, in March 1492, Ferdinand and Isabella also decreed that all Jews should leave their domains within six months. Many people deluded themselves that a wholesale expulsion would not happen. After all, the 300,000 openly professing Jews comprised the backbone of the mercantile class in Spain.[19] Their number also included prominent figures like Don Isaac Abrabanel, who once had served as minister of finance for Juan II of Portugal. Jewish leaders hoped to forestall expulsion by bribing the Spanish monarchs. But far from enjoying great influence, they encountered a wall of indifference. In the last days, Jews sold parcels of land for a silk kerchief. Debts were renounced. Shipboard passage was frantically arranged. And on July 31 1492, a 1600-year-old civilization came to an end.[20]

Now the Marranos watched and sympathized. They heard tales of privation and extortion on the high seas, of Jews given no food or forced to pay double the agreed rate to reach safe harbor. They learned how Jews arriving in Oran, Algiers, and Fez were slaughtered by Berbers who believed they were hiding gold in their stomachs. They observed the fate of Jews who hoped to remain in Iberia by crossing the border into Portugal. Initially, King Juan II was receptive to bribes (eight *cruzados* per person) But after eight months, he cracked down on the refugees, tearing infants from their parents, treating them like slaves, and sending them off to populate San Thomas and other island possessions. Juan's successor was even worse. Manuel married the daughter of Ferdinand and Isabella and, not surprisingly, emulated his in-laws by ordering the expulsion of all Jews by November 1497. Jews were too valuable, however, and before most could flee at Easter in April 1497, Manuel seized Jewish children and had them baptized. Their parents were given an option: emigrate with nothing after being penned up in corrals where they were given no food or water for three days or convert and keep the faith. Thousands of these pitiful souls became New Christians, as Portugal's Marranos were known.[21]

Marranos in Mexico and Peru

As bad as conditions were in Spain, at least the Marranos were still at home. They also had a choice: adhere to the rules of Christianity or flee to the new lands opening in the Western hemisphere. Many chose the latter, staying with a language and culture that was familiar, while secretly cursing the religion that had compromised their way of life.[22] Seymour Liebman states that Marranos may have accompanied Cortes to Mexico in 1519. Liebman further suggests by 1545 there may have been 300 Jews, many of them claiming to be Lutherans, living among the 1385 Spaniards in Mexico City. Additional numbers of Jews came in the next century from Italy, Salonica, France and Amsterdam as Spanish monarchs welcomed any European settler to their possessions for a price of 20,000 ducats.[23] Some of these invididuals prospered during the period 1580–1642 (what Liebman calls the Golden Age of New Spain). One, Luis de Carvajal, became governor of New Leon, the territory southwest of San Antonio. Marranos settled as far afield as Guadalajara, Caracas, and Manila. They developed silver mines in Mexico, founded the city of David in Panama and made the trek across Brazilian forests to Buenos Aires. Some were even granted immunity to settle in Yucatan if they served as slave brokers.[24] In the entire seventeenth century, a handful (Juan de Torres de Rivera, Fernando Rodriguez, Juan de Ayllon, Francisco de Albuquerque, Enrique Rios Obregon, Juan de Aranjo, and Miguel Nunez) were listed as traffickers in slaves.[25]

For practicing Jews and Marranos, life was not pleasant in the Americas. As early as 1515, a Marrano, Pedro de Leon was taken back from Hispaniola to trial in Seville. A decade later, Bishop Juan de Zumarraga introduced a local form of the inquisition to the New World. In October 1528 Hernando Alonso, who had fought alongside Cortes in the conquest of Mexico, and another man were burned at the stake in the first *auto da fe* (public act of faith). In 1537 Paul III issued a papal bull forbidding apostates and conversos in the Indies. Philip II introduced the first full-fledged Inquisition in 1569. A few years later, in 1603, Pope Clement VIII issued a Bull of Pardon, granting backsliders two years to return to the true faith. Sincere converts, denigrated because of their impure heritage, were hounded throughout their lives for the slightest hint of impiety. All the old means of interrogation, scourging, breaking on the wheel, fire, were applied in the New World. As late as March 1648, holy warriors were exhuming bodies and burning the dead in effigy. Dozens of men and women were flogged, exiled, sentenced to a lifetime in prisons or galleys, or hanged for no other reason than they burned candles on Friday, prayed toward the east, or lapsed into Hebrew prayers for their relatives.[26]

The Inquisition operated in the New World until the Latin American republics declared themselves free from Spanish tyranny in 1820. In just one quarter century, 1575–1601, there were 879 trials involving the condemnation of 767 persons. One of the single greatest persecutions took place in Mexico City in 1649 when 109 persons were publicly denounced (one burned alive, several garrotted).[27] Numbers cannot convey the torment of individuals persecuted in this period. It is, perhaps, legitimate to relate the suffering of a few:

Clara Enriquez: born in Fondon, Portugal, this widow was charged with having celebrated the festival of Passover. Her daughter Justa Mendez, born in Seville Spain, was charged with observing the Sabath and praying in accordance with "the dead Law of Moses." The women did not eat bacon, fat, or pork. Their punishment in the auto-da-fe of December 8, 1596: life imprisonment and confiscation of all property.

Manuel Gomez Navarro, born in San Martin de Trebajos, Portugal. A merchant, he used clean linen on Fridays, prayed facing the east and denied the Holy Trinity, as well as the eucharist. He was given 200 lashes, six years as a galley slave without pay and ordered to wear the sambenito for life in jail in Seville.

Leonor Martinez, fourteen years old, when she was denounced to the Inquisition in Mexico. According to the charges, Leonor began judaizing at the age of eight or nine. When she had new shoes, she would first wear them on the Sabbath. She would not eat anything cooked in lard. She attended weddings of couples married without benefit of Christian clergy. When her father left on a trip, he would bless them with Davidic psalms. Her punishment: reconciliation and placement in a house of the Holy Office in Spain where she would be given instruction in Catholicism for the rest of her life.

Pedro Fernandez de Castro, born in Valladolid, Castile, the descendant of New Christians. An itinerant merchant in Mexico, Castro was denounced in January 1647. Nicknamed "Sombrero" because he wore a head covering in his prison cell, de Castro admitted to having once visited a synagogue in Ferrara. His home in Mexico was open to Jews from Spain, Peru and the Philippines. Worst of all, he had undergone circumcision, allegedly to impress a Jewish woman. His punishment: 200 lashes, service in the galleys for five years, and life imprisonment in Spain.[28]

Manuel Bautista Perez, identified as the *capitan grande* of Lima Jews. He and his brother-in-law Sebastian Duarte had been active in the slave trade as early as 1612. While accumulating a half million pesos, Perez faithfully sent his children to Catholic schools and made substantial donations to the church. Denounced during the Inquisition of 1635–37, he remained impenitent after several suicide attempts. Following his execution in prison, he was also burned in effigy.[29]

The last victim burned was Maria Anna de Castro in December 1736.[30] Like David Dras Pimienta, a Cuban priest from the Order of Mercy, those condemned may have had no true understanding of their actions. After living a life of confusion, praying twenty times daily as a Jew, twenty times as a Christian, Piemienta was finally burned at the stake in Seville in July 1720.[31] By the middle of the eighteenth century, the church had grown, as Seymour Liebman says, "lax and venal."[32] There was no great need to continue the public displays of inhumanity. Jews and Marranos had either been exterminated or driven underground to the Mestizo villages of Venta Prieta, Toluca, or Apipilco, Mexico.[33] As late as 1889, only a few thousand Jews could be found in all of Latin America. For the most part, these were were recent immigrants, a dissimilar mix of Sephardim and Ashkenazim who encountered hostility in Mexico where only 100 Jews were naturalized in the last forty years of the nineteenth century, in Peru where only the Catholic religion was tolerated to 1915, and in Argentina where the Inquisition sat beyond 1813.[34]

The Dilemma of Identifying Marranos as Jews

It is impossible to determine how many of these victims truly attempted to deceive authorities. But it is equally specious to ascribe all the actions of Marranos to Jews. Jose Faur recently noted that there were four different types of Marrano-Conversos: (a) those who truly wished to be counted as Christians; (b) those faithful to Judaism; (c) a third group willing to accept Jesus as the messiah while retaining Jewish traditions; and (d) the apathetic who wanted no part of either religion.[35] There were the *Chuetas* (pork-eaters) of Majorca, hounded from the mainland, rejected by their neighbors, forced to be ultra-orthodox Christians, yet retaining vestiges of their Jewish traditions. There were individuals who did not know of a tainted ancestry until a search of their family tree failed to yield the necessary seven generations of pure blood. And there were people who simply lamented: "I am neither a Jew, nor a Moor, nor a Christian. I am nothing. I pray God to kill me in some horrible manner."[36]

Any attempt at identification of these troubled souls is bound to be frustrating. As John Longhurst has written,"Genealogy is a difficult art under the best of conditions. When it is further complicated by the mystique of blood purity, it becomes a bottomless pit."[37] Nevertheless, reputable scholars continue to debate whether it is legitimate to label Marranos, especially those in the New World, Jews. Perhaps it was martrydom that appealed to some Jewish historians who identified the Marranos as Jews. According to Graetz, they preserved their "love for Judaism and their race" in the depths of their hearts.[38] His position seems to be supported by Henry Kamen (who says most Marranos were never reconciled to baptism),[39] Yitzhak Baer (who suggests Marranos adhered to a living Jewish tradition),[40] the anthropologist Melville Herskovits and historian Geshon Cohen (who insist that no matter how Christianized the Marrano way of life may have become, these individuals remained Jews "historically, socially, or even religiously").[41]

Cecil Roth, the foremost authority on Marranos, offers a number of bleak observations: (a) the fundamental rite of circumcision was "obviously an impossibility" for Marranos; (b) any knowledge of Hebrew, the traditional language of prayer was "almost out of the question"; (c) possession of Jewish works, even in translation, "exposed the owner to persecution"; (d) observance of holidays which was risky, uneven from place to place, often disappeared. Concludes Roth, "Uninstructed and isolated, cut off from the outside world, and deprived of the guidance of literature, it was impossible for them to preserve the traditions of Judaism in anything like entirety." But even Cecil Roth will not renounce the Marranos, noting their penchant for Jewish cuisine, funeral rites, emphasis on charity.[42] Says Roth, "Despite all oppression, all characteristic features of traditional Judaism were preserved; and the appellation 'Jew' applied by the Inquisitors to the Marranos in scorn, may be vindicated for them as their rightful due."[43]

A number of scholars take a diametrically opposite view. Ben Zion Netanyahu flat out calls the notion of Marrano Judaism a myth,[44] a position supported by Salo Baron who emphasizes the Talmudic definition of a Jew (e.g., born of a practicing Jewish mother). David Brion Davis concedes there were some Marranos from Majorca who developed sugar plantations. But Davis questions the propriety of calling these forced converts who were ignorant of Jewish rituals Jews. "The Marranos were Jewish," writes Davis, "to the extent that they were never free from persecution as Crypto-Jews."[45] Seymour Liebman points out the survival of a number of odd anachronisms among the descendants of Marranos (a peculiar circumcision ritual, spitting out the wafer of the eucharist, superstitions concerning the curative powers of matzos, dietary practices, the burning of a piece of dough in the oven before baking bread, no sabbath sales, observance of a "Quipur" holiday)[46] and concludes, "Judaism could not survive on inheritance of blood or mere professions of faith. Jewish prayers must be recited and ritual must be practiced, covertly if necessary but affirmation must take place."[47]

The most reasonable resolution of the problem, it seems to me, comes from Judith Elkin who calls the pursuit of Judaism among Marranos a chimera. "This tradition, where properly investigated, has proved to be without substance," writes Elkin. "All overt manifestations of a colonial Jewish presence were legally extinguished and genetically submerged."[48]

The New Christians from Portugal

Scholars are equally perplexed over how to assess the New Christians from Portugal. I.S. Revah of the College de France says "the name Portuguese was often synonymous with New Christian and most often with secret Jews." Liebman concurs, stating that New Christians remained Jews while Marranos did not.[49] Yosef Yerushalmi, on the other hand, distinguishes between Spanish and Portuguese marranism, noting that Jews in the Portugal converted in toto.[50] C.R. Boxer suggests that the threat of confiscation of property meant everything, "the stigma " of being identified with Judaism very little to New Christians.[51] The task of verifying who was a New Christian, let alone how well they adhered to Jewish rituals, has proved daunting for scholars. Not for the Spanish who conquered Portugal in 1580. They made no distinction between New Christians and Old Christians, the latter who had no taint of Jews in their bloodlines. A Spanish proverb held that a Portuguese, any Portuguese was "born of a Jew's fart."[52]

The estimated number of New Christians in Portugal diminished from 100,000 in 1497 to 60,000 in 1542 and 30,000 in 1604. For good rea-

reason. Life for these people was a living hell. The Inquisition, introduced in 1531, continued to function well into the seventeenth century. Gordon Merrill reports forty-seven autos da fe between 1621 and 1640 in Lisbon, Coimbra and Elvora.[53] Many New Christians leaped at the opportunity to move to the New World after Pedro Cabral discovered Brazil in 1500. Indeed, Cabral's pilot, Gaspar da Gama, may have been a Jew from either Granada or Poland who adopted the name of the navigator who sailed to Goa in 1498.[54]

New Christians were permitted to settle in the west by Manuel I who hoped to develop Brazil as the center of Portugal's sugar trade. Sugar had first been brought back from Asia during the Crusades. Such a rare delicacy originally was sold in pharmacies for medical purposes. When Portugal expanded its empire in the fifteenth century, it transplanted cane from Sicily to Madeira, the Azores, and then to Sao Tome off the coast of west Africa. Among the colonists forced to these islands to develop *engeñhos* (sugar mills) were *degredados* (criminals, dissenters, nonconformists) and *cristoas-novos* (New Christians).[55] Some of the latter, including women, intermarried and bore children with Africans.[56]

The first large band of colonists, 600 to be exact, came to Brazil under Duarte Coelho in March 1534. The settlers learned to grow manioc (cassava) from the Indians, but then concentrated their energies on planting sugar cane. By 1550 there were five sugar mills in operation in all of Brazil. Forty years later, the number had grown to 200. Of these, only one, the Santiago, may have been operated by Jews.[57] Without question, some of the new arrivals were New Christians. Their attempts to cling to vestiges of their old faith so outraged the governors (none of whom were Jews) that the Inquisition was introduced into Brazil in 1580. Thereafter, those accused of the most incidental offenses (pouring water on their hands outside the house of a family in mourning, placing their hands on the heads of children as a sign of blessing) were sent back to Lisbon where they might be shamed, poisoned, or burned.[58]

While the Portuguese monarchy encouraged Jews to settle in Brazil (Judaizers were expelled to this land in 1535, King Juan IV enlisted New Christians among stockholders of his *Compania General de Comercio* in 1649) it persecuted those who did come and prosper.[59] According to Seymour Liebman, intolerance made Brazil in the seventeenth century "hell for blacks, purgatory for whites, and a paradise for Mulattoes."[60] How ironic, since Liebman declares, "In its early years, Brazil was built by Negro slaves (400,000 between 1570 and 1670) and the acumen, hard work and calculating perserverance of the Jews."[61]

It should follow that Jews were very active in the slave trade which supplied manpower for Brazil's sugar plantations or in the operations of the *engeñhos* themselves. Brazilian historian Gilberto Freyre, who once lectured at Harvard, makes the preposterous statement that Jews had a "natural bent" for slavery.[62] The assumption is not borne out by serious inquiry. Professor M.B. Amzalak of Lisbon, writing to Rabbi Bertram Korn in 1970, declared: "I don't know of any Jew having dealt in slavery and in researching in libraries I never found references about it. Not even the antisemites wrote anything about it!"[63] Antonio Marques Bessa agreed, noting that while he had "tried hard to find information on Jews in the slave trade" in "an enormous amount of books," "results don't come to light."[64] Professor Bessa did allow that New Christians were established in the port of Pinda in the Congo,"exactly the place from where the biggest quantity of slaves came." This Portuguese scholar attached a document from the priest Belchior de Sousa Chichorro to the king of the Congo in July 1553 which denounced the "wicked" activities of New Christians and which resulted in the expulsion of New Christians. Not even Bressa, however, could vouch for the accuracy of names listed or whether the traders were in fact New Christians, let alone Jews.[65]

Writing in 1970, the British antiquarian M.L. Ettinghause declared, "In the sixteenth to eighteenth centuries, the export of Africans as slaves to Brazil and the Cape of Good Hope was regarded as no more unjust than the export of tobacco from Brazil to Portugal. It was regarded as a legitimate and honest trade and Africans were, I believe, considered by the Portuguese and other nations as well as animals and consequently as without any souls."[66] Ettinghause stressed the role of Catholics, but scholars agree that New Christians also were engaged in the slave trade. Citing the research of Stephen Birmingham and articles in *L'Arche,* Dr. Edouard Roditi of Paris granted, "It would appear New Christians like other Portuguese merchants traded with Africa and were engaged in the slave trade."[67] The Dutch scholar Jan Vansina concurred, noting the presence of forced converts at Fernando Po and in Angola.[68]

Rabbi Korn spent more than a decade researching the subject and, much to his chagrin, uncovered several lists detailing the names of New Christians involved in the slave trade to Brazil. In the seventeenth century, these included members of the Ximenes, Rodrigues d'Evora, and Mendes de Brito families, Caspar Angiu, Manuel Alvares, Alvaro Dinis, Antonia Gomes da Costa, Gasparo da Costa, Joao Sousa, Andre de Fonseca, Gaspar Nunes, and Antonio Nobre in Lisbon; Simao Pinel,

Estevao Rodrigues, Simao Rodrigues d'Avora, Diego da Silva, Diego das Querido, and Simon Lopes Rosa of Amsterdam; and Fernando de Mercado, Gabriel da Costa, and Isaac LeMaire of London, perhaps fifty names in all.[69] Such lists may have prompted C.R. Boxer to conclude that "Marranos and ex-Marranos were in the slave trade up to their eyes."[70] But even Boxer says the allegation that Jews monopolized the trade of Spanish America "'from the vilest African Negro to the most precious pearl,' was obviously exaggerated."[71]

It is one thing, as we have already pointed out, to identify Marranos or New Christians. It is a giant leap, however, to equate these Crypto-Christians with Jews, or to suggest that, confronted with the twin threats of expulsion or Inquistion, they willingly served as brokers for the royal families of Spain and Portugal. There were no openly professing Jews in Brazil until the Dutch conquered the land in 1630. Then, responding to Dutch proclamations of freedom of religion, some of the New Christians returned to their ancestral faith.

The Dutch Haven in Brazil

In the short-lived Dutch era of toleration, Jews from Poland, Turkey, and the Barbary States emigrated to Brazil. Their numbers remain in dispute. Liebman believed the total to be only 1500 in 1640, while Gordon Merrill estimated 5000, C.R. Boxer 600 in Recife by 1654.[72] Using official Dutch census reports, Wiznitzer maintains the number of professing Jews in Brazil peaked in 1645. Of 12,703 persons counted in Recife, Mauricia, Itamaraca, Parahiba, and Rio Grande, no more than 1450 (11 percent) were Jews.[73] According to Wiznitzer, the figure actually was halved by emigration during the next decade as Jews were harassed and vilified by Portuguese Christians who plotted ceaselessly against the Dutch. According to Herbert Bloom, at the very moment when Johan Maurits was governor and Brazil was enjoying its greatest prosperity (1637–1644) "anti-Jewish prejudice was rampant."[74] In Maurits' first year, a number of so-called Old Christians (whose ancestry was untainted) called for the expulsion of all Jews. Four years later, 66 *Portuguese* merchants submitted a petition to the governor and Supreme Council accusing "this cheating and dishonest race" of giving special advantage to their kinsmen and of speaking ill of Christianity.[75] "Four infamous Jews and four Flemish knaves" were even accused of plotting a revolt of slaves in 1645.[76] Before the Portuguese recaptured Recife in 1654 and gave Jews three months to leave Brazil, a host of restrictions had been imposed upon Jews, banning intermarriage, the construction of synagogues or charging more than 3 percent interest on loans.

Portuguese Catholics especially resented any intrusion into the principal industry of Brazil—sugar. In the twenty-five years of Dutch domination (1630–54), Jews worked mainly in retail and brokerage, as engineers and lawyers, not as *Señhores de engeño*. The oft-misquoted Arnold Wiznitzer makes that point very clear. In 1639, he writes, there were 166 sugar mills in Dutch Brazil, 120 of them in operation. Sixty percent were owned by Portuguese Brazilians, 34 percent by Dutchmen, and about *6 percent by Jews*. Wiznitzer concedes that some families in Brazil may have been of Jewish origin, but notes that suspect names like Pereira, Oliveira, Carneiro, Mendes, and Pinto were common to Old Christian families. If, during the Dutch interregnum, New Christians did not formally embrace Judaism, writes Wiznitzer, "there would seem to be no basis for designating them Jews."[77] The worst example of misidentification is Jorge Homen Pinto, often cited as a prominent Jewish planter who owned nine sugar mills, 370 slaves, and 100 oxen in the 1640s.[78] Evidence suggests Pinto was anything but a Jew or a Jewish sympathizer. In 1637, Pinto was nominated to serve on the *Conselho de Escabinos*, the Council of Jurymen in Paraiba along with three other merchants. Only professing Christians free of Jewish ancestry were eligible for the Council. After several raucous debates over the lineage of one candidate, the other three were turned down. Only Pinto was selected. During the next ten years, Pinto actively plotted with João Fernando Vieira hoping to bring about the downfall of the Dutch in Brazil. His seizure of several forts earned him the *Ordem do Christo* (Order Of Christ), a distinction once again reserved for devout Catholics, from the Portuguese crown in September 1644.[79]

To those who suggest that Jews dominated the sugar industry (and indirectly, thereby, the slave trade upon which cane plantations relied), Wiznitzer replies, "It cannot be asserted that the Jews played a dominant role as 'Señhores de engeño' in Dutch Brazil."[80] Jacob Marcus concurs, stating that "there is no evidence that Jews or persons of Jewish ancestry ever dominated the industry, and only a few New Christians had been planters."[81]

A World Without Jews

The end of the Dutch era also meant the end of Jewish economic influence in Brazil. Portuguese authorities dealt brutally with New

Christians who reverted to Judaism. When cities fell, Jews were separated from other prisoners, to be sent back to Lisbon. Rather than face death at the hands of the Inquisition, many committed suicide at sea.[82] Some New Christians tried to flee into the hinterlands of Rio Grande do Norte or the state of Paraiba. New Christian physicians in Bahia tried to escape detection by prescribing pork as a health remedy for friends and families. Such efforts proved useless. Inquisitions in 1710–20, 1726–35, and 1811 decimated the New Christians.[83] Absent its Jews, Brazil continued to prosper in the eighteenth and nineteenth centuries. Stockraising ranches and gold mines, cacao, cotton, tobacco and coffee plantations, sugar mills and ports continued to need manpower.[84] After 1720, the General Company of Brazil (directed by non-Jews Jean Dansaint, Manoel Domingos do Paco, Francisco Nunez da Cruz, Noel Houssaye, Laurenco Pereira, and Bartholomeo Miguel Vienne) dominated the slave trade.[85]

What Seymour Drescher wrote recently of slavery in Brazil might well serve as an epitaph for Hispanic Jewry. The bulk of the Luso-Brazilian (Portuguese) slave trade took place in the last two centuries, eight to twelve generations after the initial mass of conversions of the New Christians and Marranos. Scholars have not assigned a Jewish role of any kind to that period of the slave trade which accounts for five-sixths of the Africans landed in Brazil. For good reason. As Liebman, Elkin, Yerushalmi, and others have already noted, few descendants of converts regarded themselves as Jews. "Modern scholars, overwhelmingly rejecting this racist and biologizing definition treat the problem of Iberian Jewish identity as a historical process," concludes Drescher, with each generation of New Christians probably having fewer members who regarded themselves as Jews or having any desire to revert or convert to Judaism.[86]

Spanish Jews paid for the voyages of Columbus not with the proffer of gemstones to Isabella, but through the confiscation of their wealth, seven million maravedi, five times the amount needed to underwrite exploration of the New World. Jews were expelled from lands where they resided for as much as sixty-eight generations. Marranos and New Christians were deprived of their homeland, their freedom and their lives into the nineteenth century. They were hunted down, tortured, and punished for attempting to cling to any vestige of their culture. How ironic, then, that Jews today should bear responsibility for deeds of Spanish and Portuguese slavers.

5

Haven: Holland and the Dutch West Indies

Origins of the Dutch East and West Indian Companies

Persecution and expulsion may have been the hallmarks of the Jewish experience in Spain and Portugal, but what of Holland? According to the editors of *Secret Relationship*, there were a number of affluent Jews who lived in Amsterdam in the seventeenth century. Men like Diego Dias Querido, David Querido, and Jacob Belmonte "frequently" despatched slave ships to the coast of Africa. Other Jews supposedly enriched themselves as brokers or magnates in Surinam, Guiana, and Curacao. In this age of commercial experimentation, when the joint stock company was just coming into being, Jews supposedly controlled both the Dutch East India and West India Companies. "Jewish slave traders procured Black Africans by the tens of thousands and funnelled them to the plantations of South America and throughout the Caribbean."[1] Like everything else in the *Secret Relationship* , the charges are one part fact and nine parts fable.

Technically, there was no fully independent Holland until Austria reluctantly granted independence under the 1648 Treaty of Westphalia. Through a mottled series of intermarriages and endowments, the Low Countries found themselves bequeathed in 1555 to Philip II of Spain and then to Charles V. Rule of these devout Catholic princes proved insufferable to the Dutch Calvinists. In 1568, seven northern provinces revolted, leaving what is now Belgium to Hapsburg control. In 1579 representatives of these rebellious provinces acknowledged the rule of William of Orange in the Union of Utrecht.

In this time of turmoil, it was virtually impossible to distinguish trade from brigandage. Attacks on foreign commerce were considered a patriotic duty. If a nation could profit through illegal trade, as an example circumventing the asiento, it would. The English and French smuggled thousands of slaves to Brazil, Mexico, Venezuela, and the

Antilles. So did the Dutch. A few rare souls did express concern about the institution of slavery. When the first Africans arrived in Holland in 1596, Burgomaster Ten Haeff of Middleburg argued that they "could not be kept by anyone as slaves and sold as such, but had to be put in their natural freedom without anyone pretending [to have] rights to them as his property." Then in 1615, the poet Gijsbrecht Bredero denounced slavery as an "inhuman practice, godless rascality."[2] Despite such misgivings, the Dutch established a base at Fort Nassau in Africa, ostensibly to protect their interests in gold and ivory.

Fearful of losing control of the spice trade from Indonesia (which they had dominated since the middle of the sixteenth century) to British privateers, the States General, chartered a Dutch East India Company in 1602. A few years later, in 1621, the Dutch parliament drafted articles of incorporation for a West Indies Company (hereafter referred to as the DWIC). The brainstorm of Willem Usselinx, a non-Jew from Antwerp and Middleburgh, the DWIC was designed to further Dutch adventures against the hated Spanish, to capture their ships and silver from Peru. Not until 1638 did the DWIC receive a monopoly on wood, war materials, and slaves.

The DWIC became fully operational in 1628 when the States General established its board of directors. The XIX or Herren, as they were called, were selected in the following manner: eight from Amsterdam, four from Zeeland, two from the Maas, two from West Frisian towns, two from the provinces of Groningen and Friesland, and one at large by the parliament. The original directors consisted of Ionnas de Laet, Samuel Blommaert, Samuel Godijn, Albert Coenraets Burgh, Kilaen van Resselaer, Michael Pauw, Pieter Boudaean Courteen, Jan de Moor, Geleyn ten Haeff, Joost van der Hooghen, Cornelis van Beveren, Adriaen van der Goes, Adriaen van der Dussen, Boudewijn Hendricksz, the Lampsin brothers, and a representative of the van Peere family.[3] Commenting on the makeup of this original board of directors, C.R. Boxer notes that the DWIC was largely the work of emigrant Calvinists from Flanders, "whereas it would be difficult to recall a single Jew in this connection."[4]

This is not to say Jews were oblivious to what was going on about them. Just as great merchants like Balthazar Cooymans, Laurens Real, Pieter de Graeff, ministers of the Dutch Reformed Church, Gentile bookkeepers, knifemakers, pharmacists, housewives and maid-servants, indeed "anyone who was eager for quick gain,"[5] eighteen Jewish residents of Amsterdam subscribed 36,000 florins (perhaps $10,000) to the DWIC in 1623. The figure represents 1.2 percent, approximately one-hundredth of the total capitalization of 3,000,000 florins contributed[6]—and with good reason. There were only a few Jews in Holland at the time and they were not wealthy.

The Union of Utrecht which created Holland in 1579 was notable for another reason. In an age when men burned men for burning candles on the wrong day of the week, the Dutch, themselves imperiled because of their Protestant faith, proclaimed universal religious toleration as a fundamental article of their new government. Not surprisingly, Jews, Marranos, and New Christians who had contacts in what previously had been part of the Spanish empire, including the descendants of those who had settled in Antwerp as early as 1512, now fled to Holland. It was not a flood, as some would have it. More a trickle. Fifty years after the revolt, in 1624, there were only 800 Jews in Amsterdam, less than 1 percent of the total population.[7] While many were of Portuguese background, the Jews who came from Germany and Poland were impoverished, earning a fraction of what the average Dutch urbanite brought home.[8] Despite the promise of religious freedom, they remained second-class citizens, forced to live by peddling and menial trades, excluded from government posts and guilds until 1796.[9]

According to researchers of the Nation of Islam, the actual involvement of Jews in the DWIC cannot be reckoned because complete lists of shareholders and their investments in that early period are unavailable.[10] Herbert Bloom was able to make an assesment of several lists from later in the seventeenth century, however, and discovered that in 1656 there were seven Jewish names listed among 167 principal investors. If all seven were professing Jews (an unlikely circumstance), they would have constituted 4 percent of the major shareholders of the DWIC. Of 169 names in 1658, perhaps 11 (6.5 percent) were Jews. Of 192 names in 1671, 10 were Jewish (5 percent of the total.)[11] Bloom's findings were sustained by Samuel Oppenheim who discovered a list of 111 investors dating from 1674, just four years before the DWIC was terminated. 11 names (10 percent) may have been Jewish. The actual contributions of 72 are listed, with Jewish investments ranging between 30,000 and 40,000 guilders (again $10,000).[12] According to Professor Pieter Emmer, total Jewish investment in the DWIC may have amounted to 0.5 percent of the company's capital.[13]

Jews may have invested in the DWIC, but, as Robert Swierenga has noted, none served as directors monitoring operations during its fifty year existence. None were elected to the States General which, recognizing the 240 percent profit turned on each slave, committed Holland to extensive slave trading by 1647.[14] Jews most certainly were not accorded a "righteous part," 10 percent of the company's profits, as the Prince of Orange received.[15] No patents were issued to Jewish captains to establish forts along the coast of West African in the seventeenth century. That was accomplished by the likes of Philip van Zuylen, Van Yperen, and "Peg Leg" Jol. There were no Jews among the military commanders (Jacob Willekens, Jan van Dorth, Elias Trip, Piet Heyn, Pieter Schouten, Jan Dirckszoom Lam, and Andries Veron)[16] who carried out the conquest of Brazil between 1624 and 1630. No Jews are mentioned in the frequent letters sent back to Amsterdam by Matthias van Beck, vice director of the DWIC stationed at Curacao between 1657 and 1659.[17] Perhaps five of the more than 500 Dutch captains that commanded 1200 ships making the transatlantic crossing between 1675 and 1803 were Jews.[18] Cornelis Goslinga suggests that Jewish participation in the affairs of the DWIC "increased in significance as the old company drew to a close."[19] C.R. Boxer concedes that some Jewish speculators were active in the slave trade after the Herren XIX decreed cash-only transactions in 1644. But he dismisses the "ignorant and prejudiced" notion that Jewish capital and industry were responsible for the commercial revolution in Holland. Citing the works of Dutch scholars Watjen and Van Dillen, he calls such assertions "greatly exaggerated."[20]

The Guianas and Surinam

Jews and New Christians may have comprised one-half of the white population in New Holland (Brazil) between 1630 and 1654. Here, as we have seen, they were resented by both the Portuguese who had temporarily been subjugated and Dutch Christians who wished to revive the Theodosian Code (i.e., prohibitions against Jewish employment or conversion of Gentiles, intermarriage, participation in certain trades, ownership of slaves or land). Jews fleeing Brazil after the Portuguese restoration crossed the border into territory which the Dutch referred to as the "Wilde Kust" and which the Indians called "Surina." Citing Marc Raphael (who spoke of the slave trade as "a major feature of Jewish economic life" in Surinam/Guyana), Farrakhan's scholars offer an impressive indictment of Jewish persecution of Africans in this region. This includes a chart of alleged Jewish slaveowners (no source given.) *The Secret Relationship* speaks of Jewish cruelty toward Africans, of branding troublemakers through the tongue, or ceaseless rapes that created a substratum of "Maroons," of runaways to the bush who became "freedom fighters." A document from 1730 is also cited, stating that 400 plantation masters in Surinam possessed 80,000 African slaves.[21]

There is evidence that the first Jews crossed into Guyana as early as 1639. The region was vast, relatively uncharted and in dispute among the Dutch, British and French. All three imperial nations were interested in developing this jungle area as a counterpoise to Spanish sugar possessions in the West Indies. A few Jews may have emigrated as far west as Paramaribo in 1644, but it was not until 1652–57, when the situation fell apart for Jews in Brazil, that complete families made the trek to the Essequibo and Pomeroon Rivers. In January 1658, David Nassy (also known as Joseph Nunez de Fonseca), a Jewish merchant from Brazil received a patent from the DWIC as patroon for a colony at Cayenne. The charter promised all necessary manpower (slaves) to develop the mines and plantations of what the Dutch called Novo Zeelandia. Lured by promises of religious freedom and instant wealth, several hundred of his co-religionists from as far off as Livorno, Italy, and London joined Nassy and his family. Whatever prosperity they may have enjoyed was short-lived. In 1664 the French conquered Cayenne and expelled the Jews.[22]

Once again, the Jews moved north and west—to Surinam—or what some British colonists called Willoughby Land, after a prominent governor of the day. In 1667 the British ceded Surinam to the Dutch in exchange for New Amsterdam (New York) in the treaty of Breda. Two years later, David Nassy was granted the right to create another Jewish colony sixty miles south of Paramaribo. Called *Joode Savaane* or *Joden Savaane* (Jewish meadow), the colony had its own synagogue and cemetery (with as many as 400 graves) before it was abandoned early in the nineteenth century. By that time, the number of Jews had grown from 130 in 1675 to more than 1300 by 1791, approximately one-third of all the whites in Surinam. These included 834 Portuguese Jews, 477 Germans, and 100 mulattoes. Of their involvement in the slave trade, Bloom writes there can be no doubt.[23] As early as 1667, 18 Jews owned 15 plantations with 414 slaves. By 1694 92 Sephardic and 12 Ashkenazic families (570 persons in all) held 40 estates with 9000 slaves. In February and March 1707, Jews purchased one-fourth of the slaves sold by the DWIC in Surinam.[24] As late as 1750, there were still nine flourishing plantations in the Jews' Savannah.[25]

Such statistics are at once damning and misleading. 9,000 slaves is not 80,000, as suggested by the *Secret Relationship*. Nor does the purchase of one quarter of slave imports constitute domination of the trade.

Oppenheim stresses that having lost Brazil, the Dutch were bent on making the colony in Surinam a success. Because of the importance of sugar mills, "the demand for slaves was brisk." The Christian directors of the DWIC viewed slavery not as an evil but as "the sole salvation" for the colony and slaves "as valuable as burnished silver."[26] To entice settlers into the region, the company offered special inducements to anyone who would establish sugar plantations—twelve years of tax relief for those employing fifty slaves, nine years for anyone with thirty slaves.[27] Two separate searches of the Notarial Archives of the city of Amsterdam conducted for Rabbi Bertram Korn in 1970 yielded a total of fourteen references to Jews or Portuguese involved with trade to the West Indies and New Spain between 1601 and 1698. According to Dr. E. M. Koen, head of the Archiefdienst in Amsterdam, slaves constituted only a portion of the cargoes.[28]

It has been argued that of all the slaving Europeans, the Dutch treated their slaves most kindly, "meticulously" insisting upon cleanliness of quarters, regular exercise and food.[29] Once in the Western Hemisphere, only one segment of the Dutch colonies demonstrated humanity toward their chattels. Among blacks, there was a saying,"Who enters a Jewish home is blessed by God."[30] For good reason. Only Jews insisted upon enforcement of DWIC decrees that slaves should not work on the Christian sabbath or holidays (some sixty-four days per year).[31] In the West Indies, it was customary for Jews to emancipate several blacks in their wills.[32] Still, life in Surinam, with its dense jungles, wild animals, perpetual heat and fevers, was rigorous for master and slave. Despite several attempts to reach an accord with "Bush Negroes,"[33] Jews also had to contend with full-scale rebellions in 1690, 1717, 1718, 1726, 1738, 1743, 1749, 1750, 1772, and 1774 that left scores of men, including notables like Manuel Pereira and David Nassy dead.[34]

The Dutch made life more miserable by withdrawing benefits that had enticed Jews to Surinam. Sunday closing laws were enforced in 1695, the same year Jewish leaders were deprived of representation in the colony's religious council. In 1704 marriages performed according to Jewish religious law were no longer recognized. Eight years later, a mob profaned the lone synagogue in the savannah by sacificing a pig outside its door. Jews were barred from the militia, prohibited from attending the theater, and denied access to administrative posts which their mulatto progeny could hold. In 1768, Dutch authorities even publicly discussed the prospect of constructing a ghetto in Paramaribo.[35]

Because of uneven crop yields, raids by hostile runaways and continuous pressure of anti-Semitism, the number of Jews operating plantations actually declined in the last part of the eighteenth century. From
115 of 401 planters in 1730 (approximately 25 percent), Jews in Surinam
fell to 46 of 591 (a little more than 7 percent) by 1787. Of those farming magnates most (30) were not in sugar, but in timber.[36] As Herbert
Klein aptly puts it, by 1791 the decline of Jews in Surinam was so great
as to make them an "insignificant element in society."[37]

Curaçao

The Dutch enjoyed temporary control over Brazil and Guyana in the
seventeenth century. At the same time, they established more permanent bases in Surinam, Tobago, St. Marten's, St. Eustatius, and Curaçao.
The latter, an elliptical isle 40 miles off the coast of Venezuela and 300
miles northwest of Caracas, was discovered by Spanish explorers in
1499. Ceded to the Dutch in 1634, Curaçao was, in the words of Jacob
Marcus, "eminently unfit for farming."[38] The directors of the DWIC
reasoned that the island might serve as a central depot for the needs of
the rest of the Dutch empire in the west. As a result, Curaçao played
host to the greatest number of ship chandlers in the Caribbean. Transatlantic commerce involved slavery, hence Curaçao became the chief
market for African slaves bound to other Dutch colonies.

The editors of *Secret Relationship* accuse Jews of transforming
Curaçao into a huge slave market, declaring "the Jews had become
notorious for their perceived ability to control trade and for flouting
established rules of trade. And when they attempted to buy still more
slaves, the [DWIC] company refused."[39] This notion of Jewish domination was seconded by *Washington Post* journalist David Mills who in
1993 entered the debate on Jews and slavery, quoting several historians
to the effect that Curaçao Jews were "numerous" (2000 by the mid-
1700s),"prosperous" (each owning between one and nine slaves for their
own personal use) and serving as "the predominant insurance underwriters for ships plying the Caribbean," including slave ships.[40]

In fact, the first twelve Jewish families reached Curaçao in 1650, a
decade after the DWIC decided to concentrate its trading operations on
the island.[41] Just as the Jews in Surinam, the new arrivals were refugees
fleeing Portuguese persecution in Brazil. They arrived in Curaçao with
very little and were not initially welcomed. Governor Peter Stuyvesant
denounced them as "usurious, covetous" and "generally treacherous."[42]

Stuyvesant wanted to bar them from participating in the slave trade but was overruled by the directors of the DWIC, who advised the governor on July 24, 1653 that if the West Indies should "ever...arrive to any degree of grandeur," agriculture should be developed through "the import of *more* slaves and restriction of emigration of all servants."[43]

Over the next twenty-five years, the Jewish population in Curaçao did increase. Willemstad, the principal city on the island, had its own Jewish quarter with Jewish and Synagogue Streets. By the mid-1700s, there were 200 Jewish households (more than in New York City at the time).[44] The exact ratio between Jews and non-Jews on the island in the eighteenth century is still unclear. One survey from the DWIC suggests there were seven Jews to every Christian. Another, cited by *Post* reporter Mills, puts the figure at 50 percent. A third census done in 1747 and running 101 pages claims Jews constituted 14 percent of the island's population. A fourth study done in 1942 states there were only 700 Jews among Curaçao's 70,000 people.[45] More recently, Robert Swierenga has estimated the number of Jews in 1764–65 to be 1500, approximately the same number found in Surinam.[46]

If there is some confusion over, even exaggeration of the number of Jews on this pleasant island, there can be no disputing that Jews on Curaçao did buy and sell slaves. Isaac and Suzanne Emmanuel refer to a number who secured patents from the DWIC and the monarchs of Portugal and Spain to bring Africans to the West Indies.[47] The fact that several of these (Don Manuel Belmonte and Jacob Calvo d'Andrade) were commissioned by "the Catholic Majesty" of Spain at the end of the seventeenth century, two hundred years after the Jews were expelled from that country, suggests a vestigial trace of Marranism.[48]

A number of Jews were brokers (17 of 25 to be exact), middle men disposing of DWIC property on Curaçao in 1794. Forty of 45 insurance underwriters were Jews.[49] Jews entered this field because Gentiles disdained the risks of piracy, wars, navigational errors and natural disasters which might cost a firm as much as 30,000 £ sterling ($150,000 per year.) Insurance underwriters and brokers dealt with sugar, cotton, tobacco, indigo, ginger, cocoa, hides, dyes, tar, candles, and wines, in addition to slaves.[50] Prominent slave traders included the cantor David Pardo, David Lopez Fonseca, Philippe Henriques and the physician Isaac da Costa. It is invalid, however, to paint most Jews as wealthy slavers. According to Isaac and Suzanne Emmanuel, Jews had no interest in the import or export of slaves by 1730.[51] For the most part, Jews on Curaçao were clerks, translators, shopkeepers and merchants. When the French attacked Curaçao in 1676, Goslinga notes Jews supplied an infantry company of 40 planters and "as many poor Jews."[52] A tax assessment from 1713 lists 9 percent of Curaçao's Jews belonging to the magnate class, 67 percent to the lowest income bracket.[53]

Despite warnings about the soil, a few Jews were counted among the plantation class (sugar, tobacco, cattle) which exploited slave labor. Some estimates of their wealth are just far-fetched. Moses Penso, for example, is said to have owned 403 slaves, more than twice the number ascribed to any slaveowner in an official government survey conducted in 1764. The same survey showed eight Jews who owned 20 or more slaves (the highest figure of 80 owned by Abraham and Isaac de Marchena). By way of contrast, 53 Gentiles owned 20 or more slaves. The Marchenas were the only Jews among the top 28 slaveholders on the island. (See chart below.) Of 5,534 slaves on the island, Jews (supposedly 50 percent of the white population) owned 867 or 15 percent of the slaves in Curaçao. As in Surinam, the percentage declined markedly over the next several decades. Barred from active participation in the slave trade by the DWIC, discouraged from farm activities by natural conditions and the animosity of competitors, and harrassed by Christian neighbors who accused them of disloyalty and race mixing,[54] Jews abandoned farming or Curaçao altogether. The first batch of Jews to land in New Amsterdam in September 1654 came from Curaçao. The British seized the island a decade later, but did not grant Jews political rights until 1825. The astonishing thing, therefore, is that there were any Jews on the island (there were 965) in 1863 when Curaçao emancipated its last slaves.[55]

A Postscript on Jews and the Baltic States

From audacious beginnings, the DWIC had deteriorated to little better than a corrupt agency clinging to a decrepit empire. By the time it went out of business after the Peace of Nijmegen in August 1678, the "soul of the company," its reason for existence, was *de slaffsche handel*.[56] The century that had promised so much for Jews ended with repeated expulsions, not only in Europe, but also in the New World. Gordon Merrill likens their wanderings to that of the Acadians expelled from Nova Scotia, "only no one has mourned—other than Longfellow" who left a short poem reminiscent of "Evangeline" on the Newport Cemetery.[57]

The editors of *Secret Relationship* insist that Jews continued their involvement in the slave trade in a circuitous fashion, through involve-

TABLE 5.1
Major Slaveholders—Curacao 1764

Jan Martin	200
Pieter Diedenhoven	170
Nathaniel Ellis	160
Casper van Uytrecht	150
Dirk van Uytrecht & Co.	140
Widow Fredrik Wm. Hermes	120
Cornelis Berch	100
Dirk van Uytrecht	100
Widow Daniel Lesire/family	100
Jurrian de Pool	90
Widow Claas Reyninck	83
Anna Kenningum	80
Widow Rudolph Bughij	80
Abraham & Isaac de Marchena	80
Widow Isaac Lamont	76
Jan Hendriksz	70
Widow Wigboldus Rasvelt	70
Widow Samuel Striddels	70
Widow Willem Kock	70
Jacobus van Brandt	64
Widow Gerard Schonenboom	61
Johannes Ellis	60
Widow Matthias Schotborgh	60
Lourents de Mey	60
Wigbodlus Reyninck	50
Jean Rodier	50
Maria Lupke	50
Widow Pieter Redoch	50

Source: Isaac and Suzanne Emmanuel, *History of the Jews of the Netherland Antilles* (Cincinnati, OH: American Jewish Archives, 1970), II, pp. 1036–45.

ment with Swedes, Danes, and Germans. Again, legitimate scholars inadvertently lend support to such notions. According to Dr. Pieter Emmer of the University of Leyden, Portuguese Jews probably antedated the Dutch by a decade or more in conducting slave traffic to the Antilles. It was unlikely that they continued their involvement with the DWIC because of the "Calvinist attitudes" of the directors. "Much more

likely," writes Emmer, "is Portuguese Jewish participation in the Swedish, Danish, and Brandenburg African Companies."[58]

Professor Emmer may be correct in suggesting New Christian contact with north Europeans, but any suggestion of large-scale slaving
ventures must be dismissed. In the middle of the seventeenth century,
Austria attempted to establish a company "on the line" to Guinea. Only
two slave ships ever made the journey for the Holy Roman Empire.
Few Jews could have been involved in the enterprise since Jews had
been expelled by the Hapsburgs in 1670, 1705, and 1710. About the
same time (1695–1703), the Elector of Bandenburg made overtures about
renting slave ships. but as Rabbi Korn notes, the idea was "merely a
project."[59] The same might be said of the misadventures of the Swedish
African Company following its establishment in 1647.[60]

Dutch investors helped underwrite the first West African ventures of
the Swedes. Willem Usselinx, architect of the Dutch West Indies Company, also proposed the creation of a joint overseas trading company to
King Christian IV. In January 1625, the Danish monarch, jealous of the
wealth enjoyed by Hamburg and other Hanseatic cities, authorized
granted an eight-year trading monopoly to Guinea, the Antilles, Brazil,
and Virginia to a consortium headed up by Jean de Willum.[61] A decade
later the king awarded a letter of patent to the brothers Jean and Gobert
Braem, creating the Company of Africa and Guinea. Between 1640
and 1661 men like Jean Lassen, Samuel Smidt and Jost Kramer sailed
from the Baltic port of Glückstadt, raiding enemy fleets and establish-
ing bases in Africa at Frederiksburg and Christiansborg.[62] During the
remainder of the seventeenth century, Danish imperialism took several
different names and forms. In July 1661, the African company was re-
organized as the Company of Gluckstadt under the direction of Martin
Baers and Gerard Bremer. A decade later (March, 1671) King Christian authorized the creation of the West Indian and Guinea Company
with six directors, three of whom were Baron Jens Juul, Count Pedersen
Lerke, and Bishop Hans Nansen.[63] In 1680, the organization took a
different name—the Company of the Antilles and Guinea, to the delight
and profit of men like Holger Pauli, Nicolas Jansen, and Jean Lykke.

The Danes not only fended off attacks by the Dutch, English and
French and mutinies of their slaves, they expanded their possessions in
Africa and the West Indies. Augustaborg, one of the principal embarka-
tion points for slaves to the New World, was established in 1787.[64]
Akwapim, Akim and Awuna peoples were being victimized in the
slavekassernes of Christiansborg. Throughout much of the eighteenth

century, Danish governors in Africa (Iversen, Kioge, Schielderup and Wrisberg) were shippping as many as 3000 blacks per year to St.John, St.Croix, and St.Thomas. Between 1671 and 1733 Denmark acquired the Virgin Islands almost by default[65] and as late as 1809 Governor Muhlenfels in Guinea was talking of sending another 10,000 slaves to colonies in the West Indies.[66] In all, the Danes shipped 333 cargoes with at least 100,000 slaves across the Atlantic before 1847 when total emancipation for blacks was proclaimed.[67] Not one of the individuals mentioned above was Jewish.

There were a handful of Jews in the Virgin Islands,[68] even less involved in the overall trade of Denmark. Jews helped develop Atona's trade with Greenland.[69] Four members of the deMoura family (Lopo, Antonio, Fernâo, and Francisco) sailed from Baltic ports to Guinea, India, Brazil, and Madeira as early as 1611. Hamburg records cite "sporadic" sailings of the Azevedo family to Tangiers and Angola, while Glückstadt documents speak of slaving activity of Moses Henriques in the seventeenth century.[70] In the end, however, these efforts were "without any lasting success" and "the voyages ceased to Guinea in the 1690s."[71] Jews are not mentioned among the principal Danish slavers to West Africa in Ivor Wilks' study of the Akan and Asante.[72] Their presence in the Danish West Indies was, at best, tolerated.[73] Even if Jews had been the principal go-betweens for the Danes, Swedes, Germans and Austrians, their role in the overall slave trade would have been puny. For as Seymour Drescher points out, "All the Baltic states together accounted for less than 0.7 percent of Africans transported to the New World."[74]

6

Unwelcome Visitors:
France and the Code Noir

Colbertism

The Secret Relationship says very little of Jewish involvement in the French slave trade. This is especially ironic since slavery was one of the building blocks of colonial empire in the sixteenth and seventeenth centuries. This was the age of mercantilism, when European governments nurtured domestic industry and raised economic barriers against foreign competition, when colonies existed for the good of the mother country, purchasing what was produced by the imperial nation and sending back raw materials, gold, silver, and sugar. For much of the seventeenth century in France the concept of mercantilism was known as Colbertism, after Jean Baptiste Colbert, the chief adviser to Louis XIV between 1661 and 1683. Controller-general of finances, secretary of state for the royal household, overseer of both the French navy and army, architect for the Tuileries Gardens and the Hotel des Invalides, Colbert was also the founder of the French East and West Indies Companies.[1]

The creation of these monopolistic joint stock companies came about in 1664, long after the Dutch and British set about dismantling the empires of Spain and Portugal. The French were every bit as eager to grab territory from the West Indian islands of Santo Domingo, Martinique and Guadeloupe to the farflung reaches of Senegambia, Pondicherry (India), and the Ile de Orleans (what was to become Louisiana). The French had already established a fort (St. Louis) at an islet leading into the Senegal River as early as 1638. In the next century, the West Indian Company would give way to the Company of Senegal (1679) and the Guinea and Africa Coast Company (1681) all of which sought to bring slaves from Sierra Leone and Cape Lopez.[2] Historians stress the role of Normandy and Rouen merchants, not Jews, in the early ventures to Sierra Leone and Cape Lopez.[3] The French chartered 3, 000 slave expeditions between 1716 and 1792 to develop tobacco, then sugar in the colonies. Fourteen-hundred ships came from Nantes, known as "the city of slaves."[4] By 1775 black slaves outnumbered whites by more than six to one on Guadeloupe and Martinique. The numbers were even more disproportionate on the island of "Saint Domingue" with 40, 000 whites and 450,000 black slaves.[5] Prominent in the activities of the Company of Senegal which brought nearly a million Africans to the French islands were Sieur d'Apougny, Andre Brue, Maurice Egrot, Francois Francois, Claude Jannequin d'Rochefort, Sieur Villault de Bellefond, Francois Raguenet, Jean Oudiette, Hippolyte Noel, and Count d'Estrees, none of them Jews.[6] France owed its claim on Louisiana to aristocratic Christians—Robert Cavalier (Sieur de La Salle), Jean Baptist LeMoyne (Sieur de Bienville), and Pierre Le Moyne (Sieur d'Iberville.) Werner Sombart was so hard-pressed to find any prominent Jew in France to support his thesis of Judaism=capitalism that he had to settle for Samuel Bernard (an eighteenth-century Christian with a baptismal certificate) who *may* have had Jewish ancestors.[7]

The virtual absence of Jews from the mercantilist miracle was itself hardly remarkable. What Jacob Marcus had written of Jews generally in the seventeenth century—"the Jew was everywhere looked upon as an inferior, a second class citizen at best and no government had as yet enfranchised him anywhere in the world"[8]—was especially true in France. But for the momentary respite enjoyed under the Carolingians, Jewish existence in France was marked by centuries of ridicule, exceptional measures, confinement in ghettos, pogroms, and expulsions. Over 100 French and north Spanish congregations had been devastated by the Shepherds' Crusade of 1320. Jews were slaughtered in the wake of the Black Death before being expelled from most of France in 1394 and Provence between 1481–86. Henry II issued *lettres patentes* to New Christians in 1550, but these individuals endured a precarious existence in coastal towns to the end of the seventeenth century. The 500 Jews in Bordeaux and Bayonne were married by parish priests and had to present their children for baptism. Yet between 1622 and 1670 there were several instances where individuals were attacked and slain for blasphemy, host desecration, and ritual murder.[9]

Despite the issuance of the Edict of Nantes by Henry IV which offered freedom to Protestant Huguenots in 1598, Catholic France remained committed to a policy of clericalist bigotry for the next 300 years. Henry's successor, the weak-willed Louis XIII reneged on the promise of toleration. Invoking the image of St. Louis (Louis IX who expelled Jews in the 13th century), Louis XIII ordered the ouster of all Jews from his realm within one month in April 1615.[10] It would not be the last such decree of the century. In 1685, Louis XIV followed up with a ukase expelling Jews from all parts of the French Empire. The few thousand Ashkenazic Jews who had straggled into Alsace-Lorraine were expelled in 1761, despite protests on their behalf attempted by Isaac Pinto and Jacob Pereira.

Expulsion from Martinique 1685

The frequency of such decrees reveals the ineptitude of their execution. While there were no substantial numbers of Jews in France until after the Thirty Years War (with the annexation of Alsace-Lorraine), New Christians in Bordeaux and Bayonne who could claim immunity from the reign of Henry II managed to avoid expulsion. Some later emigrated westward when France seized Martinique, the eight islands of Guadeloupe, and portions of Santo Domingo after 1635.[11] Here they encountered other Sephardic Jews avoiding the clutches of the Inquisition and Dutch emigres fleeing Brazil. An overworked legend, attributed to Abbe Gregoire, credits one of the Brazilian Jews, Benjamin d'Acosta, with having introduced the art of sugar cultivation to the West Indies in 1650—a wonderful achievement considering the fact that, according to a census report from Ft. Saint Pierre, d'Acosta was twenty-nine years old in 1683. He was not even born in 1650.[12]

Article IV of the newly formed *Compagnie des Iles d'Amerique* declared that all inhabitants of the newly acquired colonies should be instructed in the apostolic Roman Catholic faith. Jews were not the only dissidents in the French islands. Protestants, too, had sought sanctuary across the Atlantic. For a time, the two groups managed to gain admittance to the French colonies.[13] As everywhere, in the Indies man-power was crucial and for a price proprietary lords were willing to bend imperial rules. Thus, in 1654 a shipload of Jews and "heretics" from Brazil was rebuffed by M. Parquet, senior proprietor of Martinique, but welcomed to Guadaloupe by M. Hovel who rewarded them with land grants, livestock and slaves if they promised to develop sugar cane on his island. Not to be outdone, Parquet subsequently received a group of 300 Dutch refugees "with open arms."[14]

Jews enjoyed relative tranquility in the French islands for nearly twenty years.[15] At Cap Haitien on the northwest coast of Santo Domingo, there was a Jewish quarter (known as Calvary) with its own mikveh and cemetery.[16] Jewish numbers never presented any threat. There were only 23 families (94 individuals) on Martinique by 1694. Most of the earlier immigrants either returned to Holland or succumbed to tropical fever.[17] Jews constituted no economic threat, either. A handful, like Jacob Gabay and Jacob Luis still planted cane or ginger, while the rest were small merchants or brokers. Proof that they had been accepted supposedly came with Abraham d'Andrade who reached Martinique in 1671, bearing a letter from Louis XIV which promised religious freedom in all of the French Indies. The document read:

> Ayant été informé que les Juifs qui sont établis à la Martinique et les autres iles habilées par mes sujets ont fai des depenses assez considérables pour la culture des terres et qu'ils continuent à s'appliquer à fortifier leurs établissement, je vous fais cette lettre pour vous dire que mon intention est que vous teniez la main à ce qu'ils jouisssent des mêmes privilegès dont les autres habitants des dites iles sont en possession et que vous leur laissez une entiere liberté de conscience en faisant prendre néanmoins les precautions necessaires pour empêcher que l'exercice de leur religion ne puisse causer aucun scandal aux Catholiques.[18]

In actuality, the letter instructing that Jews "should enjoy the same privileges as all of the other inhabitants of those islands, " was issued by Colbert acting in the name of the king.[19] Minister Colbert followed up with a separate letter to Lieutenant-General Charles deBaas, governor of Martinique, clarifying the monarch's intentions of extending special protection to the Jews. Whether these letters were motivated as Petitjean-Roget suggests from Louis' desire to win Jewish support for his war with Holland, we may never know. What is certain is that the thought of Jews' securing protection of the crown, let alone equal rights with non-Jews in the islands, was a mirage.

From the moment Jews were identified on French soil, rival merchants (there were so many Bretons on Santo Domingo the island was dubbed "La Bretagne Noire") and priests (Capuchins, Carmelites, Jesuits, Dominicans) waged a campaign of derision against them. Already in 1654 Abbe Biet was complaining that Jews had bought their way into Martinique by bribing proprietor Parquet and his wife.[20] When seven Jewish families arrived in 1664, Pere du Tertre was outraged at their effrontery in demanding land.[21] Throughout this "idyllic" period, the small Jewish community of Martinique was compelled to sit through conversionary sermons. Charges kept mounting: the Jews had too many stores; the Jews had shifted the principal market day to Wednesday to avoid profaning their Saturday sabbath; they publicly assembled with their rabbis and buried their dead in Jewish rituals; despite their "hereditary hatred" for Jesus Christ, their children played with Christian tots; they corrupted innocent Christian women and daughters; they owned slaves and led them astray from observance of Catholic holy days and the catechism.[22]

While Louis hinted at toleration, his governors responded with repression. When Martinique's Jews petitioned for free practice of their religion in June 1664, Governor-General de Tracy tried to enact a series of punitive measures. Failure to observe the Christian sabbath could result in a fine of 300 livres of tobacco, failure to instruct blacks in the catechism cost 120 livres. Anyone who spoke against the Catholic church in public could be fined 60 *livres*. A child found carrying any book which contained verses contrary to the Catholic religion or eucharist was to be given twelve blows by his father at the gate of the church and his parents fined 2000 livres. de Tracy's edicts were not implemented because the general commissioners of the Compagnie at Martinique and Guadeloupe (Du Buc and Rouvelet) were Protestants![23]

De Tracy's successor was General de Baas, who received more complaints about Protestants failing to baptize correctly, of Jews working their slaves on Sunday, and of cabarets being open during prayer services. Armed with Louis' letter of May 23, 1671, de Baas was able to fend off the forces of bigotry until his death in 1676. His successor, Charles de Bourbon, Comte de Blénac, was neither so fortunate, nor as principled.

Blenac's previous experience as governor in the Antilles did not prepare him for the continuous assaults against Protestants and Jews authored by Jean-Jacques Farganel, the Jesuit curé of Ft. Saint-Pierre. Farganel lamented the economic power of Jews friendly to the Dutch, all of which worked to the detriment of French trade. He found Jewish prayer services "deplorable" and was especially exercised by the fact that some Jews were not only instructing their slaves in Jewish dogma, but were actually circumsizing them as well. The solution to Martinique's problems, said Father Farganel, was to restrict public worship of Protestants and to expel Jews altogether from the island.[24]

De Blenac finally yielded to such pressure in November 1680, complaining to the Ministry of Marine that Jews had so increased in numbers, landed property and wealth during the administration of his predecessor (de Baas) that they now controlled nearly all of the island's commerce. His petition went nowhere for two reasons: first, because Colbert, who appreciated the contributions of Protestants and Jews to the development of French trade, was heading the Ministry at the time. Secondly, there had been no great surge in the Jewish population of Martinique. According to the *recensement* (census) of 1680, there were only 81 Jews (including 40 over the age of 18) on the island. Three years later, the figure was 94, two of whom were listed as planters. The most that Colbert would concede was an instruction to Jean-Baptiste Patoulet, Intendant of Justice for the colonies, suppressing the public exercise of non-Catholic worship.

The colonial bigots were not assuaged. In December 1681, Father Farganel began preparing a lengthy memorandum directed against the Jews. Received by Louis XIV in February 1683 the poorly drafted document was divided into five sections containing an assortment of accusations plus a list of recommendations. It was accompanied by editorial observations of de Blenac's own intendant, Michel Begon, a fair-minded administrator who had been appointed by Colbert. The first section of Farganel's report complained that Jews were "notorious sacreligious apostates" whose families had been baptized in deceit. (While several families were mentioned—LeJuif, Lopez and Molina—Begon warned this accusation would be difficult to prove.) Part two of the indictment complained that Jews, whose "hatred and furor against the divine sacraments" was well known, were blaspheming against Jesus, enslaving Christians for their sugar mills, and denying them the opportunity to observe Christian festivals and Sunday worship. (Begon was unwilling to comment on the general charge of Jewish animosity toward Christianity, but noted slaves were permitted to observe Christian holidays.) Father Farganel next accused the Jews of "moving with impunity" among Christians, and of "corrupting innocent Christian women and girls. " (Begon's response to casual social interaction was that it had always been permitted. Sexual contact was another matter. "If that happens, " the Intendant wrote, "they should be punished. ") Section four of the indictment was a preposterous hodgepodge of charges. Jews and their Dutch kinsmen monopolized the island's trade and shut down all commerce on their sabbath. (Begon would not comment on this.) Further, they observed the holidays of Passover and Tabernacles and even invited Christians to eat with them in their cabanas. (Again no comment from Begon.) Present at such rituals were leaders like the "sacrificer" Braijnda (Begon pointed out he actually was a butcher) and the "circumcizer" Louis Le Juif (another error, according to Begon, since Manasses Perere peformed this task). Father Farganel denounced Jews for the pomposity of their weddings, even the "eclat" of their cemetery inscriptions. (To which Begon responded their rituals were no more pretentious than Gentiles. Moreover, the only inscriptions found on their tombstones were proper names.) The Jesuit indictment next accused the Jews of "licentiousness," of introducing the most detestable crimes and "damnable superstitions." Jews supposedly engaged in all kinds of marriage with in-laws and close relatives, even incest, and could repudiate their wives whenever they wished. (If true, said Begon, they ought to be punished.)

The last section of this denunciation consisted of an equally outrageous series of demands. Father Farganel urged that no new Jewish immigrants be admitted to the island and that those resident be tolerated only for the sake of commerce. Jews should not be permitted to practice their religion, observe the Sabbath or holidays, practice circumcision, or congregate. (Begon's observation was that this would be impossible without expelling them.) Since residence was depending upon the mercy of the king, all marriages and divorces should conform to the laws of the state. (This would be observed, noted Begon.) No Jew might insult a Christian and the scandal of apostate Jews, "a crime so destestable that it attracts the indignation and vengeance of heaven," must not be tolerated. Each week or month, Jews on the island should be obliged to attend instruction of the Catholic faith. (Begon conceded these points as well.) To more readily distinguish Jews from Christians, Jewish men and women were to wear a distinctive *marque* on their outer garments. (Begon called the evocation of the medieval badge "inutile"—pointless.) Finally, Jews should be forbidden to own slaves. At the time, the 94 Jewish men, women and children on Martinique held 132 slaves. (Once more, Begon called the suggestion "impractical.")[25]

Martinique's Jews responded to the threats against them. In 1682, Benjamin da Costa wrote Colbert seeking affirmation of the privileges extended to Jews in Louis XIV's letter of May 1671. This time the Jews were to be disappointed. Pressed by the Jesuits, his mistress Madame de Maintenon, and ministers Michel Letellier, Francoise de la Chaise, and Louvois, Louis issued another decree from Fontainbleau on September 24, 1683 just days after the death of Colbert. The negation of previous charters, It read:

Sa majesté ne voulant pas souffrir le mauvais exempte que les Juifs établis dans les Îles francaises de l'Amerique donnent à ses sujets par l'exercice de leur religion ni permettre qu'ils demeurent plus longtemps, elle mande et ordonne aux dits Juifs de sortir de l'entendue des dites Îles un mois après la publication du présent ordre.[26]

Because of their presumptuous behavior, Jews in the French West Indies were given one month to leave. Louis' promise of equal rights lasted little more than a decade. Martinique's Christian zealots were denied a complete victory, however. For one thing, the Jews were given three months, not one, to leave the island. Rather than emigrate, most publicly abjured. (On Guadeloupe, all but two families "converted easily." Not so on Saint Christophe where the entire Jewish population of 64 men, women and children quit for the British West Indies.)[27] Local administrators reported that the expulsion decrees had been "punctually executed," but, coaxed by bribes, they ignored Jewish subterfuge. As early as 1693, Isaac da Costa boldly petitioned the king for a letter of naturalization . The following year (1694) Comte de Blanac permitted six Jewish families to return to Martinique.

Anti-Jewish discrimination was institutionalized in the Code Noir of 1685 which worked against Protestants as well. The Code Noir was, in the words of Louis Sala-Molins, "the most monstrous legal text produced in modern times."[28] Article III forbade the public pracice in French territory of any faith but the Catholic. Article IV outlined punishment for masters who did not instruct their slaves in the Catholic religion. Article V ruled all non-Catholic marriages invalid, all children born of such unions bastards.[29] Such proclamations were repeated in the Code Noir of Louisiana in 1724 which established the slave system in that territory while simultaneously barring Jews.[30]

The Santo Domingo Crisis of 1765

Jews continued to reside in France and its colonies throughout the eighteenth century, but never with a sense of security, never again with a champion like Colbert. The vast compendium of laws on French colonies in the Western Hemisphere between 1550 and 1785 contains twenty-one pages of regulations which testify to the negative treatment of Jews.[31] One of these, enacted in October 1727, was an interdict against the naturalization of any foreigners in colonial possessions.

Objects of constant denunciations, Jews watched helplessly as their property was awarded to non-Jews.[32] In January 1694, Father Labat visited a cocoa plantation which belonged to Sieur Bruneau, Juge Royal of Martinique. It had previously belonged to Benjamin da Costa. The latter requested compensation from the crown for its seizure. To no avail.[33] Jews everywhere were also forced to pay shakedowns of the kind paid by their kinsmen in Bordeaux (11, 000 livres per month) or Santo Domingo

(50, 000 livres in special funds toward a "hospital, " "fountain" or "public utilities") for the privilege of remaining on French soil.[34]

The harrassment from corrupt administrators, jealous trading rivals, and bigoted priests came to a head on the island of Santo Domingo in the spring of 1765. Jews had fled there in the wake of the persecutions of the previous century. By 1760 there were forty tax-paying Jews on the western end of the island (what now is called Haiti.)[35] One of these, the elder d'Aguillard, petitioned for reinstatement of traditional rights which Sephardic Jews had enjoyed under patents dating to the mid-sixteenth century.[36] Such effrontery was apparently too much for gentiles on the island, who reacted with a memorandum of their own to the Governor-General Comte d'Estaing in April 1765, reminding him of anti-Jewish decrees issued in 1615, 1685, and 1727.

The complaints of French islanders in Santo Domingo were virtually identical to those of their predecessors on Martinique. Gentile merchants resented Jewish competition and planters like the Belin family, Stanislas Foache, and the Marquis de Gallifet (five plantations, 950 slaves) saw an easy opportunity to acquire more land. So, they complained, there were too many Jews on the island spread out everywhere. Not only had the general populace suffered through their presence, so had the welfare of France itself. For these Jews were no more patriotic than transient strangers. They were not members of the body of the nation, not subjects of the king, just transplanted foreigners who conducted a ruinous, fraudulent trade with kinsmen at Curacao and Jamaica.[37]

Santo Domingo's Jews responded with their own memorandum, pointing out that the many decrees of expulsion had never been implemented on the island. Portuguese Jews, especially, argued that they had been immune from persecution. In 1723, Louis XV confirmed their rights and privileges, distinguishing them from East European Jews.[38] Their loyalty to the crown was unquestioned, especially as they had recently contributed manpower to the defense of French Guiana. D'Aguillard's application, symbolic of Jewish residence, had been upheld as recently as 1758. Surely, his son and others like him must enjoy similar rights.[39]

Publicly, d'Estaing, who enjoyed a reputation as a liberal before coming to Santo Domingo in 1764, displayed personal distress over the affair. In February, just before he received the Christian memorandum, the governor wrote d'Aguillard thanking him for assistance in building a new barracks. A second note informed d'Aguillard of accusations made by the Christian merchants and suggested that it might be helpful if the Jews contributed 10, 000 livres to a special donation. To officials in Paris, d'Estaing praised Jews as "industrious men" who "give charity to the hospital" and "contribute to the growth of [the colony's] wealth. " Santo Domingo's Jews, he reported, fell into two categories: tradesmen and farmers, neither of whom found religion to be a major obstacle in their lives.[40] It was with great reluctance, therefore, that the Governor-General turned the Christian accusation over to the *juge du cap* (the chief magistrate on the island) on April 3, 1765 for a decision. One week later, April 10, 1765, the judge issued his decision: "each and every Jew" must depart from his jurisdiction within three months.[41]

In reality, d'Estaing welcomed the decision as a means of bleeding Santo Domingo's Jews. Four months earlier (January 18, 1765), before this entire charade was played out, the governor obtained permission from his superiors in Paris to suppress the Jews of Santo Domingo. His diary for this period snipes at what he termed fraudulent Jewish bankruptcies and exudes enthusiasm for the accusations of the Christians:

March 24, 1765. Leading merchants have come to me seeking to present a request against the Jews established in the colony. I told them I would give the greatest attention to their request.

March 30, 1765. The traders presented their request against the Jews, demanding expulsion. The request is well done, seems reasonable to me, and I have sent it to the ordinary justice. We should be ready to receive the order of the court. If the expulsion of the Israelites is ordered, it will be carried out.

April 3, 1765. The Jews are working to stay in the colony. The riches of the Jews are due to their selling at 10–15 percent cheaper than others. Christians can't sell at half the price.[42]

Instead of clarifying anything, the decree of expulsion merely confused matters. In the following months, officials in Paris and Santo Domingo debated whether to make special allowance for Sephardic Jews or to rid themselves altogether of "this truly odious resource."[43] In June, Governor d'Estaing announced he would issue "letters of relief" from the expulsion sentence—for a price of 25,000 livres. The latter came too late for d'Aguillard, the onetime spokesman for the Jews, whose true-life tragedy approximated the tale of Shylock. Financially destroyed when his gentile creditors, confident of their own immunity from lawsuits, refused to pay their debts, d'Aguillard embraced Christianity in order to remain on the island. For years, he pleaded with the treasury for compensation. But it was not until September 1787, long after his death, that the government reimbursed his heirs. By that time, the decree of 1765 was a memory and the French government "preferred to let everything fall into disuse."[44]

For the handful of Jews who continued to reside in France or the West Indies down through the time of the French Revolution, the situation remained "full of danger."[45] Taxed arbitrary sums by capricious governors, subjected to arrest, deportation, and confiscation of property, the Jews continued to send their demarches back to Paris. They had little impact upon the *ancien regime*. Says Abraham Cahen, "The force of inertia was very opposed to the march of ideas."[46]

The Gradis Family and the French Slave Trade

There is no special chapter dealing with French Jews and the slave trade in *The Secret Relationship* because, as Seymour Drescher points out, "the Jewish role ranged from marginal to virtually nil."[47] French slavers out of Bordeaux and Nantes did transport hundreds of thousands of Africans to the New World. But the religious background of these merchants was very important in Catholic France. Only a small number of non-Catholics were tolerated in the important commercial centers. Of 500 large business houses in Bordeaux, perhaps thirty were Jewish and no more than three or four of these engaged in colonial trade.[48] Writes Robert Stein: "With one exception, the minorities were Protestant. The exception was at Bordeaux, where a handful of Jewish mechants also participated in the slave trade. This participation was on a small scale and had slight impact. Only two Jewish families, Gradis and Mendez, fitted out more than one slave ship each during the entire eighteenth century: both families were of Portuguese origin and both managed to overcome local hostility to achieve prominence in the Bordeaux commercial community."[49]

The founder of this trading dynasty was Diego Rodriguez Grandis, a Sephardic Jew who came to Bordeaux at the end of the seventeenth century. His sons, Antoine, Samuel, and David, became so wealthy through the import of cocoa and production of armaments that Jews repeatedly offered non-interest loans to the city in times of famine (1709, 1710, 1712, 1715) and were able to pay a special tax of 100 million livres by 1723. A daughter's marriage to a Mendes sealed the alliance of these two great trading families. In 1732, a grandson, Abraham, travelled to Martinique to establish the western branch of the firm.[50] On August 21, 1779 Louis XVI officially acknowledged the company's contributions to France in a letter of appreciation. The French monarch thanked Gradis-Mendes for its "considerable advance of money to the nation in time of war. " He also saluted the trading house for serving as chief provisioner of American and African colonies since 1748.[51]

Among the cargoes exchanged between the homeland and Cayenne, Santo Domingo and Martinique were wine, alcohol, meat, sugar and indigo.[52] As for slaves, Madame Pierre Glotin of the *Archives Departementales de la Gironde* (the repository of the Gradis family archives) informed Rabbi Korn, "I don't believe that one would find in this collection any documents concerning the slave traffic."[53] Francoise Thésée likewise makes only three passing references (none dealing with slavery) to the Gradis family in her book *Negociants bordelais et colons de Saint-Domingue (1783–1793).*

In fact, a memorandum of Abraham Gradis on the Louisiana colony dated May 21, 1748, establishes that the firm of Mendes-Gradis was involved in the shipment of slaves as well as foodstuffs and other goods. Writing from Bordeaux, Gradis suggested the importation of 2, 000 slaves per year to Louisiana. However, he warned that shipping slaves directly to Mississippi and Louisiana would drive down prices and might even diminish profits from the colonies once slaves outnumbered free settlers. Gradis urged that slave ships stop first at Santo Domingo. Because the island was closer to Africa, slaves would arrive in better condition and higher prices might be asked. Gradis even outlined what he believed to be the ideal composition of slave ships.[54]

It is impossible to adduce from one memorandum how many slaves may have been transported by the Gradis-Mendes clan. We know that with its varied enterprises, the firm only had six ships at sea in 1725, hardly enough to dominate the French slave trade.[55] We also know that the few Jewish moneylenders in western and southern France in the eighteenth century were of no consequence in financing the traffic.[56] There were also no Jewish slave traders. According to Gabriel De Bien, regarded by some as the principal historian of the French Antilles, "I do not recall having come across any Jewish slave traders.... If there were any, I have the idea that they were not numerous. One would have to study the English slave trade for information on the subject."[57]

De Bien grants that Jews "as everyone else" in the Antilles did own slaves, but suggests that most were *esclaves de casa* (domestics). There were some plantation slaves.[58] Marie-Antoinette Menier, conservateur of the Archives Nationales, examined the records of the Mendes-France family which owned property at Seneschasy, Petit Goave, and Fond des Negres near Port-au-Prince in the eighteenth century. What she found was a series of purchases of new slaves (in 1768, 1770, 1772, 1778) and sales (30 in 1777, 53 in 1779), but no monopoly.[59]

There were other Jewish slaveowners. The 94 men, women and children on Martinique who owned 132 slaves in 1683, and whose low per capita rate confirmed DeBien's suggestion that most slaves owned by Jews were domestics. The 200 Jews of Guadeloupe (12 of them sugar factors) who owned 900 in 1685. Four members of the DePas family petitioned Governor d'Estaing of Santo Domingo in 1764 for the right to import slaves. Most of their 280 slaves were willed to Michel DePas, a mulatto, and Jacob Toussaint, a wealthy black who may have been related to Toussaint L'Ouverture, the black revolutionary who brought freedom to Haiti between 1791 and 1804.[60]

Jewish slave activity still pales when compared with the numbers attributed to a few Christian planters on Santo Domingo. Surveys conducted for the the *Institut francais d'Afrique Noire* between 1961 and 1967 yielded lists of prominent farmers, the names of their plantations, and slaveholdings for the year 1796. Among the sugar planters were Marquis de Laubriere (134 slaves), Jean-Louis, Comte de Bailleul and Jean-Baptiste Francaise, comte de Beaunay (79), the Blanchard plantation at Cul-de-Sac (84), the Toussaints at Haut-du-Cap (154), and the family Chappotin (34). Coffee and indigo magnates included Louis Andre Bartholomee (117), Sieur Arnous (58), Pierre and Gabriel Fromentin (43), Charles Arnould Hanus de Jumecourt (88), Rene Leroi (102) and that of the family Mornes (102).[61] It must be stated again that none of these planters were Jews.

We may safely conclude that Jewish involvement in the trade of the French West Indies has been much exaggerated. Any investment in planting required large sums of money and Jews had little. Says Jacob Marcus, "Most of the Jews were not great sugar planters, but supported themselves as shopkeepers and merchants."[62] What Marcus says about sugar (there is no evidence Jews made any outstanding contribution to the development of the industry which supplied France with more than 200,000,000 pounds of sugar in by 1789),[63] might be said of Jews as merchants, factors or carriers of French slaves. Native French Catholics and transplanted Dutch, Irish, German, Swiss, and Scottish financiers were far more important during the 200-year period (roughly 1600–1800) when the French were actively pursuing mercantilism in the New World.[64] On the eve of the French Revolution, there were only 40, 000 Jews in a French population of 20, 000, 000. For them, life was, as Abraham Cahen wrote, *"pleine de dangers."*[65]

7

The Age of British Mercantilism

British Joint Stock Companies: Gentile Institutions

Unquestionably, the English were the most active purveyors of Africans during the seventeenth and eighteenth centuries. Late to the slave trade, they envied Spanish wealth and sought to strip their rivals of possessions in the West Indies. The triangular trade (slaves from Africa, sugar from the islands, rum from New England) became the linchpin of British mercantilism. While the British may have despised the Spanish, they pursued control of the monopoly on slavery to the Spanish and adopted Spanish terms (asiento, Negro) to describe its features.

It is estimated that 2,000,000 blacks were shunted to British colonies between 1680 and 1786. The peak year may have been 1768 when 104,000 were uprooted.[1] The British first challenged the Portuguese monopoly on African slaves when William Towerson docked at Guinea in 1556. Six years later, John Hawkins, one of Queen Elizabeth's favorite raiders, snatched 300 slaves from Sierra Leone and carried them for sale in Hispaniola. After a century of dispute, at Utrecht in 1713 the British won the right to bring approximately 5,000 slaves per year to Spanish colonial ports for thirty years. By this time, a number of joint stock companies were operating in the trans-Atlantic trade, including the British East India Company (chartered by Elizabeth in 1600), the Company of Adventurers of London (established in 1618), the Royal African Company (chartered in 1660) and the South Sea Company (established in 1711). Merchants from London, Liverpool and Bristol were active in shipments of slaves until Lord William Wilberforce convinced his countrymen that the slave trade should be abolished in 1807.

An examination of the lists of those who contributed to the stock companies and the principal slaving merchants yields a striking conclusion. Few, if any, were Jews. There were no Jewish privateers competing with Hawkins and Sir Francis Drake for the affection of Queen

Bess. There were none among the various lords (Robert Rich, Earl of Warwick, Sir Richard Young, Sir Kenelm Digby, George Kirke, Humphrey Slaney, Nicholas Crisp, William Clobery) holding special grants from James I to pursue the African slave trade before 1625. None listed among the special letters of marque issued by the British East India Company in the 1650s to Sir Nicholas Crisp, Prince Rupert, Rowland Wilson, Thomas Walter, John Woods, Thomas Chamberlaine, Maurice Thompson, John Frederick, or Samuel Vassall. None among the twenty-seven names listed in the new charter of Charles II for the Royal Adventurers in 1660. (The original list included James Duke of York, Maria Princess of Orange, Princess Henrietta, Prince Rupert Duke of Cumberland, George Duke of Buckingham, George Duke of Albermarle, James Marquis of Ormond, Philip Earl of Pembroke, Henry Earl of St.Albans, Edward Earl of Sandwich, John Earl of Bath, Thomas Earl of Ossory, George Lord Berkely, William Lord Craven, John Lord Berkeley, Charles Lord Brandon, Sir George Carteret, Charles Howard, William Coventry, Sir Charles Sidley, Sir John Warner, Sir Charles Berkely, Henry Jermyn, William Legge, John Denham, Sir Anthony de Marces, Sir Ellis Leighton, Sir Edward Turner, Edward Gregory, Richard Nicholls, and Cornellis Vermuyden.) By 1667 this list had quadrupled to more than 110 investors, none of whom were Jews.[2] One Jew (Joseph Cohen) was listed as a director of the Scottish Company in 1698–99. Of the 249 directors and creditors of the Royal African Comopany who petitioned Queen Anne in 1711, exactly three (Phineas Gomes Serra, Abraham da Costa and Daniel Hays) or 1.2 percent were Jews.[3] Of 66 merchants (including the mayors of Liverpool and Bristol) who complained to George II of Spanish attacks against their ships during the War of Jenkins' Ear in November 1739 none were Jews. Of 72 Liverpool merchants who appealed to George III to extend the slave trade with Africa in 1807, again, none were Jews.[4]

Jews played little or no role in the establishment of the first British colonies in the Leeward Islands. Ralph Merrifield, a London merchant, underwrote the expedition to St.Christopher's (St.Kitt's) in 1624. A transplanted Dutch Protestant, Sir William Courteen, took control over Barbados that same year and was ousted from his position of privilege four years later by a syndicate headed by Marmaduke Rawden. Other settlements followed at Nevis (sponsored by Anthony Hilton and Thomas Littleon), Antigua and Montserrat (under trade warrants issued by the Council of State to Robert Wilding, Samuel Atkins, and Martin Noell). Noell, Maurice Thompson, and Thomas Povey were the chief advocates (and beneficiaries) of the seizure of Jamaica which was taken by force in 1655.[5] No Jew served as governor of Antigua, Nevis, Jamaica or Barbados. Among those credited with revolutionizing the process of grinding cane and thereby increasing sugar productivity in the West Indies were the British engineers Smeaton, Woolery, Garnett, Collinge, Fawcett, Rennie and Thistlewood, none of them Jews.[6]

Dozens of Englishmen (like William Miles of Bristol, Bryan Blundell of Liverpool and James Knight) made fortunes in sugar in the West Indies and brought their wealth back to the British Isles.[7] William Beckford, twice Lord Mayor of London, owned 22,000 acress of land in Jamaica in 1754. Anthony Wymmer owned more than 8,000 acres, Nathaniel Bayly, four sugar plantations at the time. Henry Lascelles returned from Barbados where he had served as Customs Collector and opened his own trading house (Lascelles and Maxwell) in London. Bryan Edwards did the same in Southampton. All of Jamaica's top families (the Barclays, Baylys, Beckfords, Bourkes, Briscoes, Campbells, Chambers, Dawkins, Fullers, Grants, Grays, Hibberts, Jacksons, Longs, Pennants, Vaughans) maintained close connections with commission agents and/or banks in London.[8] They banded together to form mutual self-help organizations like the Societies of West India Merchants in Bristol, London, and Glasgow.[9] These millionaires did more than share information on tilling and milling. Between 1730 and 1775, seventy of the so-called "West Indians" were members of Parliament, England's ruling body to which no Jew could be admitted.[10]

The wealth of the Indies was generated by slavery. Between 1710 and 1795 England's slave fleets sailed from three ports: London, Bristol and Liverpool (see table 7.1 below). 90 percent of the vessels bound from Bristol were involved in the transatlantic slave trade. Writing to Rabbi Korn in January 1974, David Richardson of the Department of Economic and Social History of the University of Yorkshire, advised,"regarding the Bristol slave trade venture agents, I do not believe that there were any Jews among them."[11] Rabbi Sefton Temkin of the Department of Judaic Studies at SUNY, went further, saying, "I don't think the Jews of the two seaports in question [Bristol and Liverpool] had reached the mercantile status to enable them to engage in such far reaching operations."[12]

After 1750 most slave ships cleared Liverpool where merchants undercut competitors by 12 percent by hiring on boys as deckhands, issuing annual not monthly payrolls, and offering flat commissions to factors. Ninety-seven percent of the vessels bound from Liverpool were en-

TABLE 7.1
British Slave Ships to West Africa 1789–1795

Year	Liverpool	Total Clearances London	Bristol
1789	61	15	18
1790	93	16	25
1791	97	25	31
1792	131	22	42
1793	48	12	12
1794	110	14	17
1795	70	14	12

Source: D.P. Lamb, "Volume and Tonnage of the Liverpool Slave Trade 1772–1807," in *Liverpool, The African Slave Trade and Abolition*, Roger Anstey and P.E.H. Hair (eds.) (Historic Society of Lancashire and Cheshire, 1976), p. 93.

gaged in the transatlantic slave trade. Eighty-eight ships from Liverpool carried 24,730 slaves to the New World in 1752. Liverpool was so deeply involved in slavery that abolitionist George Crooke reproached, "Every brick in your infernal town is cemented with an African's blood."[13] The names of John Bolton, John Tarleton, J.Aspinwall, Francis Ingram, Thomas Clare, John Shaw, John Clarke, and Thomas Leyland appear among the Liverpool traders who outfitted 150 vessels to bring 52,557 slaves in 1798, another 132 vessels that transported 45,281 slaves in 1799.[14] According to B.K. Drake, seven firms (T.and W. Earle, Francis Ingram, J. France, J. Blackburne, G.Hodson, Earles and Molyneaux, and Allanson and Barton) controlled the slave trade. Several of Liverpool's outspoken abolitionists, William Rathbone and William Roscoe even permitted their own West Indian freight to be carted back to England aboard slave ships. None of the owners or captains of these ships were Jews.[15]

Such statements did not hold true for London. The British South Seas Company conducted much of the trade to South America and the Caribbean out of the seaport/capital. In her classic study of slave documents, Elizabeth Donnan cited some of the principal directors of the company in 1713, including William Heysham, Richard Harris, William Tryon, Edward Chester, William Chapman, Dudley Woodbridge, and Charles Rowland.[16] None were Jewish. Donnan found only incidental references to Jews (petitions of an individual named Mendes— no first name given—and Isaac Fernandez Nunez from 1715). Donnan was not looking specifically for references to Jews, but Rabbi Korn was. In 1970, Korn poured over the ninety-one volumes of papers of the South Seas trading Company dating from 1711 to 1856 and, like Donnan, found a few, isolated notations in the minutes of the company. None of the seven entries between January 25,1716, and March 14, 1720 dealt with slavery.[17] Amid the South Seas Company papers, however, Korn did identify thirty-one names of possible Jews/ Marranos who were qualified to vote in elections for the board of directors. These included Menasseh Mendes, Moses Mendes, Abraham Mendes, Alvaro da Fonseca, Francis and Solomon Pereyra, Isaac Nunez, Alfonso Rodriguez, and five members of the da Costa family.[18] A separate list of important Jewish merchants in London in 1700 turned up twenty whose business transacions amounted to more than £1000, another twelve whose net worth was more than £4000 ($20,000).The list included Alvarez de Fonsca, Menasseh Mendes, Isaac Nunez, Francis and Solomon Perreira, Joseph Rodriguez, Alfonso Rodriguez, Rodrigo Ximenes, and Alvaro, Joseph, Anthony Sr. and Anthony Jr. Da Costa.[19]

The Jewish Return to Britain

Considering the history of Jews in England, it is remarkable that any could have achieved such prosperity by the end of the seventeenth century. England's insular nature worked as a barrier to any but the hardiest of Jewish merchants before the Norman Conquest in 1066. Thereafter, only a handful attempted to settle in the British Isles. Their story was one of rejection by the guilds, denial of land tenure by the nobles, and massacre at the hands of mobs like the one at York in 1190 which cost the lives of 150 people. In the end, Britain's Jews, too, suffered the fate of their Spanish, Portuguese and French cousins. In the summer of 1290, between 2,000 and 3,000 people (less than 1 percent of the total population) were expelled.

Jews could not have controlled any aspect of the economy because officially there were none in the British Isles for the next 350 years. A rare Marrano perhaps, but it was not until February 1656 that the revolutionary government of Oliver Cromwell saw fit to readmit Jews. Even then, there was no formal revocation of the old expulsion decree, no general proclamation of amnesty from Parliament. Motivated by Calvinist millenarianism and the anticipation of expanded trade with Holland, the government simply dropped what had previously been effective barriers to Jewish immigration. When Charles II was restored to the throne in 1660 he also disdained issuing any official decree.[20]

Jews came to England and they kept coming: 414 by 1684; over 800 by 1695; 6,000 in 1734; 7000–8000 in 1753; 25,000 in 1800; 35,000 in 1851; 60,000 in 1880; 100,000 in London alone between 1870 and 1914.[21] They came seeking sanctuary after the Portuguese reclaimed Brazil from Holland in 1654. 99 came between 1721 and 1732 when Portugal reinstituted the Inquisition. They came, fearing the Spanish during the War of Jenkins' Ear in 1739–42.[22] They came fleeing tsarist pogroms of the nineteenth century.

For the most part, they were *Betteljuden* , weary, destitute people who arrived with parcels of clothing and little else. As Harold Pollins writes, "The idea that 'Jewish capitalists and their representatives at once flocked into England' is a gross exaggeration."[23] Until the end of the nineteenth century, Jews were funnelled into rickety firetraps between Whitechapel and Commercial Lanes where they languished in poverty. Unfamiliar with the language and lacking skills, they improvised, becoming petty traders, street peddlers, ragmen, boxers, and pickpockets. Some became familiar with the confines of debtors' prisons and the Old Bailey jailhouse. Others became printers, bakers, tailors, perfumers, butchers, barbers, hatters, fishmen, engravers. Because of connections with relatives in Holland, a few even became rather adept at the diamond trade.[24]

Despite such minimal achievements, Jews in the Georgian period (and the Victorian era) were, as Todd Endelman writes, "desperately poor."[25] This was true in Ireland where 150 of 200 Jews on the island in 1852 were dependent upon charity. It was true of Manchester where in 1841 79 of 88 Jewish shopkeepers sold clothing, hardware or stationery. It was true of Liverpool where the Hebrew Philanthropic Society was sustaining dozens of families to 1857. It was true of Bristol where relief was a principal concern of the Jewish community. And it was true of London where the Sephardim had a difficult time raising funds to maintain a synagogue in the 1670s and where 30 percent of the newly arrived immigrants of the nineteenth century required public assistance.[26]

Jewish bankers like Samson Gideon who helped restore the Credit Bank of England in 1745, the Prager brothers who came from Holland in the 1790s, Benjamin Goldsmid and Nathan Rothschild, jewelers like Moses and Lewis Samuel, contractors like Mendes da Costa and Abraham Prado, insurance magnates like Moses Montefiore did manage to achieve wealth. But their success is misleading. Jews were missing from the development of great industries—textiles, steam, coal, iron, steel, shipbuilding—in England. Only one served as a member of the board of directors of the Bank of England. Only 5 percent of the 138 members listed on the London Stock Exchange in the 1880s were Jews.[27] According to Endelman, no more than ten Jewish families who lived in England in the middle of the eighteenth century could be chastized for an "opulent " lifestyle. Perhaps ten Jews possessed great fortunes or engaged in large-scale foreign trade.[28] To the present day, London's Jews claim as their biggest contribution to British culture not money but "business acumen," scholarship, and the development of the cheap clothing industry.[29]

There were a number of reasons for the generally depressed level of existence of British Jews. The first, and most obvious, was theological hatred, the byproduct of New Testament polemics and the Psalter. Populist demagogues like William Cobbett incited the masses with their charges of Jewish pretentiousness, greed, and cheating.[30] Gentile merchants pressed for measures that would impair the rights of Jewish competitors. Parliament, which was unwilling to publicly disclaim Jewish expulsion in the seventeenth century was less laconic in imposing double taxes and special duties upon alien Jews in England. Jews were restricted in making charitable donations, lending money, purchasing land, and especially in seeking denization (residence rights) or endenization (trading privileges).[31] Seymour Drescher reports that resentment against "swarms of Jews" flared to such a point that some British demagogues were urging special registration, collective liability, even deportations between 1764 and 1770. Hostility against Jews was so severe, that a French schoolteacher, mistaken as a Jew, was nearly lynched.[32]

Relations with the crown were just as bad. Charles II (1660–1685) established the pattern for dealing with Jews shortly after his restoration and only five years after the Jews returned to England. In July 1661, the British monarch denied the application of three Jews seeking the right to trade in "his Majestys Plantations."[33] Charles was obviously impressed with the complaint of rival merchants who warned that "Jews were so subtle in matters of trade, they will ingross trade among themselves and divert it elsewhere." Using like charges of "treacherous behavior," "fraudulent inducements," and "cheating," he ordered several Jewish ships seized and at least ten men banished from the islands of Barbados and Jamaica between 1665 and 1668.[34]

"The proportion of the total trade of London handled by Jewish merchants," writes Pollins,"was small." Their role in the overseas trade with South America and the British West was likewise "relatively un-important."[35] They were not involved in the tobacco trade, which devolved into the hands of Scottish merchants. They could not monopolize traffic in commodities (wine from the Canaries, cloth from Northern Europe, sugar from the West Indies, or fish from Newfoundland.) Jewish merchants in Liverpool and Bristol may have supplied slavers with supplies, clothes and food for their journeys. but it is folly to speak of Jewish control of any aspect of the British economy, let alone the slave trade.

Jews in the Trade of the British West Indies

Farrakhan's scholars concede nothing about the Jews of England, stressing instead the involvement of insurance underwriters, stockbrokers and merchants, all of whom profited from the "invisible" aspect of the slave trade. Even more villainy is ascribed to Jews who actually resided on the other side of the ocean. *The Secret Relationship* charges that "Jewish slave traders procured black Africans by the tens of thousands and funnelled them to the plantations of South America and throughout the Caribbean." This was supposedly so in Barbados where Jews brought in so many Africans, that Gentiles finally had to limit their involvement in 1679 for fear of black rebellion.[36] It was so in Nevis where five Jewish families owned 43 slaves. It was so in Jamaica where "Jews were highly active" and "significant" in the slavocracy.[37]

Some Jews in Barbados and Jamaica did dabble in underwriting insurance for transatlantic ventures. Richard Sheridan of the University of Kansas claims Sephardic Jewish refugees taught the British cane culture and lists a Kingston merchant (Aaron Baruch Lousada) as the biggest creditor on Jamaica between 1766 and 1775.[38] Four Jewish companies (Aguilar and Copello, David Henriques, Alex Lindo, and Hyman Levy) were listed as slave traders in the principal journals of Kingston between 1779 and 1806.[39] Steven Fortune claims,"Jews did deal in the slave trade and were also local slave brokers and kept slaves for hire."[40] Fortune offers examples of large scale transactions on Jamaica in 1689 where Jewish brokers imported 14000 worth of sickly slaves (approximately 500 Africans) to be sold at 8–10 £ each and on Barbados after 1700 where Isaac and Moses Mendez brought in another 522.[41] There is also incidental evidence from records of the South Seas Company and the Royal Guinea Company implicating shippers like Isaac Nunez, David Henriques, Alexander Lindo, Hyman Levy, Alvares Noguera, and Isaac da Costa between 1699 and 1780.[42] Rabbi Korn researched the invoice books of the Royal African Company to the West Indies between 1676 and 1729 and chronicled the import of more than 1000 slaves by Jews.[43] He also discovered a dismayingly long list of slaves owned by Jews on the island of Jamaica in 1838, when courts were awarding compensation for emancipation.[44]

Closer scrutiny does not sustain charges of extensive Jewish wrongdoing. Fortune's own statistics (below) indicate there were approximately 40,000 slaves both on Jamaica and Barbados by 1700. The 500 slaves imported to Jamaica by Jews in collaboration with Christian subbrokers in 1689 represented 2 percent of the slaves on this island at the time. The same was true for the large deal on Barbados by the firm of Mendez noted above.

Korn's citations from the invoice books of the Royal African Company are flawed because they do not list the total number of ships, let alone a complete number of slaves on all boats coming to the Indies during the fifty years under examination. Individual Jews did make large purchases (28 by Joseph Mendez in January 1694; 46 by Benjamin Carbello, 41 by MosesCordoso in January 1695; 169 by Aaron Lamego in December 1708; 146 by Isaac and Benjamin Bravo in March 1723) but these were anomalous transactions. Where we have a complete accounting, Jews purchased a fraction of the slave cargoes. Five Jews bought 29 of 108 slaves (27 percent) aboard the *South America* in 1681.[45] Three Jews purchased ll of 376 slaves (3.5 percent) aboard *John's Bonaventure* which arrived in Jamaica in October 1682.[46] Two Jews purchased 33 of 134 blacks (24 percent) landing on the same island in

TABLE 7.2
Slaves in Jamaica and Barbados

	Barbados		Jamaica
1629	29	1661	514
1643	6,000	1670	2,500
1655	20,000	1673	9,504
1673	33,000	1677	20,000
1690	40,000	1703	45,000
1712	41,900	1722	80,000
1734	46,360	1739	99,239
1748	47,025		

Source: Fortune, *Merchants and Jews,* p.58.

February 1684.[47] Eight Jews from Port Royal purchased 68 of 495 slaves (14 percent) in Jamaica on December 10, 1684.[48] Twenty-seven of 111 slaves (14 percent) aboard the *Return to Jamaica* were purchased by Moses Cardoso in October 1686.[49] Twenty-six of 221 (12 percent) bound for Nevis aboard the *Edward and William* in October 1699 were purchased by Isaac Pereira and Abraham Bueno de Mesquita.[50] Thirty of 443 (7 percent) bound for Barbados aboard the *Royal Africa* in November 1703 were purchased by Joseph Mendes.[51] Mendes also purchased 60 of 442 slaves (14 percent) aboard the *Royal Africa* which docked at Barbados in May 1707.[52]

Reprehensible as these purchases may be, they reveal no Jewish domination of cargoes, let alone the entire slave trade. In the British islands, as elsewhere, Jews purchased small numbers as domestics. This is borne out by review of the compensation claims from Jamaica and Barbados in 1838. Of 30 masters (with 417 slaves) on the island of Barbados, 18 owned three or less and eight owned one or two. In the parish of Kingston, Jamaica, there were 315 claims for compensation on 1486 slaves. Of these 191 involved masters with less than four slaves. In the parish of St. Catherine, there were 66 cases involving 382 slaves. Of these 38 claims related to cases of four slaves or less.[53]

Critics of the Jews may hasten to point out that there were also some great slaveholders among those seeking compensation for emancipating blacks in 1837–38. Alexander Bravo owned 488 of the 489 slaves owned by Jews in the parrish of Vere. Judah Levy owned 140 of 161 in Port Royal. The combined slave holdings of Hyman, Judah and Henry Cohen in St. Elizabeth, Manchester, St. George and St. Andrew parishes totalled nearly 1400. Such numbers could not be rationalized as house slaves. They were the last vestiges of an earlier time when Jews were influential, not dominant, in the sugar, indigo, and vanilla plantations of the islands.

The Jews of Barbados

The original British contingent to Barbados in 1627 consisted of 80 whites and 10 blacks. By 1643, the island's population numbered 18,000 Europeans (a few of whom may have been Crypto-Christians) and 6000 slaves. The destiny of Barbados changed with the arrival in 1656 of the first professing Jews—Dr. Abraham de Mercado and his son David. Refugees from Recife, Brazil, the Mercados introduced a new style of sugar mill to the British colonies.[54] Before the end of the century, 50 percent of the 166 square miles of land surface on the island would be devoted to sugar. There were 300 large plantations and 400 sugar mills all in need of slave labor, 175 planters, many of them from Madeira, Spain and Morocco, owned 60 or more slaves; 18,700 Africans were imported between 1627 and 1650 when the new mills were introduced. Thereafter, the lords of Barbados, important cogs in the triangular trade, bought and sold 353,068 black slaves.[55]

Jewish names appear among slaveholders and importers on Barbados. Of 8,580 Africans dragooned to the island aboard 53 ships between 1698 and 1704, 522 (6 percent of the total) were consigned to Isaac and Moses Mendez.[56] Such citations, however, are rarities. A counting undertaken in 1650 shows 150 blacks (approximately 1 percent of all slaves on the island) owned by Jews.[57] No Jews are included in the list of 175 prominent planters who owned 53 percent of the land, 54 percent of the slaves in 1679–80.[58] By this time there were 260 Jewish men, women and children on Barbados. They owned 317 slaves (exactly 0.7 percent) of all the blacks on the island.[59] Many of these slaves belonged to just four men (David da Costa, David Namias, Benjamin Bueno and Daniel Bueno Henriques) who were listed as planters.[60] But their farms (ranging in size from 10 to 40 acres and manned by 15 or 20 slaves) could not compare with the plantations of aristocrats like Samuel Newton from Christ Church who owned 267 slaves, John Gittens, the Anglican Rector of St.John's Parish, and the attorney Forster Clarke.[61]

Not only was the level of Jewish slave ownership small in the 1600s, it actually declined in the next century. For good reason—the Jews were very poor and they faced constant harrassment. In Bridgetown, the census of 1680 listed 45 Jewish taxpayers, five of whom were counted in the higher income bracket, 31 in the lower brackets.[62] At the same time, there were more Jewish children (185) than slaves (12) among the 52 Jewish families of St.Michaels.[63] Examination of some 90 Jewish wills on file at the American Jewish Archives reveals no important Jewish planters, few Jews who did not manumit their slaves.[64]

Jews had always been upopular on the island. A visitor to Barbados in 1657, Henry Whistler, described it as a "dunghill" populated by all sorts—"English, French, Duch, Scotes, Irish, Spaniards thay being Jues."[65] In official correspondence, Jews were described in the same terms used by King Charles as "very treacherous" and pro-French or Dutch in their trading activities.[66] Early on, Jews were denied the right to employ Christian indentured workers. Jews were barred from taking Christian debtors to court. By the end of the seventeenth century they could not import any goods, let alone slaves, unless they were naturalized or denized. The only way any managed to stay on the island was by periodically taking "loathesome oaths" of allegiance[67] or making gifts of mock baked goods to administrative officials. Known as "Jew pies" or tarts, these delicacies were crusted with piles of gold coins.[68]

Just as elsewhere in the West Indies, Jews on Barbados were an insecure minority, most of whom were relatively poor shopkeepers with their families, each day confronting overt hostility and each night dealing with the spectre of expulsion. Jacob Marcus allows that Jews did play a part in the development of the sugar industry. But having found no Jewish plantations listed on a map of the island dating from 1657, having identified no more than six or seven sugar and indigo farms owned by Jews at any time, Marcus writes, "One suspects that as the industry became a big business, Jews were given fewer opportunities to participate in it."[69] Gordon Merrill is more direct. He writes, "One must conclude that the Jews were not as important as agriculturalists on Barbados as they had been in Brazil and Surinam."[70]

By 1750, 100 years after they supposedly masterminded the sugar revolution on the island, the Jews of Barbados were described as "a feeble folk, numbering scarce half a dozen, headed by the Baezas." In 1789, Jews made up only 1/20th of the population. At a time when Barbados was importing its greatest number of slaves, Jews owned 1/100th of the property on the island.[71] In the next century, there would only be 100 Jews left in Bridgetown, safeguarding the remaining synagogue with its overcrowded cemetery.[72]

The Jews of Jamaica

The lot of Jews in Jamaica was virtually identical with that of those on Barbados. Before the end of the seventeenth century, they faced discrimination in securing endenizaion. They were denied the right to vote, could not serve in the militia or civil offices. Their testimony was excluded in a court of law. There were problems in transferring property through inheritance. Jews were not permitted to hire indentured servants or legally own more than two slaves. (Most managed to get around this.) Jamaica's Jews were forced to pay special taxes, again in the form of propitiatory pies. On occasion, a Jew accused of presumption might have to get down on his hands and knees in public and beg forgiveness.[73] Following an earthquake or hurricane, Jews might be required to pay a lump sum atonement fine, as if they were responsible for the natural disaster.[74] Segregated into "Jew Streets," they operated shops where all kinds of "vendibles" (hats, shoes, fabrics) were sold. Jews were also listed as tailors, bricklayers, seamstresses.[75] Whatever virtues they possessed were transformed into liabilities. Thrift became penury and Jews were ridiculed as "damned disagreeable people" or "peddlers of scotch."[76] Jews were accused of smuggling. Their willingness to sell to blacks led Christians to accuse them of encouraging blacks to steal, gamble, drink, rebel, and run away.[77] And, periodically, they were subjected to violent attacks, as in 1739 when gentiles burned down the Speightstown synagogue.[78]

All of this is ironic since Jews were relative latecomers to Jamaica. They also presented no real threat to the island's economy. There were Marranos on the island around 1580 when the Braganza family united territories of Spain and Portugal. A crypto-Christian may have served as mayor of Kingston. Professing Jews did not arrive in Jamaica until after their expulsions from Brazil and Surinam in the 1660s. Of 717 landowners listed in a 1670 accounting, only one had a Jewish name. A number of land grants were issued to Jews between 1665 and 1694.[79] On Jamaica, an island twenty-six times larger than Barbados, there were five plantations owned by Jews.[80] By the end of the century, there were 80 Jewish families in Jamaica, fewer than were found at the same time in Barbados. The great plantations on Jamaica, 500 controlling one million acres by 1750,[81] belonged to wealthy aristocrats like Lord Seaford (who owned three properties), John Baillie (with a huge estate at Roehampton), Sir Henry Fitzherbert (absentee proprietor of sugar mills), John Gladstone of Liverpool, attorney Henry Goulburn, Edward Lascelles, Sir Edward Hyde East (who ran a coffee plantation near Kingston), Richard Beckford (owner of five plantations and 1,000 slaves), the Radnors (206 slaves), the Irwin family (231 slaves), Sir Rose Price, J.F. Barham (whose slaves had an abominable attrition rate of 352 per 1,000), and Thomas Roughley, a modern would-be Cato who drafted an instructional guide for the treatment of plantation slaves.[82] There were 313,000 slaves in Jamaica when slavery was abolished in 1834. Exactly 6,060 (less than 2 percent) belonged to Jews.[83] Merrill declares, "One is forced to conclude that planting was not widespread among the Sephardic Jews of Jamaica."[84]

Despite adverse conditions, there were as many Jews in Jamaica in 1775 (2500) as in all the British colonial possessions of North America.[85] They most assuredly were not shippers or planters. Writing to the Duke of Newcastle in July 1738, Governor Edward Trelawny confirmed that only a small percentage paid taxes as planters. "Their way of business," wrote Trelawny, "is chiefly in disposing of dry goods and in keeping of shops."[86] Trelawny, of course, painted a much more sanguine picture of Jewish existence on the island, declaring that their exclusion from jury duty and other civic responsibilities was actually a boon, freeing them for other enterprises, and suggesting that Jews enjoyed freedom of the profession of their religion. The governor of Jamaica did, however, feed notions of Judaeophobia when he reported that Jews, the principal importers of alcohol, were selling spirits, and possibly gunpowder, to rebellious blacks on the island.[87]

Jews were not engaged in some secret cabal with blacks on the island. Neither were they the principal dealers in African flesh. Jews lacked the wealth and resources necessay to sustain investments, let alone possible losses in the transatlantic slave trade.[88] "Though Jamaica was one of the world's great slave marts," writes Marcus,"there is very little evidence that Jamaican Jewry was engaged in that traffic except, of course, in the purchase and sale of servants for use in their own homes and shops, at the wharves and on the plantations."[89] Whether in Jamaica or any of the other islands, Jews generally were unfamiliar with farming techniques. Their wills testify to the small numbers of slaves held at any time. Reference in manumission documents to blacks who were trained as artisans and tradesmen suggests less brutal treatment of slaves Marcus concludes, "Planting was based on slavery and most Jews simply possessed insufficient capital to involve themselves in the industry. Few were merchant shippers because it required wealth and resources beyond the capacity of more than a handful of Jews."[90]

Britain did come to dominate the transatlantic slave trade in the eighteenth century. But those who see in the brutal uprooting of millions of Africans the heavy hand of Jews are being disingenuous. When England embarked on empire-building under the rule of Queen Elizabeth, there were no practicing Jews in the realm. Their absence, combined with their generally miserable state throughout the world, inspired noble sentiments from Christopher Marlowe and William Shakespeare. Three hundred years later, the pervasive state of misery enjoyed by Victorian Jews would lead Charles Dickens to stereotype Jews in the British Isles in the person of the petty thief/fence Fagin, hardly a Rothschild, still less an international slavebroker.

8

The First Jews in America:
New York and the Middle Colonies

Pilgrims from Curaçao

At the end of July 1654, the bark *St. Catherine,* carrying twenty-three Jewish refugees from Curaçao, docked at New Amsterdam.[1] While historians agree the permanent settlement of Jews in North America began with the arrival of these four men, six women and thirteen children in the Dutch colony, there is evidence to suggest Jews arrived much earlier. There may have been Marranos among the Spanish settlers of St. Augustine in Florida in 1565 or Santa Fe, New Mexico when it was established in 1610. The names Torres, Rodriguez, and Abraham, favored by Crypto-Christians, are fairly common among Spanish settlers in the Southwest.[2] Joachim Gause, a Jewish metallurgist, accompanied the doomed Roanoke expedition at the end of the sixteenth century. In 1621, Elias Legardo reached Virginia aboard the *Abigail.* Three years later, a Rebecca Isaac was listed among the residents of that British colony. On July 8, 1654, three weeks prior to the arrival of the twenty-three Jews from Curaçao, Jacob Barsimson, identified as a Jewish debtor, was permitted to land in New Amsterdam.[3]

Awarding the distinction of first Jews in America is almost as difficult as attempting to enumerate how many Jews there were at any given time. For reasons of safety, status or commerce, some Jews continued to conceal their identity, not just from potential Inquisitors but from the supposedly more benign British as well. In virtually every colony, documents are lost, some illegible. Census records, which continue to miss people in the twentieth century, may not reflect the movement of transients. Census tracts give us names, not religion. Scholars have come up with an assortment of numbers of Jews in America during the colonial period. Earl Grollman and Joseph Rosenbloom attempted to list every Jew in North America between 1654 and 1700 and identified 77 "indubitable Jews" and an overall estimate of 462 people who might be tinged with Jewish ancestry.[4] If there were 70,000 Europeans (as Jacob Marcus estimates),[5] Jews would have constituted 0.6 percent of the total white population in 1700. The number of Jews cited by Marcus and Rabbi Korn for the time of the American Revolution is 2,500 or less than 0.3 percent of the population in 1776.[6] Ira Rosenwaike, one of several scholars who closely scrutinized the first official U. S. census in 1790, suggests that such numbers may be inflated. Culling lists from households, congregational membership lists, tombstone inscriptions, marriage and death notices, Rosenwaike (whose name is frequently invoked by the editors of *The Secret Relationship*) found only 1300 to 1500 Jews in the United States), less than 0.01 percent of the population.[7]

What kind of people were these pilgrims in the New World? Were they the bold and daring, the achievers in European society or the frightened and the weak, running from familiar torment to something hopefully better? Were the Jews, as NOI scholars maintain, "savy businessmen whose wealth far surpassed that of many immigrants"?[8] Or were they accurately portrayed by Korn when he wrote that the typical American Jew of the mid-eighteenth century was "of German origins, a shopkeeper, hardworking, enterprising, religiously observant, frequently uncouth and untutored, but with sufficient learning to keep his books and write simple business letters in English."[9] Korn's colonial Jews kept kosher, contributed to the upkeep of synagogues and cemeteries, and even made regular donations to institutions in Palestine.[10] Professor Marcus has described them as a mixed group of paupers sent by London charities, their relatives who came after, suttlers who accompanied soldiers, and venturesome businessmen, weak in capital but strong in ambition, many of whom were incompetent, but all of whom were "seeking a world of lesser competition and greater opportunity."[11] As farming was "not the metier of these immigrants," the typical Jew was "a businessman who owned a small home."[12]

This hardy band had to be extraordinarily stolid. Far from being welcomed, Jews experienced anti-Semitism from the moment they set foot in North America. This was not surprising. As Professor Marcus writes, "Judaeophobia was indeed deeply rooted in every group. All immigrants brought their medieval anti-Jewish prejudices across the Atlantic with their baggage."[13] If Jews were reviled and persecuted throughout Europe and the Middle East, if such attitudes were communicated to South American and Caribbean colonies, why shouldn't such bigotry also operate in North America?

Peter Stuyvesant had tried to frustrate the settlement of Jews in Curacao before being appointed governor of New Amsterdam. Confronted with the first shipment of refugees in 1654, Stuyvesant appealed to the directors of the Dutch West Indies Company, claiming that Jews were "repugnant," "a deceitful race" of "godless rascals" who would cause trouble. Their indigence would become a burden upon the colony. Some might divert trade away to New Sweden. They would demand free and public exercise of "their abominable religion" (a cemetery, reversal of sabbath worship), the right to serve in the militia, and soon the colony would be overrun with "aliens and nonconformists."[14] Stuyvesant was seconded in these complaints (which were rejected by the DWIC directors) by Dom Johannes Megapolensis of the Dutch Reformed Church, who castigated Jews as "servants of Baal" and urged that if they were admitted they be confined to a ghetto.[15]

While Jews may have been permitted to land, they suffered a number of disabilities under the Dutch. Initially, they could not buy land or hold public religious services. They could not vote, hold office or serve in the military.[16] They were barred from trading with the Indians and were latecomers to slave ownership, which had been introduced by Dutch Calvinists to the Mohawk Valley as early as 1624.[17] Somehow, though, Jews managed to account for five of the twenty wealthiest men in the Dutch colony. A few more eked out a "relatively modest" lifestyle trading in beer, wine, and tobacco.[18] Many more found Dutch rule intolerable and emigrated, leaving the colony with perhaps fifty Jews out of a total of 1,000 persons when the British seized New Amsterdam (renamed New York) in 1664.

This transfer of authority did little to improve their lot. Throughout the British colonies, Jews were denied citizenship, could not serve as lawyers, let alone testify in a court of law, were denied the franchise or right to hold office. They still could not engage in transatlantic commerce because the British Navigation Act of 1660 required that goods traded with an English colony be carried on ships built and owned by Englishmen. The Conventicle Act of 1664 gave special recognition to the Church of England and resulted in prosecutions of Jews in England who conducted public services. Though the Duke of York instructed Governor Edmund Andros to preserve "liberty of conscience" in New York, it was not until 1696 that Jews, along with Huguenots, were granted limited rights. These remained in dispute, along with questions of naturalization, through the 1740s.[19] The Jews of New York managed a permit for their first synagogue in Jew's Alley in 1730 (seventy years after they first arrived in this major port.) The press regularly vilifed them as "devilish" and complained about their "cheating" business practices.

Synagogues, homes and cemeteries were desecrated not only in New York but also at Philadelphia and Newport. Some zealots suggested creating a ghetto for New York's Jews, but more moderate churchmen favored constitutional barriers against the entry of "Jews, Turks, Spinozists, deists, and perverted naturalists."[20]

The Jews of New York

Despite official and personal hostility, the number of Jews in New York City grew—from 10 households in 1678 to 17 in 1700, 20 by 1722, 31 in 1728, 40 by 1790. At the same time, there was also a consistent decline in the percentage of Jews in the overall population, from 2.3 percent in 1728 to 0.73 percent in 1790 (when 242 Jews were listed among the city's 33,131 residents) to 0.4 percent in 1820 (when there were 550 Jews in the official count of 123,706 residents.)

The Secret Relationship allows that Jews in colonial New York may have been few in number, but charges they were very powerful as "dealers, owners, shippers, or supporters of the slave trade."[21] NOI editors offer as proof a list of fifty prominent eighteenth century Jewish traders, including David Franks, Jacob Franks, Daniel Gomez, Haym Salomon, Jacob Fonseca and Moses Levy, plus an 1830 listing of twenty-six Jews who owned a total of thirty-two slaves, and through selective references from "Some Aspects of the New York Jewish Merchant and Community, 1654–1820," a study done for the American Jewish Historical Association by Leo Hershkowitz in 1976.

Jacob Marcus tells us that some Jews did enjoy "well-appointed homes, silver, fine linen, expensive glassware, good cutlery, rugs and carpets."[22] According to Hershkowitz, Jews at one time did constitute a major segment of the mercantile population and "were an important part of the colonial trade."[23] One, Isaac Franks, left £300,000 when he died in England in 1737.[24] Moses Levy and Abraham Lucena supplied the British expeditionary force against Canada in 1711. Sampson Simpson, Hayman Levy, Benjamin Seixas, Judah Hays, and Isaac Moses owned ships and were members of the Marine Society. Between 1719 and 1772 the family of Daniel, Luis, and Moses Gomez outfitted several vessels that carried earthenware, clothing, gunpowder, silks, pork,cheese, sugar, grindstones, coal and pewter between New York and the West Indies.[25] Uriah Hendricks, a shopkeeper who came to

America in 1755, dealt in such arcane goods as stock muskets, blunder-busses, swivel guns, green ratteens, swan skins, raven's duck, osnabrigs, penniston, blue and red strouds, bays, dowles, clouting diaper, plumb-colour grazets, ferrits, silk romals, pee longs, black alamodes, black padusoy, fine French vetery, Irish dowlas, castor hats, women's callimancoe, hyson tea, muscavado sugar, glaubert salts, ratesia and capilair in cases, Jesuits' bark, fine and common Russian drilling, stone blue in casks, steel chapes, scarlet and blue rattinets, tobines, gensa velverets, huckabacks, Florentines, sattinets, buff-colored Jennets, In-dia dimity, cane for ladies' hoopos, hair shaggs, white dimothee, log lines, boulting cloth, fine Yorkshire and bath coatings, worden rop, as-sorted queen's ware, diapere doweling, chip hats, Indian strouds, Rus-sia duck, nests of India kettles, caks, cotton cards, curls and bells, white taby, women's stays, strept mantuas, ticklenburg, velvet corks, bead foals, Holland Rope oil, and Flanders bed ticks. All of these men also traded in slaves. Slaves are mentioned in fourteen of the forty-one sur-viving wills of early New York Jews.[26] They are also cited in advertise-ments of Jewish commercial agents. There is a reference to "a couple of very likely Negro boys" in an adverisement from the *Independent Gazeteer* of March 4, 1783. The source is Haym Salomon, the Polish-born Philadelphia shipper who has been lionized by American Jews for his financial generosity to the Continental Congress.[27]

A century ago, in 1894, Max Kohler tried to address the issue of Jewish slaveholding. He wrote, "Until about 1750...every New York family of any wealth or comfort held slaves, and in keeping and even in dealing in them the Jews were neither being better nor worse than the Christian inhabitants."[28] Kohler was not being disingenuous. Rather, he was trying to point out that wealthy Jews (and the operative word was wealthy) emulated their Christian neighbors by keeping one, two, or three house slaves during their lifetime.[29] Two of fourteen Jewish wills that make reference to slaves offer manumission to such servants.[30]

When Jews died, they bequeathed no great fortunes on the order of Isaac Franks. Joseph Torres Nunez died in 1704, leaving an estate of pewter buttons, ribbons and guns valued at £700. The estate of Moses Levy (d. 1728) was valued at £6800, that of Aaron Louzada (d. 1764) at £468 and David Hays (d. 1812) at $3,658. 98. Even the eclectic Uriah Hendricks, who also collected roubles, was worth a little better than £9000 when he died in 1798.[31] In New York, as every other community we have surveyed, most Jews were not rich. The city directory for 1799 lists fifty-nine Jews, fourteen of whom were merchants, four auctioneers, two bookbinders and stationery merchants, two brokers and commission agents, two fig blue and chocolate manufacturers, two coppersmiths, two women's mantilla makers, and one each harnessmaker, insurance broker, grocer, dry goods dealer, hairdresser, accountant, shipwright, mariner, druggist, carpneter, smith, boatman, pilot, and curer of rheumatics.[32] Many merchants suffered bankruptcy or were imprisoned for bad debts. Only one (Sampson Simpson) ever sat on the prestigious Chamber of Commerce created in 1768.[33] Whatever success Jews enjoyed trading for cocoa, rum, wine, fur and fabrics was shared with gentile partners. Hershkowitz emphasizes that Jewish participation in the overseas trade (including slaves) practically disappeared in the first half of the eighteenth century. In 1701 nine Jewish merchants accounted for 12 percent of the colony's total commerce. In 1764 there was only one Jew still active and he accounted for less than one-half of one per cent of the international trade.[34]

Jews played an equally inconsequential role in the slave trade in New Amsterdam-New York. In 1629, the Dutch West Indies Company promised to supply colonists "as many blacks as they conveniently can."[35] There is no evidence that Jews figured in the trade until at least 1661 and then only rarely. Of the more than 100 newspaper announcements of slave runaways or sales cited by Samuel McKee in his *Labor in Colonial New York 1664–1776,* only three relate to Jews.[36] The advertisement involving slaves attributed to Haym Salomon is unique among twenty-five cited by Nathan Kaganoff in the *American Jewish Historical Quarterly.* A representative sample of more than 1000 advertisements placed in the *Pennsylvania Packet, Pennsylvania Journal,* and *Independent Gazeteer,* reveals that the ads stress not slaves but sales in gin, china, hogsheads of sugar, tiles, houses, stocks, silks, and bills of exchange. (In fact, 356 ads make reference to Salomon as an authorized broker to the office of finance under the supervision of Robert Morris.)[37] When the sole ad relating to slaves appeared, Salomon was based in Philadelphia (where he resided between 1781 and his death in 1785), not New York.

Slave trading was not considered a dishonorable profession in the middle of the eighteenth century. The major slavetraders in New York at the time were Gabriel Ludlow, Philip Livingston, and Nicholas de Ronde, all Christians, described by their contemporaries as "men of unimpeachable social standing." The principal ships' masters who abided by stringent British shipping rules included members of both Dutch (Rosevelt, Vandam, Vanderhule, Van Courtland, Schuyler, Van Buskirk) and English families (Walton, Tudor, Depeyster, Hough, Smith, Clarkson, Painter, and Martin Burger). A few ne'er-do-wells like John Watts and Gedney Clarke circumvented customs by smuggling slaves into the colony. The slaves were deposited at Schuyler's, Crommelin's, Walton's and Van Zandt's wharves where they were sold off by scriveners like John Knapp and Obadiah Wells to large slaveholders like Lewis Morris (who owned 66), Frederick Philipse (40), Adolph Philipse (15), Sir William Johnson (19) and Philip Ver Planck (18). Lesser slaveholders in 1755 with six to ten slaves in their possession included Charles Brodhad and Nicholas Demyer of Ulster County; Jacobus Bruyn of Swawangunck; Derck Wynkoop and Jacobus Persen of Hurley, Solomon DuBois and Abraham Hardenbergh of New Paltz; Levi Pawling of Marbletown; Jan Arison, Pieter Prae, and Cornelis Van Brunt of Kings County; and Abraham Schenck, John Bargay, Josiah Martin, David Jones, Samuel Fish, William Walton, and the Widow Clarkson, all of Long Island.[38] The slaves were subjected to catechists like Elias Neau and John Beasly.[39] When white guilt, fear, and projection welled over, as they did in 1741, slaves were accused of arson and fomenting rebellion; 154 blacks were prosecuted, 18 hanged, 13 burned at the stake, and 70 deported at the decree of Lt. Governor George Clarke and supreme court justices Daniel Horsmanden, Frederick Philipse, and James DeLancey.[40] Not one of these individuals was Jewish.

Records from the British Naval Office list 670 slave ships bound for New York between 1715 and 1765. At first glance, the number may appear staggering. Not so, according to James Lydon who analyzed New York shipping in the eighteenth century. Writes Lydon, "The city's merchants in these years never devoted as much as *2 percent* (italics mine) of the tonnage sent overseas to the African trade, and it is doubtful that the figure was much exceeded in years for which statistics are not available."[41] The Jewish portion of that 2 percent trade is microscopic. One ship bound from Guinea in 1720 was ascribed to "the Jew Simon." The vessel never arrived.[42] Individual Jews and those who tentatively might be identified as Jews (Moses and Sam Levy, Jacob Franks, Mordecai Gomez, Justus Bosch, Jonathan Abrams, David Algeo, Isaac Low, and Rodrigo Pajacho) occasionally contracted with Gentile partners (Adolph Phillips, W. Godfrey, Paul Richard) for the joint purchase of one, two or three slaves. Jews invested in the cargoes of 33 ships of the 670 which docked in New York, approximately five per cent of the total. Jews owned or were partially responsible for 113 of the 4,004 slaves, 2.5 percent who entered the colony at this time.[43] (See table 8.1.)

TABLE 8.1
Slaves Imported by New York Jews, 1715–1765

Dates	Number of Ships	Number of Slaves	Jews and Number of Slaves
6/15–11/15	7	52	0
12/15–12/16	9	63	0
3/17–12/17	22	328	0
12/17–12/18	44	503	Moses & Sam Levy, 3 slaves on *Curacao* from Jamaica, May 13,1718
12/18–12/19	19	102	Jacob Franks and Moses Levy with H. Chuyler and Nathaniel Simpson, 3 slaves from Nevis aboard *Charlotte*
12/19–12/20	23	77	Moses Levy and Jacob Franks with Jacob van Courtland and Adolph Phillips, 1 slave aboard *Abigail* from Jamaica
12/20–12/21	21	202	0
3/22–12/22	16	91	Moses Levy, 1 slave on *Nassau* from Jamaica
3/23–12/23	20	101	0
3/24–12/24	25	64	0
12/24–12/25	34	211	Moses Levy, 1 mulatto on *4 Sisters* from Curacao
12/25–12/26	28	176	Moses Levy and Adolph Phillips, 2 boys aboard *Abigail* from Martinique; Moses Levy 1 slave on *4 Sisters* from St. Thomas
12/26–12/27	35	221	Justus Bosch and Jn. Abrams (?) 12 from Jamaica on *Anne and Elizabeth*; Moses Levy, 4 from Jamaica on 4 Sisters; Moses Levy and Adolph Phillips, 4 from Curacao on *Abigail*; Mordecai Gomez and Do. Gomez, 1 from Jamaica aboard *Jacob.*
12/27–12/28	19	117	0
12/28–12/29	45	205	Moses Levy with P. Richard, R. Livingston, D. and C. Clarkson, 1 Jamaican slave on *Prince William*; Mordecai and D. Gomez, 2 from Curacao aboard *Samuel*; executors of M. Levy (deceased) and Jacob Frank, 4 on *Abigail* from Surinam; Justus Bosch and Jon. Abrams, 9 on *Anne and Elizabeth;* Rod. Pachero and four others, 10 aboard *Mary.*
12/29–12/30	47	182	Jacob Franks, 1 aboard *Charming Philas* from London
12/30–12/31	29	296	M. Gomez and two Gentiles, 4 on *Mary* from Jamaica; Justus Bosch 1 on *Anne and Elizabeth*
12/31–12/32	44	139	0
12/33–12/34	20	52	0
12/34–6/36	22	136	M. and D. Gomez with Paul Richard, 1 slave on *Hester* from St. Thomas; Benj. Bartlett and W. Godfrey, 1 aboard *3 rothers* from Jamaica; David Gomez and Paul Richard, 2 on *Hester* from St. Thomas; Rodrigo Pajacho, 1 on *Patience*, London.

TABLE 8.1 (continued)
Slaves Imported by New York Jews, 1715–1765

Dates	Number of Ships	Number of Slaves	Jews and Number of Slaves
12/37–3/38	24	98	Paul Richard, Mordecai and David Gomez, 1 slave on *Hester* from St. Thomas 3/38–12/39 54 217 R. Pajacho among five owners of 9 slaves from Jamaica aboard *Mary;* Pajacho listed among five owners of 1 slave on *Mary* a second time; P. Richard Mordecai and D. Gomez, 11 slaves on *Elizabeth* from St. Thomas; Richard and two Gomezes, 3 slaves aboard *Hester* from St. Thomas; M. Levy, P. Richard and three non-Jews, on *Prince Frederick* from Jamaica
12/39–12/40	22	56	0
12/40–12/41	18	55	0
12/41–3/42	No entries available		
3/42–6/43	11	34	M. and D. Gomez with P. Richard, 3 slaves on *Elizabeth* from St. Thomas; Jacob Franks, 1 slave aboard *Oglethorpe* from Jamaica
6/43–3/48			No entries
3/48–1750	3	14	David Algeo ?, 4 on *Polly* from Antigua
1750–4/54	No entries		
4–54–10/54	4	65	0
10/54–4/63	Entries missing		
4/63–10/63	3	112	0
4/64–1/65	2	35	Peter Bernson, Abraham Lott and Isaac Low, 5 slaves on *Abraham* from Barbados

Source: British Naval Office lists in Donnan, III, pp. 462–510.

New York's Jews did own slaves, but never in numbers that suggest domination of the trade. The city census of 1703 lists Joseph Isacks (*sic*), resident in the East Ward with one slave, Moses Levey (sic) and Louis Gomas (Gomez) in the Dock Ward with two apiece.[44] According to Edgar McManus, there were 2,170 slaves in the colony in 1698. Jews, then, owned 0.2 percent of New York's slaves at the beginning of the eighteenth century. The percentage wavered slightly over the next century, whether in New York City or New York state. Dr. Malcolm Stern reckoned that in 1790, there were sixty Jewish households in the state of New York. Twenty of these owned a grand total of 43 slaves, or 0.2 percent of the 21,324 slaves in the state.[45] According to Leo Hershkowitz, in 1816 five Jews held 10 of the 414 slaves (2.4 percent) in the city.[46] The 1820 census lists 79 Jewish households with 7 slaves (approximately 1.3 percent of the 518 slaves in the city.)[47] There were also 29 free blacks living in these Jewish households. By an act passed in 1810, New York prohibited the sale of slaves imported after 1801. July 4, 1827 was supposed to be general emancipation day. Schemers managed to defeat the spirit of the law, bringing "transient" slaves into the state until 1841. If the figures offered by the Nation of Islam of 26 Jews owning 32 slaves in 1830 are accurate, they no more reflect Jewish control of slavery in New York than the same census which reports 21 free blacks who owned 431 slaves in the state (including 8 Negro residents of New York City with 17 slaves.)[48]

New Jersey: Zero Jews, Zero Slaves

Visited by a score of Italian, Dutch, English and French explorers, the strip of lush forests running more than 130 miles from Cape May to New York was finally claimed as New Sweden at the beginning of the seventeenth century. Peter Stuyvesant bumped the Swedes from the Delaware River and was in turn displaced by the British who renamed the territory New Jersey in 1664. Almost from the start, there had been slaves, Indian, and blacks working farms in what initially was a proprietary colony. In 1702, the Royal Governor Lord Cornbury actively encouraged the Lords in Trade and the Royal African Company to import more Africans. Perhaps 115 entered between 1718 and 1726 through the colony's principal port, Perth Amboy. In 1737 New Jersey counted 3,981 slaves. They constituted 8.4 percent of the overall population. The highest number was reached in 1800 when there were 12,422 black slaves in a total population of 211,949. Subsequently, as a result of energetic Quaker protests and the general abolitionist attitude in the North, the figure declined to 2,254 in 1830, 236 "apprentices for life" in 1850.[49] While slavery existed in New Jersey, however, it was marked by the cruel and punitive police regulations, degrading social conditions, and limp defensive rationalizations of individuals like the Reverend Moses Ogden and Colonel Richard Morris of Shrewsbury, the latter who counted sixty slaves on his mill and plantation as early as 1680. By 1700 nearly all of New Jersey's residents had slaves.[50] Before abolition, the greatest number could be found in those counties where the Dutch and Germans predominated.[51]

It would have been very difficult for Jews to control the slave trade in what was originally called New Sweden, for they were not permitted into the region by the Swedes. When the Dutch gained control of New Jersey, Peter Stuyvesant barred Jewish traders from going beyond the South Delaware River. In 1655, three Jewish (Abraham de Lucena, Salvador Dandrada and Jacob Cohen) petitioned for the right to send agents into the region. It was not until 1657, however, that Isack Masa, a Jew from the Caribbean, gained permission from the Dutch West Indies Company to trade with Indians. Even then, in 1662, the Mennonites, known for their quiet pacifism, barred "those in communion with the Roman See, usurious Jews, English stiffnecked Quakers, Puritans, foolhardy believers in the millennium, and obstinate modern pretenders to revelation" from their communities in New Jersey.[52] They needn't have bothered. With its vast woodlands and fertile fields, New Jersey hardly appealed to Jewish merchants in the eighteenth century. Not surprisingly, then, there are no Jews listed among the 184,139 residents of New Jersey in the 1790 census, only five listed (owning no slaves) in the census of 1830.[53] Jews played virtually no role in the history of New Jersey until immigrants from Eastern Europe were diverted from New York's East Side at the end of the nineteenth century.

Pennsylvania

The Swedes, Dutch, and English also competed for supremacy in what was to become Pennsylvania when William Penn chartered the first permanent British settlement at Philadelphia in 1682. What should have been a model of tolerance established by people (the Quakers) who had undergone persecution themselves proved to be as prejudiced as any of the early colonies. From the start, Baptists, Puritans, and Roman Catholics were harrassed, particularly the latter, who were accused of aiding the French and Indians along the western frontier. Officially, the first Jews did not enter Pennsylvania till 1723, but one, Arnold Bamberger, a merchant, was resident in Philadelphia as early as 1702.[54] By 1775, there were, perhaps, 250–300 Jews among the total population in the city.[55] Mostly merchants, a few hardy souls like Michael and Barnard Gratz helped open western Pennsylvania to Pittsburgh and Newcastle on the Ohio border by the turn of the century.[56]

Several Jews who lived in Philadelphia maintained businesses in both this city and New York and were relatively prosperous. They included Isaac and David Franks, Moses and Nathan Levy, Jonas Phillips, Levy Marks, Samuel Hays, Solomon Cohen, Benjamin Seixas, and Haym Salomon. In 1780 their fortunes ranged from £30,000 to £100,000.[57]

Apart from dealing in realty and bills of exchange, their list of sundries traded included pins and needles, Madeira wine, "goloshoes," "umbrelloes," tobacco, sugar, tea, indigo, spices, beaver, squirrel and raccoon pelts, handkerchiefs, men's and boys' "maccarony hats," and Barcelona denims.[58] Some also traded in slaves.

Place names such as Guineatown and Guinea Hill testify to the early arrival of blacks in Pennsylvania. There are indications that Africans were enslaved by Swedes, Dutch, and Finns as early as 1639.[59] To the end of the century, there was little difference between their treatment and that of white indentured servants. Penn's initial invitation to the Free Society of Traders acknowledged the special situation of slaves, but advised that blacks should be freed at the end of fourteen years of servitude. The illusion of equality, even for the growing number of free blacks in Pennsylvania, evaporated in a series of restrictive laws passed by the colonial legislatures between 1725 and 1773. Meanwhile, the number of blacks in Philadelphia and Pennsylvania increased from 2,500–5,000 in 1721 to 11,000 in 1751 (6,000 in Philadelphia).[60]

Probably the peak year for imports of slaves to Philadelphia was 1762. The promise of an end to the French and Indian wars spurred notions of prosperity and 500 black Africans were brought in that year. Two hundred of these brought in from Guinea between August 1761 and August 1762 may be traced to one Jew, David Franks. Franks, a general wholesaler, had imported three slaves between 1737 and 1742. Franks also petitioned Governor James Hamilton in March 1761 to suspend the duty on imports of slaves because of "the inconveniences the inhabitants would suffer from a want of laborers" and the hardships and impending dangers such a tax would wreak in the colony. Franks is one of the Philadelphia Jewish slaveholders cited by NOI scholars,[61] along with members of the Gratz, Simon, Levy and Etting families. What they fail to mention, however, is that Franks and his principal partner, a non-Jew William Plumsted,[62] were joined in this particular venture by two other gentiles Thomas Riche and David Rundle.[63] It is also noteworthy that Franks was one of twenty-four merchants (including two other Jews, Benjamin Levy and Joseph Marks) who petitioned Governor Hamilton for suspension of the tax on slave imports.[64] Commenting on the slaving activities of the Franks and Levy families, Edwin Wolf and Maxwell Whiteman write, "Aside from the occasional sale of a Negro slave, the Levys never ventured as heavily in the slave trade as did other merchants along the Atlantic seaboard."[65]

TABLE 8.2
Slaves in Pennsylvania and Philadelphia

	Pennsylvania			Philadelphia		
Year	Free Blacks	Slaves	Population	Free Blacks	Slaves	Population
1790	6,537	3,737	434,073	2,102	387	54,391
1800	14,564	1,706	602,305	6,795	85	81,009
1810	22,492	795	810,091	10,514	8	111,210
1820	32,153	211	1,047,507	11,884	7	135,637
1830	37,930	403	1,348,233	15,604	20	188,787
1840	47,854	64	1,724,033	19,831	2	258,037
1850	53,626	0	2,311,786	19,761	0	408,762
1860	56,949	0	2,906,215	22,185	0	565,529

Source: Turner, The Negro in Pennsylvania, p. 253.

Jews did own slaves in colonial Philadelphia. Dr. Malcolm Stern reckons that there were thirty-one Jewish heads of households in 1790. Three of these owned a total of 6 slaves.[66] The U.S. census for that year lists 3,787 slaves for all of Pennsylvania. Jews, therefore, held 0.2 percent of the slaves in the state, hardly a stunning figure. By 1820, Philadelphia remained the nexus of Jewish settlement in Pennsylvania, although some Jews were listed in Berks, Bucks, Lehigh, Northampton and Susequehanna Counties. According to Ira Rosenwaike, there were 12 free blacks living among the 76 Jewish households in the greater Philadelphia area—no slaves.[67]

Several Jews (Benjamin Nones, Israel Jacobs, Philip Moses Russell, and David Nassy) had been among the first to manumit slaves in Pennsylvania.[68] Despite the evangelism, temperance and exclusivism of antislavery societies, Jews were also prominent in such groups in Philadelphia and New York. In 1787, the partially disabled Revolutionary War veteran Solomon Bush was the first Jew to join the Quaker Society for Promoting the Abolition of Slavery in Philadelphia. A decade later, Moses Judah became a member of a similar society in New York City. The antislavery sentiments of Gershom Seixas, Solomon Simpson, Naphtali Judah and Benjamin Nones were so pronounced, particularly during the slave rebellion of Toussaint L'Ouverture in Santo Domingo, that some American conservatives were already denouncing the "Jew press" as early as 1800.[69]

Any suggestion that Jews dominated the slave trade in Pennsylvania must be rejected. If one seeks major slaveholders in the colonial period, they would include such individuals as Jonathan Dickinson of Philadelphia, Judge Langhorne in Bucks County, and John Harris, founder of Harrisburg, each of whom owned more than thirty before 1740.[70] Historian Charles Blockson maintains that the Revolutionary War patriot Captain Archibald McAllister owned more than any other master. As for slave traders before Pennyslvania shut down the practice on the eve of the Revolution, the Philadelphia firm of Charles Willings and Robert Morris was importing hundreds of Africans in the period 1754–1766. They were, wrote Blockson of Willings and Morris, "one of Pennsylvania's most persistent participants in the commerce of slaves."[71] Once again, none of these individuals was Jewish.

9

Jews in the Triangular Trade: Colonial New England

Sugar, Rum, and Slaves

The colonies of New England were crucial to the success of Great Britain's triangular trade. Slaves were purchased in Africa and taken to sugar plantations in the West Indies. Sugar and molasses were then made into rum at more than thirty distilleries in Rhode Island, another sixty-three in Massachusetts. By 1723 rum would surpass brandy, gin, trinkets, and dry goods as the medium of exchange in securing slaves from Africa.[1] It was also the principal manufacture of New England before the Revolutionary War. Few Englishmen other than Richard Baxter, the novelist Mrs. Aphra Benn, Samuel Sewalls, actor George Crooke, the former slaver John Newton, or the dilettante Lord Wilberforce fretted over the system.[2]

In America, too, there was little stigma associated with the trading of blacks before the American Revolution. Slaves were part of the economic lifeblood of the empire. Not only were they needed in the West Indies, they were also wanted by Narragansett planters and dairy farmers, by warehousers and shippers as dockhands, by judges, postmasters, and members of colonial assemblies for housework.[3] According to a contemporary French visitor in 1687, every New England town had at least five or six slaves. Of Boston, he wrote, "You may also own Negros (cost 20–40 pistoles) and Negresses; there is not a house in Boston, however small may be its means, that has not one or two."[4] Looking backward, from the perspective of 1887, William Weeden noted, "We are amazed and humiliated when we consider how little people knew what they were doing."[5]

Boston had been familiar with the peculiar institution almost from its founding days. Some of the early colonists enslaved Indians during the Pequod War of 1637. White indentured servants were common during the middle of the seventeenth century. Even before that, however, Samuel Maverick, the son of an Anglican clergyman in Chelsea, acquired two African slaves in 1625. By 1644 Boston traders were sailing directly to Africa for gold dust and slaves. Two of these, John Endicott and John Saffin, were so successful in supplying other northern colonies they made Boston into the official slave port by 1700.[6] When Parliament opened the trade to all Englishmen, a number of merchants leaped at the opportunity to participate in what was regarded as "an honorable vocation."[7] Although they were at a disadvantage compared with powerful European trading companies, many New England merchants thrived by buying and selling blacks.[8]

The numbers are not overwhelming—fewer than 4,000 slaves were owned in the six colonies of New England by 1790. But slave traders and owners profited by the institution. They included Jonathan Blecher, Cornelius Waldo, George Cabot, Andrew and Peter Fanueil of Boston, Isaac and Jacob Royall of Charleston, William Pepperell of Kittery, George Crowninshield of Salem, John and Obadaiah Brown of Providence, Rowland Robinson of Narragansett, slave dealers who "enjoyed the highest social position and held public offices of the greatest trust and responsibility."[9] They included Connecticut farmers like John Pantry of Hartford, Henry Wolcott of Windsor, Rev. William Hart of Saybrook, Captain John Perkins of Norwich, Godfrey Malbone of Brooklyn.[10] The list of the top 162 slaveholding families in Massachusetts, Rhode Island, and Connecticut in the seventeenth and eighteenth century includes such luminaries as the Rev. Jonathan Edwards, Oliver Wolcott, Rev. Ezra Stiles, Dr. John Cobbett , Andrew and Peter Fanueil, John Hancock, Cotton and Increase Mather, James Otis, John Alden, and Dudley Saltonstall.[11] Those who profited from the slave trade included the masters and captains of twenty-one ships that travelled to and from Africa between 1746 and 1757 and the masters/captains of twenty-three more vessels that carried slaves to Boston in 1771–74.[12] The exploiters also included thirty-one slave brokers or agents (Pym, Atkinson, Maccarty, Long, Robinson, Holmes, Wadsworth) who advertised "several Negros" for sale in the *Boston News Letter* or *Boston Gazette* between April 1715 and May 1721.[13] None of the individuals mentioned above were Jews. For good reason: as the French visitor to Boston in 1687 noted, "There are no Jews in Boston—anymore than Baptists or Quakers."[14]

Warning Out the Jews

Though Jews were generally unwelcome in the Western Hemisphere, they still managed to enter colonies and prosper, to a limited extent. This was not the case in New England. One would think that having suffered persecution at the hands of intolerant European lords, Protestant refugees would have established havens of tolerance on this side of the Atlantic. Instead, the benighted Pilgrims and Puritans introduced a host of "blue laws" which regulated many aspects of behavior. Sunday was the Sabbath and church attendance was deemed mandatory. Gambling, drinking, dancing, joyous celebrations of any kind (May Day, Christmas, one's birthday) were prohibited. Publications were censored, trade regulated. Violaters of these decrees might be flogged, branded, ducked, exposed in stocks, hanged, or burned. In a caste system which delineated how rich and poor might dress, as well as where the people might sit in church, there was no room for deviant religious thought. Baptist preachers were beaten and expelled from Massachusetts Bay in 1646. The Puritans then warned all atheists they faced death in 1652. The Pilgrims of Plymouth executed four Quakers between 1659 and 1661. Between 1647 and 1662, fourteen persons were hanged in Massachusetts and Connecticut on charges of witchcraft, thirty years before the infamous witchcraft trials in Salem took the lives of twenty men and women and two dogs.

Only the most daring/foolhardy Jew would have ventured into such a countryside. There were none in Vermont, a state which counted sixteen slaves in a population of 85,539 in 1790. One Jewish family in New Hampshire(that of Abraham Isaac) in a state of 141,885, including 158 slaves. No Jews in Maine where there were 96,540 people and no slaves in 1790. Several Jewish families in Connecticut among 237,946 Gentiles who held virtually all of the state's 2,764 slaves.[15] Only one Jew among 379,787 people in Massachusetts—Moses Michael Hays, an insurance man and Mason who came from Lisbon via Jamaica. There were no slaves in Massachusetts in 1790. Hays' residence in Boston was all the more remarkable because Jews had been "warned out" of the city by the Puritans in the 1640s.[16] Their only other noteworthy appearance in Boston came in June 1716 when three merchants from London (Isaac Lopez, Abraham Gutatus, and Jacob Ruggles) made a temporary stopover in the city.[17]

According to Ira Rosenwaike, in 1790 there were no more than 150 Jews in all of New England, perhaps 0.01 percent of the 1,009,522 persons in the six states.[18] Five Jewish households owned twenty-one slaves, approximately 0.5 percent of the 3886 slaves held in New England.[19] In a region where most people found chattel slavery personally distasteful or unworkable, Jews who were few in number, played an equally minor role in the slave trade.

The Jews of Rhode Island

An exception might be argued for Rhode Island. Most Jews in New England lived in the tiny packet of peninsulas and islands founded by Roger Williams because it was the only colony which made an effort at practicing religious toleration. *The Secret Relationship* paints an almost idyllic picture of Jews living in Rhode Island. Before the Revolution, Jewish families supposedly dominated not only the slave trade, but diamonds, coral, and candle-making as well. Virtually all Jewish homes owned slaves. Loyalists to the British cause, somehow after the conflict, they managed to secure equal rights, increase in number, and continue to finance the "enslavement, shipment and murder of Black Africans."[20]

It is unclear exactly when the first Jews came to Rhode Island. Marcus suggests that a group may have arrived from Curacao between 1656 and 1658, certainly no later than 1677.[21] Kohler places the date closer to 1694.[22] According to Ezra Stiles, president of Yale and a man who enjoyed a close relationship with the Jews of Newport , there were between fourteen and twenty Jewish families (perhaps sixty persons) in Rhode Island in 1760. Constituting 1 percent of the 6,000 residents of the colony, they were, said Stiles,"almost the only ones [Jew] in New England."[23] The peak number was reached in 1774 when Rhode Island counted nearly 200 Jews. Seventeen families resided in Newport which dedicated a small, but elegant colonial synagogue in December 1763.[24] During the Revolutionary War, many of these Jews emulated their cousins and business associates in New York and fled British occupation, siding with the colonial patriots in Providence.[25] Their trade with England ruined by their allegiance to the new United States, the number of Jews in Rhode Island declined in the next several decades. There were only seventy-six (twenty-eight adult males) by 1790. Few were counted among the 461 families in Rhode Island that owned 958 slaves in that year.[26] By 1820 the official census listed not a flourishing community which had deviously secured special benefits, but only two Jewish males in Newport.[27]

Without question, Rhode Island's Jews prospered. Apart from small shopowners and skilled craftsmen, by the middle of the eighteenth century they operated twenty-two distilleries, four sugar refineries, five ropewalk and furniture stores. Their seventeen sperm oil and candle factories gave them a virtual monopoly on these important items. A few also participated in Rhode island's vast slave trade.[28]

Rhode Island's Slave Trade

Slaves were not unknown in Rhode Island during the seventeenth century, but by statute of May 19, 1652 "no blacke mankind or white being" could be held in servitude for more than ten years.[29] The handful that were imported came from the West Indies, not directly from Africa.[30] Humane laws soon "passed into absolute neglect and forgetfulness."[31] There were 400 slaves in the colony in 1708, 3800 by 1782.[32] Limited by size and thin, stony soil, the residents of Rhode Island made a conscious decision to surpass Massachusetts in the import and sale of what their contemporaries deemed a useful commodity. The crucial year seems to be 1717. Despite opposition from Quakers, Rhode Island passed its first fugitive slave law. More important, trade in Indian slaves was now outlawed. The profit protential in African slaves was enormous.[33] According to Jay Coughtry, who has made the most comprehensive study of Rhode Island's role in the transatlantic trade, the scheme succeeded. For nearly a century (1725–1807) the American slave trade was virtually synonymous with that of Rhode Island.[34] Throughout the eighteenth century, Rhode Island merchants controlled between 60 and 80 percent of the American slave traffic. Between 1709 and 1807 this translated out to 934 voyages to Africa, bringing back 106,594 slaves.[35]

In the age of mercantilism only British subjects were entitled to trade between Africa and the colonies. To assure tax revenues, the British Shipping Office made valiant, if vain, efforts at keeping meticulous records. We know the size of the ships, the exact cost in rum, powder or calico for slaves, how many slaves were aboard the vessels, the mortality rate—and the makeup of the crews and their ownership.[36] None of the first eight ships dispatched directly to Africa between 1725 and 1728 was owned or captained by Jews.[37] Nor are there any Jews associated with the twenty vessels listed by British authorities for the period 1731–39[38] or the thirty-seven listed between 1747 and 1755.[39]

According to John Spears, typical Rhode Island slave captains of the eighteenth century were David Lindsay of Newport, William Boates, one-eyed Hugh Crow, John Paul Jones, John Griffen, George Scott, Daniel Cooke, Luke Collingwood, John Newton, George Douglass, John Whittle, Gilbert Cooper, and Philip Drake. They sailed on ships outfitted by William Johnson, Jansen Eykenboom, Appleton Oaksmith, and Thomas Leyland.[40] Other major owners included distillers like John Gidley and Geoffrey Malbone, the London insurance houses of Hayley and Hopkins and Tomlinson and Trecothnick, and Newport merchants such as Samuel Sanford, Caleb Gardner, Francis Malbone, Peleg Clarke, James, Robinson, James D'Wolf, and John Slocum.[41] Peleg and Audley Clarke, Benjamin Mason, and Peleg Thurston operated the principal slave brokerages from Rhode Island to the West Indies.[42]

Long after the Continental Congress banned the import of slaves in December 1774 and after the U.S. Congress banned slave trading with the West Indies in 1794, some Rhode Island merchants (Caleb Gardner, Nathaniel Briggs, John Stanton, Cyprian Sterry, John Brown, John cook, Freeman Mayberry, Paul Brownell, John Thurston) were still engaged in the illegal practice.[43] Between 1784 and 1807 when no more slaves could be legally imported anywhere into the U.S., 204 Rhode Island citizens collaborated in financing 229 voyages to Africa. Nearly half of these were underwritten by familiar names including seven members of the D'Wolf clan (88 voyages), the firm of Briggs and Gardner (22), Clarke and Clarke (22), Cyprian Sterry (17), Vernon and Vernon (10), Jeremiah Ingraham (10, and Bourn and Wardell (9).[44]

The activities of the D'Wolfs are especially notable. Beginning with Mark Anthony D'Wolf, a Protestant slave captain from Bristol in 1769, three generations of this family (sons Charles and James, then John, William, Levi, Samuel, and George) operated fourty-four vessels out of Newport between Africa and slave markets in Havana and Charleston. Coughtry says of them, "Without a doubt, then, the D'Wolfs had the largest interest in the African slave trade of any American family before or after the Revolution."[45] *The Secret Relationship* makes much of the D'Wolfs (DeWolfs) offering a two-page sketch of their activities in the biographical section listing "Jews" responsible for the black holocaust.[46] When I mentioned the D'Wolfs at a seminar on Jews in the slave trade held at Hebrew Union College in May, 1995, Jacob Marcus asked, "Who?" I repeated the charge made by NOI editors. To which the ninety-nine-year-old dean of American Jewish scholars responded, "I never heard of them."[47] In fact, the D'Wolfs had been practicing Christians for several generations, members of the Episcopal parish of St.Michael's,[48] and their inclusion in *Secret Relationship* as Jews is invalid.

Aaron Lopez

Not one of the individuals or companies mentioned thus far that played a prominent role in the Rhode Island slave trade was Jewish. But Aaron Lopez was. A Portuguese-born crypto-Christian who came to Rhode Island in 1752, Lopez figures prominently in *Secret Relationship*. The five pages devoted to him in the biographical section of Jews responsible for the black holocaust tell of a singleminded merchant who kept thirty to forty ships at sea plying the slave trade even after American rebels tried to get him to join them defying British tax policies. Lopez supposedly was uncooperative in upholding the nonimportation response to the Townshend Acts of 1770. Among those who allegedly "fingered him" for this unpatriotic behavior was the Rev. Ezra Stiles of Yale.[49]

A number of legitimate scholars have tried to analyze the character of Aaron Lopez. About the only thing they agree on is that he was the wealthiest Jew, if not citizen, in Newport at the time of the American Revolution.[50] Beyond that, the man was a mass of contradictions. Given, at first, to Loyalist proclivities, like a number of his insecure Jewish neighbors (Isaac Hart, Myer Pollock, Moses Hays, Hazzan Touro), he abandoned his home, ships, and warehouses in 1776 and joined the rebels in Leicester, Massachusetts for the duration of the war. As Jacob Marcus declares, "There can be no question of his readiness to sacrifice in this matter or of his ultimate devotion to the Continental cause."[51]

A maddening record-keeper whose different ledgers sometimes duplicated entries, Lopez did, on occasion, smuggle tea and other commodities. No one seems to know exactly how many vessels he and business partners Jacob Rivera (his father-in-law) and son-in-law Abraham Pereira Mendes had at sea between 1752 and 1775. The Rhode Island Historical Society has stated that it would be impossible to determine exactly how many ships Lopez actually owned, but estimates somewhere about 30.[52] From his memoranda, account books and sailor's invoices we can count the following: *America, Diana, Mary Thresher, Industry, Greyhound, Aaron, Hero, Tamar, Betsy Ann, Pitt, Savannah and Sarah, Joseph, Hope, Hopestill, Dove, Jacob, Hannah, Priscilla, George Allen, Fanny, Rhoda, Sally, Ranger, Sloop, Dolphin, Cecilia, Abigail, George, Neptune, Cleopatra, Flora, Active, Swan, Two Brothers, Draper, Ocean, Endeavour, Lovely Lass, Africa, Reliance, Sprey, Ann, Royal Charlotte, Three Friends*, and *Sally*, many of which were actively engaged in the slave trade with Africa between 1761 and 1774.[53]

When Lopez died (in an accidental drowning in June 1782), far from being chided for his involvement in the slave trade, he was eulogized by the same Rev.Stiles of Yale as a merchant of the first eminence who was "the most universally beloved man I ever knew." Stiles lauded Lopez' "sweetness of behavior," his "calm urbanity" and "politeness of manner," his "sincere, pious and candid mind," and declared that his beneficence to family, nation and world were "almost without a parallel." Far from being a villain, Lopez was for Stiles a mythic figure in history akin to Menasseh ben Israel, Pope Clement XIV, and Socrates.[54]

An equally glowing epitaph was offered by the residents of Leicester who remembered Lopez as "a merchant of eminence, of polite and amiable emanners. Hospitality and benevolence were his true characteristics, an ornament and a valuable pillar in the Jewish society of which he was a member. Knowledge in commerce was unbounded: and his integrity irreproachable. Lived and died—much regretted, esteemed and loved by all."[55] Wrote Stanley Chyet of Hebrew Union College, "Clearly we see, in places as remote from Rhode Island as South Carolina, South America, Spain and England, the name of Aaron Lopez was something of a synonym for honesty and integrity—even to people who never laid eyes on its bearer."[56]

Lopez left no diary or autobiographical memoir, but his letter books reveal a man who was interested in every detail of commerce down to pins, spectacles, black plumes, leather inkpots, and Swedish steel, as well as a man who was concerned with world affairs.[57] To the very end, Lopez fretted about the quality of rum and wine being transported in his name, whether his shipments of iron would be arriving on time. He offered to settle a bad debt by letting the customer pay in realty rather than "suffer him to be imprisoned." He saluted the inhabitants of Virginia and South Carolina for their "glorious conquests" and prayed for the termination of "calamitous wars." And yet, as Professor Chyet points out in two separate essays, Lopez suffered a terrible blind spot when it came to slavery. In one instance Chyet says, "Lopez regarded slave-trading as did most eighteenth century businessmen—as 'a very gainful and advantageous commerce.'"[58] Elsewhere, Chyet writes,"We are forced to conclude that what Edith Hamilton wrote of the Roman poet Horace applies equally to Aaron Lopez of Newport: He was wise and good, yet he lived with a monstrous evil and never caught a glimpse of it. So does custom keep men blinded."[59]

Aaron Lopez owned twenty-seven slaves when he took his family to Leicester.[60] We gather from his ledgers that he tried to treat them fairly—

excusing them from work on holidays and election days.[61] His accounts, however, reveal no similar compassion for slaves transported from Africa for resale. Between 1761 and 1775, Lopez and Jacob Rivera outfitted a number of slave ships from Newport (see table 9.1). Correspondence with bankers and insurance brokers in London suggests that Lopez knew the risks of such enterprise.[62] He was on fairly intimate terms with some of the more notorious slaving captains of New England, including Nathaniel Briggs, Peleg Clarke, Nathaniel Waldron, and William English.[63]

From the moment in 1761 that Lopez and his father-in-law Rivera (whom he called "Couz"), subscribed the brig *Greyhound* to transport 134 slaves to South Carolina (they arrived in Charleston on January 25, 1763),he was involved with the day-to-day operations of the slave trade. Lopez was fully aware of difficulties negotiating purchases in Africa, conditions aboard ship in the Middle Passage, and problems associated with sale of slaves. He commented on the need for repairs of ships.[64] His log book for the ships *Sally* and *Cleopatra,* two of his principal slaving vessels, reflect changing costs in cloth, onions, chocolate, coffeee, flour, and tea in barter with "the chief of blacks" at Lagos.[65] In 1765 he instructed Captain Briggs that "his "preferrances" were for slaves aboard the sloop *Betsy* to be taken to Jamaica.[66] Later, he would complain of discrepancies in the manifests of ships sailing to Barbados and Kingston under the command of Captain English.[67]

Far from showing compassion for his chattels, Lopez instructed his captains to use leg irons and handcuffs on Africans, for they were "less than human" and because this was "their natural habitat."[68] There is no indication of concern when his son-in-law Abraham Pereira wrote back from Jamaica in November 1767 complaining on several occasions about the terrible condition of newly arrived slaves.[69] Lopez cared only whether the price would be £27 or 45 per head.

Lopez' business ledgers indicate substantial dealings in other commerce, of course. There are scores of entries for whaling oil, lumber and staves,[70] foodstuffs (rice,pork, beef, wheat, salt, fish, molasses), raccoon and deer skins,[71] sundries (cotton, leather, dry goods, Havana snuff and sassafrass),[72] and an arcane assortment of psalters, mahogany wood, limes, oranges and kosher cheeses.[73] Rather than slaves, a typical bill of lading for Lopez might have come from the sloop *Friendly* which, in May 1773, carried 106 casks of molasses, 2,000 pounds of coffee, and 20 barrels of sugar.[74]

TABLE 9.1
Slave Ships Chartered by Rhode Island Jews, 1709–1807

Departure	Vessel	Captain	Slaves (start/finish)	Arrival
Lopez and Rivera				
1761	Br. Greyhound	Wm. Pinnegar	150/134	Charleston 1/25/63
7/64	Sl. Spry	Wm. Pinnegar	unknown	unknown
5/65	Br. Africa	Abraham All	unknown	Jamaica 7/66
7/65	Sl. Betsy	Nat. Briggs	unknown	Jamaica 5/66
8/66	Br. Sally	Nat. Briggs	120	Barbados
10/66	Br. Africa	Abraham All	unknown	unknown
5/68	Br. Hannah	Nat. Briggs	126	Jamaica
1769	unlisted	Wm. Bardon	112/100	Barbados
6/70	Sl. Mary	Wm. English	unknown	Barbados
7/70	Sh. Cleopatra	Nat. Briggs	108/96	Barbados
7/71	Sh. Cleopatra	Nat. Briggs	257/230	Barbados
12/72	Br. Ann	Wm. English	118/89	Jamaica
1772	Royal Charlotte	Benj. Wright	unknown	unknown
5/72	Cleopatra	Nat.Briggs	unknown	unknown
1772	George	Peleg Greene	unknown	unknown
5/73	Sh.Africa	Nat.Briggs	183/171	Barbados
7/73	Cleopatra	James Bourke	101/90	St.Christopher
1773	Active	Capt. Taggart	unknown	unknown
1773	Sl.Charlotte	Eb.Shearman	unknown	unknown
1774	unlisted	Peleg Greene	unknown	unknown
8/86*	Sh. 3 Friends	Eb.Shearman	116	unknown
				*Rivera and partners
Moses Levy				
11/65	Br. Greyhound	John Thurston	unknown	unknown
Moses Seixas				
5/1806*	Sh. Union	James Manchester	188/168	Charleston
8/1806*	Br. Hiram	Thom. Hudson	103/92	Charleston
1/1807*	Br. Eagle	John Clarke	109/97	Charleston
				*Seixas and 4 non-Jewish partners

Source: Coughtry, *Triangular Trade*, pp. 241–85.

According to Jay Coughtry, the Rhode Island slave trade assumed its greatest proportions after the Revolution, when those merchants involved did everything they could to save it.[75] As the attached chart reveals, few Jews continued the practice after the War for Independence. Lopez was already dead. If we add all of the confirmed sailings underwritten by Rhode Island's Jews, including Lopez, Rivera, Moses Seixas and Moses Levy, the total is 25 out of 934 slave ships chartered for the entire state between 1709 and 1807. Jews then owned 2 percent of the ships involved in Rhode Island's slave trade. Most of these vessels were 90–100 ton brigs or schooners which could accommodate no more than 150 slaves. If we project a total of 2,500 slaves imported aboard "Jewish" ships, that would still represent 3 percent of the 107,000 Africans shackled to these shores in the eighteenth century.

With all his faults, Aaron Lopez was no Jewish Mephistopheles directing flotillas of slave ships out of Newport before the Revolutionary War. Perhaps the fairest evaluation of his (and all of Rhode Island Jewry's) involvement in the slave trade comes from popular historian Stephen Birmingham who has written: "All the 'best people' were involved in it, and a great many of New England's oldest, finest and most redoubtable fortunes are solidly based on human cargo." Slavery was not a Jewish preoccupation, said Birmingham who cautioned, "One should not point to the Jews and ignore the Christians."[76]

10

The Old Dominions: Virginia and Maryland

The First Blacks in North America

Guide books offer glowing accounts of the virtues of the Middle Atlantic states. Virginia, Maryland, and Delaware all are blessed with mild climates, vast beaches graced by ocean breezes, green forests and fertile valleys. It is a region rich in tradition and hospitality. Two centuries ago, Virginia was not only the largest state in the newly created union but also its most populous with 747,610 people. Virginia also counted the greatest number of slaves of any of the original thirteen colonies (292,627) in 1790. Its neighbor Maryland trailed only Virginia, New York, South and North Carolina in population (with 319,728) and was third in slaves with 103,036. Surely, if Jews dominated the slave trade anywhere it had to be here where slavery was introduced to North America.

The editors of *Secret Relationship* attempt to show that this was the case. Relying upon the research of Ira Rosenwaike, NOI scholars offer two pages of statistics that supposedly demonstrate Jewish power in Maryland and Virginia. By the middle of the 18th century, five Jews owned plantations in Virginia. In 1788, Jews constituted 17 percent of the Old Dominion's population and all but one Jewish householder possessed slaves. The editors also offer two charts listing all of the Jewish slaveholders and their slave possessions in Virginia and various southern communities (Baltimore and Richmond included) in 1830.[1] Once again, such efforts are misleading.

Historians often cite the landing of Peter Menendez at St. Augustine in September 1565 as the first instance of slaves coming to what would become the United States. Evidence suggests, however, that Lucas Vasquez de Ayllon, another Spaniard who discovered Chesapeake Bay while seeking the Northwest Passage, may have employed slave labor when he tried to establish the colony of San Miguel de Guandape near

129

Cape Fear in 1526. The first permanent African inhabitants of North America arrived at Jameston in August 1619. John Rolfe made note of "a dutch man of warre that sold us twenty Negars."[2] We do not know where the slaves came from (whether directly from Africa or the West Indies). We don't know the name of the captain or whether the ship was a privateer or man of war.

What we do know, however, is that the governor of Virginia, Captain Samuel Argall (a non-Jew) owned a ship (the *Treasurer*) which sailed against the Spanish and carried a slave woman named Angela to the colony in 1625. Five years later, the *Fortune,* commanded by Captain Grey, brought a group of slaves from Angola. Twenty-six Africans arrived in 1635, seven in 1642, seventeen more in 1649 listed amidst hogsheads of rum and molasses,wooden staves, foodstuffs, cloth and iron goods and nothing more. It was not until 1636 that the first full-time slaver, the *Desire*, operated out of Marblehead, Massachusetts.[3]

What had once been a trickle of slaves (23 according to the census of 1625, fewer blacks than white servants as late as the 1670)[4] became a torrent when England wrenched the Asiento from Spain at the conference of Utrecht. Ships like the *Neptune* and *Dophin* sailed out of Bristol, Liverpool, Boston, London, and Barbados, bringing slaves to Virginia. According to Elizabeth Donnan, between 1710 and 1718 eight ships carried 174 slaves to the Potomac River district. None of the 17 masters were Jews. At the same time, 43 ships carried 2,657 slaves to the district of the York River. Again, none of the 43 masters were Jews. Twenty-two ships carried 674 slaves up the Rappahanock. None of the 23 masters were Jews. Fifteen ships took 166 slaves to the upper district of the James River. None of the 27 masters were Jews. Sixty-three ships carried 732 slaves to the lower district of the James River. None of the 63 masters were Jews.[5]

Between 1718 and 1727, 59 ships, chief among them the *Greyhound*, *Mayflower*, *John and Mary*, brought 8,572 slaves to the York River district. None of the masters were Jewish. (Isaac Hobhouse is listed as the owner of the *Greyhound*.) No Jews are listed among the brokers or captains who brought 251 blacks to the Lower James. Nor are there any Jews among the masters of fourteen ships that brought 2,186 slaves to the Rappahanock during this decade.[6] The lists of English merchants certified by the Lords of Trade to engage in the slave trade to Virginia between 1723 and 1729 contain thirty-six names, none of them Jewish.[7]

The pattern is replicated for the period 1727–1769, during which time Donnan claims 644 ships brought 39,596 Africans to Virginia.

One Jew, Samuel Jacob of Bristol, is listed as master of two ships (the *Nancy* and the *George*) which made two voyages each between June 1741 and May 1743. 987 people were dragged from their homeland on these four voyages, 2.5 percent of all the slaves transported to Virginia in this forty-three-year period.[8] A time of imperial rivalry with France and pre-Revolutionary turmoil in the colonies, it was also the period of closest scrutiny and most accurate recordkeeping by the British Naval Office. Which is why scholars at the Virginia State Library felt constrained in 1984 to update Donnan's earlier findings. Apparently the Wellesley professor had counted only slave ships coming directly from Africa, omitting those from the West Indies. The new list showed more than 69,000 slaves aboard 900 vessels for the period 1699–1775. Samuel Jacob's name appeared as owner of the *Nancy* and *George*, which made four entries in Virginia between June 1741 and September 1746. Jacob had also underwritten two earlier voyages from Bristol—the *Commerce* in August 1727 and *Castle Galley* in March 1728. Over two decades, Jacob imported 1357 slaves. Another Jew, Solomon Joel was responsible for four slaves who came from Barbados and Bermuda between December 1741 and March 1747. According to these corrected figures, Jews accounted for 1361 slaves of 69,006 slaves imported to Virginia— 2 percent of the total—pretty much what Donnan's figures had demonstrated fifty years earlier.[9]

The Plantation Gentry

The Secret Relationship recites the names of John Levy, Manuel Rodrigues, David Da Costa, Michael Israel, and John Abraham, as if to suggest that Jewish planters were the principal beneficiaries of the transatlantic trade to Virginia. The authors are either unable or unwilling to list the number of slaves owned by each, but they do indicate the size of these estates (ranging from 80 to 300 acres), leaving the reader to reach his/her own conclusions. Reputable historians offer a different story. U.B. Phillips notes that from its beginnings, Virginia was a colony operated by the London Company which created a "plantation gentry" of the Burwells, Randolphs, Pages, Nelsons, Braxtons, Fitzhughes, Wythes, and Lees.[10] The Carter dynasty, started with Robert "King" Carter in 1663, produced wheat on several plantations to the time of the Civil War and counted 509 slaves at Nomini Hall in 1791.[11] The Massie family of Pharsalia employed more than 130 slaves in tobacco production.[12] William Bowling owned three plantations, the celebrated Byrds of Westover at least that many into the nineteenth century.[13] Edmund Scarborough, who owned more than thirty slaves in 1655, was regarded as one of the most distinguished planters on the Eastern Shore.[14] George Mason, James Mercer, and Philip St. George Cocke owned more than 100.[15] Even George Washington inherited and used slave labor at Mt. Vernon.[16] Other prominent plantation magnates in Virginia listed by Kenneth Stampp included Bickerton Lyle Winston, Edmund Ruffin, Jeremiah Morton, Hamilton Brown, William Waller, John Ambler, and Jeremiah Morton.[17] In Maryland, Stampp mentions W.J. Bingham, Col. Edward Lloyd (who owned 275 slaves), Elizabeth Ann Boswell, John Ensor, and Joseph Martin.[18] The lists include some of the most important families in American History. The plantation gentry were Episcopalians, Presbyterians, Methodists, and Baptists—a tightly knit aristocracy—but none of them were Jews.

Stampp notes that many of these same magnates were engaged in industry, either in Virginia or a neighboring state. Already in revolutionary times, slave labor was employed in iron works that manufactured guns and heavy weapons, ploughs, farming equipment, pots, kettles and other essential items. There were 161 slaves at Charles Ridgely's Nottingham Company, 80–120 at William Byrd's Spotswood Tuball Works, 220 at David Roth's Oxford Works in Bedford County, 40 used by John Tayloe, 70 by William Weaver, more owned by the Quaker Isaac Zane, Thomas Johnson, James Baker Johnson, Samuel Hughes, Charles Carollton, and James Hunter. Probably the greatest number, however, perhaps as many as 1,000 at any given moment ,were forced to work at forges, furnaces, coal mines, and wharves belonging to Joseph Anderson's Tredegar Iron Works.[19] In the century before the Civil War, slaves worked for more than forty coal companies along the eastern shore. A large percentage of the more than 3,000 slaves in Kanawha (what later would be West Virginia) were forced into coal or salt mines owned by David Ross, David Hancock, Harry Heth, A. S. Wooldridgre, and Christopher Tomplins.[20] There were more than 5000 slaves laboring in 200 hemp factories in Kentucky (several of which were owned by Robert Carter). They worked in dozens of gristmills in Maryland and Virginia (prominent among whose owners were Gallego and Haxall). By 1860 there were 13,000 slaves laboring in Virginia's tobaccories. Prominent among these were the Richmond tobacconists James Thomas who owned upwards of 150 blacks,[21] James Grant (110), T. and S. Hardgrove (108), Talbott and Bros. (78), Christian and Lee (89), Turpin and Yarborough (97), and J.H. Gentry (65).[22] The only Jewish name that appears among these leading businessmen is that of Samuel Myers, whose tobacco company owned 82 slaves.[23]

Jews were every bit as anomalous among the speculators who served as slave merchants in colonial and ante-bellum Virginia. Initially, as in New England, society attached no stigma to those who dealt in human flesh. Some of Virginia's elite, Colonel William Byrd, George Taliaferro, Jeremiah Morton, and Edmund Ruffin hired out slaves. Later, a number of companies came to specialize in selling slaves—including R.C. Ballard and G.W. Apperson in Norfolk,[24] Seth Woodruff and W.A.J. Finney in Lynchburg, Francis Everod Rives of Petersburg, Floyd Whitehead of Nelson City, Abner Robinson, Pulliam and Slade, Dickinson, Hill & Co., Silas and R.F. Omohundro in Richmond.[25]

Frederic Bancroft, whose study of slave trading in the Old South is considered the definitive work on the subject, listed no Jew among the eighteen full-time slave agents in Richmond before the Civil War.[26] One Jewish commercial house (that of Davis, Davis and Ash Levy) appeared among thirty-four slave auctioneers. There were also three Jews—Solomon Davis, Ash Levy, and Samuel Reese—listed among seventy slave traders (individuals who bought or sold slaves at various times) in ante-bellum Richmond. Actually the number is higher if one counts all of the Davis brothers, Ansley, Benjamin, George and Solomon, immigrants from England who operated a dry goods store in Petersburg and Abraham Smith of Richmond who was listed as a full-time slave merchant.[27] Their activities pale when compared with the great gentile slave traders of Richmond.

Through much of the ante-bellum period, Virginia and Maryland helped supply slaves to the rest of the South. Between 1830 and 1860, 300,000 slaves were "exported" from the Chesapeake centers of Richmond, Alexandria, Norfolk, and Baltimore.[28] The single most notorious slave trading firm in Virginia on the eve of the Civil War was that of Price, Birch and Co. which maintained a filthy pen at the corner of Duke and Paine Streets in downtown Alexandria.[29] Originally a simple two-storey house constructed by General Young, this brick structure was converted into a fortress of padlocked gates, manacles and chains, capable of holding 1,000 slaves in 1828 by Isaac Franklin of Natchez and his nephew by marriage John Armfield. The former was lionized as a typical Southern gentleman, while Armfield was described by a northern visitor as "a man of fine personal appearance and of engaging and graceful manner."[30] Both men feigned concern about the physical well-being of their slaves and insisted that families sent South be kept together.[31] In the process, they also became millionaires.[32] Between 1828 and 1837, when they sold the business to George Klephart, one of their agents from Montgomery County,[33] Franklin and Armfield dispatched more than 10,000 slaves by foot, wagon, or boat to Mississippi.[34] They had become "the most eminent slave trading firm in the South."[35] In a typical year (1832), the owners shipped separate coffles of 117, 109, and 134 slaves to Natchez from which they trudged on, twenty-five miles per day, to their ultimate destinations.[36]

The relative absence of Jews as importers, planters, and brokers may be readily explained. According to Rabbi Korn, Jews lacked the necessary wealth to become planters. Barred from owning land in Europe, they lacked the know-how with which to train their own children in farming. They also felt safer in an urban setting among their own people.[37] Leon Hühner suggests that because of historical persecution, Jews had survived as a mercantile people ill-fitted for the agricultural nature of the land in Virginia and Maryland. The two colonies were controlled by a cavalier class which jealousy guarded its power. Jane Turner Censer, associate editor of the Frederick Law Olmsted Papers has pointed out that the planter class in the south was a tightly knit collection of individuals, linked by religion, common attitudes, and intermarriage. There simply was no room for Jews in such a rigidly conformist structure.[38] Both Virginia and Maryland were established as proprietary colonies, the former reserved for members of the Church of England, the latter for Catholics.[39] Unlike New England, there was no need of warning out of Jews in the seventeenth century. The laws took care of that. Virginia equated the practice of any form of Christianity other than Anglicanism with blasphemy and automatically freed any Christian white servant owned by a black, Indian, Jew, Mohammedan, or "other infidel."[40] As late as 1784, Patrick Henry was urging the state's constitutional convention to mandate that all citizens tithe to the Christian religion.[41]

Despite these adversities, some Jews came to Virginia fleeing religious persecution in the seventeenth century, natural calamities (earthquakes) in 1755. The first Jews mentioned in papers of the Public Records Office in London are Elias Legardo, age thirty-eight, who arrived in 1621; Joseph Mosse and Rebeca Isaacke, listed in 1624; John Levy who received a land patent of 200 acres in 1648; and Moses Nehemiah involved in a lawsuit in York Couty in 1658. Several others served in the French and Indian Wars and as part of the militia who fought alongside Washington in the Revolution.[42] According to Jacob

Marcus, it was not until 1769 that Isaiah Isaacs, a silversmith from London, became the first permanent Jewish settler in Richmond. A decade later there were three Jewish males listed on tax returns of the city. By 1786 Richmond was a modest town of 2,000–3,000 persons, including ten Jewish householders.[43] Three of these were listed as fairly well off, six lower middle income, and one of the lowest income.[44] Their numbers continued to grow slowly. From personal memoirs and tax records, Rabbi Malcolm Stern was able to develop a list of thirty-six adult Jews in Richmond and six others in outlying communities like Roanoke, Frederick, and Charlottesville by 1800.[45]

The figures pretty well conform to records of Beth Shalome, the first synagogue in Richmond. According to the oldest minutes book extant, there were thirty adult Jewish males in Richmond in 1791.[46] Official U.S. census reports place the population of Richmond in 1790 at 3,761, of whom at least 1,000 were slaves.[47] According to Jacob Marcus, Jews in Richmond owned exactly ten of these. The German-born Isaacs, nicknamed "the Dutchman," and his business partner Jacob Cohen owned three slaves. Six other households owned one domestic servant each. Malcolm Stern has determined that 45 more slaves were owned by six Jewish households in King William, Henrico, York, and Culpepper Counties[48] In 1790, then, the Jews owned approximately 0.9 percent of all the slaves living in Richmond. There were 292,627 slaves in all of Virginia. Jews, then, owned 0.02 percent or two-hundredths of one percent of the slaves in the state at the time.

Accusations of widespread Jewish involvement in slavery in Virginia are not sustained by later census reports either. Rosenwaike notes that in 1820 37 of the 49 Jewish families in Richmond, Norfolk, and Petersburg owned a total of 149 slaves.[49] At the time there were 4,387 slaves in Richmond, 3,261 in Norfolk.[50] Jews, then, owned 1.9 percent of the 7,648 slaves in these two largest Virginia cities. In 1830, the 28 Richmond and 24 "residual" Jewish households in Virginia held 83 and 38 slaves respectively.[51] Allowing for no increase whatever in the number of overall slaves in Virginia between 1820 and 1830 (and this was by no means the case), the 121 slaves attributed to Jews would have constituted 1.6 percent of the total slave population in Virginia.

On the eve of the Civil War, most Jews in Virginia lived in Richmond and they were not wealthy. The city directory for 1852 listed the following occupations for Richmond's Jews: thirty dry goods dealers, fifteen clothiers, nine salesmen, five tailors, two jewelers, two shoemakers, two shoe dealers, two confectioneers, two auctioneers, two traders, two shoe dealers, two bank cashiers, two milliners, and one member of the U.S. Navy, a single grocer, merchant, painter, butcher, coachmaker, bookbinder, printer, banner maker, clockmaker, city watchman, attorney, collector, reverend and postman.[52] Three years later, the Jewish community counted an additional 14 clothiers, five dealers in dry goods, three more tailors, two confectioneers, two salesmen, another grocer, a fruit seller, optician, and a surgeon-barber. Hardly the stuff of millionaires.[53]

Jews and Manumission

Some Jews, like 100 from Richmond who enlisted in Confederate ranks or the Reverend Maximillian Michelbacher of Orthodox Congregation Beth Ahabah enthusiastically endorsed the existing way of life in the South.[54] Rabbi George Jacobs of Beth Shalome equivocated, praying for peace at the crucial moment in January 1861. Examination of thirty-three Jewish wills from colonial Virginia reveals, however, that "some Jewish Southerners were deeply sensitive to the human character of their Negros and thought of them as fellow men rather than as cattle or merchandise."[55] Rabbi Korn refuses to apply the word "kindness" where people are treated as property,[56] but these wills offer unique glimpses of the relationship between blacks and Jews. Jewish masters instructed their heirs to treat their slaves "with lenity."[57] They offered financial rewards to slaves who nursed them back to health[58] and those who tended family graves.[59] Where possible they commanded that slave families be kept intact.[60] They encouraged slaves to purchase their own freedom or simply manumitted them and provided them with cash to start them in business.

As Isaiah Isaacs declared when he freed his slaves, giving each $20 in clothing in 1799, "Being of the opinion that all men are by nature equally free, and being possessed of some of those beings who are unfortunate, doomed to slavery, as to them, I must enjoin upon my executor a strict observance of the following clause in my will. My slaves hereafter named are to be and they are hereby manumeted and made free so that after the different periods hereafter mentioned they shall enjoy all the privileges and immunities of freed people."[61] A few years later, Jacob Cohen instructed that five adults and their children be freed and given $25 each. If they did not desire freedom they could choose their own master.[62]

Many Jews in Virginia were horrified by the ill treatment accorded blacks, especially in the wake of the bloody Nat Turner rebellion. According to Myron Berman, statements condemning such cruelty were "quite common among the papers of Richmond Jews."[63] Reacting to the torture of blacks who were dragged by horses, mutilated, and burned on the feet, Emma Mordecai wrote, "If the conduct of the blacks was outrageous, that of the whites was more barborous towards many of them who were arrested."[64] Even after Southern states made it illegal to manumit in 1841, Jews continued to purchase slaves for the purpose of offering them protection from brutal system. Writes Korn, "Probably many Jews as well as non-Jews, were caught in the dilemma of purchasing slaves just because they did not believe in slavery; since emancipation was virtually impossible all they could do was to become the most generous masters possible under the circumstances."[65]

Commenting on the Jewish attitude toward slavery, Myron Berman has written, "The role of the Jewish population of the South, whether native or immigrant in the entire slavery issue has been greatly exaggerated, however, and was a reaction to, rather than a catalyst of events."[66]

Calvert's Maryland

The history of Jews in neighboring Maryland is remarkably similar to that of Virginia. Confronted with an agrarian (tobacco) economy and an alien social system (initially there were no major urban centers in the proprietary colony), few Jews ventured into Maryland before the middle of the eighteenth century. Provincial records note the presence of itinerant traders like Mathias de Sousa, Mathias de Costa, Isaac de Barrethe, David Fereira, and Jacob Leat between 1633 and 1641, but it was clear that Jews were not welcome in this Catholic, then Protestant, colony. Maryland's original charter of June 20, 1632 warned that no religious interpretation be admitted that might cause prejudice or diminution of "the truely Christian religion."[67] The provincial legislature followed this up with the misnamed Toleration Act of 1649 which guaranteed freedom of religion for those who professed belief in the divinity of Jesus Christ and decreed the death penalty for the broadly defined crime of blasphemy.

In the summer of 1657, the punitive aspects of the Toleration Act were put to a test for the first time. Dr. Jacob Lumbrozo, a Portuguese Jew associated with a Quaker settlement, was charged with blasphemy for suggesting that Jesus and his disciples had been ordinary magicians and body snatchers. Lumbrozo was ordered to recant in formal court proceedings held in February 1658. Only the intervention of Richard, son of the Lord Proprietor, secured his release from the sheriff.[68] Five years later Lumbrozo won his letter of denization and in 1723 Maryland amended the code on blasphemy providing for boring through the tongue for a first offense, branding the letter B on a malefactor's forehead for the second offense, and then execution in the case of a third offense.[69]

England's Glorious Revolution in 1688 which entrenched Protestants in power merely substituted one gang of oppressors for another. The association of Protestant landholders which brought an end to proprietary government in 1689 three years later made the Church of England the established church in Maryland.[70] Thirteen Jewish names appear in government records before 1699 when Jews and Unitarians and Jews were legally barred.[71] Those who managed to secure naturalization were forced to swear by a special Jewish oath. Discrimination was institutionalized in the Maryland constitution of 1776 which granted religious liberty only to Christians. (The restriction remained in force till 1851.) When President Thomas Jefferson named Ruben Etting to the post of U.S. marshall at the turn of the century, no Jew could be admitted to the bar, hold public office, or serve in the militia in Maryland. Some of that state's political leaders defended such restrictions as legitimate responses to the evil that the Jews' ancestors had done by killing Christ.[72] It was only in 1826, after an thirty-year battle, led the last eight years by State Senator Thomas Washington that Maryland formally granted civil rights to Jews.[73]

We marvel at the fortitude of those early Jews who braved what Eric Goldstein termed a "forbidding environment."[74] Some, like Isaac Navarro and Moses Morecai who came to Annapolis or Henry Lazarus and Levy Cohen who settled in Fredericktown between 1740 and 1760, then Sampson Levy, Jacob Hart and Benjamin Levy who subsequently served as the core of Baltimore Jewry, were simply merchants, peddling pots, kettles, shoes, and spinning wheels to the rural inhabitants of the colony.[75] Many others, however, were involuntary settlers like Benjamin Moses, condemned in 1726 for stealing a silver tankard and expelled to the shores of Chesapeake for his crime. More than 50,000 British subjects were sent to the colonies in the first decades of the eighteenth century under the terms of the Transportation Act: 160 Jews, some of them imporverished workmen, tailors, craftsmen, suffering poverty in England, were accused of such abominable crimes as theft of a wig, a linen hanky, some lace, a silver sword; nineteen of their number (including one woman) came to Maryland as bonded criminal laborers.[76]

By 1790 there were no more than fifty Jews residing in Maryland, most of them in Baltimore.[77] A random assessment of slave ships bound for this harbor demonstrate that Jews played virtually no role in the trade of Africans. According to Elizabeth Donnan, seventeen ships carrying 2,290 slaves came to Maryland between midsummer 1698 and Christmas 1707. The following year six ships brought 648 slaves.[78] Between October 1753 and January 1765 ten ships brought 238 more slaves to Annapolis.[79] The principal masters and owners of these vessels were Samuel and John Smith, John Hollins, Samuel Galloway, James Hamrick, Perry Browne, William Van Wyck, and, for Lord Baltimore, his agent Richard Kemp. None of these vessels were owned or operated by Jews. The major slave merchants in the Potomac area in 1685 were Edward Porteus, Christopher Robinson, Richard Gardiner, none of them Jewish. Between 1711 and 1838, Jesuits priests kept hundreds of slaves on six estates in "wretched condition."[80] The leading planters in 1790 were Robert Gilmour, William Patterson, Robert Oliver, and Colonel Jon Howard.[81] Maryland's shipbuilding industry (e.g., the construction of 500-ton clipper ships) the largest in the slave states, was concentrated in the hands of the Bell brothers, Edward Johnzey, and Richard Henry.[82] The state's great factors and bankers between 1770 and 1830 included Samuel Smith, James Buchanan, Alexander Brown, Samuel Chase, Robert Oliver, Hugh Thompson, and George Grundy, a merchant who also traded in slaves.[83] Among the enterprising young business tycoons who transformed Baltimore into the center of the railroad industry in the 1840s were George Peabody, Johns Hopkins, John Garrett, Thomas Kensett, Benjamin Latrobe, Jonathan Knight, John Child.[84] None of these individuals was Jewish.

Just as in Virginia trading in slaves to be sold to the Deep South became big business when the import of African slaves was banned in 1808. A small investment could turn a profit of $30,000 in just a few months. Though the Maryland slave trade was concentrated, for the most part, in the hands of the six Woolfok brothers, who set up pens in Baltimore, Easton and other cities of the eastern shore,[85] a number of Baltimore slaving magnates took out advertisements in newspapers to impress prospective clients. These included John Denning who claimed to have 200–300 blacks available for shipment at his South Frederick Street prison; Joseph Donovan who claimed to have 500 accessible to the railroad depot and steamboat landing; Jonathan Wilson and G.M. Duke, with contacts in New Orleans; Bernard and Walter Campbell, originally from Mobile, and so influential that they were invited to Washington when Congress deliberated compensation for freeing slaves in 1862; and Hope H. Slatter, a Clinton, Georgia native, sometimes referred to as Baltimore's biggest slave dealers. Slatter's slave pens, maintained at Hoard and Pratt Streets for more than twenty years, were described as "hot as hell." It was here, before the courthouse, that brutal beatings were administered and families were separated. Slatter, Denning, Donovan, Duke, Wilson, the Campbells and the Woolfoks, none of them was Jewish.[86]

In the nineteenth century, Maryland's Jewish community inched upward in numbers, wealth and importance—from 150 in 1825, to 300 in 1835, 1,500 in 1847, 7,000 by 1859.[87] On the eve of the Civil War, most of Maryland's Jews (an estimated 5,000) lived in Baltimore. Many (Henry Sonnenborn, the Ettings, Friedenwalds, Hutzlers, Hamburgers, Levys) were recent German immigrants and, like their counterparts in Richmond, were clothiers or small merchants. The Cohen brothers (Jacob, Mendes, David, and Philip) did make a fortune in the lottery business. Joshua Cohen, a University of Maryland physician, was also instrumental in removing legal barriers to black testimony in a court of law.[88]

Despite their upward mobility, Maryland's Jews were not among the leading slaveowners in the state. According to Rabbi Korn, three Jewish heads of Baltimore households in 1790 owned a total of three slaves. They represented 0.003 percent (less than three-one-thousandth of a percent) of the 103,036 slaves in Maryland counted in the official census of 1790. In 1820 seven of Baltimore's twenty-one Jewish households owned a grand total of eleven slaves.[89] They represented 0.2 percent of the 4,357 slaves in Baltimore at the time.[90] A decade later, there were only four male house slaves among the thirty Jewish homes in Baltimore, approximately 0.08 percent of the slaves in the city.[91] In 1860 there were 2,218 slaves in Baltimore. Nine belonged to the Eschbach, Felgman, Groverman, Isaacs, and Jacobs families, approximately 0.04 percent of the slaves in the city.[92] Among more than 600 Baltimore slaveowners were five Jewish families. When Ralph Clayton compiled a list of 138 "longterm slaveholders" in Baltimore for the decade between 1850 and 1860, he counted only two Jews—Samuel Jacobs and Richard Isaacs, both of whom owned two slaves.[93]

Rabbi Einhorn and the Biblical Debate on Slavery

Just as in Virginia, Maryland's rabbis were divided over the issue of slavery. Bernard Illoway emulated Rev. Michelbacher calling for a peaceful separation from the Union. Benjamin Szold, like George Jacobs, called for reconciliation. There was, however, one individual in Baltimore who had the courage to speak out against the institution of slavery—Rabbi David Einhorn. The editors of *Secret Relationship* mention him briefly and grudgingly. In the turbulent years preceding the Civil War, Einhorn, a Reform rabbi, offered some of the most forceful denunciations of slavery. It was a time when America's Jews were fearful of what the breakup of the Union might mean for them as outsiders. As a result, many welcomed the sermon of Rabbi Morris Raphall of New York's B'nai Jeshurun temple which counselled quietism on January 4, 1861. Hoping to head off the impending conflict, Rabbi Raphall explored three questions relating to slavery: (a) how far back did it exist; (b) was it a sin; and (c) what was the status of ancient slaves. Those who embraced the institution took comfort in learning that slavery predated the Bible and that it had never been condemned in either Old or New Testament. Less comforting for contemporary slaveholders was Raphall's contention that biblical slavery bore little resemblance to that practiced in his own day and his recommendation that Southerners modify their practices along biblical lines.[94]

Raphall's suggestion that Jews adhere to the law of the day enraged Michael Heilprin, a Polish-born immigrant who had come to the U.S. in 1852. A gifted linguist and contributor to the *New American Cyclopedia* , Heilprin attacked Raphall in Horace Greeley's *New York Daily Tribune* on January 15, 1861. It was, wrote Heilprin, "ridiculous and sacrilegious" to suggest that two oblique references in the Ten Commandments condoned slavery. It was also incorrect, both from a linguistic and practical nature to compare biblical slaves with those of the ante-bellum South. The first *evedim* to serve Noah were not slaves but servants. According to Heilprin, there had not been a single slave rising in ancient Jewish history, remarkable for fifteen centuries punctuated with constant warfare, revolution, civil strife and catastrophe. Why? Because biblical slaves had been "voluntary followers, pupils,and friends enjoying all the privileges of free persons, the advantages of mutual protection and assistance and the blessings of a wise rule." By way of contrast, chattel slavery in the South destroyed human dignity and "reduces the slave to a thing."[95]

At least Raphall and Heilprin, residing in the North, enjoyed some personal safety as they debated. Not so, the Bavarian-born Rabbi Einhorn who came from Pesht only in 1855. As a Jew in Baltimore, he experienced the daily tensions of life for a minority in the South and accepted the risks when he entered the abolitionist controversy. While most Southern rabbis tried to rationalize slavery or straddled the issue, almost immediately Einhorn spoke out in sermons and essays in his German-language journal *Sinai*. As early as 1856, Einhorn labelled slavery *diesem Krebschaden der Union* ("this cancer of the Union") and called for its repudiation. He conceded that the Bible tolerated slavery of non-Hebrews as a necessary evil, but reminded his readers of the overriding biblical principal which teaches equality of origins (*gleichen Gottesebenbildlichkeit aller Menschen*) and final judgment (*Verdammungsurtheil*) of all peoples before God.⁹⁶ Three years before Lincoln was elected president, Einhorn said of slavery:

> Is it anything else but a deed of Amalek, rebellion against God to enslave beings created in His image, and to degrade them to a state of beasts having no weill of their own? Is it anything else but an act of ruthless and wicked violence to reduce defeseless human beings to a condition of merchandize , and relentlessly to tear them away from the hearts of husbands, wives, parents, and children?

Einhorn was not impressed with the argument that slavery was mentioned in both Old and New Testaments. Said the Baltimore rabbi:

> It has ever been a strategy of the advocate of a bad cause to take refuge from the spirit of the Bible to its letter, as criminals among the ancient heathen nations would seek protection near the altars of their gods. Can that Book hallow the enslavement of any race, which sets out with the principles, that Adam was created in the image of God, and that all men have descended from *one* human pair? Can *that* Book mean to raise the whip and forge chains, which proclaims with flaming words, in the name of God: 'break the bonds of oppression, let the oppressed go free, and tear every yoke!" Can *that* Book justify the violent separation of a child from its human mother, which, when speaking of birds' nests, with admirable humanity, commands charitable regard for the feeling even of an animal mother?⁹⁷

Einhorn responded swiftly to Raphall's 1861 exposition on slavery with four essays of his own in *Sinai*. The issue, he wrote, in February 1861 was not whether Abraham and other Biblical figures owned slaves but whether Americans in the nineteenth century would embrace such an archaic practice any more than polygamy or blood vengeance. The biblical spirit, wrote Einhorn, sets individuals free to make their own moral choices. Slavery is a moral evil and "we do not want it in our time." He was outraged that a descendant of the slaves of Egypt would defend such an institution and suggested that if a Christian minister in Europe had delivered a comparable sermon, Orthodox and Reform rabbis would have immediately united in rejecting "such untruths, such insults, such profanation of God's name." Einhorn's message was motivated as much from self-preservation as altruism. He foresaw no tolerance, no acceptance for Jews or any minority group as long as slavery was practiced in this land. (The Jew, he wrote, "wants freedom at any cost and trembles more than anyone for the preservation of the Union, as much as a devoted son for the life of his deathly ill mother.") If blacks were to be enslaved forever, foreigners would also be perpetually degraded as second-class citizens.[98]

A month later, Einhorn was again chiding Raphall for his faulty interpretation of the Bible, pointing out that slavery could not be justified under a so-called curse of Ham. Only Ham's youngest son, Canaan, and his descendants, the peoples of ancient Palestine and Syria, were subjects of the ancient Israelites. All Jewish authorities as well as general historians agreed that Ham's other sons—Cush identified with Ethiopia, Mizraim who became Egypt, and Put who is associated with Libya—were destined for greatness. In this essay, Einhorn questioned Raphall's training and suggested he might be better off seeking a biblical justification in the New Testament. Subsequently, he likened the debate to the Mortara Affair and argued that Jews react with equal vigor to the disregard of what he termed "the holy natural law."[99]

Einhorn's next essay was composed from afar. When the *New York Post* published a translation of his first article denouncing Rabbi Raphall in April 1861, white Southerners went on a rampage against Jews in Baltimore. They wrecked the printing presses of *Sinai* and threatened the rabbi, so much so that young members of his congregation had to escort him on the streets and at his home. The situation became so dangerous that Einhorn finally had to quit the city for Philadelphia a week later. He never returned to Baltimore, but he continued to contribute to *Sinai*.

In June 1861 he explained why he could not remain silent at this profanation of Judaism.[100] The following month, he warned: "The rebellious South wants to overturn the principle of all the innate equality of all beings created in the image of God, in favor of the opposing principle of innate servitude, and to see slavery and the law of might recognized as a force in the formation of states, as the basis of civilization. It wishes to tear the glorious Stars and Stripes to pieces, to trample it into the mire, and to set up in its place the bloody corpse of international freedom as an ornament."[101] And again, later in 1862, he affirmed that the future of America would not rest on slave chains or belittling its adopted citizens, but in the words of the Prophets, the constitution, and "the fight against prejudice."[102]

David Einhorn had the courage to say what was in the minds of many of the 7,000 Jews of Maryland, the 2,000 Jews of Virginia, indeed of all 35,000 Jews who resided in the South on the eve of the Civil War. North or South, Jews who owned *few* slaves knew the institution to be obsolete, inefficient, and morally wrong.

11

The Carolinas

Charleston: Slave Entrepot for the Southern Colonies

In 1663 Charles II issued a crown grant to Lord Ashley Cooper (Earl of Shaftesbury) and a number of nobles to develop the expanse between Norfolk, Virginia and the land of red clay controlled by the Spanish, what now is known as North and South Carolina. Its principal port would be named after the king. From such humble beginnings arose Charleston, the magnificent city perched at the estuaries of the Ashley and Cooper Rivers. Once a dangerous backwater where Europeans were likely to succumb to any of several marsh fevers, Charleston was transformed into the nation's third largest city (population 16,359) after only New York and Philadelphia in 1790. By 1860 this city of palmettos and mansions, festival balls and military batteries, had even played host to a national convention of the Democratic party.

Charleston owed its elegance and luster to one thing: the slave trade. Sir John Yeamans may have brought the first African to his Ashley River plantation in 1670–71. Three years later, a Mr. Percival is recorded as trading for blacks with the Spanish. A report of the Commons House of the Assembly of the Province of South Carolina reports slave imports of 300 men, 200 women, and 600 children grown to 1800 by 1709.[1] British naval office lists suggest that approximately 80 percent of the slaves brought into South Carolina came directly from Africa without a stopover in the West Indies.[2] Gambians were favored because they were already familiar with rice production which became the first staple crop of the Carolinas.[3] Colonial entrepreneurs, committed to the development of rice, hemp, and indigo plantations also believed that Africans enjoyed a natural immunity to the sun and swamp.[4]

Charleston was, quite simply, the main port of entry for slaves shipped from Africa and the West Indies for resale through English colonies in the Old South. Writes W.Robert Higgins, "South Carolina had the larg-

145

est and most widely developed slave trade of any of the continental English colonies. Very few of the Negroes brought into the province entered ports other than Charles Town."[5] For Robert Rosen, Charleston (a city he likens to an extension of the Caribbean world rather than colonial New England)[6] was more committed to the institution of slavery than any Southern city. Tens of thousands of Africans were funnelled through Sullivan's Island, "the Ellis Isle for black Americans" in the eighteenth century, as Charleston became America's major slaveport.[7]

The exact number of slaves that entered Charleston during its heyday may never be known. Before 1790 a complete census was rarely attempted in any of the Southern colonies. Record keeping was irregular. There are no official records because prohibitive duties in 1741–1743 and 1766–1768 and nonimportation protests in 1770 made imports virtually impossible. As a result, scholars have had to do the best they could in making their estimates. Elizabeth Donnan combined data from the *South Carolina Gazette* and the letters and notebooks of Henry Laurens, perhaps the single most important slave merchant in Charleston in the eighteenth century. Daniel Littlefield contrasted figures of the British Naval Office and South Carolina Treasury records for the period 1735–1775. During the summer of 1993, my son Jason and I scoured shipping documents from the British Public Records Office contained in the Thomas Tobias Papers of the South Carolina Historical Society and the registry of ships for South Carolina on file with the Charleston City Library. While there may be arithmetical differences in these accountings, there is no disputing the miniscule activity of Jews in the slave trade to Charleston/South Carolina.

To prevent frauds and abuses in the plantation trade (collusion with customs authorities, smuggling, the illicit traffic of those who were not English) the Navigation Acts of 1696 required that masters of every boat seeking to trade in British ports obtain a licensed certificate. It mattered little whether barque or schooner, 14 or 200 tons, whether it carried calico or slaves, as long as the vessel was headed into South Carolina, it had to be registered with the Naval Office in London. Of 789 ships officially listed between 1734 and 1780, eight were fully or partly owned by Jews, exactly 1 percent. These included the 30-ton schooner *Lindo Packett* and the brigantine *Hannah* (listed in part to Moses Lindo); the 25-ton schooner *Heron* and 20-ton schooner *Molly* (owned in part by Solomon Isaacs); the 45-ton sloop *Philip* (owned by Philip Hart), the 40-ton brigantine *Carolina* (owned by Isaac DePass) and the 45-ton sloop *Carolina Packett* (shared by Isaac Da Costa and three non-Jews).[8]

Donnan's survey of slavers coming to South Carolina is equally telling. The data is admittedly spotty, random in places. Where exact numbers are not available, Donnan estimates cargoes of 300 Africans per vessel. Between 1733 and 1807 more than 600 ships carrying nearly 90,000 slaves entered Charleston harbor. Jewish merchants (Solomon Isaacs and Isaac da Costa with his partner Thomas Farr) are listed in three transactions (0.5 percent) involving 363 slaves (0.4 percent of the total). As the following chart indicates, there was a flurry of activity at the beginning of the nineteenth century when the legal import of slaves was about to cease. Between February 1804 and December 1807, 164 ships docked at Charleston. They carried more than 26, 000 slaves. Not one of the slavers was owned or operated by Jews (see table 11.1).

Donnan's figures are sustained by other scholars. W.R. Higgins analyzed records of 405 merchants or factors in the eighteenth century and found six Jewish individuals or businesses that dabbled in the slave trade, approximately 1.3 percent of all the slave traders in Charleston. These included John Hart with one cargo in 1751, Solomon Isaacs three in 1755, Isaac Da Costa one in 1765, Nathan Levi one in 1772, Jacob Aarons one in 1772, and the firm of Isaacs and Henderson one in 1775. The total duty paid for these eight slave cargoes was 925£ sterling. At Higgins' estimate of 10£ sterling per slave, the total number of slaves imported by Jews was less than 100.[10] Jim Hagy, chairman of the History Department at Charleston College and the author of *This Happy Land: The Jews of Colonial and Antebellum Charleston,* the definitive work on Charleston Jewry, reached basically the same conclusion. Hagy found six Jewish slavers (the firm of Emanuel Cortissoz and Emanuel Abrahams, Isaac Da Costa, Isaac De Pass, Philip Hart, Solomon Issacs, and Nathan Levy) who subscribed nine cargoes between 1752 and 1772.[11]

It is a mistake to assume that all vessels passing in or out of Charleston harbor were solely plying the slave trade. Ships entries registered in the British Public Records Office list a wide assortment of products: frames for houses, staves, bricks, mahogany planks, shingles, pine boards and redwood timber, barrels of tar and pitch, ploughshares, salt, rice, beef, cider, molasses, flour, wine, coca, apples, pork, oysters, sassafras, beeswax, casks of beer, rum, lime juice, coconuts, and bread; horses, leather, skins, turpentine, Irish linen, candles, and "sundry European goods."[12] Using the same Naval Office records for the period 1717–

TABLE 11.1
Number of Slaves Imported by South Carolina 1733–1807

| Period | Estimates of Elizabeth Donnan | | |
	Ships	Slaves	Jewish Masters
Jan.1733–Jan.1738	57	17,100 (est.)	0
Mar.1739–Oct.1744	13	3,900 (est.)	0
June.1749–Dec.1751	11	1,345	0
Jan.1752–Dec.1754	36	3,732	0
Mar.1755–Dec.1755	16	1,305	Solomon Isaacs, 3 slaves
Jan.–Sept.1756	14	2,239	0
Feb.–Aug. 1757	4	1,207	0
1758	na	2,477	0
June–Nov.1759	10	1,577	0
Jan.–Dec.1760	18	3,573	Da Costa and Farr, 200 slaves
Jan.–Dec.1761	9	2,000 (est.)	0
Feb.–Nov.1762	3	640	0
Jan.–Sept.1763	7	1,110	DaCosta and Farr, 160 slaves
Feb.–Dec.1764	18	1,992	0
Jan.–Oct.1765	48	6,243	0
Jan.–Sept.1769	29	3,228	0
Feb.–Dec.1771	19	2,688	0
Apr.–Dec.1772	24	3,717	0
Feb.–Nov.1773	41	5,473	0
Jan.–Oct.1774	14	1,944	0
Sept.–Dec.1783	4	194	0
Jan.–Dec.1784	16	2,240	0
Jan.–Nov.1785	18	1,262	0
Mar.1786–Mar.1787	12	na	0
Feb.–Dec.1804	31	4,565	0
Jan.–Dec.1805	32	5,079	0
Jan.–Dec.1806	45	2,179	0
Jan.–Dec.1807	56	15,676	0[9]

1767, Daniel Littlefield counted 380 ships carrying 32, 663 slaves to Charleston.[13] That is less than 10 percent of the 3,800 vessels that entered Charleston harbor. Of these, only two are confirmed by the Naval Office as belonging to Jews—the *Lindo Packett*, bound from Barbados in November 1757 with 49 slaves and the very same brig *Greyhound* owned by Aaron Lopez and Jacob Rivera of Rhode Island which entered Charleston on January 25, 1763 with 134 slaves (see table 11.2). (The *Lindo Packett* made six voyages in and out of Charleston about this time—only one of which involved Jews. By the end of 1757 it was

TABLE 11.2
Ships Entries Port of Charleston

	No. of		No. of	
Period	Ships	Slavers	Slaves	Principal Owners
Dec. 1716–June 1717	76	6	351	Wragg, Howell, Gibbon, Higginson
July–Dec. 1717	66	7	122	Kent, Clark, Gibbon, Delaroundos
Dec. 1717–Mar. 1718	51	3	56	Perry, Luce, Powell
Mar. 1718–June 1718	32	5	183	Sanderson, Holmes, White
June 1718–Sep. 1718	33	5	762	Logan, Barron, Bradley, Allen
Sep. 1718–Dec. 1718	19	4	75	Allen, Gibbon, Logan, Porter
Dec. 1718–Mar. 1719	34	5	29	Hake, Harrris, Randall
Mar. 1719–June 1719	31	4	32	Goddin, Laugher, Murdock, de La Conscillere
June 1719–Sep. 1719	23	5	211	Wragg, Gibbon, Allen, Burnham
Dec. 1721–Mar. 1722	58	3	36	Lee, Bant, Barfoot, La Roche, Matthews
June 1723–Sep. 1723	35	2	220	Lansdale, Johnstone
Sep. 1723–Dec. 1723	33	0	0	
Dec. 1736–Mar. 1737	74	4	673	Wragg, LeRoche, Clark, Hobhouse
Mar. 1737–June 1737	49	1	206	Darlington
June 1737–Sep. 1737	33	3	421	Atkins, Ogden, Foster
Dec. 1737–Mar. 1738	52	1	360	Allen, Grant, Saunders, Lloyd
Mar. 1738–June 1738	53	3	769	Gray, Naysmith, Wallace, Whittaker, Butler
June 1738–Sep. 1738	38	6	808	Wragg, Segourney, LaRoche, Hobhouse
Dec. 1738–Mar. 1739	59	0	0	
Mar. 1739–June 1739	60	3	547	Atkins, Grant, Ewing, Saunders, Foster
Nov. 1752–Dec. 1752	38	3	280	Grant
Dec. 1752–Apr. 1753	70	9	119	Brown, Booth, Armstrong, Barber, Hutton
Oct. 1757–Jan. 1758	52	2	100 est.	**Moses Lindo, 49 on Lindo Packett
Jan. 1758–Apr. 1758	72	6	241	Saunders, Faulkner, Johnson, Wallett
Apr. 1758–July 1758	79	8	1,117	Smith, Hardman, Whaley, Farr, Rigby
July 1758–Oct. 1758	58	9	1,672	Knight, Barber, Boyd, Grant, Deane
Oct. 1758–Apr. 1759	127	0	0	
Apr. 1759–July 1759	39	4	312	Banks, Hanna, Black
July 1759–Oct. 1759	na	6	1,071	Sergeant, Grant, Barber, Oswald, Watson
Oct. 1759–Jan. 1760	82	3	496	Deane, Jenkins, Heyward, Bannister
Jan. 1760–Apr. 1760	65	2	62	Cowan, Johnson
Apr. 1760–July 1760	45	2	407	Sargent, Hill
July 1760–Oct. 1760	49	11	1,607	Biggin, Clarke, Smith, Morris, Maddock
Oct. 1760–Jan. 1761	77	6	2,101	Deane, White, Dunbar, Hartley, White
Jan. 1763–Apr. 1763	102	1	134	**Lopez, Rivera on Greyhound
Apr. 1763–July 1763	103	3	201	Savage, Nicolson, Bampfield, Smith
July 1763–Oct. 1763	74	4	85	Rogers, Amory, Wharton, Morris
Oct. 1763–Jan. 1764	126	1	na	
Jan. 1764–Apr. 1764	106	5	160	Robinson, Harquier, Nonton, Bright
Apr. 1764–July 1764	74	13	965	Smith, Knight, Gordon, Savage, Todd
Oct. 1764–Jan. 1765	50	9	685	Griffith, Herbert, Savage, Slocum
July 1765–Oct. 1765	88	21	2,081	Stead, Smith, Turney, Gordon, Oswald
Oct. 1765–Jan. 1766	57	8	242	Savage, Stead, Pierpont, Smith, Simpson
Jan. 1766–Apr. 1766	124	2	101	Laurens, Todd, Lewis
Apr. 1766–Mar. 1767	376	0	0	
Apr. 1767–June 1767	66	1	9	Savage, Young
July 1767–Sep. 1767	63	0	0	

Source: Thomas Tobias Papers 11-417 and 11-418, 2-10. South Carolina Historical Society.

no longer registered to Moses Lindo but to a prominent slaver John Gordon.)[14] Numbers may be juggled about, but if we limit our analysis for one moment to 1757–1767 for which we have a complete record, the number of slaves imported by two Jewish ships (183) constitutes exactly 1 percent of all the slaves (17,815) brought in to Charleston during that decade.

The South Carolina Slavocracy

Whatever list is examined, certain names stand out. W.R.Higgins points out that between 1735 and 1775 twenty-four men imported more than ten cargoes. They included William Savage, George Austin, Henry Laurens, John Simpson, George Lord, Miles Brewton, Joseph Wragg, Pouag, , LeGare, Powell, Hopton & Co.[15] None were Jews. In Donnan's calculations, Joseph Wragg and Benjamin Savage were the predominant slave traders between 1717 and 1744, accounting for better than thirty-six vessels and 10, 000 slaves.[16] Wragg was especially active, his name also appearing twenty-five times in the minutes of the Royal African Company between 1722 and 1727 with reference to slave shipments from Gambia.[17] Until the Revolutionary War, the firms of George Austin and Henry Laurens (with at least twenty-three ships and a minimum of 3,000 slaves) Thomas Middleton and Samuel Brailsford (twenty-nine ships, 4,000 slaves) Miles Brewton and Roger Smith (thirty-six ships, 7,000 slaves) predominated.[18] Between 1760 and 1768 the number of slaves employed in the back country more than doubled (from 2,417 to 6,548). Many of these went to hemp and indigo planters like William Harrison (with twenty-eight slaves), Samuel Wyly (25), Daniel Nail (40), the Anglican merchant Joseph Kershaw, Robert Goudey (more than 100), and John Chestnutt (who owned 135 by 1790).[19] In the last flurry of activity before slaving was barred (1804–1807), the names of Thomas Tunno (16 ships, 2,500 slaves), William Boyd (22 ships, 6,079 slaves), Gibson and James Broadfoot (12 ships, 2798 slaves) crop up repeatedly. In my own tallies for the period 1717–1773, the names Sam Ward, William Gibbon, John LaRoche, Edmund Saunders, Abel Grant, Andrew and Samuel Allen, Isaac Hobhouse, Thomas Deane, John Sargent, John Knight, and Samuel Wragg appear most frequently. Adventurous aristocrats, eager middle class English merchants, Huguenots and Irish Catholics seeking a haven, not one of the gentlemen responsible for importing upwards of 70, 000 slaves into Charleston in the eighteenth century was Jewish.

The colonial patriot Henry Laurens was typical of these slave magnates. Onetime president of the Continental Congress, imprisoned by the British in the Tower of London until he was exchanged for Lord Cornwallis, member of the American delegation at Paris which hammered out peace terms in 1783, Laurens privately held reservations about slavery.[20] Publicly, however, he was one of the greatest, if not the greatest, slave trader in South Carolina in the eighteenth century. The correspondence of Bristol, Liverpool, London, and Barbados companies between 1748 and 1774 is literally punctuated with 151 notes from Laurens, complaining about the mortality of slaves transported to Charleston, the capricious rise and fall of slave prices, problems of obtaining profits from cargoes accompanying slaves and the meddling of king's officers.[21] At one point (May 1773) Laurens had twelve cargoes with 1900 slaves in harbor. His interest in these Africans did not cease once they were landed and sold. Records maintained at the South Carolina State Historical Library in Columbia show thirteen members of the Laurens family in forty transactions involving 443 slaves until 1851.[22] Laurens and his heirs needed their own personal contingent of slaves to run Mepkin, the mansion on the Cooper River, and the town house at Ansonborough. In this they were no different from other planters who exploited slave labor for agriculture and domestic purposes.

According to Robert Rosen, the average plantation in colonial Carolina ranged from twenty-seven to 1,610 acres and required approximately 120 slaves to operate it.[23] These included Charles Pinckney's Snee Farm in Christ Church, Middleton Place, Drayton Hall, Edward Fenwick's Fenwick Hall, the Oaks owned by the Manigaults, descendants of of Samuel Wragg, Saluda Mill near Columbia, James Hammond's farm which served as a breeding grounds for slaves,[24] the rice and wheat fields of the Pettigrew family in both North and South Carolina, and the several cotton plantations of Wade Hampton.[25] David Williams started with a plantation force of 100 and when he died in 1830 he owned 500 slaves.[26] Slavery was the economic lifeblood of the Carolinas. Attorney Rosen reports that on a single day in 1860 two Charleston newspapers advertised 2,048 slaves for sale. Five years later, when the Civil War ended 400,000 slaves in South Carolina were emancipated. According to Rosen, "thousands" took surnames like Pinckney, Hayne, Middleton, Manigault, or Gadsden.[27]

The selection was not accidental. Bills of sale filed in Columbia confirm that the most prestigious families in Charleston were active in the buying and selling slaves for their own personal use. The first sizable estate noted was that of Clement Lemprier with 38 in July, 1787.[28] When John Axson died in 1851, his estate counted 79 slaves.[29] Philip Prioleau had 116 when he died in December 1846.[30] Between 1785 and 1849, nine members of the Van der Horst family, including its founder Thomas Cooper Van der Horst from St.Helena, were involved in the buying and selling of 212 slaves.[31] There are seven pages of transactions for the clan of Thomas Heyward dating between 1774 and 1852, including 265 slaves bought and sold by William C. Heyward in the last four years of entries.[32] The Drayton family, which produced ministers and governors, bought and sold 200 between 1799 and 1860 to staff the charming farmhouse and surrounding grounds which have inspired tourists to photographs, poems, and marriage vows.[33] The topiary gardens of their neighbors, the Middletons, were trimmed by some of that family's 100 slaves. Between February 3 and May 2, 1837, 233 slaves belonging to Henry Middleton were sold. On a single day, April 19, 1843, 323 slaves belonging to John Middleton were disposed of.[34]

There were some Jews in South Carolina who claimed to be planters. Jim Hagy discovered thirteen individuals in city directories aspiring to such a grand title.[35] These same men also listed incomes from activities as shop merchant, accountant, gorcer, auctioneer, vendue merchant and broker. Not every sale or purchase involving slaves was recorded, but evidence from those that were suggests few, if any, Jews belonged to the planter aristocracy. Only three of these so-called planters recorded more than ten slave purchases or sales (see table 11.3 below). The official records in the State Library at Columbia show, for example, that Jacob Barrett only purchased two slaves in 1838–39.[36] Like most of the other so-called Jewish planters, he is not even listed as being involved in ten or more slave transactions. Barnet Cohen sold 6 between 1815 and 1829.[37] David Daniel Cohen was involved in four transactions with 7 slaves between 1836 and 1844.[38] Mordecai Cohen bought and sold 33 between 1799 and 1835.[39] Solomon Cohen sold 9 in 1840.[40] Isaac Dacosta is listed as selling two slaves in 1809.[41] Myer Jacobs sold 14 between 1820 and 1848.[42] Isaac Lyons sold four in the period 1810–15.[43] Josiah Moses sold 4 in 1829.[44] Nathan Nathans sold two in two separate transactions in 1814 and 1852.[45]

My own research jibes with Professor Hagy's conclusion that the most active Jewish slave traders averaged between one and four slaves bought or sold in each transaction. Even the greatest activity on the part of Jews pales next to that of Gentile planters. Isaiah Moses bought and sold 66 slaves in 19 transactions between 1809 and 1854.[46] The entire

TABLE 11.3
Purchases/Sales by Jews in South Carolina

Name	Directory Listing	Slaves	Period	Trans.	Avg.
	10 or More Recorded Transactions				
Barrett, Isaac	Merchant, factor	34	1817–29	10	3.4
Cohen, Mordecai	Merchant, planter	51	1795–1838	27	1.8
Davis, Hannah	Shop	29	1803–35	23	1.2
DeLeon, Mordecai	Physician, Vendue Agent	12	1813–20	11	1.1
Lazarus, Marks	Shop	34	1786–1834	11	3.3
Levy, Lyon	Accountant, Planter	11	1792–1824	10	1.1
Levy, Solomon	Shop, merchant	30	1809–28	21	1.4
Mordecai, Benjamin	Broker	48	1847–60	29	1.6
Mordecai, Moses	Account, merchant	19	1827–49	14	1.4
Moses, Esther		10	1795–1817	10	1.0
Moses, Isaac	Shop, auctioneer	21	1794–1820	13	1.6
Moses, Isaiah	Grocer, planter	58	1809–45	14	4.1
Moses, Levy	Store	35	1803–37	12	2.9
Moses, Simon	Store, broker	37	1813–32	27	1.4
Nathan, Solomon	Shop	14	1799–1817	10	1.4
Sasportas, Abraham	Merchant	27	1799–1806	13	2.1
Tobias, Abraham	Merchant, Vendue Agent	24	1816–37	16	1.5
Woolf, Rachel	Shop	15	1814–25	16	0.9

Source: James Hagy, *This Happy Land*, p. 95.

Levy clan of South Carolina (including 48 persons listed under Levey, Levi, and Levy) bought or sold 150 slaves in the period 1783–1858.[47] By way of contrast, General James Hamilton, from Charleston's elite aristocracy, bought 173 on a single day, May 2, 1837.[48] Catherine Verdier, a Christian lady of some esteem, disposed of 161 slaves on April 26, 1855.[49]

There is no mention of either General Hamilton or Mrs. Verdier in *The Secret Relationship.* But there is of Jacob Ottolengui, supposedly the Jewish master of a plantation near the Savannah River that employed a thousand slaves. Hagy has exposed this claim of a great Jewish plantation as myth, based on a poorly documented book published in 1884.[50] In fact, the records at the South Carolina Depatment of Archives and History list only three references involving slaves which might be attributed to Ottolengui. The first, in his exact spelling, details the sale of 9 slaves to C.J. Beckman in February 1845. The second, under the heading Jacob Ottolingui, tells of the sale of 4 slaves to B. Mordecai on June 11, 1860. The third, under Jacob Ottolingui, as executor, tells of the sale of 4 slaves in July, 1859.[51]

The Secret Relationship also alludes to Moses Lindo in its list of Jews responsible for the "Black American Holocaust, " offering support from the *Jewish Encyclopedia* that he was "a wealthy planter." While serving twelve years as indigo agent for the colony, Lindo supposedly profiteered through a 500-acre plantation which employed 60–70 slaves. As with Jacob Ottolengui, this is the stuff of nonsense. Lindo came to South Carolina in November 1756 with a scientific expertise in dyes. Appointed by Governor Thomas Boone to the post of surveyor and inspector general for "indico, drugs, and dyes, " Lindo was responsible for the boom in indigo dyes (600,000 pounds, 150,000£ sterling per year) from South Carolina. Far from oppressing blacks, he is credited with discovering the cure for yaws, the skin disease that afflicted so many Africans.[52] There is no evidence to suggest that he ever owned a plantation. He is not mentioned among the principal planters or dealers listed by Lt. Governor William Bull in the middle of the eighteenth century, a list which included Henry and Thomas Middleton, John Drayton, William Moultrie, Peter Manigault, John Colleton, James and Henry Laurens.[53] According to Barnett Elzas, one of the earliest chroniclers of South Carolina Jewry, "there is nothing to show that Lindo planted at all."[54] State records in Columbia reveal applications in his name for two remote pieces of land in the upper part of the state. Lindo is also reputed to have purchased two young men "probably...his personal servants" in two separate transactions.[55]

These are not the numbers of ante-bellum colonels. And for good reason. While Lindo and other Jews may have fantasized about entering the planter aristocracy, just as everywhere else in the Western Hemisphere, they were neither paticularly welcome nor indispensable to this slave society. Latecomers to South Carolina, no matter what their self-perceptions about "the Happy Land," Jews have always had to battle their image as outsiders.

Locke Welcomes the "Jues"

It was not supposed to be that way. Unlike the northern bastions of religious intolerance, the initial grant to Lord Ashley Cooper in 1665 stipulated: "We will grante in as ample manr as ye undertakers shall desire freedomes and libertye of contience in all relligious or spirrituall things and to be kept inviolably with them, we haveing power in or charter soe to doe."[56] Four years later, this pledge was refined in a constitution drafted by John Locke which guaranteed rights of "heathens, Jues and other disenters." Regardless of their ignorance or mistakes, advised Locke, Jews and other strangers to truth must not be expelled or "used ill," but won over to Christianity by respect and "imbrace."[57]

Not everyone was so eager to welcome the Jews. Already in 1660, Thomas Violet, a customs official, petitioned King Charles urging their expulsion from British colonies in the new world. Wrote Violet: "It would be to the great damage of our merchants whose trade they engross and eat the childrens' bread and in the Barbados they do so swarm that had no care been taken to banish them, in twenty years they would eat out the English, but by the care of this blessed Parliament, they are within a year to be banished thence."[58] While Carolinians did not bar Jews, their reactions were rather cool. Business relations between Jews and Gentiles were formal. There were incidents of religious desecration. (Hoodlums stole the silver spice box and tossed torah scrolls about in Beth Elohim, the oldest synagogue in Charleston on September 18, 1787.) Bigots were upset that "Jews, strangers, sailors, servants, Negroes, and almost every french man in Craven and Berkely County" participated in the election of 1703.[59] And the colonial assembly retained the standard restrictions against disbelievers participating in government (e.g., voting, sittting in the legislature) until Charles Pinckney made an impassioned effort to remove such disabilities in 1790.[60]

Still, the Jews came to Carolina, which remained a united royal province till 1729. The first, mentioned in tax assessments of 1694, was Mordecai Nathan. The following year, a report from Governor John Archdale mentions a Jew from Charlestown acting as interpreter between the English and Spanish who were trying to sell four Yamassee Indians as slaves. (When it turned out that the three men and one woman were Christians, they were freed.)[61] In 1697 there were four Jewish merchants in Charleston, none of any substance, mentioned in the *Carolina Gazette* before 1734.[62] Joseph Tobias, president of the first Jewish congregation in Charleston, managed to secure naturalization in 1741. But as late as 1750, there were fewer than fifteen adult Jewish men in the community.[63]

Those numbers increased dramatically in the last half of the eighteenth century. Marcus estimates that by 1776 there were forty to fifty Jewish families, perhaps 200 persons in South Carolina.[64] In 1790, Charleston counted one-sixth of the 1500 Jews in America. Ten years later the number was up to 400. And by 1820 Charleston had the highest number of Jews of any city in America—800—more than New York (550) or Philadelphia (450).[65] Jews flocked to Charleston because of its climate, its relaxed atmosphere, and the business opportunities which this bustling port city offered. Some like Isaac Da Costa were importers with connections to the Lopez-Rivera firm in Rhode Island.[66] Others were jewelers, clerks, physicians and vendue masters—merchants commissioned to sell practically every sort of incoming goods. Professor Hagy has chronicled the diversity of jobs: from attorneys and blacksmiths to tailors and umbrella makers.[67] The predominant trade listed, however, was shopkeeper.

They came to Carolina and embraced the concept of slavery— Sephardic Jews because it was an accepted way of life in the West Indies, Ashkenazic Jews because it was a means of gaining acceptance with the general white populace. An urban people, the Jews owned slaves, but, as Hagy notes, "not [in] great numbers."[68] They rationalized that only blacks could work in such a climate.[69] They experienced feelings of guilt but were hampered by state laws which made manumission difficult by 1800 and all but impossible (only through legislative act) by 1820. Still at least ten Jews freed slaves between 1772 and 1811, some out of state.[70] And they shared white fears of blacks in the aftermath of the Stono Rebellion of 1739 and the alleged conspiracy of Denmark Vesey in 1822.[71]

According to Hagy, the first transaction involving slaves and Jews occured in 1696 when Simon Valentine sold one to Samuel Mincks.[72] A century later, the census of 1790 listed 73 households headed by Jews. Of these 34 owned 151 slaves, less than 1 percent of the slaves in the state, and a figure consistent with the notion that Jews owned few slaves and generally for domestic purposes. In 1830, 104 Jewish households owned 420 slaves.[73] There were 12, 652 slaves in Charleston in 1820. Assuming no increase in the number of slaves (an unlikely circumstance), Jews would have owned 3 percent of the slaves in the city. The numbers become more disparate when it is pointed out that ten Jewish families owned more than ten slaves in 1830 while 390 Christian families had ten or more. Eighty-seven Christian families owned more than twenty slaves. The lone Jewish family with such numbers was that of Mordecai Cohen which owned twenty-three.[74]

In the decades preceding the Civil War, the Jewish population of Charleston not only stagnated, it began to decline. In 1830 the numbers were down to 650 as New York and Philadelphia left the once promising community in their wake. By 1850 Charleston counted 500 Jews.

Hagy has listed fifty-one individuals who owned 288 slaves in that year (eleven of whom owned more than 20.)[75] The figure accounts for approximately 2 percent of the 14, 000 slaves in Charleston. Spread over the entire state, where there were fewer Jews and tens of thousands more slaves, as in Virginia or Maryland, the percentage dwindles to insignificance.

The Jew as Vendue Master

Whether Jews imported slaves or owned them in great numbers as vendue masters, the charge is made they played a crucial role peddling them in the slave marts. representatives of Benjamin Mordecai and Jacob Cohen served as middle men in the area bounded by Broad, Bay, Queen, and Meeting Streets in Old Charleston. In Columbia, Jacob Levin, a self-proclaimed rabbi, served as auctioneer in a number of estate sales involving as many as fifty blacks between 1844 and 1866 and was even singled out by name in a commentary to *Uncle Tom's Cabin.*[76]

As Sol Breibart, resident archivist at Beth Elohim, points out, not all vendue masters were involved with slave trading, and even those that were may have dealt as a sideline.[77] In his seminal essay on slavery, Rabbi Bertram Korn mentions three kinds of slave traders: (a) the normal slaveholder ("there was hardly a slave-owner who had not bought and sold"); (b) the dealer or speculator in all kinds of commodities; and (c) the professional slave trader whose sole income derived from full-time efforts in the slave market.[78] In Charleston, Korn distinguished between Cohen (a speculator) and Mordecai (who qualified as a full-time slave merchant even though he derived income from other sources because his warehouses were located in the center city next to the slave pens).[79] Korn identified other so-called brokers who advertised slaves for sale on at least one occasion, including Myer Moses, Abraham Mendes Seixas, H.H.DeLeon, Ralph dePass, Jacob Ottolengui, and Jacob Jacobs.[80] Four of these men (Cohen, Mordecai, DeLeon and Ottolengui) appear in the 1859 Charleston City directory among forty-four traders, auctioneers, or brokers.[81] Only one (Benjamin Cohen) appears on a list of the thirteen most prosperous slave traders in Charleston for 1860. Cohen's commissions from slave sales amounted to less than one-fourth those of old guard aristocrat Louis de Saussure.[82] Working from census tracts, Michael Tadman identified fifty-five slave traders in South Carolina, 37 from the Charleston area. These included aldermen Alexander McDonald, S.J. Riggs, Thomas Ryan, Ziba Oakes, and A.J. Salinas, the

TABLE 11.4
Traders, Auctioneers or Brokers in Slaves

Charleston 1859–180		
Alexander, Thomas	Gourdin, Wm.	Riggs, J.S.
Austin, Robert	Hume, Thomas	Rodgers, T.L.
Baker, J. Russell	Laborde, J.P.	Ryan, J.S.
Bennett & Rhett	Lee, Hutson	Ryan, Thomas & son
Bowers, J.E.	Lockwood, P.L.	Salinas, A.J.
Capers & Heyward	McBride, M.	Shingler bros.
Cohen, Jacob and sons	McCall, B.	Simons, Wm.
DeLeon, H.H.	Marshall, R.M.	Spencer, Seth
DeSaussure, Louis	Mordecai, B.	White, Alonzo
DeWitt, G.	Nipson, Francis	Whitney, T.A.
Drayton, Charles	Oakes, Z.B.	Wilbur & son
Faber, Joseph	Olsen, C.M.	Willis, Henry
Ford, J. Drayton	Ottolengui, J.	Willis, Henry Jr.
Gadsden, Thomas	Porcher & Baya	
Gilchrist, J.M.	Rhett & Fitzsimons	
Willis, Henry Jr.		

Source: Bancroft *,Slave Trading in the Old South,*pp.175–76

TABLE 11.5
Prosperous Slave Brokers

Charleston 1860	
Name	**Commissions**
DeSaussure, Louis	$10,983
Riggs, J.S.	8,707
Capers & Heyward	5,000
Oakes, Z.B.	5,000
Bennett & Rhett	4,000
Ryan, Thos. & Son	4,000
Marshall, R.M.	3,800
Porcher & Baya	3,500
Gourdin, Wm.	3,028
Cohen,Jacob & Son	2,500
White, A.J.	2,500
Hume, Thomas	2,000
Salinas, A.J.	2,000
Wilbur & Sons	2,000

Source: Bancroft,*Slave Trading in the Old South,*pp.189–90.

banker Thomas N. Gadsden, sheriff Thomas Weatherly, and Joseph Crews (who later became a Scalawag). The lone Jew to make Tadman's list was Benjamin Mordecai.[83]

Of all the Jewish slave brokers, Cohen held the greatest number of slaves in his Charleston home—15.[84] By way of contrast, the de Saussure family (onetime unionists in the days of the nullification controversy) maintained 42 slaves in its series of Charleston mansions. By far the most prosperous slave broker in the city (see table 11.5), Louis DeSaussure hosted the last slave auction in Charleston. Among other Christian families, the Heywards counted 88 city slaves, Thomas Middleton 48, the Ravenels 43, Dr. Thomas Prioleau 21, Dr. James Moultrie 20, William Pringle 35, the Holbecks 69, John Baker 112, the Gibbses 72, the Bees 63, Colonel Charles Blum 56, the Pinckneys 27, Mrs. Eliza Ball 54, the Legares 35, the Browns 39. the Blacks 34, James Gantt 32, the Gadsdens 30, the Warings 40, the O'Neils 31, Jacob Miller 34, F.W. Edwards 35, the Webbs 44, Rodger Adger 32, the Marshalls 44, the Macbeths 37, and Thomas Lucas 160.[85] Trading slaves in Charleston might have been lucrative practice, but the profession was neither dominated nor monopolized by Jews.

The case against Jewish slave brokers in Columbia is equally flimsy. Jacob and L.T. Levin may have taken out a number of advertisements announcing the sale of blacks in 1852–53, but the ads also mentioned furniture, featherbeds, wash stands, crockery, and articles of glass.[86] According to Bancroft, the Levins served as auctioneers disposing of property belonging to deceased planters in order to settle debts among heirs.[87] The principal slave traders in Columbia included the house of Allen and A.R. Phillips which annually bought and sold several hundred slaves[88] or that of Charles Logan and Alexander Forsythe who maintained brick slave pens at Assembly and Senate Streets.[89] An Irish-born shoemaker, Logan would eventually retire as a philanthropist, dabbling in horses and real estate as a result of his slave gains.

Those who bought the slaves in Columbia were non-Jews like William Clarkson who had 210 by 1860, Frank Hampton who owned 260, or the various branches of the Adams family which owned 1,100.[90] As for Jacob Levin, he was a man of middling importance—secretary-treasurer of the Hebrew Benevolent Society of Columbia between 1834 and 1843, onetime bookkeeper for the Exchange Bank and Secretary of Columbia Gas Co., member of the Masonic council.[91] It was in this last capacity that he earned his one reference in John Hammon Moore's *History of Columbia*, complaining in November 1861 that "the lowest dregs of the meanest people on earth" (Yankee prisoners of war) were being permitted to attend meetings of the local Masonic lodge.[92] For Columbia's Jews, Levin is a forgotten name. In August 1993 Hyman Rubin, a retired state senator who doubles as a community historian, told me: "I have no knowledge of Jews in the slave trade. It would be totally strange. Certainly if it existed at all, it was very minimal."[93] Just to be certain, Rubin scanned a four-volume history of South Carolina looking for Levin's name. It wasn't there.

Jews in South Carolina are passionate in affirming their love of their state. Says Charleston attorney Robert Rosen, "Jews came to the South and got political liberty unknown to that time. Freedom to practice their religion, freedom to practice commerce. By way of contrast, in New England which was founded as a hotbed of religious liberty, the people had freedom to oppress."[94] Hyman Rubin says practically the same thing, boasting of Columbia and South Carolina: "It really is a great city, a great state. The people are most genteel, wonderfully mannered. We had major problems in the state when segregation was so important to some people. But having crossed that threshold, we are in a very fortunate state and we thank Him who placed us here beneath this sweet Southern sky."[95]

South Carolina may be Solla-Sallew for Jews today, but that was not the case 100 years ago. As elsewhere, they were a vulnerable minority, some of whom owned slaves, all of whom, to paraphrase John Moore, "had less impact upon the local scene during the opening decades of the nineteenth century" than Episcopalians, Baptists, Methodists, and Presbyterians.[96]

12

Georgia: The Land Closed to Slaves, Rum, and Lawyers

The Battle to Legitimate Slavery

Every schoolchild learns that Georgia, the last of the original thirteen colonies, was founded in 1733 by General James Oglethorpe as a haven for English paupers and felons.[1] In fact, Oglethorpe was not the first to attempt a colony here. Proprietors in Carolina recognized the need for a buffer against incursions from hostile Indians and the Spanish in Florida. In 1717, Sir Robert Montgomery received a grant to establish a Margravate of Azilia between the Savannah and Altamara Rivers. It failed after three years, just as the abortive settlement of Purrysburg founded by the Swiss Jean Pierre Purry had in 1732. Military outposts having proved unsuccessful, George II and his advisers concluded that what they needed was a fixed population and that was readily available in lawbreakers and the needy.[2]

Tradition has it that when Oglethrope received his charter, it contained three restrictions: no alcoholic beverages, no slaves, and, according to local legend, no lawyers.[3] In reality, the third restriction involved land tenure (none to any trustee, and no grants to be over 500 acres).The prohibitions on drink and slavery were enacted on April 3, 1735, and supposedly were designed to make the colony more defensible. Georgia's trustees, sitting in London, believed that slaves were inherently unstable, given to running away and fomenting rebellion with the Spanish. The import of rum or brandies might only exacerbate the situation along the frontier.[4] Besides, some of Georgia's first settlers, fiercely independent farmers from Scotland and Salzburg, resented the competition of slave labor.

In the next fifteen years, aspiring planters badgered the Privy Council for a reversal in policy.[5] In December 1738, 117 prominent citizens of Savannah petitioned London claiming that without Negroes, "the colony must sink."[6] Two years later, they renewed their application, stating that "if Negroes were allowed, the colony would people apace."[7] Among the petitioners were James Habersham, one of the colony's foremost merchants; George Whitfield, Savannah's leading minister; Patrick Telfair, an apothecary surgeon; John Brownfield, registrar; Hugh Anderson, overseer of public gardens; Andrew Grant, Robert Williams, and Benjamin Mackintosh. Whitfield and Habersham stressed the positive moral impact of exposing blacks to Christian society.[8] They apparently convinced two men who initially were opposed to the introduction of slavery—Colonel William Stephens, the first president of Georgia colony, and Pastor Martin Bolzius. Both Stephens and Bolzius, having reluctantly concluded it was God's will, added their names to the petition.[9] More than 400 slaves would be brought into Georgia illegally after the War of Jenkins' Ear (1739) which convinced the trustees to repeal the prohibition on slaves in July 1750.

Between 1755 and 1771 326 slaves entered Georgia aboard 158 vessels, another 1479 on 14 vessels between 1796 and 1798.These ships were listed to more than 200 owners, some of whose names are mentioned repeatedly, including Carolinians Miles Brewton and Henry Laurens, and Georgians James Spencer, Edward Telfair, Jeremiah Meyler, John Ellis, and David Montaigut.[10] The lone Jewish name that appears is that of Solomon Levy of Jamaica who was a partner with James Wright. Levy's eighteen slaves brought in aboard the schooner *Esther* in 1766 constituted 0.3 percent (less than one-third of one percent) of the 5,720 slaves tabulated by Donnan in the eighteenth century.[11]

Ascertaining the extent of slave trading activity in Georgia after 1808, when Congress banned the importation of Africans, is more problematic. Captains entering or leaving American ports had to fill out forms swearing that slaves aboard their vessels had either been legally imported or born in the U.S. Such manifests confused individuals who were personal manservants with gangs being transported for sale. We may assume that large numbers reflect slave transports. A survey of ships clearing Savannah harbor in the nineteenth century suggests that the principal slave traders included James Johnston, who shipped out more than 100 slaves between 1812 and 1820, R.J. Haversham, responsible for 25 in 1820, William Jones of Virginia who sent 30 to Wilmington, North Carolina, and I.H.King of Suffolk, who sent 64 to Charleston in December 1864. The manifests include several Jewish owners (Jacob DeLamotta, David Yulee, Anna Delyon, A.A.Solomons,

I. Nathans) travelling with single slaves. The sole instance where Jews were responsible for a large shipment came in September 1820 when Moses Sheftall and Isaac Cohen outfitted the sloop *Caroline* to Beaufort, South Carolina, with 15 slaves aboard.[12]

Such numbers by no means reflect Georgia's exact slave population. Many more slaves were brought overland from South Carolina or Florida. The *Georgia Gazette* estimates there were at least 7,800 slaves in the colony by 1766. A decade later, there were 16,000 slaves and 34,000 whites in the colony/state. By 1790 the number of slaves had increased to 29,264. And on the eve of the Civil War, Georgia counted 462,198 slaves among its total population of 1,057,286 making it second only to Virginia in the number of slaveholders and slaves. From 1755 forward, Georgia's slaves were subjected to a brutal code modelled on that of South Carolina. Any slave caught without a special identity ticket might be subjected to a whipping. Because slaves were valuable property, runaways were to be returned to their masters. Even the once tolerant Salzburgers agreed that white masters who killed their chattels in the heat of passion should only be fined a maximum of £50.[13]

Slaves were imported because they were crucial to the development of rice and cotton plantations which became the backbone of Georgia's economy. Before the invention of the cotton gin, Georgia's white farmers owned an average of twenty to thirty slaves.[14] The first plantations south of Savannah were established by colonists from New England and Virginia—John McIntosh, David Joseph Butler, John Barnard, and Jacob Lockerman.[15] Julia Smith offers the following examples of rice planters: Governor James Wright who owned more than 500 slaves on 121 plantations sprawling over 19,000 acres; James Habersham who counted 200 slaves on his 12,000 acre plantation southeast of Savannah; and Lieutenant Governor John Graham who owned 27,000 acres of land.[16] In the Ogeechee River district, Dr. John Cheves owned 234 slaves on a 1,500-acre plantation. George Anderson had 129 on 1,200 acres, Ralph Elliott 232 on 1,500 acres. In the same Chatham County district, Arthur Heyward owned 352 slaves, Stephen Habersham 181. In the Savannah River district, William Gibbons and James Potter owned more than 300 each, while George Harrison, Charles Manigault, Mitchell King, John Tucker, Zachariah Winkler, Dr. James Screven, George and Thomas Screven owned 100 to 300 and Robert Habersham owned 213. In Bryan County, Joseph McAllister owned 271, Eliza Clay 230, Richard Arnold 195, James Middleton 180, Joseph Hines, William Patterson, Charles and William Rogers, and Ralph Elliott 75–150. In Liberty

County, George Walthour owned 300 in 1860, Nathaniel Varnedoe 200. Other large slaveholders included John Stevens, George Waldburg, Thomas Quarterman, John Barnard, Charlton Hines, John and Joseph LeConte, and Thomas Mallard. In McIntosh County Pierce Butler owned 505, including 114 slave children, Thomas Spalding 242, P.M. Nightingale 170. In Glynn County, Francis and Richard Corbin owned 235 slaves each. In Camden County, Stephen King was the largest slaveowner with 311. George Owens had 256 and others included Duncan Coinch, F.M. Adams, John Bailey, J.B. Guerrard, L.W. Hazelhurst, George Lang, and E.A. Riley.[17] James Couper of St.Simon's Island was produced more sugar cane than any of the other 100 plantations in the Altamha region (which included Thomas Spalding, Pierce Butler, Thomas Butler King, and Roswell King).[18] Couper and his brother James also owned more than 500 slaves on their Hoopeton rice plantation above Darien. None of these individuals was Jewish.

Between 1786 and 1788, Thomas Spaulding and Alexander Bissett introduced "sea island cotton" and demonstrated how to separate cotton fibres from seeds. Five years later, Eli Whitney, a Yale graduate living in Georgia, invented the cotton gin. In Georgia alone, the number of bales of cotton increased from 1,000 in 1790 to 40,000 in 1811 and 521,472 in 1860. There was a commensurate increase in plantations and the call for slaves.[19] Among Georgia's new cotton elite were Charles Spalding Wylly (grandson of Thomas Spalding) who owned 600 slaves on 1,500 acres; Colonel Farish Carter of Baldwin County who owned 426 slaves on 33,000 acres; James Abingdon Everett of Fort Valley who counted 242 slaves on his three plantations; Robert Toombs, a prominent Whig politician who was a staunch defender of slavery; his Democratic counterpart Howell Cobb; John Basil Lamar, Cobb's brother-in-law and business manager of six plantations around Macon; Judge Joseph Lumpkin, railroad magnate Alexander Pope, Alexander Telfair, Mallory King, Thomas King, Dr. John Wilson, Joseph Tooke of Houston City, John and Henry Dubignon of Glynn County, and Joseph Bond, a millionaire from Macon who in 1859 owned six plantations with 369 slaves.[20] Not a single one of these great planter barons or the thirty in Liberty County listed by Clarence Mohr was Jewish.[21]

A Northern minister, Jeremiah Evarts made the crossing from Savannah through the backwoods country of Georgia in March-April 1822, imposing upon the hospitality of planter magnates and small farmers from Savannah to Athens. Evarts raved about the varied Georgia terrain in spring—its pleasant yards, berries, trees, and gardens. He complained about the perpetual rain. He also lamented the state of slaves which was, he wrote,"as abject beyond my powers of description."[22] Nevertheless, Evarts tried to convey the sense of despair which prevailed among plantation slaves. They had, he wrote, few conveniences for any kind of labor. ("They are obliged to do everthing by the hardest.") Their clothing was coarse, dirty, wretched, worn, old. There seemed to be no enjoyment in these places. "The young appear cheerful—the aged miserable," he wrote. "Their poor bodies appear to be worn out, by hard service and scanty fare."[23] Evarts had stayed on several occasions with ministers like Dr. Southworth Harlow, Goulding Wallis, and Dr. Waddel, president of the University of Georgia, Sheriff Burke, Thomas McDowall, Greville Ewing, Major Walker, Timothy Edwards, and the Eaton, Moseley, Dudley, Hillhouse, Bennell, Lowell, Leach, Mongin, Pierce, Grieves, Wilburn, Ketchum, and Pace families. Baptists, Methodists, Presbyterians, and "Dutch Germans," not one of the slaveholding families he encountered between March 31 and April 26, large or small, were Jews.

One might be tempted to dismiss Evarts' experience, as he was a man on a specific mission, to save souls through the catechism. Yet his findings are sustained by black scholars in Georgia. The African-American Family History Association of Atlanta began researching slave bills of sale in 1977. The task was made more difficult by destruction of documents brought about by Sherman's march to the sea. The two volume Slave Bills of Sale Project, however, does list 2,539 slave references and 1,368 buyers and sellers. The most notorious slave merchant listed was Zachariah Lamar of Baldwin County involved in the purchase and sale of 118 slaves in eight separate counties between 1796 and 1833. The only other individuals who come close are James Grubbs of Burke County, 13 transactions involving 42 females and 13 males between 1840 and 1859; Lindsey Durham of Clarke County (18 transactions, 1820–49); William Hardin of Henry County (13 transactions, 1826–52), W. Beedles of Oglethorpe County (6 transactions, 1788–97), Allen Inman and the McAlpin family both of whom sold 27 slaves.[24] There are no significant references to Jews in these documents. Nor are there any Jews listed among the 89 slave owners for Warren County in 1798,[25] or the 314 grantors/grantees listed in Jones County between 1791 and 1864,[26] or among the dozens of names listed of slave importers to Columbia County 1817–1838,[27] or Franklin County's importation of slaves 1818–31,[28] or the 26-page slave register of Morgan county

1818–24,[29] or in the Court of Ordinary Slave Record for Pulaski County 1818–1865.[30]

Initially, the brokers who traded in slaves belonged to the elite society of Georgia. As in Virginia or South Carolina, men like Joseph Clay, James Habersham, and John Graham had no compunctions about dealing in what was for them a profitable sideline.[31] After the importation of slaves was banned, slave trading in Georgia took on "a disesteem so great as to produce a social ostracism."[32] The prototypical slave merchant was coarse, ill-bred, of shabby dress, a half-literate cretin standing before a ramshackle hotel who, following the Civil War, was given to lamenting the good old days when he bought and sold 600 or more blacks.[33] "Preeminent in villainy and a greedy love of filthy lucre stands the hard-hearted Negro trader," wrote Dr. D.R. Hundley of Alabama.[34] In the 1860 census only five individuals—Walter Campbell of New Orleans, B.F. Logan in Caddo, Louisiana, James Worth and John Gordon in Alabama, and W.S. Cothron of Floyd,Georgia would admit to this rather ignoble profession.[35] There were others in Georgia, including Clark & Grubb (the major house in Atlanta), Charlie Stubbs, A.J. and D.W. Orr, John Jossey, Charles Collins, Rafe Phillips, and James Dean in Macon, the cotton brokerage of Greenwood and Morris, Hatcher, and McGehee, and Harrison and Pitts in Columbus, Benjamin Fort, Robert Bentley, the auctioneer T.J. Walsh, Captain Joe Bryan, the wealthy merchant J.B. Allgood, and the house of Miller and Waterman which advertised in Savannah.[36] Some of these men maintained stables for 200 human beings and mules for as long as twenty-five years. All were Gentiles.

The only Jewish slave merchants mentioned by Rabbi Korn were the firms of D. Mayer, Jacobs and Co. of Atlanta, and Solomon Cohen of Altanta/Augusta.[37] A third man, Levi Cohen, may have purchased slaves in several Georgia counties during the Civil War. None are cited by Bancroft, Phillips, Stampp, Menn or any other authority as being of especial importance, and for good reason. David Mayer arrived in Atlanta in October 1839. Advised to "carry a bundle" (e.g., become a travelling salesman), he tinkered in a variety of enterprises—a music store, dentistry, hotels—before opening an auction and commission house with a Mr. Jacobi which dealt in slaves and other commodities.[38] Solomon Cohen's announcements of "75 likely Negroes" for sale appear in the Atlanta *Daily Intelligencer* only between September and November 1862.[39]

It is relatively simple to look at the present sprawling metropolis of Atlanta and impute the same kind of economic importance to the city

100 years ago. Slavery was not preeminent in the thoughts of Jews of Georgia. As Stephen Hertzberg, author of the definitive study of Jews in Atlanta has written, "Slavery probably exerted selective influence on Jewish settlement in the South." Many Jews who were disquieted by the institution departed for other regions. Others stayed, because, says Hertzberg, fear and hatred directed against blacks "acted as a lightning rod deflecting prejudices which might otherwise have been manifested against Jews."[40] Jews accepted slavery because it was the norm among their Gentile neighbors, serving as an escape valve for frustrations of poor whites, offering protective coloration for the foreign born. Hertzberg might also have added that Jews stayed because they were among the first peoples enticed into the Georgia colony.

1733 Georgia: A Majority of Jews

From the start, Oglethorpe was receptive to the idea of having Jews participate in his new colony. The notion supposedly appealed to his Masonic sense of fair play, as Crypto-Christians continued to be harrassed by the Inquisition in Portugal.[41] But more, the proprietor believed that Jews, especially Sephardic Jews, were gifted in vitriculture and silk production, two industries that might prove profitable to the new colony. Thus the trustees celebrated the virtues of the southern climate throughout the West Indies. As one advertisement which sought to induce Jews to come to Georgia proclaimed:

> Nature has not blessed the world with any tract which can be preferable to it. Paradise with all her virgin beauties may be modestly supposed at most, but equal to its native excellencies. It lies in the same latitude with Palestine herself, that promised Canaan which was pointed out by God's own choice to bless the labors of a favorite people![42]

The first boatload of 130 settlers (no Jews) arrived in Georgia on February 1, 1733. Four months later, July 11, 1733, the *William and Sarah* bound from London discharged 42 weary passengers (39 Portuguese and 3 German Jews) at Savannah. Four of their companions had died during the Atlantic crossing.[43] Many Sephardic Jews, like Abigail DeLeon (who arrived in November) bore marks of torture at the hands of the Portuguese Inqusition. Some like Benjamin Sheftall, Isaac Henriquez, Raphael Bornal, and David DePass went on to become the founders of Georgia's most illustrious Jewish dynasties.[44] The first native-born Georgian was Philip Minis, son of Abraham Minis.[45] Most important, however, was Dr. Samuel Ribiero Nunez, once personal physician to the Grand Inquisitor in Lisbon. The beggared Nunez family arrived in London just as plans for the journey to Georgia were proceeding. According to Horace Folsom, "The roseate accounts of liberty in the New World were as tinkling cymbals to this stricken Hebrew family and they responded to the call." More than that, Dr. Nunez took charge of a sanitation program—constructing latrines, controlling insects, securing fresh water, devising the first pharmacy—that helped control yellow fever and cholera, two diseases that were ravaging the new colony.[46]

Initially, Georgia's trustees sitting in London helped outfit this Jewish ship. But fearing they had been tricked into creating a Jewish-dominated haven (even today the legend persists that Jews outnumbered Gentiles in that first year),[47] the trustees appealed to Oglethorpe to intercept the Jewish ship. When this proved impossible, the trustees rebuked the proprietor for "doing little or nothing to discourage Jews from remaining in Georgia."[48] For his part, Oglethorpe ignored the warnings, pointing instead to the benefits of Dr. Nunez' curative cold baths and cooling drinks. Hoping to calm their fears, he reported that one of the Jewish colonists had converted to Christianity.[49] And quietly, he permitted the Jews to have their own cemetery and to organize a congregation Mickva Israel.

The trustees need not have fretted about Georgia becoming a Jewish colony. On October 13, 1735, a third ship reached Savannah with 220 Gentiles, thereby guaranteeing a Christian majority. Many of the original Jewish settlers died of disease or were so dismayed by the hard life and steaming climate (even today, Savannah is perpetually hot and humid) that in the words of Levi Sheftall, "they went away."[50] In the year 1740–41 the synagogue was disbanded because the only Jews remaining in Savannah belonged to the Sheftall, Minis, and Delyon families. Ten years later, an unofficial census for Georgia listed 2000 whites, 1,000 blacks, and 16 Jews (Abraham and Abigail Minis and their 8 children, Daniel and Moses Nunez, and Benjamin and Hannah Sheftall and their two children.) All the others had gone to Charleston.[51]

Despite efforts by Gentiles to shut down the Jewish cemetery in Savannah and convert the downtown land into something more profitable, several speculators of Jewish background did try their luck in Georgia. Between 1750 and 1800 a number engaged in shipping and dry goods out of Savannah. Abraham Delyon is credited with introducing viticulture to Georgia about this time. In 1774 Joseph Ottolengui, the very same individual whose Christian missionary activity earned him the title of reverend, used an annuity of $500 in a futile attempt to make Oglethrope's dream of silk culture a reality.[52] *The Secret Relationship* highlights the activity of James Lucena, the major importer of Castille soap when he lived in Newport. A cousin of Aaron Lopez, Lucena came to Georgia in 1767 and became prominent as an attorney, member of the grand jury, and serving on the commission for roads. By 1770 he acquired more than 1,000 acres of land and twenty slaves. He also ran several advertisements in the *Georgia Gazette* seeking return of fugitive slaves.[53] A loyalist to the English crown during the Revolution, Lucena returned to London and then to Portugal before he died. It would be a mistake to identify him as a Jew, however. Lucena swore an oath to the "true faith of Christianity" when he was naturalized in Rhode Island in December 1760. An Anglican the rest of his life, he was, writes Jacob Marcus, "not the least bit interested in asserting a Jewish identity."[54]

There were a few observant Jews who were also planters and, therefore, slaveowners. One of the original settlers in 1733, Benjamin Shetfall from Bavaria, owned five slaves when he died in 1760. His son Mordecai, who served as commissary general for the state of Georgia had nine on a plantation of 1,000 acres.[55] Isaiah Moses, whose descendants were responsible for the development of the Muscle Shoals hydroelectric power stations, was a planter at Goose Creek and Bushauree plantations.[56] One of those descendants, Major Raphael Moses, chief commissary for General James Longstreet of the Confederacy, owned 47 at Esquiline Hill near Columbus.[57]

Some of these Jewish-black relationships were very poignant. Moses Nunez had a son by his first wife, three sons and a daughter by his second—a mulatto. According to Marcus, "Nunez made no distinction in his will between his first born and the other children, but to protect the quadroons he emancipated them formally in his will."[58] Francis Sheftall wrote a touching letter to her husband on July 20, 1780 telling of death of "little Billey," a black youth who died of yellow fever despite the efforts of doctors to save him.[59] David Leion, a Jew from Hamburg who married Hannah Minis in 1798, acknowledged a relationship with "a free woman of color," endowed her with a lifetime stipend which enabled her to own slaves and left bequests for their offspring Rita and David Jr. when he died in 1842.[60] For better than a decade in the mid-nineteenth century, the *shamash* (caretaker) of Temple Mickvah Israel was a black named Henry.[61] There were also blacks who converted to Judaism in this period.

Perhaps the best known story of black-Jewish interaction was that of Major Raphael Moses and his slave "Old London." As Major Moses later recounted,"When the War broke out I had 47 slaves and when it ended I had forty-seven freed men. All left me except one—Old London, he stayed with me until he died." Moses' grandchildren recalled a half-bald man with a wooly white ring on his hair known as Uncle London. When Raphael explained that Lincoln had freed the slaves, Old London replied that he had seen his master buy him on the block at Darien and that until he saw Mr. Lincoln refund the purchase price he would still consider himself a slave. He asserted that he was no free black. The only reward he asked was that his master should "preach his funeral sermon" and say that he had been a loyal slave. Old London was buried in the black section of the little private cemetery on Esquiline Hill a few feet away from the graves of Raphael and Eliza Moses. According to memoirs on file with the Atlanta Jewish Community, Raphael preached the funeral sermon and, "with tears streaming down his cheeks," told how long and faithfully London had served him.[62]

Jewish Demographics in Georgia

People like Major Moses, the Nunezes, Sheftalls, and Minises were rarities. Jews were few and far between, no more than 2,500 out of 1,057,286 people in antebellum Georgia, less than two-tenths of one per cent of the total population in 1860.[63] Most of the early Jews in Georgia had very little wealth, like Isaac Polock, Samuel Morecai, Isaac Benedix, and David Cardozo who dealt in dry goods in Savannah. They were joined in midcentury by refugees from Central European persecution, men who ventured into remote communites. The only Jews in Sandersville were members of the Pincus Happ family. Sam and Louis Bashinski, from Poland, worked as bank tellers in Tennille. Isaac and Adam Hermann, storekeepers from Alsace, braved life in Fenns Bridge.[64] David Steinheimer worked as a clerk in Macon before leaving for Pittsburgh in 1860. Lazarus Strauss tried to eke out an existence in Thomasville until 103 citizens of that town petitioned for the expulsion of all Jews in 1862.[65]

The first Jews arrived in Marthasville, a dusty railway junction, in 1845. Two years later, the town changed its name to Atlanta and, despite health problems attributed to cholera, grew to more than 10,000 people by the time of the Civil War. There were several dozen Jews in Atlanta. No millionaires, no plantation magnates or slave brokers but, for the most part, poor German immigrants like Aaron Alexander who failed as a druggist before leaving for Philadelphia, Isaac Cuthman and Abraham Landsberg who helped establish a B'nai B'rith lodge, Herman Levi, Jacob Haas and Herman Haas who established the retail firm of Haas and Levi, the Cahn brothers who were clerks, the Goldberg family, Henry Hirsch who travelled with sacks of salt as far south as Marietta, Calvin Pay, and the Essig brothers.[66]

Jews played an insignificant role in the import or sale of slaves in Georgia. They also owned very few. Two of the passengers aboard the first Jewish ship in 1733 were Abraham and Abigail Minis, a family which produced some of the most distinguished doctors, attorneys, bankers and philanthropists in Georgia. When Abigail died at the age of 93 in October 1794 (she had been widowed in 1757) her estate in four counties included 20 slaves (9 of them house servants).[67] Their descendants in antebellum Georgia averaged between 6 and 10 slaves.[68] A grandson Isaac owned 26 in 1845.[69] At the same time, Mordecai Myers, a fourth generation Minis who graduated from Princeton, held none on his 2,000 acre farm.[70] The combined holdings of all 77 descendants of Abraham and Abigail Minis could not match the 19,000 acres and 500 slaves owned by James Wright, a Christian who was governor of colonial Georgia.

In 1820 there were twenty-one Jewish households in Savannah. Seventeen owned slaves, a total of 116 blacks. There were 3,075 slaves in the city. The wealthiest, best-established Jewish families in Georgia, owned 3.7 percent of all the slaves in Savannah.[71] This percentage actually declined by 1860 when there were 7,712 slaves in the city. The story was much the same in Atlanta. In 1850 four of Atlanta's six Jewish households owned slaves. Jews owned 7 of 493 slaves in Atlanta, less than 1 percent of the city's total. Ten years later, only one of Atlanta's Jewish families owned any of the 1,939 slaves in town.[72]

Rabbi Saul Rubin, author of a history of Savannah Jewry, concedes there were Jews involved in slavery—"some, but too small a percentage." Rubin notes Hofwyl (a rice plantation run by the Troup Dent family) as the only plantation in which Jews had an interest. (Solomon Cohen's daughter married Dent.) "Jews were mainly commercial," he told me, "merchants along the river. Every citizen owned town lots and farm lots, but the farms were only five acres, too small for slaves. Savannah was not a center for growing crops. Many of the Jews had house slaves, but they were treated totally different. Some could even buy their freedom. Dr. Minis had a slave who was a master bricklayer. He paid him the going rate for his profession."[73] According to Rabbi Rubin, a few of Georgia's Jews (V.B. Pember, Eugenia Philips, and Sam Yates Phillips) were fanatical Southerners. "Most Jews, however, were not content to sit back and let things happen. They were not totally free to oppose racism but I'm sure it stuck in their throats, like segregation. Some acted behind the scenes. Salomon Cohen was powerful in 1862. R.D.C. Lewin was a wild-eyed reformer, very radical for that time. As a result, people in Thomasville, Talbot and Waynesboro petitioned to expel the Germans and the Jews."[74]

Rubin's impressions are confirmed by two leaders of Savannah's black community, W.W. Law and Carroll Greene, Jr. Law, founder and co-chairman of the Afro-American Historical Association of Savannah, declared,"All Jews did not own slaves. Basically they were merchants, professionals. Some controlled the bars and brothels, but they were not rice or cotton planters. A few Jewish families owned slaves, no question about it. Many of the early crowd were so interested in assimilating that they, like Northerners, outdid Southerners in the spirit of the times. There might have been Jewish slave traders. Some were doing everything. But many provided for their slaves. In the Minis family, Phillip never married. He kept a black slave woman and had children and provided for them." For Law, the notion of antagonism between blacks and Jews is alien. "In early Savannah the two communities lived side by side. They shopped at the same stores. The children played together. There never has been any anti-Semitism among blacks here. Jews gave them every opportunity to rise. One of the most decent men in Savannah is H. Sol Clarke, a retired Georgia Supreme Court Justice. Early in his career, he created a legal aid society to defend people unable to provide for themselves." Law laments the fact that the two communities are no longer in close proximity with one another and that Jews who are now lawyers and doctors "don't always employ blacks." At the same time, he affirms that relations are fairly good.[75]

For Carroll Greene, director-curator of the Acacia Historical Arts Collection, the issue is very complex. "Here the Jews were in the midst of such a terribly Christian, church-centered society. They developed a largely segregated, parallel society, centered around the synagogue, Sunday school, temple organizations. Some were better off financially and were on boards of major community organizations. No Jews or blacks could belong to the Oglethorpe Club. Some were proud of their distinctiveness, but others, in the words of Ludwig Lewisohn, were trying to be prototypical Southerners. Jews who were poor lived in or catered to black communities. They were proud of their distinctiveness, but also disturbed by slavery. We know from the diary of Elizabeth Levy that seeing blacks in slavery upset her."

Greene points out that no one had been able to translate such moral outrage into social action in the south where emphasis on conformity was and is so great. "We're so deep in the South here," says Greene, "anyone who did not toe the mark was out of here. Any kind of liberalism in the Cotton Kingdom would not have been tolerated. Maybe in a more metropolitan area like New Orleans it would have been possible. But not in Savannah. Not in Atlanta/Marthsaville, which had no sense of cosmopolitanism." Slavery eventually overwhelmed everyone. "The system was very persuasive. Salzburg Germans came here. One leader [Pastor Bolzius] was against slavery and the way the economy was set up. With all the pressure, he gave in. So did the Quakers and the Unitarians. The Quakers went to Maryland and the oppression was so great they had to leave. The Unitarians had to cool their rhetoric. Only one of their churches survived in Charleston." One of the few individuals to concede black ownership of other blacks, Greene points out that there were a number of black slave masters in Georgia, people who owned relatives, wives, children, as "the only way to protect them from the peculiarities of the laws."[76] Jews came to Georgia and like everyone else they bought blacks, educated some and manumitted others. To those who single them out as the principal villains in the slave trade, Carroll Greene asks rhetorically, "Where do we get the notion that Jews transcend human experience?"

13

Louisiana: The Sugar Kingdom

The French in Louisiana

Carroll Greene referred to New Orleans as the sole cosmopolitan center in the Old South. This seems a fair observation, based upon the checkered history of that city and of Louisiana. Spanish explorers first charted the coastline of this colony between 1519 and 1528. A century later, Robert Cavelier, Sieur de La Salle, took possession of the entire region on behalf of Louis XIV. Louisiana was a land cursed with sixty inches of annual rainfall, floods, swarms of mosquitoes, and perpetual epidemics of yellow fever, malaria, smallpox, and cholera.[1] Following a number of failed settlements at Natchez, Biloxi and in Mississippi (under the Englishman John Law), Jean Baptiste Le Moyne, Sieur de Bienville, founded New Orleans in 1718. Designated a crown colony in 1731, Louisiana was awarded to Spain at the end of the French and Indian War in 1762–63. Napoleon wrested control back from the puppet government of Spain in the treaty of San Il De Fonso in 1800. Three years later, his dreams of a revived empire in the Western Hemisphere dashed by the revolt of blacks in Haiti, Napoleon sold the vast colony with its ill-defined boundaries to the United States.

By this time there were all sorts of people in Louisiana—six tribes of Indians (Caddo, Natchez, Atakapa, Chitimachan, Muskogee, Tunican) in the backwoods, Englishmen in Apilachicola (West Florida) and Mississippi, Rhineland Germans upstream from New Orleans, Acadian refugees (French families from Nova Scotia) in the marshy bayous south of New Orleans, Spanish and Swiss deserters, and a host of French prostitutes, paupers, and criminals who had been beaten and shackled in transports between 1717 and 1721.[2] New Orleans became the second most important port of entry to America in the nineteenth century, as thousands of Irish, Germans and Italians swarmed to this charming city.[3] The blend of these cultures is reflected in the sounds that may be heard on any street of the French Quarter—the infectious rhythms of Cajun music, classical French symphonies, American pop, and, one more which symbolizes New Orleans—Dixieland. There were also African slaves in Louisiana, 680 in the New Orleans and Mobile areas according to a census in 1721, more than 331,726 by 1860.[4]

The first blacks were transported to Louisiana from the coast of Guinea and Angola in July 1718 aboard vessels commanded by Captain Herpin, Sieur de Laudouine and Sieur du Colombier. These actions were authorized by directors of the French West Indies Company (Despremenil, P. Saintard, and Godeheir) and the governor of Louisiana (Bienville deVillardeau). Requests for slaves came from planters like d'Ausseville (who asked for 20), Sinard de Bellisle (2), LeBlanc (150), d'Artaignan (40), Lusser (20), and Dalcour (200).[5] Constant warfare with the Natchez and Choctaws convinced French colonial officials like Etienne de Perier and Edme Gatien de Salmon that black replacement labor was needed for indigo and rice plantations.[6] In that early phase of Louisiana history, the richest man in the colony was Joseph Dubreuil de Villars, who owned 43 black and two Indian slaves.[7] Disease and death rates were high because of Louisiana's subtropical climate, but owners did not care. As an example, Jacques Charpentier dit LeRoy, an overseer for Raymond Dauseville in 1727, brutalized his slaves, working them from pre-dawn until late at night in all kinds of weather, giving them very little to eat. All were weak and emaciated. Pregnant women were forced to work in the fields until they dropped.[8]

Conditions were no better when Louisiana was retroceded to Spain between 1763 and 1790. Cuban, Scots, British, and American slave traders flocked to the territory when a series of royal decrees reopened the slave trade with the West Indies. The exact numbers are difficult to determine because the Spanish kept no accurate customs records, but it is clear there were more than 20,000 slaves in Louisiana by 1790. Many of these had been brought to Pensacola, Natchez, New Orleans, or Baton Rouge by gentile slave traders like Robert and David Ross, George Profit, Jerome and Charles La Chapell, Jean Raymond et Cie, and Dr. Benjamin Farar (the latter a transplanted South Carolinian who owned 225 slaves when he died in 1790).[9]

In 1796, the Creole Etienne de Bore demonstrated the potential of refining sugar cane and syrup into granulated sugar (he earned $12,000 that year).[10] In 1843 the Creole black Norbert Rillieux perfected the process of boiling cane juice in vacuum pans and using the vapor from one pan to heat another. By this time, adventurers, many of whom had failed elsewhere, headed to Louisiana to make their fortune in sugar. All that was needed to start a plantation or mill was a loan of $40,000. Claudius Le Grand sold his plantation in Maryland and went to seek his fortune in the Louisiana Delta in 1836. Andrew and John McCollam arrived penniless from New York in the 1830s and became wealthy planters by 1860. Judge Alexander Porter came from Northern Ireland and amassed 2,000 acres and 160 slaves in Bayou Teche. In 1841 Leonidas Polk was appointed bishop for the Episcopal church in Louisiana. Polk reluctantly sold his cotton plantation in Maury County, Tennessee, but he took his 400 slaves with him to farm Leighton in Bayou la Fourche.[11] According to J. Carlyle Sitterson, such self-indulgent, profane men became addicted to wealth through the acquisition of more land and blacks.[12] What had once been a trifle of investments grew to $34 millions in 1834, more than $60 million by 1860.

At one time there were no fewer than 1,400 sugar plantations in Louisiana, each averaging 100 slaves.[13] Many plantations were built around gaudy, rambling, "Greek Renaissance" style mansions where owners like William Minor, Duncan Kenner, Henry McCall, and Thomas Moore held balls and enjoyed raising horses as a sideline. Their colleagues in sugar planting included the likes of William Ruffin Barrow, Isaac Osgood, Effingham Lawrence, William Porcher Miles, Benjamin Winchester, P.M. Lapice, E.J. Forstall, and Henry Clay Warmouth. According to J. Carlyle Sitterson, most of the Creole planters (with names like Bringier, Triste, Landry, Tureaut, Broussard, Deblanc, Dugase, Delahoussaye, and Declouet) were Catholics. "Among the non-Creoles," adds Sitterson,"the Methodist faith was more numerous than any of the other Protestant sects, among which were also sizable numbers of Episcopalians and Presbyterians."[14] These included such prominent families in the sugar belt of Ascencion County and Bayou Lafourche as the Prestons, Mannings, Duplantiers, Doyals, Shaffers, Barrows, Gibsons, Cages, Palfreys, Richardson, Cofferys, and Fosters. Louisiana's major planters were Colonel Joseph A.S. Acklen (owner of six plantations, 20,000 acres, and 659 slaves), Valcour Aimes (15,000 acres, 215 slaves), Thomas Pugh (250 slaves on his Madewood plantation), Dr. John P. Stone (owner of Evergreen in Iberville Parish), John Burnside (an immigrant from Northern Ireland whose five plantations in Ascencion and St.James Parish counted 937 slaves and were valued at more than $2,000,000),[15] L.R. Marshall with 932, Meredith Calhoun with 709, Alfred Davis with 637, John Manning with 616, O.J. Morgan with 501.[16] Louisiana's greatest slave magnate was Wade Hampton, formerly of South Carolina, who established himself at the head of Bayou LaFourche in 1811. Twenty years later, Hampton owned nearly 700 sugar plantations and 36,000 slaves.[17] None of these men were Jewish. For good reason: Louis XIV had tried to banish Jews from parts of the empire in 1685. The infamous Code Noir which caused so much hardship in the West Indies was introduced to Louisiana in 1725. Jews were not supposed to dwell in these regions.

There were no Jews in Shreveport or Baton Rouge until 1858. In the early days of French settlement, however, some Jews managed to slip past authorities to New Orleans. One of the first censuses from Louisiana in 1719 includes Jacob David, Romain David, Robert-Genevieve Jacobs "and wife," and Louis Salomon, listed as tailors, shoemakers, and soldiers.[18] They possessed no wealth and stayed only temporarily. There were no more than six Jewish families in New Orleans in the administration of French governor, Louis Kerlerec (1743–1753). In 1748 Abraham Gradis, the Jewish trader from Bordeaux, secured a commission to import 10,000 slaves over five years to Louisiana. But French colonial officials on the scene wanted no trade of any kind with Jews. A single ship carrying innocent goods arrived from Curaçao in 1748. Ten years later, Commissaire Ordonnateur Vincent Gaspard del Rochemore railed against Jews as spies and barred further trade with Jamaica. When West Florida was transferred back to French authority following the treaty of Fountainbleu in 1763, the French ordered the expulsion of several Jewish merchants (Joseph dePalacios, Samuel Israel, Alexander Solomons) from Mobile and Isaac Mendes from Pensacola.[19] The new Spanish governor of Louisiana, General Alejandro O'Reilly was equally hostile to Jews in his territory, and there was a rush to baptize adults and children in New Orleans after 1769.[20]

The Monsantos: Jews Who were Not Jews

Despite such handicaps, the *Secret Relationship* declares Jews settled permanently in New Orleans as early as 1758. That was the year that Isaac Monsanto, founder of a fabled dynasty, arrived in the port city. The editors of *SR* make much of the activities of this wealthy family, devoting three pages to the Monsantos in their biographical sketches of Jews responsible for the black Holocaust.[21] In reality, Isaac Monsanto was a shrewd clerk/merchant from Curaçao who secured power of attorney for an assortment of business ventures including handkerchiefs, guns, canvas, lumber, cordage, indigo, sugar, limes, and skins. Only one of his shipments involved slaves. At one time he also served as official translator for the Superior Court of Lousiana. He did not come from wealth (his father David was too poor to pay for his wife's funeral) and when he died in 1778 he was described as a pathetic , broken man, living in poverty.[22] Over the next several decades, Isaac's descendants prospered. Benjamin, Jacob, and Manuel Monsanto were involved in all sorts of successul business transactions (dry goods, food, salt, meat, ship's cable). They also dealt in slaves, "in the manner of the times" and mostly for resale.[23] Family records indicate that the Monsantos were not great slaveowners. Benjamin owned 17, Angelica 8, Eleanora 4, Manuel 12.[24]

The whole question as to the number of slaves held by the Monsantos may be moot. Few, if any, of Isaac's descendants were practicing Jews. Rabbi Korn notes that Isaac himself lived twelve years in the city and never had any contact with organized Jewish life. Not surprisingly, his three daughters, Angelica, Gracia, and Eleanora married non-Jews and "Judaism no longer meant anything to them." Angelica became a devoted Episcopalian. Another descendant, Fastio converted to Roman Catholicism. Only Benjamin married a Jewish woman, but they were married in a Catholic church in 1787 and probably became baptized Catholics.[25]

The practice of labelling anyone with a Jewish ancestor a Jew is, as we have seen in the case of Joseph Ottolenghui or the DeWolfs, typical of the editors of *Secret Relationship*. So Jean Lafitte, the celebrated pirate who fought alongside Andrew Jackson in the battle of New Orleans, is transmuted into a Jewish villain because of a garbled reference to Lafitte's Spanish-Jewish grandmother which appears in what is reputed to be Lafitte's journal.[26] So, too, the Nation of Islam might denounce Joseph Solis and Antonio Mendes, credited with the development of sugar plantations when the Spanish controlled Louisiana in the 1790s. Both men were suspected of having Jewish ancestry, but, writes Korn, "there is no evidence that members of the [Solis] family considered themselves to be Jews or Marranos." As for Mendes, he applied for a *limpieza de sangre* in 1784 and "surely was not a Jew in terms of personal religious affiliation, conviction or knowledge, even if distant ancestors had been 'new' Christians."[27]

Even more than in Georgia or other parts of the South, the pressures upon Jews in Louisiana were almost unbearable. The French made it clear through the Code Noir that practicing Jews were unwelcome. Under the Spanish, there was always the possibility of the Inquisition.

After Louisiana became part of the United States, many Jews opted for secularism or intermarriage. As Rabbi Korn wrote, they were motivated "to be free of restrictions of Judaism" and "to escape from the degradation associated with being Jewish."[28] In the 1830s, approximately 50 percent of the Jews in New Orleans married non-Jews. Many were single men who had come to New Orleans to seek their fortunes. Virtually all of their children were raised as Christians.[29] Typical of such stories was that of Manis Jacobs, first president or "rabbi" of Shaarai-Chasset (Gates of Mercy) synagogue in New Orleans. Born in Amsterdam, Jacobs came to New Orleans with his first wife in 1809. When she died, he married a Catholic woman. All of his descendants were Catholic.[30] Another immigrant, Benjamin Levy, a bookseller came to New Orleans in 1812. When he died in 1860, insurance and banking investments left him rather well-to-do, with one slave. Levy married a Catholic woman and his children were baptized in that faith.[31] Samuel Hermann, a successful banker and civic leader from Frankfurt, owned 18 slaves. He married a prominent French woman and his two sons and daughter were baptized at St. John Baptist Church.[32]

Judah Benjamin: The Jew Who did not Wish to be Jewish

Even the most famous of all the Jews in Louisiana tried to escape the burden of being Jewish. *The Secret Relationship* devotes two pages to Judah P. Benjamin, master of 140 slaves at Bellachasse plantation, secretary of war for the Confederacy, hailed by Max Kohler as "the most distinguished statesman, orator, and lawyer that American Jewry has ever produced."[33] Born in Charleston, Benjamin came to New Orleans in 1828 after dropping out of Yale University. Extremely bright and able, he rose in the ranks of the Democratic party, helping Buchanan to secure the party's nomination for President in 1856, and becoming lieutenant governor in 1859, the first Jew to hold that office. Unflagging in his loyalty to the Confederacy, Benjamin was no strident racist. Before the Civil War and after, when he chose to live in England, he expressed the view that the government had an obligation to protect property rights of slave owners. During the war, he suggested arming Southern slaves.[34]

Benjamin and Senator David Yulee of Florida had once been attacked on the floor of the Senate by Republican Senator Benjamin Wade as "Israelites with Egyptian principles."[35] But like so many other prominent Louisiana Jews, Benjamin was alienated from Judaism. As a young man, he chastized his mother for his given name (Judah) saying, "You might well have written Jew across my forehead."[36] Daniel Webster recalled a meeting with Benjamin and Isaac Mayer Wise, the Reform rabbi from Cincinnati, in the 1850. According to Webster, Benjamin, whose intellect was renowned, could not cite a single Jewish source in their discussions , while Webster was "thoroughly versed in Bible."[37] Benjamin raised no protest when in 1854 the U.S. government negotiated a treaty with Switzerland that conceded the right of Swiss cantons to discriminate against non-Christian travellers from America.[38] Even as the third highest ranking civilian in the Confederacy, he felt shunned and "surrounded by Christian distrust."[39] Perhaps, suggests Rabbi Max Kohler, Benjamin's attitude toward Judaism is reflected in his marriage of a Catholic woman, Nathalie St.Martin. At the time of his wedding, in a Catholic church, the priest omitted his given name and called him Philippe Benjamin. His daughter was reared in the Roman Catholic tradition. Benjamin was buried in Pere Lachaise, a Catholic cemetery in Paris. There was even a rumor that this man so often identified with the defense of slavery may have been a deathbed convert to Catholicism.[40] Whatever the case, Eli Evans, author of *Judah P. Benjamin: The Jewish Confederate*, notes that he was "a personality ashamed of his roots," to whom "Judaism was a burden, an inhibition to advancement."[41] Of his burial among the crosses of Pere Lachaise, Evans says,"Shunning his past, choosing an almost secret grave, with calculated concealment, he nearly succeeded in remaining hidden from history."[42]

Louisiana's Jews need not have been saddled with the burden of converts or secular Jews. There were enough observant villains among them. John Levy owned 41 slaves on his plantation in Ascension Parish.[43] Joachim Kohn held a one-ninth interest in a planation with 84 slaves in January 1842. German-born Jacob Lemann and Abraham Levi provided short-term loans to planters and even foreclosed on plantations early in the nineteenth century. (Levi took a 324 acre plantation and held the mortgage on another that ran 746 acres.)[44] London-born Edward Gottschalk owned one of the largest commission brokerages in New Orleans, selling land, rope, furniture, stocks and slaves before the firm went bankrupt in 1830.[45] Levy Jacobs and his Gentile partner George Ashbridge auctioned off slaves in New Orleans in the 1820s.[46] Worst of all was Maurice Barnett, a dry goods merchant whose Dutch father had come to Philadelphia in 1782. Barnett moved to Baton Rouge in 1806, then New Orleans. Eager to fit in to his new settings, Barnett volunteered to serve on posses retrieving slaves. He hired out carpenters and brick masons. From the veranda of the St. Louis Hotel, he and his sons also auctioned off slaves between 1836 and 1849.[47] None of these Jewish merchants, however, could compare with the business activities of factors or brokerage firms on the order of Maunsel White and Martin Gordon & Co., Maspero and Elkins, John McDonogh and Shepherd Browne, Flower and Faulkner, Laurent Millaudon, John Linton, John Hall, Hall, Rodd and Putnam, Darby and Remoulet, Miles, Adams, & Co., Adolph Fontenette, Richard Milliken, Lambeth and Thompson, or John Flathers who underwrote the slave markets on Chartres Street and who truly dominated the sugar, rice, and cotton trades in New Orleans in the nineteenth century.[48]

Judah Touro: The Jew as Saint

According to Lilian Crete, the religious Jewish community of New Orleans was so small it did not have a formal organization until 1828.[49] That achievement may in large measure be credited to Judah Touro. There is, perhaps, no more celebrated American Jewish philanthropist than this son of a cantor from Newport, Rhode Island. Touro's Loyalist family fled to Jamaica during the Revolutionary War. Judah later returned to Boston, then went to Louisiana in 1801. He was one of eleven Jews who fought against the British in the battle of New Orleans. As a shipper, Touro dealt in linens, glass, brandy, soap, olive oil, brandied fruits, gunpowder, wine, candles, beef, medicines, paving stones, herring, furniture, dry goods, mackerel, codfish, rum, onions, leather, salt, and gin. He bought realty lots and rented buildings. He concerned himself in civic affairs, funding the first synagogue in New Orleans, rescuing the Unitarian church from bankruptcy in 1822 and helping to construct the First Baptist Church. He also paid off the mortgage of the Presbyterian church, telling its grateful congregants there should be a church on that particular piece of land "until the end of time." Touro founded the first free public library and erected an infirmary in town. In 1840, he underwrote $10,000 for the first national monument on Boston's Bunker Hill. In his will, Touro bequeathed enough money to establish the Hebrew Hospital in New Orleans, donated $50,000 to support the colonization work of Moses Montefiore in Palestine, $10,000 to North American Relief to Indigent Jews in Jerusalem, a similar stipend to Jews in China, and small sums to every synagogue and Jewish charity in the U.S. He also left $10,000 to the Massachusetts Female Hospital, $5,000 to the Boys' Orphan Asylum of Boston, $13,000 to restore the Norse Stone Mill and Redwood Library of Newport, and additional sums to the New Orleans almshouse, the Society for the Relief of Orphans, St.Ann's Asylum for the Relief of Destitute Females and Children, New Orleans Female Orphanage, St.Mary's Catholic Boys Asylum, the Fireman's Charitable Association, and the Seaman's Home in New Orleans.[50]

Judah Touro amassed a fortune—more than half a million dollars—and gave it all away. The one commodity he shied away from was cotton. He may have viewed trading in cotton futures as speculative and risky. It is also possible he disapproved of the slave system that was so much a part of plantation life. Leon Hühner, Bertram Korn, and Jacob Marcus suggest that Touro was personally opposed to slavery. He is listed as owning one slave in 1805, as many as fifteen in 1809. These may have been purchased for "the sole purpose of liberating them and setting them up in business."[51] As evidence of his sympathy toward blacks, Jewish scholars cite Touro's relationship with Ellen Wilson, a free woman of color, possibly Touro's mistress, who was given $4,100 along with Pierre Cazenaue, the executor of his estate, a mulatto, who was bequeathed $10,000.[52]

Judah Touro was no different from Daniel Warburg, the eccentric millionaire developer who fathered the Creole artists Eugene and Daniel Warburg by a free Cuban black, or Samuel Kohn, the Bohemian banker who came to New Orleans in 1806 and financed trade in shipping, hides, tobacco, mahongany, hats, and skins. Before leaving for Paris in 1837, Kohn's family amassed a fortune of more than $400,000. There is no mention of its involvement in the slave trade.[53] Nor is there any reference to slave activity on the part of Hart Moses Schiff, a Jewish trader in tobacco, sugar, and cotton, who was worth $800,000 before he left for New York City[54] or the dry goods house of Goldsmith, Haber and Haber which acted as middle men between Jewish merchants in New Orleans and New York.[55]

Jews as Shopkeeper

Much as friends and foes of the Jewish people would have it otherwise, neither Judah Touro nor Judah Benjamin were representative of the Jewish people in Louisiana. There never was a large cluster of Jews in the colony/state. In 1858 Isaac Leeser estimated 8,000 out of a population of 708,000, a tip over 1 percent of the state's total population.[56] Their diverse backgrounds included hoteliers, dramatists, gamblers, educators, dentists, military men, and merchants.[57] Of 245 Jewish firms in Louisiana, better than half claimed to be clothing or dry goods stores. Many of these were shanty operations established in 31 of Louisiana's 47 parishes during the ante-bellum period.[58] Unquestionably, New Orleans with its open atmosphere and promise of success held out the greatest attraction for people who came from Germany, New York, Charleston, or the West Indies. New Orleans was the center of the Jewish population in Louisiana in the nineteenth century. But even its Jews were hardly homogeneous. The city directory for 1822 lists twenty-five Jewish family heads, including six who claimed to be bankers, three commission merchants, two general traders, one liquor dealer, two brothers in a cotton press, one grocer, one bookseller, one watchmaker, and one cigar manufacturer. Such lists are not necessarily complete, but still give a vital glimpse of Jewish life at the time.[59] For example, the city directory of 1805 lists ten individuals identified as Jews (Joseph Paillet, Isaac Boyer, Felicite Solis, George Pollock, Judah Touro, James Workman, Louis Myer, Marie Rose, Marie Joseph and Joseph Liotiau).[60] We know the list is not inclusive because neither Benjamin Spitzer and David Seixas (partners in a dry goods firm) nor Jacob Hart , a merchant-shipper who arrived from New York in 1804, are listed.[61] Government census records are also lacking in accuracy. The list from 1820 refers to a "Duchman" and a "Benjamin" (no last name) who lived in the Rue du Quartier; a "Polack" on Esplanade Street; and a "Judah" on Chartres Street.[62] The census of 1830 is even more of a mess, with people randomly identified as Jews (Widow Harby, Michael Garcia, I.L. Florance), sexes mixed up (Justine Moise is listed as Justinian Moise), and prominent figures like Nathan Hart who owned fifteen slaves once again omitted.[63]

Rabbi Bertram Korn made a meticulous study of the assortment of documents on New Orleans Jewry and came up with what must be regarded as the closest things we have to accurate numbers. He found that some, not all, of the city's Jews owned slaves. In 1820, Korn found six Jewish households out of ten that owned 23 slaves. In 1830, there were 22 households, ten of which owned 75 slaves. In 1840, 55 of 62 Jewish households owned a total of 348 slaves. For the most part, these were domestics or assistant workers. In 1830 the family of the widow Barnett (ten people) owned one slave. That of Abraham Green with seven members had two slaves. The widow Kokernote had three slaves for eight people.[64] Korn's figures are pretty much seconded by Ira Rosenwaike who indicated that 16 of the 25 New Orleans families that owned slaves in 1830 held five or less.[65]

How does this translate out into the overall picture of slave owner-ship in New Orleans at any given time? If we use the figure of 23 counted by Korn for 1820, it means that Jews owned 0.3 percent, three-tenths of a one per cent of the 7,355 slaves in the city that year. No exact account of Jewish slaves from 1860 is available, but it is fair to assume that based upon projections from 1840 Jews probably owned no more than 600 blacks or 4 percent of the city's 13,385 slaves. Korn concludes that most Jews in Louisiana were extremely poor. In a state where they only numbered 16,000 as late as 1940, Jews were not planters, slave traders, auctioneers,[66] or illegal slavers. None of the twenty-six boats outfitted in New Orleans for illegal slaving activity between 1856 and 1860 be-longed to Jews.[67] For the most part small merchants or families border-ing on indigence, they tried to live quietly, unostentatiously like most Jews in America on the eve of the Civil War.

Louisiana's Jews were no better, no worse than free blacks and mu-latto offspring of Christians and Jews who also engaged in the slave trade. Historians stress that instances where free blacks owned large numbers of other blacks were rare. Or, as in the case of Marie Louise Bitaud of New Orleans, the excuse is offered that they were purchased "to make life easier."[68] That seems difficult to reconcile with the facts. In 1830, there were 735 black slaveholders in New Orleans, including Cecee McCarty who owned 32 slaves, more than anyone else in the city.[69] Auguste Dubuclet of Iberville Parish was a wealthy man whose 1,200 acres and 94 slaves were valued at more than $200,000. Cyprien Ricard bought a plantation and 91 slaves in the same parish in 1851. Martin Donato of St.Landry bequeathed 89 slaves and an estate valued at more than $100,000 to his wife and children when he died in 1848. Mrs. Thomas Dumford of Plaquemines had 75, Antoine Decuir of Pointe Coupe 112, Mrs. C.L. Comer 61, Charles Rogues of St. Landry 47. In 1830, 14 members of the Meytoier family of Natchitoches Parish owned 306 slaves.[70] Wade notes there were even three Negro slave traders in the second municipality of New Orleans.[71] One of these, Andrew Dumford complained in 1835 of the difficulties he encountered trans-porting 25 slaves back to Louisiana from Virginia.[72]

Of the free blacks who owned slaves, Liliane Crete says, they were "reputed for their brutality."[73] That seems a harsh generalization, much the same as her characterization of the brutal behavior of Creole women toward slaves.[74] It is fairer to say that some blacks and Creoles owned slaves and abused them. The same courtesy ought be extended to South-ern Jews. Louisiana's Jews were neither saints nor devils. They all were caught up in a system where, as Rabbi Korn puts it, "neither [they] nor any other New Orleans merchants" could escape involvement in goods which "were for the use of slaves or produced by slaves."[75] Slavery was, as Georgia's Methodist Bishop James Andrew (who owned two slaves) or Louisiana Episcopal Bishop Leonidas Polk (who owned nearly 400 slaves on his plantation near Thibodaux)[76] had rationalized, a "heaven-sent institution."

14

The Cotton Kingdom

The Periphery of the Confederacy

History, economics, and geography bound the outer arc of the Old South together. Climate and soil made it possible for Florida, Alabama, Mississippi, Arkanasas, Texas, Tennessee, and Kentucky to become slave societies. Woodlands yielded to farms and plantations in each of the newly created territories. They also became part of an agricultural revolution that took place at the end of the eighteenth century. In 1792, the United States produced a total of 6,000 bales of cotton. The following year, Eli Whitney invented the cotton gin. In 1816, the single port of New Orleans processed 37,000 bales of cotton. By 1840, New Orleans would handle one million bales. The total crop passed a billion pounds by 1850. A decade later, the crop was nearly 2.3 billion pounds and accounted for two-thirds of the total exports of the United States.[1] The South produced the cotton (worth $115,700,000 in 1860), but it was transferred to northern textile firms and some in England who made fortunes off the labor of slaves, 60 percent of whom in the Deep South were employed in cotton fields.[2]

Those who hope to find some grand Jewish conspiracy to spread slavery across the South by tilling the soil for cotton will be frustrated. There are claims that a Philadelphia Jew (Abraham Mordecai) introduced the first cotton gin to the eastern region of the Mississipi territory. As a consequence, within ten years (1800–1810), the population around Natchez quadrupled. But Alabama and Mississippi were actually opened to cotton planting at the end of the eighteenth century by the Scottish trader Robert Grierson, a surveyor Joseph Collins, and Benjamin Hawkins who encouraged the Creek Indians to bring raw cotton to the junction of the Coosa and Tallapoosa Rivers.[3] A state by state analysis yields what by now is a monotonous conclusion: some Jews who lived in the Cotton belt owned slaves or profited from the slave system. At no time did they dominate the cotton trade or slavery.

Florida, Alabama, and Mississippi

When the French or Spanish controlled Louisiana, they usually held Florida, Alabama, and Mississippi as well. Propinquity guaranteed clashes between English/Americans and the French and Spanish. Americans viewed the Bourbon colonies as bastions of hostile Indians. The Spanish, who brought the first slaves to Florida in 1581, deliberately created Fort Moosa near San Marcus and Fort Blount (also known as the Negro Fort because of its number of runaways) to harass the English.[4] For their part, the French tried to establish forts at Mobile in 1701, Natchez in 1714, Pensacola shortly after, but did little to discourage attacks into enemy territory. In the 1770s, West Florida was nothing but a wilderness with several isolated small villages managed by the British Board of Trade, Privy Council, and a local council made up entirely of non-Jews.[5] Only after the Adams-Onis treaty of 1819 did the United States come into possession of the entire Gulf strip.

In Florida, the great magnates were Samuel Hairston, once described as "the richest man in Virginia," who owned between 1,600 and 1,700 slaves in Tallahassee,[6] Henry Laurens of South Carolina who maintained extensive holdings in the territory, Dennis Rolle from Charlotia, Dr. Andrew Turnbull who owned 100,000 acres of cotton farmland at New Smyrna, Colonel Orlando Rees, Colonel Louis Matair, Redding Parnell, Lancaster Jamison, William Carr, Joseph Hernandez (the first territorial delegate to Congress), Farquhar Macrae, George Noble Jones, Jacob Robinson of Jackson County who owned 65 slaves, Robert Gamble whose Wirtland plantation counted 102 slaves, Richard Harrison in Madison County with 150 blacks, S.H. Butler with 109, Jermeiah Reid with 27, J. Blue of Columbia County who owned 27 in 1850.[7] Following the closing of the slave trade in 1808 perhaps another 250,000 slaves were illegally imported into America, most of them brought to Florida from Cuba. One of the worst offenders was Zephaniah Kingsley, a planter who was enticed to Florida by the offer of 3,300 acres of land from the Spanish crown in 1803. Beginning with 74 slaves, Kingsley (who was married to a black woman) became the principal slave trader in Florida before transferring his operations to Haiti in 1830.[8]

Alabama's cotton production increased from 20 million pounds in 1821 to 440 million in 1851.[9] The major slaveholders in Alabama during this period included Charles Tait and James Asbury who owned 200 slaves each on Weldon and Springfield estates respectively, Jerre Brown with 540, Benjamin Fitzpatrick who farmed 400 acres at Oak Grove on the Coosa River, cotton planters Henry Watson and Columbus Morrison, Daniel Platt near Montgomery, James Torbett in Macon County, Henry Burgwyn, James Battle, Benjamin Yancey, Charles Matthews, Samuel Pickens, Colonel James Thornton, C.C.Clay, Peyton Burford, Samuel Townsend, and James and Samuel Pickens.[10] One of the more notorious slave traders was Peter Stokes of Sumter County who earned $2,000 per year in the 1840s.[11] Charles Davis, especially, highlights the brutal character of William Gould from Green County and James Tait. The former related in private papers how he whipped slaves and kept pregnant women working in the fields. The latter, whose slaveholdings eventually numbered 340, sounded like a modern-day Cato, offering three rules to masters: (1) never speak to blacks but on business; (2) never let blacks know the nature of their punishment; and (3) never hurry the punishment.[12]

In 1859, the state of Mississippi led the nation in production of cotton (more than 1.2 million 400 pound bales).[13] Not coincidentally, the state also counted 436,631 slaves, more blacks than whites. In the Delta counties of Issaquena and Washington, blacks outnumbered whites by nine to one. The 115 slaveholders in Issaquena averaged 63 slaves each, the highest ratio anywhere in the United States.[14] The value of slaves in this one state has been estimated at $350,000,000.[15] The names of Mississippi's biggest slaveholders are well known. In 1860 they included Wade Hampton III, the absentee landlord from South Carolina, Stephen Duncan , Gerard Brandon, John Robinson, Benjamin Roach, and J.D. Hill. Other prominent slave magnates included Peter Randolph Leigh whose plantation in Yalobusha Copunty abutted that of former President James K. Polk, Charles Wailes, F.W. Wheeless, Duncan McArn, Greenwood Leflore, Colonel Joseph Dunbar, Cornelius Vanhouten, Leonard Covington, T.S.G. Dabney, John T. Leigh, William Dunbar, Col. Antony Hutchins, Richard Ellis, Abner Green, Benjamin Farrar, James McIntosh, David Williams, Andrew Flinn, Martin Philips, Thomas Butler, John Jenkins, Clement Clay, John Nevitt, John Milliken, and Henry Watson.[16]

None of the major slaveholders in Florida, Alabama, or Mississippi were Jewish. Nor are there any Jewish names among the more than fifty names of major slave traders listed in Natchez, the principal slave market for Mississippi, between 1833 and 1859.[18] Neither the Spanish

TABLE 14.1
Mississippi Planters with 300 or More Slaves

1850	
Francis Surget	779
Stephen Duncan	668
Benjamin Roach	488
David Hunt	426
H.R.W. Hill	417
Philip Hoggatt	383
John Miller	345
William Mercer	342
Edward McGehee	333
1860	
Wade Hampton III	899
Stephen Duncan	717
John Robinson	550
Benjamin Roach	530
Gerard Brandon	512
J.D. Hill	502
Elgee and Chambers	501
Edward McGehee	471
David Hunt	468
William Mercer	452
John Miller	450
John Jenkins	424
A.J.Turnbull Estate	401
Joseph Davis	355
Levin Marshall	352
Philip St. George Cocke	329
James Metcalfe	315
A.L. Bingaman	310
Henry Turner and John Quitman	308.[17]

who continued the Inquisition to 1828 nor the French who followed the Code Noir of 1724 (banning all non-Catholics from colonies) welcomed Jews. Yet just as in Louisiana Jews tried unsuccessfully to slip past the authorities. Isaac Monsanto stayed in Pensacola temporarily in the 1760s after being expelled by the Spanish governor from New Orleans. His sons were permitted to establish plantations in West Florida, mainly because they had renounced their Jewish roots. They were more fortunate than Manuel Arias and Joseph dePalacios, two Jewish traders who tried unsuccessfully to establish residence in Mobile in the middle of the eighteenth century.

Jews did not establish themselves in Florida until that region came under American rule in 1819. One of the first was Moses Levy, founder of the New Pilgrimage Plantation in 1822. Designed along communal lines, with a central stable, cornhouse, and family residences, where workers would equally share profits, New Pilgrimage was supposed to entice refugees to the new world. Like so many utopian schemes, it failed. So did Levy's plans for his own family. His son David changed his name to Yulee, became a planter, and was one of the first senators elected by the new state of Florida in 1845. At that time there were fewer than 100 Jews among the 66,500 people in the state and few had anything in common with Yulee. Most were merchants, not slave owners. More important, Yulee disassociated himself from his Jewish roots. Like Judah Benjamin, he married out of the faith and brought his children up as Christians.[19]

The first permanent Jews of Mississippi (apart from members of the Monsanto clan) were the storekeepers Israel Mayer, Robert Abrams, Abraham Bucholtz, Wolfe Geissenberger, and the Ullman brothers who came to Natchez after 1798.[20] According to Father James Pillar, these were hard-working , enterprising men who often started out with "no more than could be carried on their backs."[21] By 1833 there were ten Jewish families in the city. According to Rabbi Julius Kerman, the movement of the John Mayer family with fourteen children from New Orleans to Natchez in 1841 provided "the leaven of Jewish life in town." The town had its first congregation, perhaps as many as eighteen families (forty-five persons), in 1861.[22] On the eve of the Civil War, the combined Jewish population of Vicksburg, Natchez, Jackson, Columbus, and Port Gibson was no more than 600.[23] Mississippi has never been a land of enchantment for Jews who as late as 1968 numbered only 4,015 out of a population of 2,315,900 (less than two-one-hundredths of one percent.)[24]

On the eve of the Civil War, Alabama had 2,000 Jews, more than Mississippi, Florida and Arkansas combined. Most of these, 75 families, were concentrated in the port city of Mobile. According to Rabbi Korn, no Jew had a permanent residence in Mobile till the third decade of the nineteenth century.[25] A few passed through the territory, like the Indian traders Francois Simon and Abraham Mordecai and the merchants Samuel Israel, Alexander Solomons and Joseph Depalocios who for a short period of time foreclosed on the LisLoy plantation in August 1777. But there is no record of Jews in the territory under the Spanish between 1781 and 1813. Only after 1821 are there Jewish names in papers, deeds, and wills.the Jewish experience in Montgomery, the state's scenic capital, and Birmingham, situated in the hills, approximates that of Mobile.[26] A Jew named Abram Mordecai established a trading post at Weathersford in 1785. But it was not until 1848, with the arrival of Jacob Kohn from Bavaria that Jews made any impact on the economy in upstate Alabama. They created a shoe factory.[27]

In 1860, many of the residents of Mobile owned slaves. Among the largest slaveholders were Thomas Saunders (124), Duke Goodman (106), brickmaker A.H. Ryland (61), Sarah Barnes (52), transplanted New England newspaperman turned farmer Thaddeus Sanford, cotton broker Gustavus Horton, merchant William Rix, Eliza Goldthwaite (widow of a state judge) and Sarah Walton (widow of a onetime mayor). None of these individuals was Jewish.[28] A few Jews in Alabama and Mississipi were involved in the operations of the slave trade. Jacob Soria of Natchez owned two slaves and was listed as a speculator.[29] So were Sol and Israel Jones, auctioneers in Mobile in the 1830s. Myer Myers was a cotton factor. Philip Goldsmith, a clothier at Church and Jackson Street, was listed as a Negro trader.[30] So, too, for two years (1823–24) was George Davis, hotelier in Tuscaloosa.[31] None of these individuals is mentioned by Charles Davis in his study of cotton in Alabama. Instead, in his section dealing with "the socially degrading traffic in Negroes," Davis writes of Peter Stokes of Sumter County and Mason Harwell, "one of the most active dealers in Montgomery," who had financial ties with the Knickerbocker Insurance Company.[32]

It would be unfair and incorrect to identify all Jews in this region as slave traders based upon a handful of names. We could just as easily recite a list of champions of black rights—including Joseph and Isaac Friedman from Tuscumbria who risked their lives, purchasing slaves to set them free in the difficult days before the Civil War,[33] Moses Levy who was famed for his discourses to Jews and Christians in 1829 arguing for abolition of slavery, and Samuel Fleischmann who was hounded by the KuKluxKlan from Marianna, Florida in 1869 because he defended ex-slaves as freemen. Fleischmann's body was found on the road to Tallahasee.[34]

In his book *Slavery in Alabama*, James Benson Sellers listed the 33 most prominent slaveholders in Mobile between 1846 and 1849, another 18 from the year 1850.They included names like Worthy, J.W.Patten, John Osment, B.W. Campbell. Sellers cited no Jews. Ironically, Sellers found references to the Chastang family with 27 slaves, Burnandez Rozieste with 14, and Madam Boshong with 16. The last three were free blacks, a fact that should not surprise since census figures established that as early as 1830 200 slaves in Alabama were owned by heads of families who were free blacks.[35] By 1850, David Barland and William Johnson, free blacks in Mississippi, owned 18 and 15 slaves respectively.[36] By way of contrast, the 1850 census for Mobile listed 31 Jewish families (less than half the number in the city) owning 90 slaves, less than one-hundredth of one percent, 0.01 percent of the 964,201 slaves in the state.

Arkansas, Texas, and Missouri

Jews in Mobile, Montgomery and Birmingham, like most Jews in the Gulf states, were merchants, lawyers, musicians, physicians, teachers, shippers. They were few in number and they were not counted among the principal slave traders or planters.[37] The same holds true for Jews in the territories that constitute the outer rim of the Confederacy. In Arkansas, Texas, Missouri, Tennessee, and Kentucky they were latecomers, poor immigrants from Central and Eastern Europe who became peddlers and shopkeepers.

The first slaves were introduced to Arkansas by French agents (Marquis du Chatel and John Law) between 1712 and 1721. A century later when the territory was organized (1820) there were 1,617 slaves in a population of 14,273. Thanks to cotton production (Arkansas ranked sixth in the Old South) the rebel state counted 111,115 slaves in 1860.[38] Most of the 11,481 slaveowners in Arkansas owned fewer than three slaves.[39] According to Orville Taylor, the major planters were Junius Craig of Chicot County (with 211) Jasper Parchal of Helena, Peter Hanger of Little Rock, Isaac Taylor of Fayettville, John Brown of Camden, Gustavus Henry, Charles Whitson, William Thorn, John Jordan of Arkansas County, Gideon Pillow in Phillips County, John Jordan in Arkansas County.[40] The principal brokers were F.R. Taylor, James Shephard who owned Waterford Plantation near Pine Bluff, and Jared Martin. None of these individuals were Jews. Nor were any of the 1,071 overseers in Arkansas. If the backwoods of Louisiana proved inhospitable to Jews until the end of the eighteenth century, imagine how Arkansas must have seemed to these urban people. Not until 1838 did

Jacob, Hyman, and Levi Mitchell come to Little Rock.[41] Twenty years later there were less than 1,200 of their co-religionists in Arkansas, Mississippi and Florida combined.[42]

Jews came to Texas with the first Americans. Samuel Isaacs was among 300 settlers led by Stephen Austin in 1821. More followed in the next two decades lured by the offer of cheap land and labor. Jacob Henry and Jacob Lyons became permanent residents of Velasco. Adolphus Sterne went to Nacogdoches where he swore an oath of allegiance to Mexico. A few went to Waco.[43] In the 1830s, Abraham Cohen Labatt and Jacob de Cordova emigrated via New Orleans to Galveston.[44] On the eve of the Civil War there were approximately 1,000 Jews in Texas and a letter in the *Occident* could relate there was "a sprinkling in every village."[45] The largest center was Houston where Jews arrived in 1836. According to the census of 1850, Houston had seventeen Jewish adults (eleven men and six women) among its 1863 whites. One was a confectioner, another a land agent, the rest were merchants. Ten years later there were 108 Jews, approximately 2 percent of Houston's white population of 3,768. Twenty-seven of the adult males were listed as merchants (retail goods and groceries), there were nine clerks, one caprenter, one druggist, and one Hebrew Church pastor.

In a state with 182,566 slaves, several Jews owned slaves. They played no role in the debate over slavery and annexation of Texas.[46] None were brokers like John Sydnor, onetime mayor of Galveston, Edward Riordan of Dallas, the fabled Bowie brothers or Colonel James Fannin who perished at the Alamo, Monroe Edwards (who was importing slaves from Cuba in 1835–36) or the firms of McMurry and Winstead or Bachelder, Samson and Company.[47] None were major landowners.[48] The distinction of being called planter (that is a farmer with 20 of more slaves) went to Leonard Groce and his family who brought the first cotton gin to the Brazos in 1825, John McNeel and his sons, John Sweeny and his seven sons, Josiah Bell, Colonel Morgan Smith and John Adriance, Dr. Anson Jones of Massachusetts, Dr. Ashbel Smith of Connecticut, Dr. James Phelps, Julien Devereux who had gone bankrupt farming in Georgia and Alabama, and a host of others drawn to Texas by cheap land and the prospect of a quick fortune.[49] A number of Christian women (Emily Perry, Elizabeth Worrall, Melinda Coffree, Sara Mims, and Rebecca McIntosh Hawkins Hagerty) bequeathed as many as 100 slaves to their heirs. None of them were Jewish. Some planters like Beverly Holocomb, Thomas League, Thomas Huling, W.W. Walton, Samuel Flournoy, Charles Tait, and Thomas Affleck opted to live in town rather than on plantations. The largest slaveowners in 1860 included cotton planters David and Robert Mills, both of whom owned more than 340 slaves each, John Clark who maintained 81 slaves on his $250,000 estate, William Stafford who established the first sugar mill in Austin's colony in 1836 and then went on to acquire more than $600,000 in slaves, William T. Scott and his son-in-law William Rose who together controlled five plantations and were the leading slaveholders in East Texas Harrison County, Abner Jackson of Brazoria, William Duncan, Morgan Smith, J. Greenville McNeel, and cotton magnates E.A. Glover (159 slaves) and William Kennedy (124 slaves).[50] Again, none of them was Jewish.

Frederick Law Olmsted toured Texas in the years just preceding the Civil War. The irascible Mr. Olmsted, who had little good to say about anyone (the Irish were "faithfuless, improvident, passionate," the "Scotch" were "cool,ambitious,penurious," South Carolina "the least democratic, worst governed, most insubordinate, most licentious and immoral" of all British colonies)[51] had this to say about Jews in Texas:

> There are a few Jew-Germans in Texas, and, in Texas, the Jews, as everywhere else, speculate in everything—in popular sympathies, prejudices, and bigotries, in politics, in slavery. Some of them own slaves, others sell them on commission, and others have captured and returned fugitives. Judging by several anecdotes I heard of them *they do not appear to have made much by it as by most of their operations.* (Italics mine)[52]

Any search for Jews prominent in slave institutions in Missouri also proves fruitless. Blacks had been brought to this upper Louisiana region in the eighteenth century to work in lead mines, as domestic servants, and in the fields. This was a territory ripe for cotton, hemp, and tobacco development. Between 1810 and 1820, Missouri's slave population increased from 3,000 to 10,000. R.Douglas Hurt's study of slavery in Missouri's principal farming belt (the seven-county area along the Mississippi from Clay to Callaway counties) turns up no Jewish slave traders on the order of William Northcutt or Thomas Selby of Columbia, John White, William Heady, J.H. Adams, T.W. Cobbs, M.B.Williams, Dulaney Coooper, N.G.Elliott, or John Talbott. More than eighty years ago, Harrison Trexler offered similar conclusions. Trexler pointed out that private disgust with slave traders like Reuben Bartlett and Corbin Thompson of St.Louis, Wright and Carter in St. Joseph and Alexander and White in Lexington was not necessarily matched by rejection of the system they represented. The slave merchant Wharton Blanton of Wright City managed to conceal the fact he was burying dead blacks in what he maintained were Indian mounds because of public indifference. The slave pens of Bernard Lynch in St. Louis were later converted into a prison building.[53] The Mount Pleasant Baptist Association of Howard County expressed regret over the existence of slavery, but declared the matter a question of states rights, beyond the purview of the U.S. Congress.[54] Even the Mormons compromised and accepted slavery as a legitimate institution.[55] Trexler makes no mention of Jews in his study—and for good reason. Ezekiel Block, the first Jew who came to this prairie state in 1796, did own slaves. Missouri counted 114,931 slaves in 1860, but none of its 500 Jews rivalled the dealings or ownership of Eli Bass of Boone County (52 slaves), W.B.Waddell, a hemp planter from Lexington, Rice Harlow of Saline County (62), John Coffman of St.Genevieve (78), William Swinney (86), J.C. Carter (43), George Cason (52) and Andrew Ashbaugh (37) of Howard County or the state's single largest slaveholder in 1860—Cynthia Smith with 106 slaves.[56]

Tennessee and Kentucky

In 1860 the two border states of Kentucky and Tennessee counted more than 500,000 slaves between them. The leading slaveholders in the Volunteer State were William Hugg King, William Lenoir, John Chester and the Polk brothers of Maury County (Lucius, William, George, and Andrew) who owned more than 400 slaves and held estates valued at more than a half million dollars.[57] Frederick Stump, a signer of the Cumberland Articles of Agreement, sold the first black in Tennessee, a 23-year-old man, for £100 to John Overton in July 1792. Fifty years later, the state was deeply inolved in the trans-shipment of slaves to the Deep South. By virtue of its location, Memphis became one of the largest slave markets in the nation. Prominent slave traders in the Bluff City included M.C.Cayce, S. and A. Fowlkes, David Saffarins, W.E. Elliott, Z.H. Curlin, B. and M. Little, Isaac Nevill, George Noel, Damascus and William James, J.C. Butler, John Staples, Edward Word and Nathan Bedford Forrest (son of a blacksmith and the future Confederate cavalry commander and founder of the first Ku Klux Klan who earned more than $96,000 per year selling slaves before the Civil War).[58] The firm of Bolton, Dickins and Co. (Isaac, Jefferson, Wade and Washington Bolton and Thomas Dickins) maintained the largest slave brokerage house in Memphis, with branches in New Orleans, Lexington, St.Louis and Vicksburg.[59] Nashville's leading slave traders included Joseph Meeks, R.W.Porter, H.H. Haynes, E.S. Hawkins, and the firms of Lyles and Hitchings, Glover and Dabbs, and Webb, Merrill and Co. The foremost slave auctioneer in Knoxville was William L. Boyd, who also maintained an office in Nashville.[60] The sole Jewish auctioneer listed in the state was Isaac Joseph.

A few Jews may have trickled west along the Holston River at the end of the eighteenth century. There were no Jews settled in Memphis till 1838, no Jewish congregation or cemetery until the 1850s. No Jews in Nashville till 1845, none in Chattanooga till 1858 or Knoxville till 1866. On the evil of the Civil War there were 9,200 Jews in the state out of a total population of 563,000. In Tennessee, as elsewhere in the South, acceptance was blocked by old-fashioned bigotry of the kind exemplified by Congressman Henry Foote, dubbed "the well-spring of slander" by a Richmond newspaper. Once a staunch supporter of the Confederacy, he would defect to the North in 1865. But only after denouncing the "evil," "unpatriotic," "shrewd," "unscrupulous," "Jewish knaves" who had flocked to Tennessee, hoping, Foote alleged, to seize nine-tenths of the land through extortion and illicit trade.[61]

The Jewish experience in Kentucky was no more alluring. A transplanted Virginian, Colonel David Meade had established one of the first plantations in Kentucky, Chaumiere du Prairie. In the next century, the typical Kentucky planter (like Henry Clay) would ship out tobacco, hemp, cotton, horses, and something else.[62] Prior to the Civil War, Kentucky ranked behind only Virginia, Maryland, and North Carolina in the sale of black slaves to the cotton states. More than 5,000 slaves were sold down river each year.[63] As one English traveller put it, Lexington was "the great place from which the South is supplied."[64] Though here, too, decent people characterized slave traders as "miserable anti-human critters,"[65] hawkers in flesh unashamedly proclaimed their wares in newspaper advertisements placed next to lawyers and banks. One of the earliest slave traders was Edward Stone of Maysville. Others that followed in Lexington included the firms of Washington Bolton, Isaac Bolton, Thomas Dickens and Wade Bolton; Blackwell, Murphy and Ferguson, W.F. White, Bolton, Dickens and Co.; Robert Thompson & Co., Griffin and Pullum, Blackwell, Murphy and Ferguson, A.B. Colwell, P.N. Brent, R.W. Lucas, Silas and George Marshall; Northcutt, Marshall & Co.; Neal McCann, W.F. White, Robert Elam, J.M. Heady and John Mattingly.[66] In Louisville, slave trading was a regular part of the business for John Stickney, J.C. Gentry, A.C. Scott, William Kelly, Thomas Powell, Jordan and Tarlton Arteburn, William

Talbott, and Matthew Garrison.[67] The most notorious slaver in all of Kentucky was Lewis Robards, a degenerate child stealer who kept all but a "choice stock of fancy girls" in eight-foot cages.[68]

There were 2,500 Jews in Kentucky at the start of the Civil War. A few crossed the Ohio River and managed to secure patents for plantations as early as 1774–1784.[69] As in Louisiana, however, these first settlers were single men, detached from their religion, eager to blend in as Americans. Many intermarried in the Anglican church. Dembitz refers to the three men named Levi listed in the Louisville directory of 1831 as "half-breeds, educated as Christians."[70] Not until 1834 did Jews conduct services in Louisville. One glimpse into their prominence in the slave trade is offered by the 1830 census. According to Rosenwaike, two Jews in Louisville (Henry Hyman and Jacob Levin) owned a total of four slaves. There were more than 1,000 slaves in the city at the time.[71] No Jew had anything like the 300 slaves of Montgomery Bell, owner of the Cumberland Works. None of the brutal slave traders in Louisville or Lexington were Jews.[72]

In his meticulous chronicles, Frederick Law Olmsted records only contacts with the few German Jews of Texas, a Jewish hat dealer in Mobile, and Jewish merchants who opened cheap clothing and trinket shops throughout the South.[73] There was another group which Olmsted compared to the would-be fashionable people of New York, a few hundred old famlies that comprised the "haughty gentry." Outwardly hospitable, they were "absudly ostentatious and extravagant." More important, this "Privileged Class of the South" was, for the most part, comprised of descendants of English and Irish immigrants, New England tradesmen, all "Christian men" who misused the Bible.[74]

15

Jews and the Great Moral Debate

The Incident at Paducah

Far from gaining acceptance, the Jews of Kentucky, most of whom were pro-Union, found themselves menaced by the very side they supported in the Civil War. Following his successful siege of Vicksburg, General U. S. Grant, sitting in Oxford, Mississippi as commander of the Army of the West, received a number of complaints against Jewish merchants. On November 10, 1862, Grant banned Jews (this "intolerable nuisance," he called them) from travelling by rail into occupied districts. One month later, on December 17, 1862, Grant, responding to complaints of profiteering (apparently emanating from General William T. Sherman) ordered the expulsion of all Jews ("a class violating every regulation of trade established by the Treasury Department") from his jurisdiction with twenty-four hours.

The first to feel the wrath of these deportation orders were the Jews of Paducah, a small town more than 200 miles down the Ohio River from Louisville. [1] Thirty men with their families were immediately expelled. (Two women, sick in bed, were permitted to stay.) Petitions from the first victims and energetic protests of Northern Jews from Cincinnati to New York prevented the deportations from becoming wholesale. General H. W. Halleck, operating upon instructions from President Lincoln, instructed Grant to reverse his decree. On January 7, 1862, this tsarist-style ukase was cancelled. [2]

What prompted the initial order was simple human greed. In the years preceding the Civil War, the price of cotton had nearly doubled. It was possible for speculators to earn 400 percent profits on small investments. [3] As Charles Dana of the *New York Tribune* wrote: "Every colonel, captain, or quartermaster is in secret partnership with some operator in cotton; every soldier dreams of adding a bale of cotton to his monthly pay." [4] Apparently that included Grant and his father Jesse.

In December 1863, the elder Grant sued Harmon, Henry, and Simon Mack of Cincinnati, claiming that he and his son had entered into an agreement with the Mack brothers in December 1862 to deliver a specific amount of cotton from the military department commanded by General Grant for sale in New York. The Grants delivered 300 bales, from which they expected a mimimum profit of $400,000. By issuing his General Order no. 11, U. S. Grant was simultaneously clearing potential competition while venting a personal animus. [5]

This ugly incident in the winter of 1861–62 symbolized the precarious existence of Jews in the Old South 200 years after John Locke drafted his liberal constitution for the Carolinas. The editors of *Secret Relationship*, however, regard Grant's Order no. 11 as a classic example of gentile society defending itself against perfidious Jews.[6] They see this as another example of Jews being on the wrong side of the crucial moral issue in American history. Somehow, through cunning cultivated over thousands of years, Jews managed to dominate the hidden or invisible aspects of slavery. They were the merchants in the cities who profiteered by selling to both master and slave. Hostile to abolitionism, Jews supposedly flouted the ban on slave imports to America after 1808. Jews lined up with the Confederacy, with treasonous bankers, both North and South, underwriting financial assistance to the rebels. Such statements are lesser libels, and like the greater claim that Jews controlled the slave trade, they are untrue.

Slavery in the Cities

Farrakhan and his lieutenant Khalid Abdul Muhammad publicly claimed in 1994 that Jews owned "three-fourths" of the 4,000,000 slaves in America on the eve of the Civil War. That statement was later amended to read that three-fourths of American Jews owned slaves, a higher percentage than the gentile population. As a source, the Nation of Islam offered Ira Rosenwaike's *On the Edge of Greatness*. In fact, any suggestion that Jews in 1860 owned significantly more slaves than Christians is a distortion of Rosenwaike's conclusions. First, Rosenwaike was using the 1830, not the 1860 census. He does, indeed, claim that the overwhelming proportion of Jewish households, three-fifths to four-fifths in southern cities (Richmond, Savannah, Charleston, and New Orleans) owned one or more slaves, but he also points out the ratio was 1 in 7 in Baltimore, zero in New York and Philadelphia, the nation's largest cities. [7] There is also a disparity in Rosenwaike's sample of 322 *selected* Jewish households (75 percent of which owned slaves) and *all* 625,000 gentile families in the South (36 percent of which owned slaves.) But Rosenwaike hastens to point out that "the relatively high ratio of slaveholding to nonslaveholding families among the South's Jews was a function not of wealth but of residence in cities and towns."[8] Virtually all urban families, Jewish and Christian, owned at least one or more slaves for domestic purposes. In Charleston, for example, the slaveowning ratio among Jews and Christians was identical, with 87 percent of the city's heads of Christian families holding slaves as compared with 83 percent of the Jewish families. Rosenwaike even offers the following chart to suggest that Jews owned proportionately fewer slaves.

Jews in the Indies, New England or the ante-bellum South lived in cities. Some owned slaves, generally fewer than their gentile neighbors. During the nineteenth century the number of slaves owned by Jews in urban settings actually declined. Whether in absolute or relative numbers, the drop in Jewish slaveholding is not surprising. In his classic study, *Slavery in the Cities: The South 1820–1860* (1964), Richard C. Wade points out an overall decline in slave population in cities. In the forty years before the Civil War, the percentage of black town dwellers in the South decreased from 37 percent to 17 percent.[9] In real numbers, Baltimore's slave population dipped from 4,357 (total population 62,738) in 1820 to 2,218 (total population 212,418) in 1860. More than one-third of Richmond's 12,067 people were slaves in 1820. Forty years later, the figure was less than 10 percent. Norfolk,with a population of

TABLE 15.1
Distribution of Slaves among Slaveholders
Southern Households and Jewish Southern Households

Number of Slaves	1830 Census	
	percent Southern Households	percent Jewish Households
1–4	18.8	16
2–4	30.2	38
5–9	24.3	26
10–19	17.1	13
20–49	7.7	6
50+	1.8	1

Source: Rosenwaike, *Edge of Greatness*, 68.

8,478, had 3,261 in 1820. In 1860, the city counted 3,284 among its overall population of 14,620. Wade notes similar declines for Louisville, Mobile, New Orleans, St. Louis, Savannah, and Washington. [10]

Relatively speaking, conditions may have been better for the half million slaves in the cities than their counterparts on the plantations. [11] Wade quotes black abolitionist Frederick Douglass who said: "The general sense of decency that must pervade [towns] does much to check and prevent…atrocious cruelty…and…dark crimes…openly perpetrated on the plantation…Very few in the city are willing to incur the odium of being cruel masters."[12] No defense of city slavery intended, Wade explains that when Douglass compared slavery in the towns with its rural counterpart, "he did so on the ground that floggings were fewer, not eliminated, and that severity, while not unknown, was less common."[13]

That is not the impression given by Douglass who said,"A city slave is almost a free citizen—he enjoys privileges altogether unknown to the whip-driven slave on the plantation."[14] Phillips agreed, declaring,"As to routine control, urban proprietors were less complete masters even of slaves in their own employ than were those in the country."[15] Wade lists a number of examples where city slaves fared better. Often, city slaves lived in the same home as their masters and not a flimsy shanty detached from the main plantation house.[16] Their clothing was better, they ate better, received better medical attention, and were excused from work on the sabbath.[17] While some worked on the docks or in the mills, many were domestics and a few, who were later freed, apprenticed next to craftsmen in their shops. Runaways headed for the ciy where they believed they could hide and lead an easier life. Still, city slaves suffered from all the inherent evils of slavery—fear of the auction block which was immediate, not remote from their daily lives, the real destruction of family ties once people were sold either through perceived need or caprice, interrogation, detention, and whippings by white patrols designated to prevent an insurrection like that supposedly planned by Denmark Vesey in Charleston in 1822 or actually executed by Nat Turner in 1837.[18] City slaves who moved about without a permit, who robbed or became intoxicated, might find themselves at the treadmill, in leg irons or even on the gallows.[19]

There was no single standard of behavior for Jews in the cities. As Stanley Falk of the Office of Chief of Military History for the Headquarters of the Army wrote Rabbi Korn in 1960, "My observation has been that Jews in the ante-bellum South were much like non-Jews, i. e., they owned slaves if they could afford them, were Whigs or Democrats, and generally shared the same attitudes and feelings as their fellow Southerners, and for the same reasons."[20] Korn himself has written that some Jews volunteered to serve on patrols pursuing runaway slaves, in the militia, as sheriff and other turnkeys.[21] In some instances, Jews had no choice but to serve, as state law required participation in the militia of all free white men.[22] Others may have mistreated their slaves. Those who have made a serious study of the subject, like Stampp, Phillips, Wade, and Bancroft offer few, if any, instances of Jewish brutality. Korn (who cites the case of Joseph Cohen of Lynchburg, convicted of killing a Negro in 1819)[23] believes this is because there were few Jews in rural areas. Attorney Robert Rosen of Charleston, who is currently at work on a book dealing with Jewish slaveholders in the Old South, suggests that just as in the Middle Ages, it was considered a relative blessing to be owned by Jews. [24] The same point was made during a conversation with Edwin Sasportas of the New York Port Authority, whom I encountered doing research at the South Carolina Historical Society in the summer of 1993. Sasportas traced his family lineage back to Abraham Sasportas, a Jew who came from Bordeaux in 1778. The French-born immigrant settled in Charleston and made nine transactions involving 19 slaves between 1779 and 1810.[25] Among these was a slave named Augustus who adopted the Sasportas name. His own son, Joseph, a free mulatto, was trained as a butcher and later became a minister, trustee of Claffin College, and slaveowner himself. Edwin Sasportas believes the progression from Jewish slave to urban freeman was typical. "I have the impression," he told me, "that the day to day treatment by Jews of slaves was better. A lot of them, the free ones in the area in the 1840s and 1850s, were from Jewish backgrounds. They were seamstresses, garment workers, shoemakers. Not on the plantations."[26]

Whether true or not, the perception existed in the West Indies, colonial America, and the ante-bellum South that somehow slavery under Jews was less oppressive. Perhaps it was because Jews in a Christian society understood the meaning of alienation. Jewish merchants were repeatedly attacked for violating the sabbath, hoarding, speculation, black marketeering, selling alcohol to blacks and accepting stolen goods from them. Charles MacKay, who toured the United States in the 1857–58, blasted German Jews ("neighborhood pests," he called them) who would squat near plantations, build a wooden shanty, and exchange whiskey, tobacco and ribbons for articles stolen by blacks. [27] In fact, despite the risks of harrassment from white bigots, Jewish traders were willing to do business with blacks.[28] As Harry Golden has written, Jewish peddlers, especially after the 1880s, were "probably the first white people in the South who paid the black people any respect at all," who called them Mr. or Mrs. and not boy, who offered them credit.[29]

Some Jews worked to ameliorate black suffering even when there was no reciprocity. Black culture had imbibed anti-Semitism along with Christian theology in the eighteenth and nineteenth centuries. Jews were fearful creatures mentioned in spirituals ("Were You There When They Crucified My Lord," "The Jew's Daughter"), responsible for deicide. Imagine the emotional impact of the following lines from "The Jew's Daughter" as they might have been sung weekly: "De Jews done killed poor Jesus and bury him in de seplecure! De grave wouldn't hold him. De Jews done killed poor Jesus but de grave wouldn't hold him. Cruel Jews, jes look at Jesus.... Dey nail Him to de cross.... Dey rivet His feet.... Dey hanged him high.... An dey stretch him wide.... O de cruel Jews dun took ma Jesus."[30] Folklorist Rudolph Glanz also offers stories of blacks who ran and hid when they learned they were being sold to Jews because they were fearful of what these people who had killed "the lord and master" might do to them. And others, curious to see what an Israelite was, returned upset because the old man proved to be a Jewish peddler, a "lowdown white man who had never been to the land of Canaan."[31]

The Illegal Slave Trade

Jews in the ante-bellum South may have been feared and loathed as city slickers, pork-haters, even Yankees, but they never were caricatured as masterminds of the illegal slave trade. After January 1808 no slaves could legally be brought into the United States from Africa or the West Indies. Much of the civilized world agreed that the trade in human beings should be suppressed. As a result, British, American, and Spanish fleets cooperated, patrolling the Caribbean, and seizing slave ships. Yet there still was a thriving market in Southern states and in Brazil where slavery was legal. Slave ships operated out of Bahía, Havana and New York, bringing between 30,000 and 60,000 slaves each year to Brazil. Between 1831 and 1855 nearly half a million Africans were uprooted and dragged to Brazil where many died of cholera, smallpox, ill treatment, or exhaustion. The principal villains in this trade were Portuguese Christians. As Leslie Bethell wrote, "At the beginning of the nineteenth century, no nation was more deeply involved in the exportation, transportation and importation of African slaves than Portugal."[32] The major slave trading installations in West Africa belonged to men like Pedro Blanco de Gallinas, Salvador Lorens, Joao Cardozo dos Santos, Jose Alves da Cruz Rios, Juan Fernandez, Francisco Felix de Souza. The principal slave auctioneers in Bahia were the mulatto Joaquim Pereira Marinho, G. A. Blosen, Joao Vigilio Tourinho, Dr. E. J. Pedroza, Joaquim Pinto da Fonseca, and Dr. Jose Joaquim Simoes. [33] Slavery was defended by aristocrats like Joaquin Jose de Sousa Breves, Gilberto Freyre, Christiano Ottoni, Francisco Brandao, Martinho Campos, Jose Antonio Saraiva, Antonio Prado, Belfort Duarte, Prudente de Morais, Casper Silveira Martins, Andrade Figueira, and Lacerdo Werneck. The institution was justified by friars, monks, and other spiritual leaders like Bishop Jose Joaquim da Cunha de Azeredo Coutinho because the church needed slaves for its properties. It was championed by Foreign Minister Visconde de Olinda and politicians Paulino Jose Soares de Sousa, Joaquim Jose Rodrigues Torres, Bernardo Perreira de Vasconcelos, and Honorio Hermeto Carneiro Leao even after Brazil yielded to British pressure and agreed to reduce the trade in 1848. All of these men were Christians and Portuguese, none of them Jews. There were no Jews in Portugal, fewer than 1,000 immigrants from Eastern Europe in Brazil when 1. 5 million African slaves, most of them brought within the previous five decades, were emancipated in 1888.[34]

Jews are also absent from the list of merchants and captains who brought slaves to the U. S. after 1808. Reports of the Twenty-first Congress indicated that during the 1830s and 1840s the worst offenders were Cubans, operating more than 200 slave ships out of Havana. [35] W. E. B. DuBois, confirmed that many of the captains were French or Spanish. None of the illegal slavers was Jewish.[36] A more accurate representation of the Jewish role in this aspect of the nineteenth-century slave trade may be obtained by scrutinizing the names of New Yorkers who continued to engage in the illegal activity down to the Civil War. Many Americans in Baltimore, New Orleans, Galveston, and Savannah were lured into the trade in "black diamonds."[37] For obvious reasons. The U. S. consul general in Havana, Henry Crawford estimated that despite the risks of intercept by British, American, or Spanish fleets and a 17. 5 percent shipboard mortality, an outlay of $160,000 was guaranteed a profit of $90,000 or 56 percent.[38] By 1859, eighty-five vessels outfitted in New York were participating in the illicit trade.[39] It was relatively easy to purchase barks or schooners and mix slave ships with the 3,000 legitimate vessels sailing from Manhattan. Traffic was so heavy that the *New York Times* of May 5, 1860 lamented how the slave trade exceeded what had been conducted in the age of Wilberforce.[40]

Perhaps the most celebrated incident of an illegal slaver attempting to defy the ban on importing Africans on the eve of the Civil War involved the *Wanderer*, a yacht despatched to Africa in February 1859, twelve months before it was sold as a blockade runner to the Confederates. The *Wanderer* was owned by W. C. Corrie, a gentile member of the New York Yacht Club. Four of the five crewmen aboard were Northerners. Their captain was J. Egbert Farnum. None of them were Jews. [41] No less notorious was the case of the slaver *Echo*. Bound to Cuba with a cargo originally listed as 473 Negroes (153 died in transit from Africa), the *Echo* was intercepted off the coast of Cuba in August 1858 by the American brig *Dolphin*. Crew and slaves were taken to Charleston harbor where state and federal authorities debated their fate. Eventually it was decided that the blacks would be returned to "salubrious" sites in Africa and subsidized (fed and clothed) at U. S. expense for one year. The commander of the *Echo* (which flew a British flag), Captain Townsend and his polyglot crew—R. T. Bates, William Henrys, Jose Gonzales Lima, Antonio Milanovich, Alexander Rodgers, Archibald Scott, Dominico Dellephene, George Aken, John Copell, Antonio Amanda, Josede Costo, Antonio Gomas, John Barber, Thomas Joseph, John Pasco, Vital de Miranda, were sent to jail. None of these lawbreakers were Jews.[42] A third example of a illegal slave ship was the schooner *Clotilde* outfitted late in 1859 to bring what may have been the last cargo of slaves to the U. S. before the Civil War. Its owner was Timothy Meaher, a Northern steamboat builder, who arranged to bring 116 slaves to John Dabney's plantation on the Alabama River near Mobile. [43] Neither Meaher nor Dabney were Jewish.

The *Wanderer*, *Echo*, and *Clotilde* affairs were typical of gentile, not Jewish attempts to flaunt the law. New Yorkers dubbed those who engaged in the illicit slave trade "the Portuguese Company" because the major dealers were C. H. S. Figaniere (Portuguese consul general in New York), his brother William Figaniere (a naturalized American citizen), John Albert Machado, and Jose da Costa Lima Viana. These culprits were not bunglers, however. According to Warren Howard, they managed to keep their own names out of transactions, using instead "dummy" or "puppet" American firms like that of Benjamin (Weinberg) Wenburg or John P. Weeks, and depending on gentile lawyers like Erastus Benedict, Charles Black, or Beebe, Dean, and Donahue to defend them from prosecution.[44] In the decade preceding the outbreak of the Civil War, sixty New Yorkers were accused of smuggling slaves. Two charges (3.3 percent of all accusations) were brought against Benjamin

Weinberg, a Jew, for his involvement with the 264-ton *William G. Lewis* in October 1856 and the bark *Panchita* in July 1857. In both instances, Weinberg was tried and acquitted of any wrongdoing. [45]

Jewish Bankers and Factors

The editors of *Secret Relationship* suggest that Jews were responsible for the hidden aspect of the Southern economy, serving as brokers and financiers, quietly involved in the exploitation of human labor in cotton fields as well as sugar. With the exception of the banking firm of Lehman Brothers in Montgomery, Alabama, headed by Mayer and Emanuel Lehman, which tried to maintain offices in both North and South, there is no supporting evidence for such contentions. Lucille Griffith cites no Jews among the operators of Alabama's principal spinning mills of the 1830s.[46] Charles Davis of Auburn University listed no Jews among the fifteen leading cotton factors in Mobile or Montgomery.[47] There are no Jews listed by John Hebron Moore as owners of the main cotton gin factories and textile mills in Natchez, Kosciusko, Prattville, and Aberdeen, Mississippi.[48]

In his recent study, *King Cotton and His Retainers,* Harold Woodman indicates that by 1838 there were no fewer than sixty-five chartered banks with eighty-one branches doing business in cotton in South Carolina, Alabama, Georgia, Louisiana, Mississippi, Arkansas and Tennessee. [49] Woodman cites a number of prominent bankers—F. H. Elmore, president of the Bank of the State of South Carolina; Leroy Pope, head of the Planter's and Merchant's Bank of Huntsville, Alabama; and Israel Pickens of the Tombeckbe Bank of Alabama. None are Jews. Nor are the any of the major factors he lists (John Hagan and Co., Peter Hickman, S. Cullom and Co.)[50] In fact, the only reference to Jews in this major text is to Jewish merchants sent by New York firms who advanced money to farmers during picking season.[51]

New England textile mills derived substantial gain from the cotton trade.[52] Analyses of the major firms in this industry reveal no Jewish names. The Quaker merchant Moses Brown and his son-in-law William Almy organized one of the first textile factories in Providence at the end of the eighteenth century. They were soon followed by Elias Derby, Billy Gray, David Poignand, Abraham Marland, Peter Dobson, John Smith, and William Sprague.[53] In 1813 Francis Lowell and eleven colleagues started the Boston Manufacturing Company in Lowell.[54] Over the next twenty years, more capital for the textile industry came from the likes of Henry Lee, George Lyman, Col. Perkins, George Howe, Henry Cabot, Dr. James Ayer, Charles Jackson, Israel Thorndike, and Nathan Appleton, none of whom were Jews.[55]

The interaction of North and South was noted a century ago by the gadfly Frederick Law Olmsted who wrote: "Cotton goods manufactured in Georgia are sent to New York for sale, and are there sold by New York jobbers to Georgia retailers, who re-transport them to the vicinity in which the cotton was grown, spun, and woven, to be sold, by theyard or piece to the planter. "[56] In *The Political Economy of Slavery,* Eugene Genovese indicts shippers (Phelps, Dodge & Co.), industrialists (David Rogerson Williams, a pioneer in cottonseed oil), textile magnates (George McDuffie and Whitemarsh Seabrook), and governors (Charles McDonald of Georgia, John Bell of Tennessee, Henry Watkins Collier of Alabama, John Motley Moorehead of North Carolina), and concludes that virtually everyone in the nation from small shopkeeprs to railroad giants profited in some way from slavery and cotton. Genovese makes no mention of Jews.[57]

One banking center where Jews might have been expected to play a prominent role in the nineteenth century was New York City. As far back as 1705, three Jews (Joseph Bueno, Abraham Lucena, and Samuel Levy) had been among sixty-six petitioners setting a standard of fair value for coins in the colony. Six more (Samuel Judah, Hayman Levy, Jacob Moses, Jacob Myers, Jonas Phillips, and Isaac Seixas) had urged tightening of the non-importation agreement in 1770. A decade later, several helped fund New York's first Lutheran church and the Bank of North America. In 1792, Isaac Gomez, Benjamin Seixas and Ephraim Hart were among the founders of the New York stock exchange.[58] By the time of the Civil War, several of Jewish banking houses had been established.[59] These included August Belmont, the American agent for the House of Rothschild,[60] Speyer and Company, and J. and W. Seligman and Company.[61] The firms of Kuhn-Loeb and Company, Lehman Brothers, J. S. Bache and Company, Landenburg, Thalmann and Company, and Goldman, Sachs and Company were established between 1865 and 1890.[62]

Jews figure prominently in New York investments and banking today,[63] but that was not the case in the antebellum period. There were no more than 40,000 Jews in New York City before the Civil War. Most of them lived in the squalor of lower Manhattan bordered by Canal, Elm, Mott and Bayard Streets, the traditional neighborhood of generations.[64] Coincidentally, both Belmonte (originally known as Schonberg) and

Seligman arrived unheralded from Germany in the same year—1837. Few Jews had been counted among New York's elite to that point. Only one Jew (Asser Levy) was able to contribute to the bond issue in 1664 designed to strengthen fortifications in the city. A decade later, Levy was estimated to be worth 2,500 florins ($1,000), a figure that paled when compared to the fortunes of gentiles like Frederick Phillips (80,000 florins), Cornelius Steenwyck (40,000), Nicolaes de Meyer (50,000) or Olof van Cortlandt (45,000).[65] A list of New York's wealthiest residents compiled in 1822 yielded such names as Aaron Burr, Henry Barclay, William Bayard, Colonel Henry Rutgers, Stephen Whitney, Orlando Harriman, Archibald Gracie, and John Jacob Astor (who left $20 million when he died in 1848). Of 673 names, only two were Jewish: Jacob Levy, director of the Bank of New York, whose personal belongings and property were reckoned at $30,000, and Jacob Mark of the commercial house of Jacob and Philip Mark, worth $20,000.[66] Circumstances did not really change over the next two decades. In 1845, the New York *Sun* issued a special pamphlet divulging the wealth of prominent New Yorkers. Of 961 individuals cited, four were Jewish: A. L. Gomez, a descendant of the colonial family described as "a true representative of the modern English gentleman in deportment and refined breeding"; David Hart, who had returned from New Orleans to live out his retirement; Hyman Solomon (sic), still trying to secure compensation for loans made during the American Revolution; and August Belmont, whose estimated wealth of $100,000 put him at the same level as the showman Phineas Taylor Barnum and the hairdresser Augustus Cavanna.[67]

For much of the remainder of the nineteenth century, New York remained a narrow-minded society dominated by a Gentile clique of Roosevelts, Bayards, Van Cortlandts, Rhinelanders, Schuylers, Verplancks, Clarksons, Beekmans, Brevoorts, Vanderbilts, and Van Rensselaers. That included business, too. Jews were not welcomed as employees of banks.[68] No Jewish establishments were mentioned in directories published by New York merchants between 1848 and 1869 listing banks, stock investors, insurance companies, or purchasing agents.[69] According to the *United States Register Blue Book for 1874,* no "Jewish" banks ranked among the top eight banks in New York City.[70] Of the 952 directors and officers listed for the city's seventy-six banks, perhaps forty-two (4. 4 percent) were Jewish.[71] None of the 105 officers of fire insurance companies were Jewish nor any of the officers of eleven marine insurance companies, which might have been expected to guarantee shipments of cotton or other materials from the South.[72] Examination of seventy-seven banks in Baltimore and Philadelphia yields identical results.[73]

Shunned by gentiles, Jews organized their own businesses and their own banks. They made money and returned it to the system which had enabled them to prosper. During the panics of 1837 and 1857 funds from the Rothschilds bolstered faltering debtor banks in the United States. Far from secretly undermining the Union cause, as is alleged in *Secret Relationship*, Northern Jewish bankers publicly embraced what they perceived as the cause of freedom. As Nathan Ausubel writes: "The Union Army and the United States Government leaned heavily on the Jewish bankers for financial assistance during the war. Especially distinguished in its devotion and helpfulness to the Northern cause was the house of Seligman which was run by seven liberal-minded brothers."[74] When withdrawals by Southern banks in the months before the outbreak of hostilities had depleted the U. S. Treasury, both the Seligmans and Belmont volunteered gifts to stabilize the government. The house of Seligman supplied the first uniforms worn by Union troops. And when Lincoln's government floated a bond issue (bearing 7. 3 percent interest) in 1862, the first major purchase of Union bonds, so necessary to sustain the war effort, came from the Frankfurt branch of the House of Seligman, which bought $200 million.[75] After the war, the firm continued to serve as fiscal agent for the government and the Navy Department.

The Great Moral Debate

There is no substance to claims that Jews in cities owned a disproportionate number of slaves, nothing to support the contention that Jews dominated the illegal slave trade, and nothing but slander when it comes to the charge of Jewish bankers secretly sabotaging humanitarian war efforts in the nineteenth century. Unquestionably, there were Southern Jews who publicly championed the slave system. There were politicians like David Yulee, Judah Benjamin, and David Kaufmann of Texas. There were rabbis like Morris Raphall of New York and the self-styled Reverend J. M. Michelbacher of Richmond who maintained that slaves were a gift from God.[76] There was the pseudo-scholarly study of "the Origins of the Black and Mixed Races" published by the Hebrew journal *HaNachash* telling that blacks were not the children of Adam, but slaves created to serve in the garden of Eden.[77] And there was the much publicized letter from Solomon Cohen, a Jewish planter from Savannah. As late as January 1866, he wrote:

> I believe that the institution of slavery was refining and civilizing to the whites—giving them an elevation of sentiment and ease and dignity of manners only attainable in societies under the restraining influence of a privileged class and at the same time the only human institution that could elevate the Negro from barbarism and develop the small amount of intellect with which he is endowed.[78]

None of the rabbis in the large Jewish communities of Charleston, Savannah, Richmond, and New Orleans dared speak out against slavery before the Civil War. One could also add the names of prominent Northern Jews who equivocated on this great moral issue. Among them were Isaac Mayer Wise of Cincinnati, founder of the Reform Jewish movement in America. A Democratic supporter (and an opponent of war), Wise endorsed the Dred Scott decision as late as 1858.[79] Max Lilienthal, also of Cincinnati, was a moderate Free Soiler who believed slavery was wrong in principle, but initially he, too, shied away from endorsing the crusade because of the tactics of some abolitionist radicals.[80] Isaac Leeser never made his personal views known but in November 1860 he did advise Jews who opposed the slave system to leave the South and move north.[81]

It would be just as simple to marshal the names of a legion of Jews who actively opposed the institution of slavery. Morris Schappes has written a series of unforgiving essays on the likes of Aaron Lopez and Judah Benjamin. But even Schappes notes the prominence of such Jews as Solomon Bush, Moses Judah, Gershom Seixas, Benjamin Nones, Solomon Etting, Napthali Judah, Solomon Simpson, Abram Dittenhoefer, and Rebecca Hart in early abolitionist societies.[82] Schappes contradicts his own statement that Jewish voices in the anti-slavery movement were "few and faint in 1853."[83] He salutes the Polish-born suffragette Ernestine Rose who said of West Indian emancipation in that same year 1853: "Slavery is, not to belong to yourself—but to be robbed of yourself."[84] He salutes Edward Kanter, Moses Solomons, and Myer Ostrander of Michigan, Adolph Loeb, Julius Rosenthal and Leopold Mayer in Illinois, all of whom signed petitions in 1854 opposing the introduction of slavery into Kansas and Nebraska. Schappes also highlights the achievements of Louis Dembitz of Louisville, a delegate to the Republican Convention in that city in 1856 who nominated Lincoln for the presidency; Moses Naar, founder of the Elizabeth, New Jersey Republican Club; Abraham Jonas, a friend and colleague of

Lincoln's from Quincy Illinois; Jonathan Nathan of New York, who brought Hamilton Fish to the Republican party that same year; and Moses Dropsie, founder of Dropsie College for Hebrew and Cognate Learning in Philadelphia, one of the organizers of the Republican party in Pennsylvania.[85] There were scores of others including Theodore Weiner (from Poland), Jacob Benjamin (Bohemia) and August Bondi (from Vienna) who fought with John Brown and the 5th Kansas Cavalry at Pottawatomie. Typical of so many European refugees from the failed revolutions of 1848, they were unable to speak the English language with clarity. But they were committed to the concept of individual liberty.[86] Another Jew from Bavaria, Louis Stix came to Cincinnati, prospered, and from the day he landed became "an outspoken opponent of all involuntary serfdom.[87] There were the five Jews in Chicago (George Schneider, Adolph Loeb, Leopold Kayer, Julius Rosenthal, and Michael Greenebaum) who blocked the capture of a runaway slave in 1853.[88] New York district attorney Philip Joachimson also intervened on behalf of fugitive slaves. There were Jewish publishers, scholars and rabbis who vigorously denounced slavery. Not just David Einhorn of Baltimore or Michael Heilprinn (mentioned above) but Moritz Loeb whose German-language journal *Morgenstern* in eastern Pennsylvania decried enforcement of the fugitive slave law in the years before the Civil War; Moritz Pinner, a scholar who circulated copies of Hinton Helper's *The Impending Crisis*; Moses Mielziner whose writings were subsequently published by his daughter Ella; and J. L. Stone of San Francisco who published *Slavery and the Bible or Slavery as Seen in its Punishment* in 1863. Shortly before coming to the United States to establish the center of Semitic Studies at Columbia University, Gustav Gottheil rebuked an audience in Manchester for the distortion and misapplication of Jewish law. Gottheil reminded that Exodus 21:16 prescribed the death penalty for kidnapping. How then, asked the professor-rabbi rhetorically, had a slave population come to exist in the republic? "Pity that the law of the Hebrew legislator had been forgotten or trampled underfoot by Christian nations professing to hold it as of divine authority. Had it been in force among them, the slave trade would have been put to an end with swift retributive justice."[89] From 1856 forward, Sabbato Morais, rabbi of Mikveh Israel in Philadelphia, denounced the institution of slavery in sermons.[90] In April 1861, Rabbi Samuel Myer Isaacs of New York exhorted readers of the *Jewish Messenger:* "Stand by the Flag! Whether native or foreign born, Christian or Israelite, stand by it, and you are doing your duty, and acting well your part on the side of liberty and justice."[91] And there was Rabbi Bernhard Felsenthal of Chicago, a strong Zionist and abolitionist who actively campaigned for the Republican candidate John C. Fremont in 1856, declaring that Jews were the heart and soul of the anti-slavery movement. "If anyone," said Felsenthal, "it is the Jew, above all others who should have the most burning and irreconcilable hatred for the 'peculiar institution' of the South." At Thanksgiving 1865, Felsenthal was jubilant that the "fetters of prejudices" had been broken and that Americans, with the help of God, had destroyed "an ugly and hateful institution."

There were Jews living in the South who risked their personal safety in ferreting blacks to safety like Joseph and Isaac Friedman in Alabama, Judah Touro in New Orleans, and Lazarus Straus in Talbottom, Georgia. And there were those who loved the South, yet recognized its flaws. Philip Phillips, a congressional representative from Alabama, boldly advocated emancipation to create a self-reliant generation for the new South. Leopold Weil wrote to his brother Josiah in May, 1861,"I think you know my feelings. We set free our slaves other than our body and household servants as soon as there were enough settlers to lease our lands. In truth, one man never has the right another man to own. But one man has no right to sell property to another and after he has invested the proceeds claim that the buyer is evil and should divest himself of his property. Yancey and the other fire-eaters, I do not hold with also. In this dispute for a man of reason is no place left. Of two evils, I choose the one more familiar."[93]

A similar letter was sent by Major Alfred Mordecai to his brother Samuel in June 1861. Governor Ellis had called for the native North Carolinian to return home, but Mordecai would not renounce his commission in the Union army. To him, Southern actions were revolutionary and useless, destined to create a horrible catastrophe. Wrote Mordecai: "I have no sympathy with the Southern feeling or doctrine…as lately inculcated. From very early youth, it seems to me from the time I first knew enought to reflect on it, I have regarded the evidence of slavery here as the greatest misfortune and curse that could havebefallen us, and it used to delight me to think what would probably be the prosperous condition of all the states north of South Carolina and Alabama, if they were as I once hoped they would be relieved from their incubus."[94]

There was little remorse in the articles published by Marx Lazarus, also of North Carolina, who came to Cincinnati in 1860. Once a devotee of the Utopian socialist Charles Fourier, Lazarus saw the question of slavery as another aspect of the struggle for free labor. He called for "Anglo-Normans" to recognize that blacks possessed many fine qualities. He urged Southern women to render the slave code a dead letter. He called for the end of the crucifixion of a martyr race. Said Lazarus: "Let all enjoy liberty." The relationship between blacks and whites should not be controlled by commands or threats "but mutual, spontaneous, polite, affectionate charm."[95]

Apparently many American Jews took Lazarus' message to heart. Perhaps as many as 15,000 enlisted in the ranks of the Union army. Another 10,000 joined the rebels. Two-thousand Jews came from the state of New York, another 1,000 from Illiniois. Eight were generals, twenty-one colonels, forty majors, 205 captains, and twenty-five surgeons. They were not simply numbers. Rabbi Liebman Adler and Arnold Fischel of Chicago became the first Jewish chaplains in the U. S. military. Dr. Jonathan Horwitz served as Surgeon General during this tragic period. Colonel Edward Solomon of Illinois, once of Schleswig-Holstein, later two-time governor of Washington state, commanded the line that stymied Pickett's Charge at Gettysburg in July 1863. Seven young Jews—Sergeant Leopold Karpeles at the battle of Wilderness, Sergent Benjamin Levy who entered the army as a sixteen-year-old drummer in 1861, Private Abraham Cohen at Petersburg, Sergeant Henry Heller at Chancellorsville, Sergeant Isaac Gause from the 21st Ohio Cavalry, Abraham Gruenwalt from Franklin Tennsessee, and Private David Orbansky at Shiloh—received the Congressional Medal of Honor fighting not for personal gain or privilege but for the principle of human equality.

Neither Saints nor Sinners

It is impossible to typecast all Jews in America in the nineteenth century as either apologists for the South or as freedom-loving abolitionists although some have tried. In the north, Judaeophobes denounced Jews as secessionists, Copperheads and rebels. In the South they were damned as "merciless speculators, army slackers and blockade-runners."[96] Some individuals or groups sided with the South. Others were Unionist partisans. Often, loyalties depended more upon the place of residence (itself an arbitrary decision) than conscience. Rabbi Korn has pointed out: "There was no such thing as an American Jewry or an American Judaism." No single Jew, not Rabbi Wise, Rabbi Raphall or

Rabbi Einhorn, presumed to speak for everyone. Unlike Baptists, Presbyterians, and other Christian sects which had national synods or councils, Jews had known no religious court since the days of Sanhedrin.

In the South Jews found themselves surrounded by true believers, not only of Christianity but of slavery. There were seventy-six synagogues in the entire United States in 1860 and only a handful were established below the Mason-Dixon Line (three in South Carolina, three in Maryland, two in Alabama, five in Louisiana, two in Missouri, one in Georgia).[97] The dominant population of the South, a mix of Anglo-American, Scots, Irish, German and French slaveholders, were, for the most part, attracted to "Evangelical Protestantism."[98] The Christian churches used the catechism to control slaves.[99] Baptist preachers in Georgia drilled into blacks the notion of sin.[100] "Episcopal orthodoxy" reigned in Eastern Virginia and the low country of South Carolina.[101] Synods and conferences like that of the Methodists held in New York in 1844 and Presbyterians in 1845 closed ranks and stifled dissent.[102] John Blasingame denounces the "loud silence" of Southern churches,[103] including the Catholic church,[104] on slavery. Such silence should not surprise. According to the annual report of the American Anti-Slavery Society for 1851, 16,346 ministers from Methodist, Presbyterian, Baptist, and Episcopalian congregations owned slaves.[105] As Unitarian minister Samuel May wrote: "The shepherds were being driven by the sheep." Of the 30,000 Christian pastors in the U.S., May declared, "not one in a hundred" openly denounced slavery or "lifted a finger to protect fugitive slaves."[106]

The Secret Relationship offers no general condemnation of the 19,816 Methodist, 5,034 Presbyterian, 2,123 Lutheran, 2,129 Episcopalian, 2,230 Congregationalist, 2,442 Catholic, 676 German Reformed, or 664 Universalist churches in America for their failure in confronting the great moral issue of the nineteenth century, but it does fault Jews, who had about as many congregations as the Swedenborgian or Moravian Christian sects in 1860.[107] As if anticipating such a denunciation, Rabbi Korn pointed out that Judaism was still in the stage of transition from a medieval, isolated faith tentative about expressing views on modern political problems (because its adherents had not been permitted to participate in the life around them) and a modern, confident religion which eventually would address specific personal and communal problems.[108] Korn acknowledged that individual Jews held a wide range of views. "But," he added, "there were probably fewer Jews, proportionately than other Americans at the extreme wings of the controversy, and more in the middle ground, because as immigrants they would naturally take less interest in political questions than in the problems of economic and social adjustment."[109]

Nowhere was this more evident than in the South. Virtually every writer has commented on the insecurity of Jews who came to this region. Myron Berman notes how Jews in Richmond were less willing to speak of secession: "Their priorities were directed toward acceptance in society and whatever support they gave to the Confederacy was a reaction rather than a catalyst of events."[110] Carolyn Lipson-Walker makes the same observation, calling the South a psychological entity, a state of mind. Quoting Laurence Fuchs, Lipson-Walker says, "To be a Jew in the American South is to be affected by the culture of the South." If this meant acceptance of slavery, so be it. "Due to deep-seated insecurities these Jews ardently adapted and adopted Southernisms."[111] Harry Golden is more blunt: "What there was in the Civil War South was anti-Semitism."[112] Such bigotry was manifest in grand juries which periodically condemned Jewish hoarding and black marketeering, newspaper accounts that blamed Jews for economic problems, demands for the removal of the Jew Benjamin from the Conferederate cabinet, the blocking of Jews from advancement in the military, and incidents of assault.[113] In such circumstances, it is unlikely that Jews could or would have taken the lead in abolitionism.

The choice for Jews in the South was either to emigrate or assimilate and accept the institutions of this society. Some, like Lazarus Straus did leave. Most, however, were timid and remained where they were, hoping to blend in without attracting much attention. Slavery actually provided a means of acceptance by white society. According to Stephen Hertzberg, "Blacks acted as a lightning rod deflecting prejudices which might otherwise have been manifested against Jews."[114] Rabbi Korn believes that if no Jews whatever had lived in the Union and Confederacy some other group—perhaps the Catholics, as in the recent days of Nativism, would have served as a major escape valve."[115] Slavery was rationalized as the law of the land. Slavery was also a most seductive institution. As Kenneth Stampp has written (quoting Cairnes), slave ownership had become "a fashionable taste, a social passion," a symbol of success like "the possession of a horse among the Arabs," offering the presumption of social position with the privileged class.[116]

Perhaps Eli Evans has expressed the dilemma of Jews in the South best. Strangers in a new land, they feared and respected white Southerners, whether the latter lived in big houses on plantations or in shanties with their broods of children. "The Southerners were not men to be challenged but men to avoid; only to sell to, never to confront." Theirs was a society based on fear and terror, the twin concepts that supposedly legitimated slavery. Jews could sense this violence "simmering just below the surface."[117] No matter how far these European newcomers progressed up the economic ladder, from packman to merchant, no matter how well their children interacted with White Christians, there was always alienation. Writes Evans: "No one crossed the Southerner in his native land. The Jew was conditioned to fear authority from the boot of the tsar and the emperor; he knew his place—the perpetual visitor, tentative and unaccepted, his primary concern to remain and survive. Subconsciously, the region would stake a claim to a corner of his soul, too; for he was white and he would acquisesce and become like them in many ways. Yet he was conscious of the differences, of the permissable boundaries of attitude and act, of just how far was too far, and protective enough of his own body and time to take on whatever colors were necessary to get through the day."[118]

Jews in the Slave Trade: A Libel Exploded

There were 697,681 slaves in America in 1790, 1,538,022 slaves in 1820. According to official census records, Jews owned 209 slaves in 1790, 701 in 1820.[119] During the formative years of the United States, then, when the import and sale of Africans was at its peak *Jews owned less than three-one hundredths of a percent, 0.03 percent of all the slaves in America.* Jews actually owned fewer slaves than native Americans, with whom the Nation of Islam feigns an alliance. According to James Oakes, the Cherokee nation owned 1,277 black slaves in 1824. Three Cherokee tribesmen owned fifty or more slaves in 1835. By 1861 the Choctaws and Chickasaws owned another 5,000, including Greenwood Leflore, chief of the Choctaws, who possessed more than 400.[120]

Despite living in societies where pressures to conform were great, Jews played a minor role in the development of slavery in the New World. Expelled or unwelcome in most European lands after the sixteenth century, wherever they roamed they encountered institutionalized discrimination of the sort embodied by the French Code Noir. Jews were not among the innovators of raiding parties off the coast of African, nor were they counted among the British noblemen who financed the first ventures to the Bay of Benin. There is no evidence to support the contention that "wealthy" English Jews underwrote insurance for slaving vessels in the eighteenth century. Quite the contrary, most Jews in Liverpool, Bristol, and London, like their cousins in Alsace or Poland, lived at the poverty level. A few Jews did speculate with the Dutch West Indies Company, no more than 10 percent of all investors. Their prosperity was fleeting, as in Brazil which the Dutch controlled for less than thirty years, in Guiana, Santo Domingo, or in other regions of Latin America where New Christians were ruthlessly hounded by the Spanish and Portuguese Inquisitions. It is a myth that Jews were responsible for the development of sugar plantations in the British West Indies. For the most part, Jews in Barbados, Curaçao, Jamaica were merchants.

Only a handful of Jews (Aaron, Lopez, Jacob Rivera, Gradis, Mendes) figured prominently in the transport of slaves across the Atlantic and even their participation is relatively small. Actual British government shipping records show that Jewish owners accounted for less than 2 percent of all slaves imported into Newport, New York, Charleston, and other port cities of North America in the eighteenth century. According to data of W. E. B. DuBois, none of the 200 illegal slavers operating off the coast of Cuba after slavery was declared illegal in 1808 were Jews.[121] Jews played no role in the import of more than one million African slaves to Brazil in the nineteenth century.[122] At no time were Jews among the major slave holders, planters, magnates, or traders in what was to become the United States. DuBois lists no Jews, not even Judah Benjamin, among the principal spokesmen of proslavery Southern conventions between 1855 and 1859.[123] According to public records, only one Jew, Solomon Polock of Philadelphia, ever served as an overseer on a plantation (near Mobile in the 1830s.)[124] As Frederick Bancroft has pointed out, 4 of 44 slave traders in Charleston were Jews, 1 of 12 in Memphis, and 3 of 70 in Richmond. There is an instance where the house of Mark, Benjamin and Henry Davis supplied an extraordinary number of slaves, 801 of 5,441 slaves, 15 percent, sent to New Orleans in the decade of the 1840s.[125] Otherwise Jews are virtually absent from the list of slave brokers who peddled hundreds of slaves in the ante-bellum period.

Karl Joseph Menn documented more than 5,000 of the great slave lords in America on the eve of the Civil War. Virtually all of these people were born in the South (less than 5 percent came from free terrritories).[126] Ten percent were women. At least 20 were Christian ministers (10 Baptists, 7 Methodists, 1 Presybterian).[127] There were no Jews among Menn's 16 greatest slaveholders. There were none listed among the 48 largest owners in Alabama, Georgia, Louisiana, or Mississippi.[128] None of the 15 greatest producers of cotton, none of the 12 largest rice planters in Georgia, none of the 12 largest sugar planters in Louisiana were Jews.[129] Wherever and whenever statistics are available, in Savannah, Charleston, Richmond, New Orleans, Jews are found to have owned less than 2 percent of the total number of slaves in a community. They generally owned fewer slaves, house slaves, and favored manumission more often than their Gentile counterparts. Concludes Rabbi Bertram Korn, "The history of slavery would not have differed one whit from historic reality if no single Jew had been resident in the South. Other whites would have owned slaves; other traders and auctioneers would have bought and sold them."[130]

16

Myth-Making and Afrocentrism

Mythopoeism: A Universal Function

It is ironic (but no accident) that Jews should play a prominent role in the mythopoeism of black nationalists. All peoples indulge in mythmaking, weaving tales that fit their conception of the universe. Folk legends are designed to help people cope with the forces of nature and, where possible, make them feel better about themselves. A reflection of religio-social behavior, the function of myth, as Theodor Gaster has put it, is "to translate the real into terms of the ideal, the punctual into terms of the durative and transcendental."[1] The myth may not be true. Indeed, it may be the exact opposite of fact as when an in-group is represented as good and virtuous or when history is radically emended to highlight the accomplishments of a particular empire. (As examples: the Romans prided themselves themselves on possessing such qualities as *gravitas, simplicitas, pietas,* and *fides.* The nineteenth-century Turkish emperor Abdal Aziz ordered the rewriting of all history texts to show that the Ottomans were victorious in all their wars.)

In a free world, people have a right to believe whatever they choose (in UFOs, secret schemes on the part of the CIA, that professional sporting events are fixed) however baseless and misguided these ideas may be *provided* such ideas not cause harm to or victimize other persons. Too often, the weavers of folk tales cross this line. Anxious to win adherents, they engage in falsification, scapegoating, and projection. Social theorists like Erich Fromm, Anthony Storr, Clyde Kluckhohn, and Rollo May have written extensively on the importance of "the Other" to a disaffected people. Normal men and women, worn down by stress or frustration ascribe failure to external forces beyond their means. Victims cope with their condition by projecting enemies "into a mythological world, inhabited not by human beings, but by demons, ogres and witches whose evil practices can only be combatted by equal malice on our part."[2]

Such, unfortunately, has been the case for some advocates of Afrocentrism. In the midst of the civil rights revolution thirty-five years ago, African-Americans seized upon the concept of "black pride" and, like so many other ethnic groups, sought to redscover their roots. Ultimately, this meant more than favoring afro hairstyles or dashikis, celebrating Kwanzaa and learning Swahili. About the same time, the newly independent states of Africa were proclaiming their own revolution in thought. Afrocentrism espoused the centrality of Africa in the evolution of the human species and the development of civilization. If anyone doubted that the black race "subjugated the white for 3,000 years," the Senegalese scholar Cheikh Anta Diop suggested they consider the black images portrayed on inscriptions at the tomb of Rameses III. Diop asserted the Greeks who succeeded Egypt in world power, were indebted to black Africa for much of their language, science, architecture, and philosophy. Like most African historians, Diop gave only passing regard to Jews whose inbreeding, he claimed, was evident in their "eyes, lips, nails and hair."[3] Diop's presentation, like that of most African Afrocentrists was made without rancor or intention of causing harm to Jews.[4] Afrocentrists in the United States have a different agenda. Finding a convenient scapegoat in the Jew and, borrowing imagery that had been refined in Europe over centuries, they transformed him into the mythic creature of wealth, power, and evil responsible for the woes of American blacks. For Michael Bradley, author of *The Iceman Inheritance* which claims whites are descendants of brutish Neanderthals, the Jews were the purest of the Caucasoid Neanderthals. If all whites were devils, the Jews were the worst of these demons.

The Dynamics of Mythopoeism: Blacks in the Slave Trade

The fable requires distortion, selective memory, and denial. The accusation of Jewish domination of the slave trade must be understood within this framework. Somehow the mythmakers omit mention of African participation in the slave trade. No legitimate scholar disputes the existence of slaves in African societies before the arrival of European whites. Just as in ancient Greece or Rome, they came through capture in war, kidnap, judicial decree (condemned because of witchcraft or debt slavery), or inheritance. There is a debate over the actual treatment of Africans owned by other Africans. Since the eighteenth century, when Olaudah Equiano (renamed Gustavus Vassa) left a memoir stressing how slaves were accepted into the family of their masters,[5] a number of writers have stressed the positive aspects of African slavery. For the most part house slaves, they were well-treated, knew no racial antagonism, and could even purchase their own freedom or become leaders in society.[6] Other historians paint a different, harsh picture of societies where recalcitrant slaves were subjected to "seasoning" (brutal regimens), women were sexually assaulted, and slaves with deformities or defects might be offered to the gods as human sacrifices.[7] Patrick Manning even reports a folk legend (not true, but told nonetheless) among the people of Benin, of slaves who were thrown into the sea and allowed to drown. Cowries would gnaw on their bodies and afterward the body would be dredged up and cowries collected.[8] The reality is that slavery in Africa was neither perpetual bliss nor torment, but as Peter Duignan and L.H. Gann of the Hoover Institute have noted, "subject to immense variations."[9]

The same might be said about the willingness of Africans to embondage other Africans to Europeans. At various times, rulers of Jolof, Asante, Oyo, Benin, and Congo opposed the export of their kinsmen.[10] Inevitably, though, avarice won out. As Lerone Bennett puts it, the slave trade was not merely a bishop in the Congo baptizing those in chains or a mother clinging desperately to her child, it was also "a greedy king raiding his own villages to get slaves to buy brandy."[11] When the first European slave traders arrived, African chieftains were not only willing but eager to trade captives for guns, textiles, tobacco, salt, jewelry, iron, kitchenware, and money, going so far as to campaign against rival tribes in the interior. According to an eighteenth-century observer, some kings were so avid for European merchandise they even attacked their own villages in the night.[12] What Manning calls "an addiction...[a] socially rational (if inhuman) activity,"[13] seduced the people of Mali and Songhay,[14] the Borno kings in Yorubaland,[15] the rulers of Dahomey,[16] and even the Oyos.[17] As Claude Meillassoux has written, "In Senegambia, in Dahomey, in Segu, in the Mawri country, in Anzourou, and so on, or wherever such wars were waged, the armies went into the field every year (sometimes more often) to capture the 'two-legged cattle'...which was to supply the kingdoms, the markets or the dealers."[18]

The trade proved so lucrative that at one point slave blacks outnumbered free in the Niger Valley by three to one.[19] The very first Portuguese slaver Antam Goncalvez who visited the coast between 1441–48 noted that the chief Ahude Meymam was eager to barter nine blacks and a little gold dust for things of little value.[20] In 1620 Richard Jobson reported on the exploitation of blacks by blacks on the Gambia River: "They [the Portuguese and mulattoes] doe generally imploy themselves in buying such commodities the countrey affords, wherein especially they covet the country people, who are sold unto them, when they commit offences...all which things they are ready to vent, unto such as come into the river, but the blacke people are broughtaway by their owne nation, and by them either carried or sold unto the Spaniard, for him to carry into the West Indies to remaine as slaves, either in their mines, or in any other servile uses, they in those countries put them to."[21] A few decades later, circa 1682, John Barbot, agent for the French Royal African Company, reported how common blacks and kings in Guinea sold not only prisoners of war but their own countrymen, "their own children, kindred or neighbors." Those who came from outside the tribal territories were "generally poor and weak, by reason of the barbarous usage, they had had in traveling far, being continually beaten, and almost famish'd; so inhuman are the Blacks to one another..."[22]

Pierre Verger describes Agaja, king of Dahomey between 1733 and 1740, as a kind of slaving genius who conquered rival tribes of Mahi, Boagry, and Juda and then demanded more substantial payments from the Portuguese.[23] The journal of slaver-turned-abolitionist John Newton is also punctuated with references to combinations of slaves, two, six, eight at times, brought to him in November 1750 by the African prince William Ansah Setarankoo or the King of Charra or the powerful mulatto Henry Tucker.[24] If such slaves were rejected by European traders because of health or other reasons, they were "murdered on the spot."[25] Slavery had become so essential to the African economy that some of the chiefs objected when the British tried to halt the trade. As late as 1838, King Anna Pepple of Nigeria argued, "It would affect myself and chiefs thus—first by stopping the revenues arising from slaves being exported; second, our own profit on slaves, and that arising from piloting slave ships up to and out of Bonny, would be lost." The king demanded annual compensation of $4,000. (He received $2,000.)[26]

In the summer of 1995 a group of African chiefs and queen mothers from Ghana embarked on a five-city tour of the United States. Their purpose was the ritual of *firhanka* (reunion) with American blacks. In reality, it was a mission asking forgiveness for the sale of Africans into slavery. As Kent State's George Garrison declared,"The people, our people, back in the early 16th century who participated in the slave trade initially may have been ignorant of the ultimate outcome of their

Myth-Making and Afrocentrism   225

actions, but as they began to see their brothers and sisters maimed, raped and butchered, many knew that had gone beyond the precipice of natural rights and values."[27] Peter Duignan and L.H. Gann rightly concluded: "The commerce in slaves did not depend solely on white men's greed. Slavery existed in Africa before the Europeans came, and it was the Arabs and the Africans who collected and sold the slaves. African traders and African chiefs supplied the human merchandise that was shipped to the New World. Long after Western European nations condemned the slave trade and sought to restrict it, Africans and Arabs continued to sell their fellows."[28]

Mythopoeism: Black Slaveholders in America

Black victimization of other blacks did not end in Africa. In the colonies, some free blacks, just as some Jews, became slaveowners. According to Eugene Genovese, a caste system permitting a class of black slaveholders existed in Brazil, Cuba, Jamaica, and Santo Domingo down to the nineteenth century.[29] Herbert Klein tells of a group of mulatto landowners who "possessed large plantations with numerous slaves" in Santo Domingo in the eighteenth century.[30] Lorenzo Greene tells of free blacks in New England—barbers, basketmakers, bakers, dockworkers—who, like Jewish merchants profited indirectly from the prosperity of the triangular trade.[31] Blacks helped build and sail the slave ships back and forth to Newport. There were even some black slaveowners in New England—one recorded in February 1756, six black families in Connecticut recorded as owning slaves in the 1790 census.[32] By 1830 the U.S. census listed twenty-one black residents of New York in possession of forty-one slaves.

As early as March 1654 the commonwealth of Virginia upheld the right of a wealthy black man, Anthony Johnson, to own slaves, a ruling subsequently upheld by all Southern states but Arkansas and Delaware.[33] Genovese allows that an indefinite number of slaves were owned by free blacks, but claims most were family members acquired for the purpose of manumission.[34] That was not always the case. When Charles Odingsells of Chatham County, Georgia, died in 1810 he left seventy-three slaves on three plantations to his children.[35] Other prominent black slaveholders in Savannah included Susan Jackson (who owned a number of slaves and twenty-three buildings when she died in 1860), Louis Mirault, a tailor who owned six slaves, Prince Candy, a cooper who owned seven, John Gibbon, a carpenter who owned five, and tailors

Andrew Morel and Joseph Dubergier both of whom owned several slaves.[36] According to the 1830 census more than 3,700 free blacks or blacks of mixed ancestry owned slaves. These included a number of black Virginians—Benjamin Taylor of King George's County who owned 71, William Brockenborough of Hanover with 46, Thomas Morton of Powhattan with 45, William Daniel with 32, Littleton Waller of Wythe with 28, and Curtis Carter of Richmond with 22.[37] We have already noted the families of Cyprien Ricard, Auguste Dubuclet, Antoine Decuir, Marie Metoyer, Charles Roques, Martin Donato, C.L. Comer, Thomas Dumford, who owned as many as 100 slaves in Louisiana. Even in Mississippi, a number of mulattoes and free blacks like Kitty Foote and Jordan Chavis of Vicksburg, William Johnson of Natchez, Nelson Fitzgerald and Robert McCary owned slaves.[38] Like Liliane Crete, Genovese has denounced their "pretensions to status" and reputation for cruelty.[39]

Apparently the pressure to conform led to more than slave ownership. In Georgia, Abraham Beasely, a free mulatto, was engaged in selling slaves before the Civil War.[40] Elsewhere, free blacks helped squelch slave rebellions in Louisiana in 1811 and Frederick, Maryland in 1814. Some fought alongside Southern whites in the Seminole War in Florida. A large number from Louisiana volunteered their services to the Confederacy in December 1860, writing the editor of the New Orleans *Daily Delta*: "The free colored population of Louisiana...own slaves and they are dearly attached to their native land...and they are ready to shed their blood for her defence. They have no sympathy for abolitionism; no love for the North, but they have plenty for Louisiana.... They will fight for her in 1861 as they fought in 1814–15...all they ask is to have a chance, and they will be worthy sons of Louisiana."[41]

In 1790 James Mitchell and four mulattos founded the Brown Fellowship in South Carolina. Affiliated with St. Philip's Episcopal Church in Charleston, the society emphasized "white blood, free ancestry and devotion to the tenets of the slave system."[42] Mitchell owned twelve slaves, Anthony Weston fourteen, William Penceel, Margaret Noisette, and the barber Thomas Inglis fifteen each. Samuel Holman, the son of a black slave trader from Sierre Leone, held forty on his Georrgetown plantation while William and James Pendarvis owned another 200 before the end of the eighteenth century.[43] Peter Desverneys, Colonel J.C. Prioleau's mulatto slave, secured his freedom and became "a brown master with the soul of a white slaver" after betraying the Vesey conspiracy.[44] By 1850,

John Garden of Colleton County owned sixty-two slaves at his Hermitage plantation, Margaret Harris forty-four on her Santee River rice plantation, Lamb Stevens thirty on his 500-acre Cherry Hill plantation.[45] In South Carolina, as elsewhere, free blacks invested in slaves for profit, employed bondsmen in the same back-breaking labor as white planters, settled debts with human chattels or bequeathed them to heirs, and even sold artisans if they were dissatisfied with their conduct.[46]

According to the 1860 census, six blacks in the South owned 493 slaves, an average of 82 per master, far exceeding the holdings of any Jew.[47] In Charleston, 130 black taxpayers were listed as owning 390 slaves. William Ellison managed to free himself, purchase a cotton plantation with sixty slaves from the governor of South Carolina, and become one of the wealthiest men in the state.[48] A member of a white church, Ellison joined the Brown Fellowship Society, and was buried in a white cemetery. Recently, one of Ellison's descendants, a physician Dr. Henry Ellison, offered an apology for his grandfather's behavior stating, "If you just look at it, he was an Uncle Tom, but he had to do what he did to survive because he lived in South Carolina and he ran a gin mill and everybody he dealt with was white. He had to be very particular and careful in how he dealt with them."[49]

Some African tribes sold their neighbors into slavery. A few blacks actively participated in the slave trade in the West Indies and in the American South. Does this mean that blacks were responsible for slavery? Absolutely not. It makes no more sense than to accuse African-Americans of supporting apartheid because they owned wedding bands which may have been molded of gold mined in South Africa. By the same token, it is improper to blame Jews, all Jews, for slavery, when there were very few in any American colony, when down to the 1880s, most Jews in the world trembled in fear of pogroms in the shtetls of Poland and Russia.

Mythopoeism: Slavery in the Middle East

Islam may be the fastest growing religion in the United States today. The *1996 World Almanac* (p. 646) estimates 5.5 million Muslims in this country, a phenomenal increase over the figure of 2 million cited in 1984. Many are blacks like Elijah Muhammad, Malcolm X, and Farrakhan drawn back to what they believe was the original faith of their West African ancestors and the universalist message of Islam which, unlike Christianity or Judaism in their way, condones neither slavery nor racism. Such images are only partially accurate. Islam was no more indigenous to the slave coast than any other region in Africa. Partisan scholars concede that no more than 10 to 15 percent of the slaves shipped to America in the ante-bellum period were Muslims.[50] Islam did not reach Hausaland till 1804, Masima until 1881.[51] Current estimates hold that 50 percent of the population of Gambia and Guinea, 20 percent in Guinea Bissau, Ivory Coast and Nigeria, 5 percent in Sierra Leone, Upper Volta, Ghana, and Cameroon, the traditional slave coast, are Muslim.[52] Exaggeration of ties to Islam has even led one pan-Africanist professor in the United States to remind his readers that Arabic is no more precious to blacks than Yoruba, Kiswahili, or Ebonics and that Mecca is outside of Africa. As Molefi Asante wrote," We out-Arab the Arabs as we have out-Europeanized the Europeans from time to time in names, dress, language, and belief."[53]

The product of seventh-century revelation in the Arabian desert, Islam was introduced into Africa by Arab missionaries. Muhammad was sent to "the Red and the Black" (i.e., all races of mankind.) Tradition has it that the first *muezzin* (caller to prayer), Bilal, was an African. The Quran prohibited enslavement of fellow Muslims and encouraged manumission for anyone who converted to the faith and could pray in Arabic before two witnesses and a *kadi* (Muslim judge). The collection of medieval fables known as the *1001 Nights* redounds with stories of loyal slaves willing to pray or sacrifice themselves for their masters. Islam offered variations of service—the *mudabbar* indentured through the life of a master and the *mukatib* who could work to achieve his freedom. Just as in ancient Rome, some emancipated slaves remained near their master, adopted his name and became clients.

Like Christianity and Judaism, the central tenet of Islam is love of one's neighbors. The application of that rule, for some, however, has proved difficult. Whether called Ethiopians, Zanj, mawla, Nubians or as-Sudan, blacks have been treated with scorn in the Arab world. The curse of Canaan was embellished in medieval times with tales of miraculous transformations of virtuous blacks who became white and whites being punished for evil deeds by becoming black.[54] In popular proverbs, slaves were stereotyped as greedy, avaricious, base, untrustworthy, impossible to educate.[55] Some of the most celebrated medieval sages ascribed negative attributes to Africans. Princeton scholar Bernard Lewis has recited a long list of these in two major studies—*Race and Color in Islam* and *Race and Slavery in the Middle East*.[56] According to Lewis, even those sympathetic to blacks were not immune to insensitivity. Al-Jahiz, writing in the ninth century, offers a picture of "cheerful, laughing" creatures with an innate aptitude for "measured, rhythmic dancing, for beating the drum to a regular rhythm." From Basra, this defender of blacks who may have been of African descent wrote: "The like of the crow among mankind are the Zanj, for they are the worst of men and the most vicious of creatures in character and temperament."[57] Several other black writers who lived through the formative years of the Arab empire engaged in similar exercises of self-hatred. Wrote the poet Suhaym (whose name meant "little Blackie"), "If my color were pink, women would love me, but the Lord has marred me with blackness." Another, Abu Dulam (d.776) commented: "We are alike in color; our faces are black and ugly, our names shameful."[58]

The Nation of Islam castigates Christians and Jews for removing blacks from their ancestral homeland, but the fact is that Arabs expanded the African slave trade 700 years before the Portuguese rounded the Bight of Benin.[59] When the fifteenth-century North African theologian Muhammad ben Abdal Kammal al-Maghili was asked by Askia Muhammad to advise on the obligations of princes, the Muslim scholar offered no comment on slavery which was "an accepted feature of Muslim/African living."[60] The renewed demand for pepper, palm oil, ivory, gold, and human slaves came from Moors and Turks at a time when feudalism had virtually eliminated the institution from West European civilization According to U.B. Phillips, "The impulse for the enslavement of Negroes by other peoples came from the Arabs who spread over Northern Africa in the eighth century."[61] Adds Alan Morehead, "No Arab regarded the trade as any more evil or abnormal than, presumably, a horse-dealer regards as evil or abnormal the buying or selling of horses."[62] John Laffin concurs, writing, "The slave trade was begun in Africa by the Arabs; they were the procurers and the suppliers.... The Arabs had many centuries of experience in slave trading before the European entrepeneurs saw money in the business, and they knew every trick of the trade—how to ambush Negroes, how to deceive them, where to find their hiding places."[63]

Such accusations might be dismissed as defensive reactions of Westerners, but the Afrocentrist Kwesi Otabil has also written: "'Afro-Arab unity' is the most pernicious hoax played on African culture and history to date. It is a hoax that economizes the macabre toll of Arab presence in Africa and serves further to conceal the painful fact that Arab hegemony is no less malign to the African world, than any other external hegemony."[64]

Arab slavers were trading in blacks as early as 641 when they arranged to import 360 Nubians per year into Egypt. Subsequently, they developed a number of special routes of supply. Berber and Tuareg tribesmen travelled from North Africa to the *souk er rekik* (market) in Timbuktu to purchase slaves. The Bournu people were bound and marched to Kuka near Lake Chad in Central Africa. Slave markets were so numerous in northern Somalia that the region across the Red Sea from Jiddah to Hodeida in Asir was nicknamed the Cape of Slaves. Between 1860 and 1873 more than four million blacks were peddled by traders in Sudan. In Sudan, an individual's wealth and respectability were reckoned in terms of the number of African slaves one possessed.[65] Those who were not used on plantations in Sudan were shipped to the Hejaz, Muscat and Oman, Zanzibar, the French Seychelles or Madagascar and India. Others were taken to Tripoli, Tunisia, and Zanzibar. The price of slaves and what they did was very much influenced by color. In East Africa where females usually brought a higher price than males, a black African cost less than a mulatto, dark Caucasian, or blond in that ascending order.[66]

R.W. Beachey described how an Arab slaver penetrated a community in the interior. He came simply at first, settling in a grass-roofed hut from which he flattered the chief with his goods and knowledge of Swahili. In return for cloth, beads, wine, and muskets the chief gave him ivory, then women, finally a regular supply of slaves. Over the years, the trader grew knowledgeable about tribal rivalries and, through his own armed band, managed to exploit them to his own advantage. As Beachey writes, "His 'ruga ruga were his dogs of war, ripe for carnage, revelling in blood, what could any individual chief or petty tribe do now?"[67] Most black slaves were prisoners of war, bartered by enemy chiefs for horses, poultry, sheep, spices, gunpowder or calico. As Leda Farrant writes,"The Arabs provided an ever-hungry market for slaves, they promoted and supported wars between chiefs, and by the power of their guns, controlled huge areas."[68] In 1949, a Hausa woman from Nigeria related: "There was always fear—war, war, war—and slavery."[69] Eyewitnesses described the brutality of raids conducted by dealers and their black mercenaries. Commenting on the Nyassa region in the 1860s, David Livingstone noted how "a deathlike silence" hung over depopulated villages. Houses were abandoned, broken by rain or destroyed by fire. Wild animals roamed farmland that once yielded corn or cotton. Corpses could be seen everywhere, including the streams where they floated as "feasts of crocodiles." Wrote Dr. Livingstone:

Wherever we took a walk, human skeletons were seen in every direction, and it was painfully interesting to observe the different postures in which the poor wretches had breathed their last. A whole heap had been thrown down a slope behind a village, where the fugitives often crossed the river from the east.... Many had ended their misery under shady trees—others under projecting crags in the hills—while others lay in their huts, with closed doors, which, when opened, disclosed the mouldering corpse, with the poor rags round the loins, the skull fallen off the pillow—the little skeleton of the child, that had perished first, rolled up between two large skeletons.[70]

Those captives who could be pacified with hippo-hide whips, butts and bayonets were chained or tied together for the march to market that might take anywhere from three days to three months. A nineteenth-century Bohemian traveller Ignatius Palme revealed how the slave masters controlled 300–600 persons in one convoy:

To avoid flight, a *sheba* is hung around the neck of the fullgrown slaves; it consists of a young tree about six or eight feet in length, and two inches in thickness, forming a fork in front; this is bound round the neck of the victim so that the stem of the tree presents anteriorly, the fork is closed at the back of the neck by a crossbar, and fastened *in situ* by straps cut from a raw hide; thus the slave, in order to be able to walk, is forced to take the tree in his hands, and carry it before him. No individual could, however, bear this position for any length of time; to relieve each other, therefore, the man in front takes the log of his successor on his shoulder and this measure is repeated in succession. It amounts to an impossibility to withdraw the head, but the whole neck is always excoriated, an injury leading often to inflammtory action, which ocassionally terminates in death.[71]

Palme went on to describe how blacks, thus shackled, were unable to sleep at night. Rarely given food, their bodies swelled with edema. If the heat of the day (a broiling 110 degrees) did not kill some, then the chill of the night would. Those whose wounds festered were left untreated. Here, too, there was a racial distinction between whites and blacks. Knowing that eunuchs would bring a higher price than a normal male at market, the traders castrated some of their prisoners. Blacks would have both testicles and penis removed; whites, however, would lose only the testicles. In either case, there would be nothing to cauterize the wound but hot sand.[72]

Knowing that they could turn a profit if only one of three or one of five of their charges made it to market, the slavers disregarded basic considerations for human life. The Africans were fed camel flesh and blood. Infant mortality was high and assaults against women common. If epidemics of yellow fever, cholera, plague, or smallpox swept through the chained gangs, the slaves would be abandoned, to fend for themselves. One European told of a scattered troop, resembling skeletons, which tottered along the road, their bony faces expressive of nothing but hunger. As a British observer from India described in 1873:

> One gang of lads and women, chained together with iron neck rings, was in a horrible state, their lower extremities coated with dry mud and their own excrement and torn with thorns, their own bodies mere frameworks, and their skeleton limbs tightly stretched over with wrinkled, parchment-like skin.[73]

After surviving death marches and transit marts, slaves might be piled into vessels bound for the island of Zanzibar, twenty-four miles off the coast of East Africa. Those who died or were unlikely to survive were left aboard ship to spare the trader from paying a dollar tariff on his useless property. Observers noted that none who died aboard ship were buried. They were either eaten by dogs or "thrown overboard to drift down with the tide, and if in their course they strike the beach and ground, the natives comoe with a pole and push them from the beach and thus their bodies drift on until another stooppage when they are served in a similar manner."[74] Survivors were peddled in several squalid squares. Troublemakers were chained by the neck to the ground outside the caliphal palace, to die exposed to the sun, their only food a broken gourd filled with gruel, flies, and other insects. Females as young as twelve years were pawed and poked by prospective buyers before being shipped off to harems.[75] Despite efforts of the British Royal Navy to stop the trade, 40,000 slaves were being imported into the caliphal port each year well into the twentieth century. In the reign of Hamed bin Mohammad, known as Tippu Tip, 5,000 Arabs on Zanzibar owned as many as 2,000 slaves each. They were untroubled by mortality rates to the island which ran as high as one in six. Small wonder that when Zanzibar gained its independence in 1962, there was a general massacre of Arab aristocrats.[76]

A harrowing 1,500-mile sea journey awaited the chattels of Zanzibar, the Ras Asir and Khartoum. Now they would be stuffed into fifty-foot long *dhows,* graceful but unstable river craft that carried them to Persia or India. If they were intercepted by British ships which prowled the ocean, all might be pitched overboard. And there was the constant threat of suffocation where:

> The Negroes are...stowed in the literal sense of the word in bulk, the first along the floor of the vessel, two adults side by side, with a boy or girl resting between or on them, until the tier is comlete. Over them, the first platform is laid, supported an inch or two clear of their bodies, when a second tier is stowed, and so on until they reach above the gunwale of the vessel. Those of the lower portion of the cargo that die cannot be removed. They remain until the upper part are dead and thrown over.[77]

Perhaps one-tenth of those who set out from the home village reached their final destinations. Some of the lucky few who survived did become house servants, butchers, or artisans. Most, however, were used in forced labor. As in the West, slaves were put to work in sugar fields and rice paddies, on galleys, and in caravans. In the Persian Gulf, some were forced into the water, to be trained as pearl divers. Slaves carried supplies, but no weapons, for the army. They extracted salt from underground mines. Periodically, like the 300,000 Zanj who lost their lives in Iraq in the ninth century, they revolted against this gruelling and demeaning servitude.

Slavery existed in the Islamic world and with a decided color bias. According to some estimates, between 1510 and 1865 12 million Africans may have been uprooted from their sub-Saharan homes by Arabs.[78] Various shaykhdoms in the Middle East and Africa continued to practice slavery after 1926 when most civilized nations subscribed to an international convention outlawing the practice. French ethnologist Germaine Tillion, writing for UNESCO in 1960, estimated that one-sixth of the Kounta tribe of Mauretania was slave. Another UNESCO study in 1965 stated that perhaps as many as three-fourths of the Tuaregs of West Africa, some 465,000 people, were not free. In 1963, a French schoolteacher, Andre Chalard, reported how 2,000 Algerians, including a seven-year-old child, had been sold into Mauretania.[79] The trade moved both ways. In 1976, Eldridge Cleaver returned a self-imposed exile in Algeria and told how he had seen black Africans living in bondage. Said Cleaver:

> Many Arab families keep one or two black slaves to do their menial labor. Sometimes they own an entire family. I have seen such slaves with my own eyes. Once I pressed an Algerian official for an explanation of the status of these people, and he ended up describing a complicated form of indentured servitude. The conversation broke up when I told him that it was nothing but a hypocritical form of slavery.[80]

Chattel slavery was legal in Guinea till 1955, in Cameroons and Nigeria until the 1960s, Saudi Arabia until 1962, Mauretania until 1980. Whatever euphemism is employed, the trade continues in house slaves, white slave girls, and field hands. No one knows for certain how many slaves there may yet be from Morocco to Yemen. The figure may be as high as 30 percent in some cities.[81] Back in 1966, the Italian journalist Fabrizio Dongo reported that Arabs in the Sudan continued what might be called "their national sport, hunting slaves."[82] Western observers deplored the continuation of slave auctions in Jibouti, Dubai, and Oman.

In 1972, Roy Pinney estimated there were 250,000 slaves in Saudi Arabia alone, a figure sustained by Andrea Rosenberg of Anti-Slavery International in 1979.[83] In September 1991 this London-based group claimed that more than 55 million children (including shepherds in Sudan, girl domestics in West Africa, underaged textile workers in Turkey, Pakistan and Bangladesh) were, in reality, slaves. In April 1992, Africa Watch, a Washington-based research group, complained that there were still more than 100,000 slaves in Mauretania, a figure borne out by *Newsweek* in its special study of slavery in May of that year. *Newsweek* also charged that slavery was "making a comeback" in Sudan.[84]

Most of the old slavers have disappeared. Hammurabi, the pyramid builders, Roman taskmasters and medieval Christians who justified involuntary servitude. The institution persists across one stretch of the world. It survives in the form of sham adoptions, debt payoffs, marriage and concubinage, as well as outright serfdom. In 1975, Don Black of the Baptist Union noted, "If you think that slavery went out with Wilberforce, you are wrong. Terribly wrong. It didn't. It is still very much alive, with all the horrors of the slave trade."[85] As one Tanzanian scholar told John Laffin ten years ago: "We thought the Arabs had changed. We hoped that they had reformed. But the slaver mentality obviously lasts longer than the slave mentality. We slave people were anxious to forget the terrible past, but the past was not terrible for the Arabs so of course they remember. They still want slaves. All that has changed is their method of getting them."[86]

When Minister Farrakhan was recently asked by reporters about the continued existence of slavery in Sudan and Mauretania, his response was, "If slavery exists, why don't you go as a member of the press? And if you look inside of the Sudan and if you find it, then you come back and tell the American people what you found." In the spring of 1996, two reporters from the Baltimore *Sun* did just that. They travelled to the village of Manyiel and purchased two young brothers in a slave market. They also reported that words like "master," "freedman," and "concubine" were common in the Sudan. According to Sharon Broussard, associate editor of the *Cleveland Plain Dealer* (July 24, 1996, p.11B) the United Nations, the U.S. State Department, human rights groups like Pax Sudan and the NAACP have all denounced the Sudanese government for its promotion of the institution. Wrote Broussard, who is black, "Farrakhan now has the proof he demanded. So far, his silence is deafening."[87]

17

Blacks and Jews: An Alliance of Convenience

Together in a St. Augustine Jail

The Secret Relationship is relentless in its exaggerations of Jewish activity in the slave trade before the Civil War. It is equally unforgiving in its rendition of black-Jewish relations following Reconstruction. In this telling, Southern Jews supposedly helped foster the Jim Crow system. Feigning friendship, Jewish merchants sapped blacks of their little cash by overpricing goods and selling cheap, shoddy merchandise. Usurious Jewish bankers helped design land laws that kept sharecroppers in a perpetual state of poverty. Jewish slumlords victimized black residents in rat-infested tenements. The Jewish press conducted a campaign against blacks who, they said, were unfit for citizenship. Jewish producers who controlled radio, television, and film ignored black achievements or deliberately portrayed them in the most negative manner. Jews blocked black advancement in public sector jobs. Jewish schoolteachers practiced cultural genocide ("menticide" said one critic) against black schoolchildren. Jewish communists, in league with the Soviet Union, aimed to subvert American society. Jewish Zionists were working closely with the racist overlords of South Africa to subjugate blacks in that country. Jewish gangsters, cooperating with the CIA, were responsible for the cocaine that flooded urban centers over the past twenty-five years. Jewish doctors secretly introduced the AIDS virus into the cities with a view toward killing blacks. No accusation, no conspiracy seems too bizarre in circles which claim that Africans, and not so-called Jews, were the original Children of Israel.

The polemic dismisses the positive interaction of these two minorities over the past century. The Russian Zionist Leon Pinsker linked the destinies of the two peoples in his pamphlet "Auto-Emancipation" which appeared in Berlin in 1882. A group of Boston Jewish lawyers, including Louis Brandeis, helped establish the National Association for the

Advancement of Colored People in 1909. Louis Marshall of the American Jewish Committee argued cases on behalf of the NAACP before the Supreme Court as early as 1923. Later on, Jack Greenberg, head of the Legal Defense Fund of the NAACP, assisted Thurgood Marshall and Roy Wilkins in legal battles resulting in the case of Brown vs. *Board of Education of Topeka* in 1954 and several Jews (Joel and Arthur Springarn, Kivie Kaplan) would serve as chairmen of the NAACP. Throughout this century, the National Council of Jewish Women published articles opposing racial bigotry. The American Jewish Congress championed job training programs for blacks and the Jewish Labor Committe worked to eliminate discrimination in unions.[1] Chicago philanthropist Julius Rosenwald underwrote the creation of the Urban League in 1910. The founder of Sears, Roebuck also contributed more than $3,000,000 to black colleges and was the financial backer for 5,000 one-room public schoolhouses that supplied education to blacks in the rural South and Native Americans on reservations between 1910 and 1932.[2] Rabbi Benjamin Goldstein in Montgomery spoke out on behalf of the nine Scottsboro youths accused of raping two white women in the early 1930s. Rabbi Goldstein, who raised money for their defense, was labelled a communist and had to leave for New York City. Rabbis like Jacob Rothschild and Charles Martinbad of Atlanta, William Silverman of Nashville, Benjamin Schultz of Clarksdale, Alabama, Perry Nussbaum of Jackson, and Emmett Frank and Malcolm Stern in Virginia were among the vanguard of the Civil Rights struggle in the 1950s and 1960s.[3]

According to Samuel Murrell of the College of Wooster, Jews provided almost 75 percent of the funding for the Congress of Racial Equality (CORE), the Southern Christian Leadership Conference (SCLC) and the Student Nonviolent Coordinating Committee (SNCC).[4] Other writers estimate that two-thirds to three-quarters of the idealistic college students who risked personal injury as freedom riders through the South between 1961 and 1963 were Jews.[5] Yarmulkehs were so commonplace they came to be known as "freedom hats." Three young men travelling together in Neshoba County, Mississippi in 1964—James Cheney, a black, and Andrew Goodman and Michael Schwerner, both Jews—were killed by Klansmen who made no distinction as to color or religion. Rabbi Abraham Heschel, the leading Jewish philosopher in America, linked arms with Martin Luther King in the 1965 march to Selma, Alabama. And forgotten somewhere in all the rage of the *Secret Relationship* was the response of Jews in June 1964, the same month when Schwerner, Goodman, and Cheney were murdered. Reverend King called for support of a demonstration against segregation in St. Augustine, Florida, the oldest city in the United States. Seventeen rabbis joined Dr. King and were jailed with him. From their cells in the middle of the night, they issued a manifesto which read:

> We came to St. Augustine mainly because we could not stay away. We could not pass by the opportunity to achieve a moral goal by moral means—a rare modern privilege—which has been the glory of the non-violent struggle for civil rights.
>
> We came because we could not stand silently by our brother's blood. We had done that too many times before. We came in the hope that the God of us all would accept our small involvement as partial atonement for the many things we wish we had done before and often.
>
> We came as Jews who remember the millions of faceless people who stood quietly, watching the smoke rise from Hitler's crematoria. We came because we know that second only to silence, the greatest danger to humanity is loss of faith in humanity's capacity to act.[6]

Such declarations once were welcomed and reciprocated by black leaders like Booker T. Washington, George Washington Carver, Walter White, W.E.B. DuBois, Roy Wilkins, Whitney Young, Bayard Rustin, James Weldon Johnson, and Roy Innis. Somehow, the voices of reason have been replaced by those who spew invective. A study of New Yorkers undertaken by the American Jewish Committee in 1992 revealed that 63 percent of the blacks surveyed believe Jews have too much influence in city life and politics.[7] The ADL conducted its own nationwide survey in 1992, putting a series of questions about Jews to a random sampling. Based upon the frequency of hostile responses, individuals were rated as not anti-Semitic, moderately anti-Semitic, or most anti-Semitic. Thirty-nine percent of whites and 14 percent of black respondents fell into the not anti-Semitic category; 20 percent of whites and 37 percent of black respondents were rated as most anti-Semitic.[8] A *Time Magazine* poll in Feburary 1994 revealed that 28 percent of blacks surveyed believed Jews wielded too much power in this country. [9]

A survey conducted by Lou Harris for the National Conference of Christians and Jews, released in March 1994 yielded similar results. The Harris poll indicated that 54 percent of blacks felt Jews would choose money when it came to choosing between people and money (as opposed to 27 percent non-Jewish whites). In the same survey, 43 percent of American blacks felt Jews had too much control over business and the media, and 45 percent believed Jews were "too preoccupied with their history of persecution, such as the Holocaust."[10] Chicago's National Opinion Research Center (NORC) which has been monitoring anti-Semitism for over thirty years suggests that 40 percent of whites and 58 percent of blacks think Jews use shady business practices.While some studies suggest anti-Semitism is decreasing in the black population, it is disturbing to note that nearly one-quarter of African-Americans under thirty subscribe to negative views of Jews and that education has had little impact on reversing this trend.[11]

Almost the Same and the Other

Concern about the collapse of a black-Jewish alliance in this country presumes, of course, that such a bond once existed. While conceding there have been some common interests, Jacob Neusner flatly declares, "There is not now, and there never has been, a special relationship between Jews and blacks."[12] Jonathan Rieder of Barnard College agrees that the two peoples never enjoyed what he terms a "symbiotic merger." Even if there had been a connection, says Rieder, it need not have been one of "unconditional love."[13] Calling the bonds between blacks and Jews "false comity," Leon Wieseltier says, "there is no law of American history according to which all its minorities will be friends."[14] Shelby Steele maintains whatever kinship the two groups felt stemmed from "a brotherhood of out-sidedness" and the common experience of rejection which carried with it an undercurrrent of shame. "But shame," wrote Steele, " is an intolerable feeling. We always distance ourselves from it, deny it, or project it onto others. I think Jews and blacks today distance themselves from each other and their kinship as a way of distancing from the shame implied in that kinship."[15]

History abounds with examples of alliances that were rooted in expedience and self-interest rather than affection. As one example, during the Holocaust, Jews and Gypsies were persecuted and murdered. Occasionally, they sympathized and even worked with one another against the common foe, but they never developed a particular fondness for one another inside or out of Nazi concentration camps. At the same time, in the United States, in the summer of 1942, L. D. Reddick was pointing out to readers of *The Negro Quarterly* that there was substantial "anti-Negroism" among Jews and anti-Semitism among blacks.[16] When World War II ended, psychologist Kenneth Clark offered a sobering warning to leaders of the Central Conference of American Rabbis who had convened a symposium on "The Negro in America." Said Clark: "It is naive to assume that because Negroes and Jews are each in their own way oppressed and insecure, this will necessarily lead to a feeling of kinship and understanding." Insecurity might well intensify ethnocentrism and bigotry, as each group sought to identify with the majority. And generalities laced with moral sentimentality would not bring about desired social change, said Clark.[17]

In February 1991, Julius Lester, a black Jew who teaches Judaic and Middle East Studies at the University of Massachusetts, examined the bonds that existed between Jews and African Americans for a Schermer Lecture audience at Youngstown State University. Both peoples, he noted, originated in slavery. Western civilization regarded Jews and blacks as outsiders and had wrenched them from their homelands. Forced to live in diaspora, both were physically separated or segregated from their masters. Both were stereotyped (Jews as minions of the devil, blacks with sexual licentiousness) and condemned by the majority white community for their very existence. Jews and blacks were reduced to pariah status by name-calling, social and economic ostracism, and physical attacks (pogroms and race riots.) According to Lester, some of the victims in both groups responded to abuse with laughter, others with self-hate, still others by attempting to pass (assimilate) into the dominant culture. As long as both peoples were perceived as victims, the bonds were strong. Before the Civil War, blacks idealized the biblical Jews. And well into the twentieth century, when a Jew like Leo Frank was lynched in Georgia and millions more murdered in European ghettos, blacks could sympathize with them. Jews responded by participating in the civil rights movement in what can ony be termed disproportionate numbers.

All was not harmony, however. According to Lester, there were major differences in the black and Jewish experiences in America. For the most part, blacks were brought to this country in chains. No matter how severe the anti-Semitic persecutions of Europe, Jews arrived as free men and women. Jews discovered that color, not religion or some other view of race, was the principal source of division in America, and that as whites they could be accepted in society. Jews divided on the slavery issue, just as some blacks ignored problems of anti-Semitism. The economic and social gap between the two peoples became greater, in part because Jews brought with them their literature, culture, religion, and education. Jews prospered, lived longer, and left decaying neighborhoods to blacks. Interaction between the two peoples declined, except where Jews were landlords, merchants, social workers, school teachers, authority figures in black community organizations. Blacks resented this one-sided relationship ("How many blacks serve on the board of the ADL?" asked Lester) and began demanding control of neighborhood institutions. As far back as 1938, residents of Harlem boycotted businesses that were not owned or operated by local blacks. Over the next two decades their resentment toward Jews was articulated by Congressman Adam Clayton Powell. When government promises of jobs and better living conditions did not materialize, black rage boiled over.

A similar assessment of black-Jewish relations was offered by Paul Berman following the appearance of Khalid Abdul Muhammad at Kean State College in New Jersey in 1993. Writing for the *New Yorker* in February 1994, Berman posed, then answered, a number of rhetorical questions: "Have the Jews and the blacks been fighting all this time over political spoils? Not especially. Over economic interests? Some peope think so, but economic competition between blacks and Jews is strictly marginal. Has it been a war over neighborhoods? Sometimes but not consistently. Is it a war between parties, Republicans and Democrats? Or between liberalism and conservatism? Not even that, for at the end of the day the blacks and Jews have trooped off to the polls and in one national election after another they have, more often than not, voted for the same candidates. So what is it—this fire that burns without logs and never goes out?"[18]

Berman suggests the answer may lie in a concept that he calls "the Almost the Same." He posits that blacks regard the Jew not so much as the Other but as a "false brother." Attempting to be fair, he divides the article into Jewish and black mindsets, trying to show how each perceived the situation. He recites all of the efforts made by Jews on behalf of black rights, but notes that these were done by "a handful of people" with their own advancement in mind. Despite their history of persecution, American Jews treated blacks with snobbishness, "a lack of genteel courtesy," or outright hostility (use of the derogatory term *shvartze* was widespread.) Parsimonious Jewish landlords and shopkeepers oppressed their tenants and customers. Jews were responsible for the breakup of the political alliance by opposing affirmative action and embracing Ronald Reagan and the conservative agenda. Partisans of the Zionist entity in the Middle East, Jews were not really brothers in the worldwide struggle against "global imperialism." They weren't even a genuine minority. "You look like an oppressed minority," writes Berman speaking for the black viewpoint, "But it is I who belong to the true minority. You are yourself part of the oppressive majority." Still worse, the black was saying,"I am you and you are an imposter. Your history is mine, not yours; and, insofar as people think that you are you, it is because you have stolen my identity. You are more than an enemy; you are a demon. Only Satan could do what you have done!"[19]

Thirty Years in a Not So Great Society

Berman's conclusions were not so dissimilar from those offered by Murray Friedman in his recent study *What Went Wrong? The Creation and Collapse of the Black-Jewish Alliance* (1995). Friedman, onetime vice chairman of the U.S. Commission on Civil Rights in Washington D.C., reminds that at one time most American Jews were poor and lived next to blacks in the nation's inner cities: "They shared many of the hopes and aspirations of urban blacks. Both blacks and Jews were largely excluded from the business and social insitiutions that dominated city life. That is no longer true. In the years after World War II, Jews made remarkable gains. Great numbers moved to the suburbs or to more protected areas of the cities, and in so doing, they left most of the blacks behind."[20] According to Friedman, now head of American Jewish Studies at Temple University, some Jews embraced neoconservatism at precisely the moment that government was cutting social programs and the black community, most of all, was experiencing the pain of the widening gap between rich and poor, as well as an epidemic of crime, teenaged pregnancies, and drug use. The upsurge of black anti-Semitism in the 1970s and 1980s, then, could be attributed to a sense of abandonment by a group that had experienced similar pain. As Cornel West declared, "black folk" had higher expectations of Jews.[21]

Bayard Rustin once noted that when social and economic conditions in a minority community deteriorate, the victims blame not so much the racists and reactionaries responsible for creating the conditions, but those nearby who worked to better conditions and failed. Rustin was commenting on the resentment manifest against moderate black leaders like himself and actual victims of urban riots that erupted after 1964, many of them Jewish merchants who serviced the inner city. Thirty years later, Henry Louis Gates was to lament that the "original sin" of Jews was their very involvement in black causes.[22] Once more, none of this was new. Ten years before Lyndon Johnson launched many of his Great Society programs, Gordon Allport predicted these very problems in a heterogeneous society. Conflict was inevitable where there was rapid social change, competition between groups, and "vertical" economic movement.[23] Allport sugested that victims of discrimination could react to their condition with passive acquiescence, obsessive concern, clowning, slyness and cunning, self-hate, or hatred against an out-group (e.g., scapegoating.)

During the 1960s some blacks adopted this last mechanism for coping with unfulfilled expectations. What Allport terms the "dynamics of prejudice" became operative in the urban ghetto. A decade after Brown vs. Board of Education of Topeka, frustration, fear, anxiety, and economic insecurity gave way to envy, anger, and aggression.[24] As Arnold Forster and Benjamin Epstein of the ADL wrote, "Inevitably, optimism gave way to frustration. coupled with a growing militancy, this frustration brought to the fore increased resentment of whites (including Jews) for the record of unkept promises. Accompanying the understandable frustration, anger, and hopelessness was the development among some blacks of nationalist and separatist sentiments."[25] According to Forster and Epstein, accessibility to mass media, indeed, the fascination of television and radio with shock characters, transformed street corner orators into national celebrities.[26] Many of these proved to be anti-Semites and the repetition of their rhetoric seemed to validate their message. In Washington, D.C. the Blackman Development Center headed by Hassan Jeru-Ahmed warned of an international Jewish conspiracy and shrilled that "black America lived for years as the blind pawn in this fantastic and deadly game, this conspiracy of Jews is playing to control America."[27] In New York, Leroi Jones (Amiri Baraka) recited anti-Jewish poetry on the air waves while the African Teachers Association lamented the death of minds of black children at the hands of Jews who dominated and controlled the educational bureaucracies of the public school system. In Los Angeles, Ron Karenga mocked the blood of "the dead Jew" Jesus. In San Francisco, the Black Panther party equated Zionism ("kosher nationalism") with imperialism and fascism.

There were 329 riots in 257 American cities during the most intense period of urban upheaval between 1964 and 1968. Despite the existence of numerous federal programs, hundreds of studies and recommendations by social theorists, efforts by community leaders, and the outlay of more than one trillion government dollars, street violence erupted in Philadelphia (where twenty-two Jewish merchants were slain between 1968 and 1972), Detroit (for years vandals have used Beggars' Night as an excuse to engage in arson), New York (tensions between blacks and Hasidic Jews resulted in the Crown Heights riots of 1991), Miami and St. Petersburg (the shooting of nonwhites by white policemen served as the sparks in both cases), and Los Angeles (where the Rodney King riot resulted in the deaths of fifty persons and more than $500 million in damages). Thirty years after the launching of the Great Society, little seems to have changed within the black community. In fact, the situation in America's inner cities may be worse today than thirty years ago. Unemployment among blacks is double the national average. There are fewer two parent families today than in 1965 when Daniel Patrick Moynihan did his study of inner city life in America. More young black males die of gunshot wounds than of any other cause. Educational, employment, and residential opportunities are still limited. While blacks consitute 11 percent of the national population, it is estimated that African Americans will make up 50 percent of the HIV cases in America by the turn of the century.[28] Forty years after Brown vs. Board of Education of Topeka, racism is still rampant in America. For some in the nation's ghettos, there is only hopelessness and despair. Others, like Farrakhan and Jeffries, seek to channel frustration and rage against society's traditional other—the Jew.[29]

The Contest for Community Control

A method of coping with victimization is alleviation, engaging in rational discourse with one's oppressors in the hope that persecution or discrimination will cease. To be effective, alleviation requires an adversary who is rational and sensitive. With few exceptions (the British in India as one example) there have been few such oppressors in history. A more familiar survival mechanism is directing rebuke upon a group in society that already is viewed unfavorably. By this means, even enemies may become allies. The small sect of Christians that struggled to survive in the first century found it much more effective to construct polemics against Jews than Romans whom they sought to convert. Thus the book of John, canonized decades after the reforms of Pauline Christianity, specified Jews, not Romans, as the principal villains in the passion story. It would be equally counterproductive for African Americans polemicists to flog the dominant culture of America—to angrily and repeatedly remind white Christians of their responsibility for slavery and racism. Just as in Rome, Jews were themselves a marginal people in American society community. And as Benjamin Ginsberg and Cornel West both have noted, Protestant fundamentalism, with its stock charges of betrayal and Christ-killing, supplied a base of anti-Semitism within black and white communities.[30]

Those seeking justification for black animosity toward Jews can find any number of real or imagined excuses. Anthropologists speak of the territorial imperative, the instinct of humans, as well as animals to stake out proprietary claim to a specific area. Immigrant groups arriving in the United States did the same, settling in ramshackle tenements in the inner city before they could afford to move on to newer and better accommodations in the suburbs. Some ethnic groups (the Irish in Boston, Italians in Philadelphia, Slovenes in Cleveland) settled down and declined to move, preferring to maintain their churches and rebuild the community. Oscar Handlin and Nathan Glazer both have pointed out that the Irish especially were opposed to abolition and black advances in housing, education, and employment in the north.[31] With a few exceptions (Squirrel Hill in Pittsburgh), Jews moved up and out from New York's Lower East Side for Brooklyn, then Long Island, in Chicago from Maxwell Street for Lawndale.[32] Jews in Los Angeles vacated Dorchester Heights for Beverly Hills, those in Cleveland went from 55th and Quincy, to East 105th, then Cleveland Heights, Shaker Heights and Beachwood.When they left the old neighborhoods, Jews rented or sold to blacks, many of whom had emigrated from the South after 1914, 1930, or 1941. What was unthinkable in other ethnic enclaves, integration, Jews considered ennobling, the embodiment of American liberalism. For their part, African Americans saw only neighborhoods hastily abandoned by Jewish residents and deteriorating buildings still owned by avaricious Jewish landlords. Thirty years ago, James Baldwin expressed the collective rage of "colored" tenants in Harlem who paid exorbitant rents to "terrible" landlords, many of whom were Jewish. And for what? Buildings that were falling apart and infested with roaches and rats, apartments that were either too cold or too hot, marked with broken windows and ceilings, stopped toilets and sinks, and piled high with garbage, "all questions of life and death for the poor."[33]

Blacks had little contact with Slovaks, Hungarians, Poles, or Italians who regarded them with contempt and physically defended their territory from outsiders. But African Americans came in contact with Jewish merchants, grocers, cleaners, bars, and recreation centers on a daily basis. Before the 1960s, many of the corner convenience stores in the inner city were operated by Jews. Occasionally, Jews permitted purchases on credit, even gave out articles free to the needy.[34] They deluded themselves in thinking this might earn them the affection of their customers. Once again, James Baldwin evoked painful memories of his youth as he recalled the neighborhood grocer ("being in debt to him was much like being in debt to the company store"), the butcher ("we certainly paid more for bad cuts of meat than other New York citizens), the local clothier ("we bought our clothes from a Jew and, sometimes, our second hand shoes"), the pawnbroker ("perhaps we hated him most of all") who were Jews. In fact, Baldwin fantasized that most, if not all of the merchants along 125th Street were Jewish ("I don't know if Grant's or Woolworth's are Jewish names").[35] Even after riots in 1935 forced the owners to employ some blacks in their stores, residents in Harlem continued to complain of insults, high prices, and the shoddy quality of goods in Jewish stores and wondered why economic control of their neighborhoods was not vested in their own kind. The anger persisted even after Jews closed their shops in the inner city. During the riots in Cleveland's Hough District in June 1966 and the Rodney King riots arsonists attacked first and foremost the business establishments of whites, Jews, Koreans, and Arabs. Consistent with the notion of territorial claims, Jonathan Rieder calls the Crown Heights clash between Hasidic Jews and Blacks in 1991 "tribal" warfare.[36]

The landlord and shopkeeper were only two sources of friction between Jews and blacks. Everywhere blacks turned, it seemed, they encountered Jewish authority figures—teachers in the public school system (in New York 70 percent of whom were Jewish by the 1960s), social workers, probation offficers, policemen, postmen, and other government bureaucrats (many of whom had entered public service believing such jobs to be "prejudice proof"),[37] doctors, lawyers, and judges. Previously, Jews themselves had collided with Italian or Irish authority figures. It was, seemingly, the American way, as one group proceeded up the social and economic ladder. Now, however, handbills in Harlem lamented how "the sons of Shylock" had their "tentacles" in grocery stores, dwellings, and schools.[38] As Baldwin noted caustically, Jews were playing the role in Harlem assigned by Christians long ago, he was doing their dirty work.[39]

Beginning in 1966,blacks demanded control of all institutions in their communities, especially the schools where they said, Jewish teachers were unable to relate to black children. In the wake of the Ocean Hill-Brownsville controversy in Brooklyn, physical intimidation and threats forced the resignation or ealry retirements of dozens of Jewish principals and school teachers.[40] Yet not even the introduction of more African-American teachers could reverse the disappointing performance of most inner city schools.

During the 1970s, blacks and Jews veered away from one another in their perceptions of access to jobs, education, and other entitlements.

For Jews equal opportunity and affirmative action meant precisely what the words said and they sided with individuals who claimed reverse discrimination as in the De Funis and Bakke cases. Jews considered goals or set-asides nothing more than euphemisms for quotas. Victimized by the *numerus clausus* in Europe, they had prospered in America under the merit system. By demanding a change in the rules, blacks were threatening our pluralist society.[41] Like most government planners and social theorists, blacks viewed affirmative action as only a start, a necessary reparative to centuries of institutional discrimination.[42] Jesse Jackson claimed that during the glory days of the civil rights revolution, Jews were willing to share decency, but they were now unwilling to share power.[43] Blacks accused Jews of abandoning liberalism for neoconservative causes, though Jews continued to vote for liberal candidates in overwhelming numbers and blacks often found themselves allied with reactionaries on issues of reproduction, homosexuality, pornography, and individual rights vs. group rights.[44]

Northwestern's Adolph Reed suggests that because of the "Reagan counter-revolution" and the ineffectual response of moderate leaders (including Jackson who became more mainstream after 1984) that more radical spokesmen came to the front in the black community. "Racial cheerleading at least offered a soothing catharsis." Thus by championing the rights of his people and embracing a Third World agenda Farrakhan emerged as "the embodiment and broker of the black race-nationalist political persona."[45] Those who claim to leadership in minority communities have an obligation to make their constituents "feel good about one's self." Doris Wilkinson suggests that what some people regard as anti-Semitism is nothing more than espousing positive images of blacks while denigrating others, a harmless attempt to put others in their place.[46] Where such feel-goodism ends and victimization of others begins, of course, is relative. Belief that Jews are egocentric, exclusivist, avaricious, subversive, unpatriotic or even responsible for the introduction for AIDS and drugs in the inner city may be soothing to some, but that does not make it so.[47]

Third Worldism

One concept that offers solace to blacks and simultaneously unnerves Jews is Third Worldism. As Paul Berman defines it, "You, the African Americans, are hopelessly outnumbered within the United States, and this unfortunate realilty cannot be wished away by a lot of talk about liberalism and rights. But on a world scale you are no minority at all. The news for you is therefore encouraging. You are many, not few, strong, not weak; time will right your wrongs." [48] Proclamations against imperialism, colonialism, and apartheid and in favor of human rights and self-determination are laudable. How such terms are defined is another matter. During the 1960s radical ideologues like Frantz Fanon and Robert F. Williams gained prominence by championing the rights of colonial peoples within decaying European empires. In the rhetoric of the day, the state of Israel was transmuted from a Little David fighting for its life against a host of Goliaths during the Six Day War of 1967 into a colonialist implant allied to racist South Africa. Most black African states, eager to curry favor with the Arab states and their newfound oil wealth, severed relations with Israel. Six years later, when Israel, which had been attacked by both Syria and Egypt on Yom Kippur, again pushed its forces into the Sinai peninsula, the few African states that maintained diplomatic relations with the Jewish state (Kenya, Ghana, Nigeria) severed them. After years of supporting anti-Zionist resolutions at international conferences in Mexico, Cuba, and Spain, it hardly came as a surprise when most African and Asian nations supported the Soviet bloc and Muslim states at the United Nations General Assembly meeting in October 1975 declaring that Zionism was racism.[49] Since then, African states have also endorsed the rights of Palestinians whether operating as "freedom fighters" along the Lebanese border, during the *Intifada,* as an entity in the West Bank and Gaza, or a projected nation state. Some black Americans, Andrew Young, and Jesse Jackson among them, claiming to be political pragmatists, favored these concepts. Others, seeking closer identification with Islam, seized upon passages in the Quran unfavorable toward Jews[50] or echoed the harsh rhetoric of contemporary Islamic sages like the Ayatollah Khomeini.[51] In the process, the lines between anti-Zionism and anti-Semitism became blurred.

American Jews found such positions incomprehensible. For them, the state of Israel, was the one functioning democracy in the Middle East. If ever there was a country that should be nurtured and protected it was this one, composed of Holocaust survivors, expellees from Arab lands, Falashas from Ethiopia. In 1967, again in 1973, Jews everywhere, including secular ones who belonged to no synagogue, vowed that they would never permit a recurrence of what had happened to their kinsmen in World War II. They recognized that the charges which had been uttered against them and the state of Israel (Israel supposedly has a God of its own that cannot be shared by other peoples, Jews have strength in the U.S. because they have great infleuence in government circles, are very wealthy, and people fear them, Zionism aims to bring about the realization of the domination of the world by Jews) were not only false, but stale. Kamil Abdul Rahim, a spokesman for the Arab League, was making use of such arguments in New York back in 1956. Only then he was addressing his message to "every public relations medium" in the press, radio, television, the lecturer's circuit, and student exchange.[52] The goal, which has never changed, was the destruction of the state of Israel.

In 1956 it was unthinkable that such propaganda would make headway in the black community. Jews and blacks were still working together to secure fundamental civil rights. Elijah Muhammad's Nation of Islam was a marginal group which taught that whites were blue-eyed devils. Much of that changed with Malcolm X. After making pilgrimage to Mecca in 1964, Malcolm successfully argued for reconciling the Nation of Islam with orthodox Islam. At the same time, he championed Third World ideology, identification with the policies of the Organization of African Unity, and the exploitation of anti-Semitism. He publicly attacked black congressmen and community leaders like Vernon Jordan as Jewish lackeys. He denigrated the Holocaust, saying, it made no sense to get "wet-eyed over a bunch of Jews who brought it on themselves." And he made it clear whose side he supported in the Middle East conflict when he said: "The Jews with the help of Christians in America and Europe, drove our Muslim brothers out of their homeland, where they had been settled for centuries and took over the land for themselves. This every Muslim resents.... In America, the Jews sap the very life-blood of the so-called Negroes to maintain the state of Israel, its armies, and its continued aggression against our brothers in the East. This every Black Man resents."[53]

Malcolm X was assassinated in 1965, but the empire begun by Elijah Muhammad continued to thrive. In 1973, Forster and Epstein reported that the net worth of the Nation of Islam was between $75 and 95 million. This included 68,000 acres of real estate in eight states and British Honduras, a publishing plant responsible for a weekly readership of 600,000, fifty mosques, and interests in everything from banks to restaurants, and barbershops. Some of this was underwritten with Middle East oil money. In 1972, Elijah Muhammad secured more than $3 million in outright gifts from Arab states including more than $2.9 million from Libya's Muammar Qaddafi. Small wonder that weekly editions of *Elijah Speaks* were peppered with articles titled "Is Life of an Arab in Israel like a Black Man's in Alabama?" Modern Israel Rivals Ancient Pharaoh in Brutality," "Israel reporter describes Nazi-like Blitzkrieg Against Arab Civilians," "Israeli War Planes, Tanks Massacre Refugee Innocents," and "Israel Building New Concentration Camps."[54]

Matters only worsened with the death of Elijah Muhammad in 1975 and the emergence of Louis Farrakhan. The press ignored some of his more outlandish escapades as when Farrakhan claimed that Elijah Muhammad descended from heaven in a UFO and blessed him atop a pyramid in Tepotzlan, Mexico in 1985. The following year, Farrakhan attributed the Challenger disaster to divine wrath for man's arrogance attempting to go into outer space.The leading spokesman for the Nation of Islam reaffirmed his belief that the white man was the creature of the devil. Six-thousand years of white hegemony had produced nothing but evil and oppression. "You cannot reform a devil," said Farrakhan, "All the prophets tried and failed. You have to kill the devil."[55] Apparently, it is permissible to deal with the devil's lackeys—for Farrakhan has received support from Lyndon LaRouche, Tom Metzger of the White Aryan Resistance, the Ku Klux Klan, and Muammar Qaddafi, while offering words of sympathy to Saddam Husssein.[56] It is also legitimate to praise the devil (Farrakhan did arouse the press when he called Hitler a great man who raised Germany from the ashes of defeat in World War I) and to emulate the devil (the creation of a uniformed bodyguard; substitution of a nationalist flag in place of the Stars and Stripes; the demand for nationalist reeducation; revision of the nation's economic infrastructure through boycotts if necessary; and rejection of interracial marriage.) Farrakhan also embraced the devil's favorite tactic—anti-Semitism—decrying Judaism as a "gutter" or "dirty" religion, lampooning the Jewish claim of being a Chosen people, attacking them for wielding too much power in black communities, the media, Congress, and even among black leaders, charging Israel with genocide against Palestinians, and, almost as an afterthought, with responsibility for the slave trade.

A few scholars have dismissed such comments as "resonant metaphors" like chants of "Kill the Jews" and "Hitler should have finished the job" uttered by mobs during the Crown Heights riots.[57] Others see a connection between Farrakhan's rhetoric and the violent lyrics of "gangsta rap music" that became popular during the 1980s.[58] One scholar labelled Farrakhan's attacks upon the media "mischievously humorous" and his accusation of Jewish involvement in the slave trade as "wickedly clever."[59] Matthias Gardell, associated with the Institute for

Comparative Religion at the University of Stockholm, offfered the broadest blanket of excuses. According to Gardell, Farrakhan's outrageous statements must be evaluated through "black sociolinguistics." When, for example, the self-proclaimed minister threatened "to kill" Milton Coleman, the *Washington Post* reporter who had revealed Jesse Jackson's comment about "Hymietown" during the 1984 primary campaign (a threat which Gardell concedes was "untactical") Farrakhan was using a black political/rhetorical metaphor which really meant "we will put you out of influence and respect."[60] In like manner, Farrakhan was not disparaging the Jewish faith when he referred to it as a "gutter/dirty" religion. Rather, he was upset with the Jews' "misuse" of world power.[61] Farrakhan's denunciations of Satan, chosen people, and America's wrongful interventions in the Middle East must also be understood from his "apocalyptic perspective.[62]

Apologetics of this kind, it seems to me, are quite dangerous. In the 19th century, Eugen Duhring, Wilhelm Marr, Theodor Fritsch, and Paul de la Garde penned nationalistic/racist screeds which painted a world of socialist, plutocrat, and Jewish conspiracies. Such pamphlets were dismissed as idiosyncratic and of little consequence. Left unchecked to feed off and reinforce one another, however, the racist ideologues watched their ideas evolve into Nazism. Some blacks in this country, particularly on college campuses, have taken a similar path.[63] Isolated to feed off one another's perceptions of truth, a disturbing number of African Americans, much as their predecessors in Central Europe, subscribe to conspiracies in which cunning, duplicitous Jews figure prominently. According to Gary Rubin, "hatemongers like Jeffries and Farrkahan thrive in an atmosphere of isolation."[64] Henry Louis Gates concurs, noting that new anti-Semitism in the black community has been generated from "the top down" (e.g., the same apostles of hate of whom Rubin spoke) and that these men "know that the more isolated black America becomes, the greater their power." And what is the most effficient way to isolate black America from those who want to be their friends? Says Gates, "Bash the Jews, these demagogues apparently calculate, and you're halfway there."[65]

"The victims of racism," Jacob Neusner has written, "learned only too well from the racists, their tormentors."[66] The distinguished professor of Judaism was not speaking of Jews. Rather he was referring to "Negro Nazis," who, he claimed constituted the one subdivision of the American population that professed racist views today.[67] And while it is popular to dismiss notions of racism in the black community because a group that is powerless allegedly cannot be racist,[68] a better insight has been offered by Cynthia Ozick in 1993: "Racism is a mob on the prowl. Racism is the tic or reflex of the benighted.... Racism is a movment, complete with leaders and followers. Racism is a widespread common belief in the deficiency of certain classes of human beings. Racism is a lie that has taken on the public appearance of a social axiom."[69]

When scholars have analyzed all the legitimate reasons for friction between blacks and Jews, black hostility toward Jews still seems deeply based in fear, myth, and lies. For the common man, lies repeated by those better educated than he, those he respects are ineluctable. Before Farrakhan, before Goebbels, the French anti-Semite Leon Bloy noted the effectiveness of the Big Lie:

> To say to the man in the street, even to the shabbiest specimen of a rottenness beyond hope: 'These perfidious Hebrews who bespatter you with mud, they have stolen all your money. Get it back from them, O Egyptian! Beat them up, if you have any guts, and chase them into the Red Sea!'—to keep on saying this, to say it everywhere, to bellow it in books and in newspapers, and even now and then to fight a duel, so that the idea will echo nobly over the hills and dales, and above all never to speak of anything else, that is the prescription and the mystification, the established tactics of the big guns which will ensure a triumphant success. No one—God help us!—can resist all that.[70]

Those who published *The Secret Relationship* understand the principle of the Big Lie very well. The charge that Jews dominated the slave trade may seem insignificant to some (as one correspondent wrote me, "the work of a fruitcake.") It is only one of many unfounded canards that have been recited against Jews. No credible research institute has yet taken a poll to determine its range of acceptance within black communities. Such attitude, it seems to me, ignores the innate seriousness of the accusation. Slavery lies at the very heart and fibre of the black experience in America and to wrongfully attribute this institution to another vulnerable minority is a cruel and inexcusable act. A number of academics have expressed concern about the corrosive impact of such an accusation. According to Robert Schmuhl of the Department of American Studies at Notre Dame; "The uses of the *Secret Relationship between Blacks and Jews* as a textbook in classes around the country also gives one pause. Fabricating 'history' is a far cry from revising it, but few students have the knowledge to make discriminating judgments about distant 'facts' that are being presented to them."[71] Harvard's Henry Louis Gates notes that the book (which Gates calls one of the most sophisticated instances of hate literature yet completed) has been marketed in the inner cities in shops that normally sell Kente cloth and beads. "Sober and scholarly-looking," wrote Gates in July 1992, "it [*The Secret Relationship*] may well be one of the most influential books published in the black community in the last twelve months."[72] Gary Rubin goes even further. The onetime director of National Affairs for the American Jewish Committee says of *Secret Relationship*, "This volume may be the single most effective piece of antisemitic propaganda produced in the United States since Henry Ford's *The International Jew* of the 1920s."[73]

If the Jewish experience in the Shoah teaches anything, it is that decent people must not stand idly by while their neighbors are insulted and menaced. Scholars, clergy, and laymen of every background must refute this old/new libel publicly and often. Blacks and Jews especially must educate their own constituents and disavow mutual contempt. In the end, we all must be reminded how for decades, for whatever reasons (altruism, moral conscience, guilt, self-help, expedience), two peoples have stood, marched, and wept together. Instead of fabricating history and villifying Jews, nationalist mythmakers would do well to read Patrick Manning's *Slavery and African Life*. There is one mention of Jews on the final page of the text. It has nothing to do with Jewish control of the slave trade. Nor is it an exercise in comparative pain (whether Jews or blacks suffered more). Rather, Manning is perceptive enough to recognize a commonality in suffering and humanity between victims of the Holocaust and slaves who endured the transatlantic crossing. In a stirring passage, Manning quotes Nobel laureate Elie Wiesel, a survivor of Auschwitz, who says: "Let us remember, again and again. For at the end that is all they wanted—to be remembered; their names, their faces, their silent songs, their secret triumphs, their struggle and their death, one as awesome as the other."[74]

Manning's message, like Elie Wiesel's, is preferable to the finger-pointing and name-calling of the Nation of Islam. In his last sentence, Manning writes,"For the case of African slaves, one may argue that the response to their sacrifice is to honor their memory and thereby ensure that no such sacrifice will be made again."[75] Unfortunately, that message is lost on the likes of Dr. Jeffries and Louis Farrakhan.

Bibliographic Comment

Any bibliography must be at once arbitrary and discriminating. Of the hundreds of books cited above, some obviously have more appeal. In the time since I began my research on the subject of Jews and the slave trade of the Americas, another volume by Tony Martin of Wellesley College has appeared in support of *The Secret Relationship*. Titled *The Jewish Onslaught: Despatches from the Wellesley Battlefront,* it makes many of the same allegations and is of similar merit. A short refutation of such libels may be found in the Anti-Defamation League's *Jew Hatred as History,* a 46-page pamphlet published in 1993. As of this writing (summer 1997), several scholars noted in the text (including David Brion Davis, Eli Faber, Harold Brackman, Leonard Dinnerstein, and Seymour Drescher) have either responded to the charges in essay form or are preparing full-length monographs.

Students seeking an introduction to the operations of the transatlantic slave trade would be wise to consult some of the following works: Philip Curtin, *The Atlantic Slave Trade: A Census* (Madison: University of Wisconsin, 1969); Davis, *The Problem of Slavery in Western Culture* (New York: Oxford University Press, 1966); David Eltis, *Economic Growth and the Ending of the Transatlantic Slave Trade* (New York: Oxford University Press, 1987); Herbert Klein, *The Middle Passage: Comparative Studies in the Atlantic Slave Trade* (Princeton, NJ: Princeton University Press, 1978); Patrick Manning, *Slavery and African Life: Occidental, Oriental and African Slave Trades* (Cambridge: Cambridge University Press, 1990); Colin Palmer, *Human Cargoes: The British Slave Trade to Spanish America 1700–1739* (Urbana: University of Illinois Press, 1981); James Rawley, *The Transatlantic Slave Trade: A History* (New York: W.W.Norton, 1981); John Spears, *The American Slave Trade: An Account of Its Origins, Growth and Suppression* (New York: Scribner's, 1900); and Robert Stein, *The French Slave Trade in the Eighteenth Century: An Old Regime Business* (Madison: University of Wisconsin Press, 1979).

The starting point for anyone working in North America must be Elizabeth Donnan's near-encyclopedic *Documents Illustrative of the*

History of the Slave Trade to America (New York: Octagon, 1965). I would also recommend Frederic Bancroft's *Slave Trading in the Old South* (Baltimore, MD: Furst, 1931), W.E.B. DuBois' *The Suppression of the African Slave Trade to the United States of America 1638–1870* (Baton Rouge: Louisiana State University Press reprint, 1969); Eugene Genovese's *The Political Economy of Slavery: Studies in the Econoomy and Society of the Slave South* (New York: Pantheon, 1961, 1965); Daniel Littlefield's *Rice and Slaves: Ethnicity and the Slave Tradae in Colonial South Carolina* (Baton Rouge: Louisiana State University Press, 1981); Joseph Menn's "The Large Slaveholders of the Deep South 1860" (University of Texas dissertation, 1964); Kenneth Stampp's *The Peculiar Institution: Slavery in the Ante-Bellum South* (New York: Alfred A. Knopf, 1956); Michael Tadman's *Speculators and Slaves: Masters, Traders and Slaves in the Old South* (Madison: University of Wisconsin Press, 1989); and Richard Wade's *Slavery in the Cities: The South 1820–1860* (Oxford: Oxford University Press, 1964). Despite recent criticism, I am also impressed by Carter Woodson's *Free Negro Heads of Families in the United States in 1830* (Washington, DC: Association for the Study of Negro Life and History, 1925).

For Jewish involvement in the Caribbean and Latin America, consult the works of C. R. Boxer: *Race Relations in the Protuguese Colonial Empire 1415–1825* (Oxford: Clarendon Press, 1963); *The Dutch in Brazil 1624–1654*, CITY????Archon Books 1973); *The Golden Age of Brazil* (Berkeley: University of California Press, 1962); and *The Portuguese Seaborne Empire, 1415–1825* (New York: Alfred A. Knopf 1969) along with Isaac and Suzanne Emmanuel, *History of the Jews of the Netherland Antilles* (Cincinnati, OH: American Jewish Archives, 1970); Judith Elkin, *The Jews of the Latin American Republics* (Chapel Hill: University of North Carolina Press, 1980); Stephen Fortune, *Merchants and Jews: The Struggle for British West Indian Commerce 1650–1750* (Gainesville: University of Florida Press, 1984); Cornelis Goslinga, *The Dutch in the Caribbean and on the Wild Coast 1580–1680* (Gainesville: University of Florida Press, 1971); Arnold Wiznitzer, *Jews in Colonial Brazil* (New York: Columbia University Press, 1960); and the many works of Seymour Liebman: *The Jews in New Spain* (Miami: University of Miami, 1970); *Jews and the Inquisition of Mexico: The Great Auto da Fe of 1649* (Lawrence, KS: Coronado Press, 1974); *The Inquisitors and the Jews in the New World* (Miami: University of Miami Press, 1975); and *New World Jewry 1493–1825* (Hoboken, NJ: Ktav 1982).

For information on the origins and status of Jewish settlements in North America, there is one authority—Professor Jacob Marcus of Hebrew Union College—and his multivolume *Colonial American Jew, 1492–1776* (Detroit, MI: Wayne State University Press, 1970) and *Early American Jewry* (Philadelphia, PA: Jewish Publication Society). See also the publications of the American Jewish Historical Society, Abraham Karp's *The Jewish Experience in America* (Hoboken, NJ: Ktav 1969) and Ira Rosenwaike's *On The Edge of Greatness: A Portrait of American Jewry in the Early National Period* (Cincinnati, OH: American Jewish Archives, 1985). The latter, an especially sound piece of scholarship, has been torturously abused by the editors of the *Secret Relationship.*

Rabbi Bertram Korn addressed the specific issue of Jewish involvement in the slave trade in his seminal essay "Jews and Negro Slavery in the Old South," published in *Jews in the South*, Leonard Dinnerstein and Mary Palsson (eds.) (Baton Rouge: Louisiana State University Press, 1973). Korn, the author of several major texts (*The Early Jews of New Orleans* [Cincinnati American Jewish Historical Society, 1969]; *The Jews of Mobile, Alabama 1762–1841* [Cincinnati, OH: Hebrew Union College Press, 1970]), intended to write a major monograph on Jews in the slave trade, but was deterred by the endless dimensions of the subject. Students seeking primary information would be well advised to avail themselves of the Korn papers at Hebrew Union College. Although records are spotty, other primary information may be culled from the archives of the Rhode Island Jewish Historical Society and the Historical Societies of Virginia, Pennsylvania, New York, Louisiana, Maryland, South Carolina, and Georgia. The task has been eased somewhat by published works of Jay Coughtry, *The Notorious Triangle: Rhode Island and the African Slave Trade 1700–1787* (Philadelphia, PA: Temple University Press, 1981); Eli Evans, *The Provincials: A Personal History of Jews in the South* (New York: Atheneum, 1973); Rudolf Glanz, *The Jew in the Old American Folklore* (New York: Waldon Press, 1961); James Hagy, *This Happy Land: The Jews of Colonial and Antebellum Charleston* (Tuscaloosa: University of Alabama, 1993); Kaye Kole, *The Minis Family of Georgia 1733–1792* (Savannah Georgia Historical Society, 1992); David de Sola Pool, *Portraits Etched in Stone: Early Jewish Settlers 1682–1831* (New York: Columbia University Press, 1952); Malcolm Stern, *Americans of Jewish Descent: A Comopendium of Genealogy* (Cincinnati, OH: Hebrew Union College, 1960), and the many essays of Morris Schappes and Leon Hughner.

For an appreciation of the widening gap between Jew and black, see Paul Berman (ed.) *Blacks and Jews: Alliances and Arguments* (New York: Delacorte Press, 1994); Jerome Chanes (ed.) *Antisemitism in America Today* (New York: Carol Publishing Group, 1995); Hasia Diner, *In the Almost Promised Land: American Jews and Blacks 1915–1935* (Baltimore, MD: Johns Hopkins University Press reprint, 1995); Leonard Dinnerstein, *Uneasy at Home: Anti-Semitism and the American Jewish Experience* (New York: Columbia University Press, 1983); Arnold Forster and Benjamin Epstein, *The New Anti-Semitism* (New York: McGraw-Hill, 1974); Murray Friedman, *What Went Wrong? The Creation and Collapse of the Black-Jewish Alliance* (New York: Free Press, 1995); Benjamin Ginsberg, *The Fatal Embrace: Jews and the State* (Chicago: University of Chicago Press, 1993); Edith Kurzweil and William Phillips (eds.) *Our Country, Our Culture: The Politics of Political Correctness* (Boston: Partisan Review Press, 1994); Mary Lefkowitz, *Not Out of Africa: How Afrocentrism Became an Excuse to Teach Myth as History* (New York: Basic Books, 1996); Abraham Peck, *Blacks and Jews: The American Experience 1654–1987* (Cincinnati, OH: American Jewish Archives, 1987); Theodore Rueter (ed.) *The Politics of Race: African Americans and the Political System* (Armonk, NY: M.E. Sharpe, 1995); Jack Salzman (ed.) *Bridges and Boundaries: African Americans and American Jews* (New York: George Braziller, 1992); Robert Weisbord and Arthur Stein, *Bittersweet Encounter: The Afro-American and the American Jew* (Westport, CT: Negro Universities Press, 1970). Cornell West and Michael Lerner must also be commended for their efforts to bring the two communities together in *Jews and Blacks: Let the Healing Begin* (New York: Putnam's, 1995) and *Jews and Blacks: A Dialogue on Race, Religion and Culture in America* (New York: Plume, 1996).

Notes

Note to Preface

1. *Plain Dealer*, pp. 1 and 6, Feb. 5, 1994. Farrakhan later claimed he was misquoted and had said 75% of the Jews owned slaves.

Notes to Chapter 1

1. *New York Newsday*, August 18, 1991, pp. 3, 25–29. For a complete account of Professor Jeffries activities, see James Traub's "Annals of Education: The Hearts and Minds of City College," *The New Yorker,* (June 7, 1993), LXIX, pp. 42ff.
2. Robert Weisbord and Arthur Stein, *Bittersweet Encounter: The Afro-American and the American Jew* (Westport, CT: Negro Universities Press, 1970), p. 55.
3. John Roy Carlson, *Under Cover: My Four Years in the Nazi Underworld of America* (New York: Dutton, 1943), pp. 155–56. Cook continued to praise Hitler till his death in 1966.
4. *The Secret Relationship* has already earned the rebuke of several professional historians who are offended by its poor methodology and scapegoating. See David Brion Davis, "The Slave Trade and the Jews," *New York Review of Books* (December 22, 1994), XLI, pp. 14–16 and Winthrop Jordan, "Slavery and the Jews," *Atlantic Monthly* (September 1995), CCLXXVI, pp. 109–14.
5. Wiznitzer, *Jews in Colonial Brazil* (New York: Columbia University Press, 1960), p. 69.
6. *Ibid.*, p. 70.
7. Elizabeth Donnan, *Documents Illustrative of the History of the Slave Trade to America: New England and the Middle Colonies* (New York: Octagon Books, 1965), III, p. 415.
8. Jacob Marcus, *The Colonial American Jew 1492–1776* (Detroit, MI: Wayne State University Press, 1970), I, pp. 73–75, 220.
9. Isidore Meyer (ed.), "The American Jew in the Civil War: Catalog of the Exhibit of the Civil War Centennial Jewish Historical Commission," *American Jewish Historical Quarterly* (September 1960–June 1961), L, p. 303.
10. Lenni Brenner, *Jews in America Today* (Secaucus, NJ: Lyle Stuart Inc., 1986), pp. 221–23.
11. Born in Italy, Ottolenghe converted to Christianity in England in 1734 and died in 1775 Ottolenghe was succeeded as rector of Christ Church in Savannah by Bartholomew Zuber.The American Jewish Archives at Hebrew Union College in Cincinnati contain eight letters dated between September 9, 1751 and June 5, 1761 from Ottolenghe to the London-based Society for the Propagation of the Gospel. In the first, he speaks of arriving in Savannah by "the mercies of God" and mentions his mission for JC" (the exact abbreviation used) "who died for the salvation of all. Later (June 8, 1752) he praises the Society for its help in carrying out his"Xn duties" and talks (September 19, 1753) of instruct-

ing slaves in "the Xn religion to make them devout Xns." Ottolenghe, Joseph file, Miscellaneous Collection no. 99, AJA.

12. Amherst, a faithful member of the Church of England, was miraculously transmuted into a "Jewish military commander" with a pathological hatred of Indians in an article—"Paradox of European Jewry" written for *Uhuru*, the publication of Black United Students of Kent State University in the spring of 1994. This incendiary piece which mixed charges of Jewish slave trading with disoriented anthropological ravings ("Caucasian Jews are also the descendants of these people of the caves [better known as the Neanderthals"]) sparked protests from Jewish and non-Jewish professors. Despite administrative efforts to mollify the situation, after more than a year there was no apology from the editors or advisers of *Uhuru*.

13. John Long. *Lord Jeffrey Amherst: A Soldier of the King* (New York: Macmillan, 1933), pp. 80, 128–29, 131, 183. See also Louis Des Cognets, *Amherst and Canada* (Princeton, NJ: Princeton University Press, 1962.)

14. Franks, David. Correspondence on Business Matters, 1761–1764, Small Collection, Box x1441 AJA. Most of the 283 pages refer to activities of Christophere Kilby who served as commissariat to March 1761, or come from Amherst's adjutant Lt. Colonel William Eyre, or are directed to Franks' partner Plumsted. There is nothing about blankets or smallpox in commercial records of Isaac Levy, Moses Israel Fonseca, Isaac Lopez, Nathaniel Simpson, Naphtali Franks, Uriah Hendricks, Benj. and Moses Levy, Rodrigo Pacheco, Moses Alvares, or William and Isaac Kops dating to the 1750s. See Records of Business Transactions of Colonial Era American Jews, 1715–1786 Box x–22, Economic File, Small Collection, AJA.

15. In fact, one of their sources tells of tremendous efforts on the part of Lillian Wald, the National Council of Jewish Women, Louis Marshall, C.L. Sulzberger, Jacob Schiff, Julian Mack, and Isador Straus to secure passage of the Mann Act at the start of this century. Francesco Cordasco and Thomas Pitkin, *The White Slave Trade and the Immigrants: A Chapter in American Social History* (Detroit, MI: Blaine Ethridge Books, 1981), pp. 13–30.

16. See articles on Muhammad in *Washington Post*, April 19, 1994, B1; *Washington Times*, April 19, 1994, C23; and *Washington Jewish Week*, April 28, 1994, pp. 6 and 30.

17. Meier and Rudwick, *From Plantation to Ghetto* (New York: Hill and Wang, 1966), pp. 33–34.

18. Davidson, *Black Mother* (Boston: Little Brown, 1961), p. 80.

19. Kay, *The Shameful Trade* (S. Brunswick and New York: A.S.Barnes, 1967), p. 1.

20. Boles, *Black Southerners 1619–1869* (Lexington: University Press of Kentucky, 1983), p. 31.

21. Klein, *The Middle Passage: Comparative Studies in the Atlantic Slave Trade* (Princeton, NJ: Princeton University Press, 1978), pp. 230–32; Rawley, *The Transatlantic Slave Trade: A History* (New York: W.W.Norton, 1981), p. 42; and Curtin, *The Atlantic Slave Trade: A Census* (Madison: University of Wisconsin Press, 1969), p. 275. According to Jay Coughtry, a sample of 100 ships between 1752 and 1807 shows mortality of 12 percent. Anything more was deemed economically unacceptable. *The Notorious Triangle: Rhode Island and the African Slave Trade 1700–1807* (Philadephia, PA: Temple University Press, 1981), pp. 145–46. See also ships lists, pp. 241–85, where the normal survival rate was 80–90 percent. See also J. Eltis, "Mortality and Voyage Length in the Middle Passage: New Evidence from the Nineteenth Century," *Journal of Economic History* (June, 1984), XLIV, pp. 301–8, and R.L.Cohn, "Deaths of Slaves

in the Middle Passage, *Journal of Econimic History* (September 1985), XLV, pp. 685–92.

22. Nora Levin, "The Relationship of Genocide to Holocaust Studies," *Holocaust Literature*, S.Friedman (ed.) (Westport, CT: Greenwood Press, 1993), p. 198.

23. Seymour Liebman, *The Inquisitors and the Jews in the New World* (Coral Gables, FL: University of Miami Press, 1974), pp. 89–99.

24. On the Protocols, see Norman Cohn, *Warrant for Genocide* (New York: Harper and Row, 1966).

25. Rawley, *Transatlantic Slave Trade*,pp. 122 and 132.

26. Roger Anstey, *The Atlantic Slave Trade and British Abolition* (Atlantic Highlands, NJ: Humanities Press, 1987), pp. 148–52.

27. Kay, *The Shameful Trade*, pp. 180–92.

28. Eltis, *Economic Growth and the Ending of the Transatlantic Slave Trade* (New York: Oxford University Press, 1987), pp. 148–52.

29. Palmer, *Human Cargoes* (Urbana: University of Illinois Press, 1981), p. 3.

30. Manning, *Slavery and African Life : Occidental, Oriental and African Slave Trades* (Cambridge University Press, 1990).

31. Graham Irwin discusses the role of Jews in the fall of the Himyarite kingdom of Yemen in *Africans Abroad* (New York: Columbia University Press, 1977), pp. 41–49. Jews are mentioned twice as slave traders without elaboration in *Slavery and the Rise of the Atlantic System*, Barbara Solow (ed.) (Cambridge: Cambridge University Press, 1991), pp. 126, 141.

32. These were Menn's principal slaveholders: John Burnside (La.) 940, L.R.Marshall (La.) 932, Stephen Duncan (Miss.) 858, Meredith Calhoun (La.) 709, James Acklen (La.) 659, Gerard Brandon (Miss.) 658, Alfred David (La.) 637, Thomas Moughon (Ga.) 623, John Manning (La.) 616, Stephen King (Ga.) 582, John Robinson (Miss.) 550, Jerre Brown (Ala.) 540, L.A. Jordan (Ga.) 522, J.F.Potter (Ga.) 504, O.J.Morgan (La.), 501. See Menn, *The Large Slaveholders of the Deep South 1860* (University of Texas dissertation, 1964, two volumes).

33. B.W. Korn, "Slave trade in the Americas," *Encyclopedia Judaica* (Jerusalem: Keter, 1971), XIV, pp. 1662–64.

34. Bancroft, *Slave Trading in the Old South* (New York: Frederick Ungar, 1931), pp. 93–94, 97–98, 175–76, 251–52.

35. Korn, "Jews and Negro Slavery in the Old South," in *Jews in the South*, Leonard Dinnerstein and Mary Palsson (eds.) (Baton Rouge: Lousiana State University Press, 1973), p. 111.

36. *Ibid.*, p. 111.

37. Eugene Genovese, *Roll, Jordan, Roll: The World the Slaves Made* (New York: Pantheon Books, 1974), pp. 252–53.

38. Meier and Rudwick, *From Plantation to Ghetto*, p. 237.

39. According to DuBois, there were 800,000 in Britain's colonies, 900,000 in the U.S.,600,000 under Spanish and Portuguese rule, 250,000 French slaves, 2,000,000 in Brazil, 50,000 under Dutch control, 27,000 in the Danish West Indies. DuBois, *The Suppression of the African Slave Trade to the United States of America 1638–1870* (Baton Rouge: Louisiana State University Press reissue of 1896 publication by Russell and Russell, 1965), p. 131.

40. Washington, *The Story of the Negro: The Rise of the Race from Slavery* (Goucester, MA: Peter Smith, 1969 reprint), pp. 1, 22; Thomas, *The American Negro: What He Was, What He Is, and What He May Become* (New York: Negro Universities Press, 1969 reprint of 1901 Macmillan edition), pp. 249, 350.

41. Jordan does offer a questionable treatment of the origins of the curse of Ham, p. 36, *White over Black: American Attitudes toward the Negro, 1550–1812* (University of North Carolina Press), see also pp. 66, 70–71, 103, 291, 329, 372.

42. Franklin and Moss, *From Slavery to Freedom* (New York: Knopf, 1947, 1988), pp. 402 and 413.
43. *Ibid.*, pp. 370, 430.
44. Quarles, *Negro in the Making of America* (London: Collier Books, 1969), pp. 164–65.
45. Bennett scores Columbus, the Portuguese, Spanish, French, Swedes, Danes, Dutch, English and Prussians (pp.34–39), but there is no mention of Jewish slave traders in *Before the Mayflower.* The only reference to *Jews in Confrontation: Black and White* (Chicago: Johnson Pub., 1965) is to the purchase of a synagogue near the University of Chicago by Elijah Muhammad's Black Muslims, p. 246.
46. Hughes' well-written, but loosely documented study is typical of the mass of books written on slavery. It chronicles the roundups in African villages, condemns Europeans for their role in the transatlantic trade and offers hope of redemption through Moses and Jesus, though neither is identified as a Jew. August Meier suggests that a joke-cracking Lincoln was viewed by blacks as a Moses. See introduction to Benjamin Quarles, *Black Mosaic: Essays in Afro-American History and Historiography* (Amherst: University of Massachusetts Press, 1988), p. 14.
47. Blasingame does speak of Jews who redeemed their co-religionists from bondage with Muslims. He offers a bleak picture of "bare-footed, half-naked" slaves, both black and white, in North African marts about to be sent to "dreaded Arab galleys." *Plantation Life and Community*, pp. 55–62.
48. See Woodson's *Free Negro Heads of Families in the United States in 1830* (Washington, DC: Association for Study of Negro Life and History, 1925) and *The Mind of the Negro as Reflected in His Letters Written during the Crisis* (Washington, DC: Associated Pubs., 1926).
49. Interview with Amos Beyan, Youngstown, August 15, 1991.

Notes to Chapter 2

1. M.I. Finley, *Ancient Slavery and Modern Ideology* (New York: Viking, 1980), p. 67. On the development of slavery in prehistoric times, see Herbert Muller, *Freedom in the Ancient World* (New York: Bantam, 1961), pp. 28–29.
2. Samuel N. Kramer, *The Sumerians: Their History, Culture and Character* (University of Chicago Press, 1963), p. 78.
3. The function of slaves in the luxurious state is clear. Slaves are the enemies of Greece taken in combat. Plato cautions, however, that Greeks should not enslave their fellow Greeks. *The Republic*, tr. Francis Cornford (Oxford: Clarendon Press, 1941), ch. VII, pp. 58–61 and ch. XVII, p. 170.
4. *Aristotle's Politics*, tr. Benjamin Jowett (Oxford: Clarendon Press, 1908), book I, chs. 3, 4, 5, 6, pp. 31–36.
5. According to St. Thomas More, slaves would be drawn from enemies captured in war, citizens condemned for heinous offenses, and foreigners who volunteered for such labor. In his *Utopia*, however, slaves who were forced to do additional labor would be treated almost as well as citizens. Sir Thomas More, *Utopia* tr. Robert Adams (New York: Norton, 1975), pp. 35, 51, 64–5.
6. Pierre Dockes, *Medieval Slavery and Liberation* , tr. Arthur Goldhammer (Chicago: University of Chicago Press, 1982), pp. 27–34 and 191–97. See also Robert Fogel, *Without Consent or Contract: The Rise and Fall of American Slavery* (New York: W. W. Norton, 1989), pp. 201–2.
7. Bernard Lewis, *Race and Color in Islam* (New York: Harper Torch, 1971), p. 102. Lewis hastens to add he is not attempting to create "a moral competition"

of offenses against humanity. Rather, his purpose is to "refute the claims both of exclusive virture and exclusive vice, and to point to the commonfailings of our common humanity. "

8. Claude Meillassoux, *The Anthropology of Slavery: The Womb of Iron and Gold*, tr. Alide Dasnois (Chicago: University of Chicago Press, 1991, pp. 101–15.)

9. Curtin, "The Atlantic Slave Trade, " in *History of West Africa.* K. F. A. Ajayi and Michael Crowder (eds.) (New York: Columbia University Press, 1972), pp. 243–51. See also Lester Brooks, *Great Civilizations of Ancient Africa* (New York: Four Winds Press, 1971), p. 165.

10. Finley, *Ancient Slavery and Modern Ideology*, p. 64.

11. See Lefkowitz, *Not Out of Africa: How Afrocentrism Became an Excuse to Teach Myth as History* (New York: Basic Books, 1996) and Lefkowitz and Guy Roger (eds.) *Black Athena Revisited* (Chapel Hill: North Carolina University Press, 1996). Mary Lefkowitz has rejected the notion that Egyptians were "Khemetic" (a term for black land, misused by some Afrocentrists. Professor Lefkowitz allowed that Egyptians were "people of color," not Europeans. Beyond that, no one could say. Frank Yurco of the University of Chicago and Frank Snowden, professor of classics at Howard, also dismiss such claims as faddish.

12. Egyptian diplomats have denounced the controversy as an American problem which has no relevance to their countrymen. Abdel Latif Aboul-Ela, cultural emissary to the U.S., told Dinesh D'Souza, "I wish people would not involve us in this kind of mess, which we have nothing to do with. They should not use us, involve us in this racial problem. " See Dinesh D'Souza, *Illiberal Education: The Politics of Race and Sex on Campus* (New York: Free Press, 1991), pp. 112 and 119.

13. According to Alan Gardiner, the earliest culture in the upper Nile valley was "essentially African." *Egypt of the Pharaohs* (New York: Oxford, 1966), pp. 391–95. The German Adolf Erman cited the Leyden Papyrus where blacks offer to protect the Egyptians from "the People of the Bow. " *The Ancient Egyptians: A Sourcebook of Their Writings*, tr. Aylward Blackman (New York: Harper Torch reprint, 1923, 1966), p. 107.

14. John Wilson, *The Culture of Ancient Egypt* (Chicago: University of Chicago Press, 1951, 1956), p. 137.

15. Cyril Aldred, *Egypt to the End of the Old Kingdom* (New York: McGraw-Hill, 1965), pp. 42, 44, 64.

16. The research of Yigael Yadin, for one, disposed of such notions. The Hyksos were a powerful band of warriors, armed with more sophisticated weaponry (chariots, sickle swords, bucklers) and knowledge of fortifications than the Bronze Age Hebrews could have possessed. Moreover, they venerated a multitude of animistic deities, including the reviled Sutekh or Set, and tried to impose their own culture upon the Egyptians. These Semitic kings (probably from Syria) dominated Egypt for more than a century until native resistance leaders Ahmose and Kamose, founders of the eighteenth dynasty, defeated them. Yadin, *The Art of Warfare in Biblical Lands in the Light of Archaeological Study* (New York: McGraw Hill, 1967), I, pp. 176–84.

17. Gardiner, *Egypt of the Pharaohs*, pp. 148–72.

18. See Harry Orlinsky, *Understanding the Bible through History and Archeology* (New York: Ktav, 1972), pp. 52–56 and Wilson, *Culture of Ancient Egypt*, p. 74.

19. Chancellor Williams susggests that many of the Israelites in Egypt were black and states that the wife of Moses was 'jet-black. " *The Destruction of Black Civilization* (Chicago: Third World Press, 1974), pp. 143 and 358.

20. John Manchip White, *Everyday Life in Ancient Egypt* (New York: Capricorn, 1963), pp. 60–61.
21. Henri Frankfort, *The Birth of Civilization in the Near East* (Garden City, NY : Doubleday Anchor, 1956), p. 110.
22. C. Leonard Woolley, *Ur of the Chaldees* (New York: W. W. Norton, 1965), pp. 175–76.
23. James Henry Breasted, *A History of Egypt* (New York: Scribner's/Bantam, 1901/1967), pp. 70–72, 256–57, 412–17.
24. *Ibid.,* p. 70.
25. *Ibid.,* p. 257.
26. Erman, *The Ancient Egyptians,* pp. 95–103.
27. I. E. S. Edwards, *The Pyramids of Egypt* (Baltimore, MD: Penguin, 1947, 1967), p. 267.
28. British copyist Norman de Garis Davies believes the slaves were being chastized. See Ian Wilson, *Exodus: The True Story behind the Biblical Account* (San Francisco, CA: Harper and Row, 1985), p. 8.
29. Wilson, *Culture of Ancient Egypt,* pp. 257–58.
30. Wilson, *Exodus,* p. 81.
31. Erman, *The Ancient Egyptians,* pp. 191, 193, 198.
32. Wilson, *Exodus,* p. 81.
33. Wilson, *Culture of Ancient Egypt,* p. 74.
34. Leonard Woolley, *The Beginnings of Civilization* (New York: Mentor, 1965), p. 598.
35. Georges Contenau, *Everyday Life in Babylonia and Assyria* (New York: W. W. Norton, 1966), p. 20.
36. Isaac Mendelsohn, *Legal Aspects of Slavery in Babylonia, Assyria and Palestine* (Williamsport, PA: Bayard Press, 1932), p. 28.
37. Contenau, *Everyday Life in Babylonia and Assyria,* p. 19.
38. Donald Harden, *The Phoenicians* (New York: Praeger, 1962), p. 165.
39. Mendelsohn, *Legal Aspects of Slavery,* pp. 43–50.
40. A. Leo Oppenheim, *Ancient Mesopotamia: Portrait of a Dead Civilization* (Chicago: University of Chicago Press, 1964), p. 75 and Sabatino Moscati, *Ancient Semitic Civllizations* (New York: Capricorn, 1960), p. 81.
41. O. R. Gurney, *The Hittites* (Baltimore, MD: Penguin, 1925, 1966), p. 71.
42. *Ibid.* , pp. 70, 99.
43. Woolley, *The Beginnings of Civilization,* pp. 178–79. Lest anyone think slaves were permitted to think independently in Sumeria, Woolley's excavations at Ur revealed the bodies of more than 100 slaves forced to accompany their royal masters to the grave. *Ur of the Chaldees,* pp. 45–67.
44. Cf. Georges Roux, *Ancient Iraq* (Harmondsworth, Eng. : Penguin, 1964), pp. 318 and 128.
45. Kramer, *The Sumerians,* p. 78.
46. James Pritchard (ed.) *The Ancient Near East in Texts and Pictures* (Princeton, NJ: Princeton University Press, 1958), 161.
47. A. T. Olmstead, *History of the Persian Empire* (Chicago: University of Chicago, 1948, 1959), p. 77.
48. D. D. Luckinbull, *Ancient Records of Assyria and Babylonia* (Chicago: University of Chicago Press, 1926), I, p. 146.
49. A. Leo Oppenheim, in *Ancient Near Eastern Texts,* ed. J. B. Pritchard (Princeton, NJ: Princeton University Press, 1950), pp. 283–84.
50. See law code of Darius I in Olmstead, *History of the Persian Empire,* pp. 119–30. See also Muhammad Dandamaer, *Slavery in Babylonia from Nabonassar*

to *Alexander the Great* (Dekalb: Northern Illinois Press, 1984).

51. Finley, *Ancient Slavery and Modern Ideology*, p. 88. See generally W. L. Westermann's *Slave Systems of Greek and Roman Antiquity*. (Philadelphia: American Philosophical Society, 1954).

52. John Fine, *The Ancient Greeks: A Critical History* (Cambridge, MA: Harvard University Press, 1983), p. 440.

53. H. Michell, *Sparta* (Cambridge: Cambridge University Press, 1964), pp. 75–84.

54. See Athenaus, *The Banqueting Sophists* , tr. G. B. Gulick (Loeb Library, 1927–1941), in Thomas Wiedemann, *Greek and Roman Slavery* (Baltimore, MD: Johns Hopkins University Press, 1981), 78–88.

55. A. R. Burn, *The Lyric Age of Greece* (New York: Minerva Press, 1960, 1967), p. 223.

56. *Ibid.* , p. 294.

57. Keith Bradley, *Slavery and Society at Rome* (Cambridge: Cambridge University Press, 1994), pp. 12 and 32.

58. Henry Boren, *Roman Society* (Lexington, MA: D.C. Heath, 1992), pp. 67–71, 222.

59. Carcopino, *Everyday Life in Ancient Rome*, p. 65.

60. J.P.V.D. Balsdon, *Romans and Allies* (Chapel Hill: North Carolina University Press, 1979) p. 79. Balsdon notes that the Romans regarded all subject peoples as *peregrini* who by definition were inferior. The Celts of Spain and France were braggarts who wwere easily vanquished. The Hyperboreans residing in the frozen north were savages, their Irish and British neighbors devoid of any redeeming virtues. Egypt was the land of superstitious animal worship, Africa the home of weak-blooded blacks. Syrians, Jews, and Arabs were "born slaves." Even the cultured Greeks were denigrated as unreliable fighters. See pp. 31–71.

61. A few intellectuals, Salvian, Strabo, Pliny, and Seneca spoke out on their behalf, suggesting that if slaves acted in these ways it was because of fear and torture.

62. Wiedemann, *Greek and Roman Slavery*, pp. 1–11.

63. Bradley, *Slavery and Society at Rome,* p. 28.

64. Carcopino, *Every Day Life in Ancient Rome*, pp. 101–2. Salvian scored the wicked behavior of masters who "went after women, each whinying like a stallion after the wife of his neighbor. " *The Governance of God*, (Columbia U. Press, 1930), 7, 4:17–20. Richard Duncan Jones talks of slaves being *vernae,* products bread on the farm. *The Economy of the Roman Empire* (Cambridge: Cambridge University Press, 1974), p. 50.

65. Boren, *Roman Society,* p. 224.

66. *Cato the Censor on Farming*, tr. Ernest Borchaut (New York: Octagon Books, 1966), II:3–7. Plutarch denounced the mean nature of this instruction. *Life of Cato*, tr. B. Perrin (New York: Loeb, 1924), p. 317.

67. Pseudolus, cited in Thomas Africa, *The Romans and Their World* (New York: St. Martin's Press, 1970), p. 87. On the plight of slaves in the mines, see R. H. Barrow, *Slavery in the Roman Empire* (New York: Barnes and Noble, 1968), p. 114.

68. Apuleius, *Metamorphoses*, 9, 12 in *The Golden Ass,* tr. Robert Graves (New York: Farrar, Straus, Giraux, 1969), p. 202.

69. Diodorus Siculus, tr. C. H. Oldfather and others (Loeb, 12 vols. 1933–67), 5:38. 1. On the misery of chained slaves, see A.H.M. Jones, *The Roman Economy* (Totowa, NJ: Rowman and Littlefield, 1974), pp. 123–28.

70. For information on the first two slave rebellions see Diodorus Siculus, op. cit, 24, 2, and 36, 1–9. On Spartacus, see Appian, *Bell. Civ.* (Loeb, 1912), 1, 14. 116–20 and Plutarch, *The Fall of the Roman Republic,* tr. R. Warner (PC, 1958), Crassus, 8. 1–11. 8. See also Arthur Boak and William Sinnigen, *A History of Rome to AD 565* (London: Macmillan, 1965, 1969), pp. 156–57 and 211).

71. Fear of slave rebellions "sent shivers down the spines of rich Romans terrified by the motley horde" according to Boren, *Roman Society,* pp. 110–11.

72. Carcopino, *Every Day Life in Ancient Rome,* pp. 57–58.

73. Balsdon, *Romans and Allies,* pp. 12–14.

74. Carcopino, *Every Day Life in Ancient Rome,* p. 61.

75. Gaius, *Institutes,* tr. F. de Zulueta (Oxford: Oxford University Press, 1958), book 1, 1:43.

76. Heichelheim, Yeo, and Ward, *A History of the Roman People* (Englewood Cliffs, NJ: Prentice-Hall, 1984), p. 288.

77. Paul Allard, "Slavery, " *Catholic Encyclopedia* , XIV, pp. 36–39. See also "Slavery, " *New Catholic Encyclopedia* (New York: McGraw-Hill, 1967–79), XIII, pp. 281–83.

78. See *The Cambridge Companion to Aquinas,* ed. Norman Kretzmann and Eleonore Stump (Cambridge: Cambridge University Press, 1993), pp. 222–29. The abolitionist Henry Ward Beecher subscribed to the same insensitivity, admonishing church audiences during American labor violence in 1877–78 that people were poor because they were sinners.

79. Allard, "Slavery, " pp. 36–39.

Notes to Chapter 3

1. For a comprehensive discussion of the so-called Curse of Ham, consult the symposium in *The William and Mary Quarterly,* 3d Series LIV (January 1997). See especially Benjamine Braude, "The Sons of Noah and the Construction of Ethnic and Geographical Identities in the Medieval and Early Modern Periods," pp. 103–142.

2. See commentary of Dr. J.H. Hertz, Chief Rabbi of the British Empire, *Pentateuch and Haftorahs* (London: Soncino Press, 1987), p. 537.

3. David Brion Davis, *The Problem of Slavery in the Age of Revolution* (Ithaca, NY: Cornell University Press, 1975), p. 523.

4. Salo Baron, *A Social and Religious History of the Jews* (New York: Columbia University Press and Jewish Publication Society, 1937–1952), I, p. 267.

5. Thousands were massacred when Pompey conquered Jerusalem in 63 B.C., at least 30,000 when Crassus sacked the Temple in 54 B.C. Josephus tells of more than one million killed in the siege of the holy city in 66–70 A.D., another 100,000 taken for the entertainment of Romans in ampitheaters and mines. Perhaps 250,000 Jews died in Alexandria, Cyprus, and Cyrenaica in the little-known War of Quietus between 115 and 117 A.D. Dio Cassius claims that at least 580,000 Jews died during the messianic uprising of Bar Kochba between 132 and 135 A.D.

6. Jews did flourish, at various times, in medieval Christian Europe. Before Visigothic hordes became entrenched in newly conquered lands, while they were yet experimenting with Arian Christianity (a sect that emphasized the human nature of Jesus), sixth century Jews enjoyed some degree of prosperity in Germany and Spain. The same was true in Italy where Jews served as physicians, craftsmen, farmers, judges, viziers before the invasion of the Lombards.

Many German tribesmen deemed Jews bearers of the once-proud Roman clture. Thus Charlemagne (768–814) authorized their trade in wine, switched the major market day in his domains from Saturday, and intervened in legal disputes out of deference to this important commercial class. Jews even succeeded in having their own special court position (*magister judaerom*) established in the reign of Louis the Pius (814–40). These moments of Jewish prosperity did not pass unchallenged. Agobard, Archbishop of Lyons (779–84), canonized as "the most enlightened man of his age," denounced the special status of Jews and plotted with Lothair, son of Louis the Pious, to depose the king. See Israel Abrahams, *Jewish Life in the Middle Ages* (Philadelphia, PA: Jewish Publication Society, 1958) and Robert Chazan, *Medieval Jewry in Northern France: a Political and Social History* (Baltimore, MD: Johns Hopkins University Press, 1973).

7. According to one eighth-century authority, Simon Qayya, intercourse with a slave girl was a violation of fourteen Talmudic rules. In the ninth century Natronai Gaon held that such practice might result in flogging and temporary excommunication for as many as thirty days.

8. Baron, *Social and Religious History of the Jews*, IV, pp. 187–95.

9. *Code of Maimonides: Mishneh Torah* (New Haven, CT: Yale University Press, 1949–), Book of Torts, tr. Hyman Klein (1954), book 11, ch.3, p. 169 and ch. IV., p. 176.

10. *Mishneh Torah*, Book of Acquisition, tr. Isaac Klein (1951), book 12, ch. 9, p. 281.

11. *Mishneh Torah*, Book of Acquisition, book 12, ch. 8, pp. 274–78.

12. *Mishneh Torah*, Book of Asservations, tr.B.D.Klein (1962), book 6, ch. 12, pp. 108, 234; and Book of Holiness, tr. Louis Rabinowitz and Philip Grossman (1965), book 5, ch. 12, p. 84.

13. *Shulchan Aruch, Yore Deah*, 267, 27.

14. Abrahams, *Jewish Life in the Middle Ages*, pp. 100–1.

15. H.S. Chamberlain, *Foundations of the Nineteenth Century*, tr. John Lees (New York: John Lane, 1912), vol. I, p. 341.

16. Pirenne also mentions Jews as sailors, physicians, bankers, shipowners, and spice traders, but few recalled these other vocations. *Mohammed and Charlemagne*, tr. Bernard Mia (New York: Barnes and Noble, 1956), pp. 84–85.

17. Reynolds, *Europe Emerges: Transition toward an Industrial World Wide Society, 600–1750* (Madison: University of Wisconsin Press, 1961), p. 317.

18. Latouche, *The Birth of Western Economy* (London: Metheun, 1961). Interestingly, there is no reference whatever to Jews in M.M. Postan's *Essays on Medieval Agriculture and General Problems of the Medieval Economy* (Cambridge: Cambridge University Press, 1973).

19. On the Radanites, see Bachrach, *Early Medieval Jewish Policy in Western Europe* (St. Paul: University of Minnesota Press, 1977), pp. 72–73 and 96. On the policies of Louis the Pius generally, see pp. 84–105.

20. Oelsner and Korn in *Economic History of the Jews*, ed.Nachum Gross (New York: Schocken, 1975), p. 272.

21. Heinrich Graetz, *History of the Jews* (Philadelphia, PA: Jewish Publication Sociaty, 1894, 1956), III, 28–29.

22. Abrahams, *Jewish Life in the Middle Ages*, pp. 97–98.

23. Baron, *Social and Religious History of the Jews*, II, 258–60.

24. *Ibid.*, IV, 193.

25. *Ibid.*, IV, 337.

26. David Brion Davis claims Syrian merchants helped guide troops of slaves across Russia, Poland and Germany to the Mediterranean. See *The Problem of Slavery in Western Culture* (New York: Oxford University Press, 1966), p. 37.

27. Dockes, *Medieval Slavery and Liberation*, p. 140.

28. Baron, *Economic and Religious History of the Jews*, III, pp. 214ff.

29. Oelsner and Korn, *Economic History of the Jews*, p. 270.

30. Baron, *Economic and Religious History of the Jews*, IV, p. 337.

31. Friedman, *Without Future: The Plight of Syrian Jewry* (Westport, CT: Praeger, 1989), pp. 4–9.

32. S.D.Goitein , *A Mediterranean Society* (New York: Schocken, 1967), p. 140.

33. Oelsner and Korn, *Economic History of the Jews* , p. 272.

34. David Brion Davis, *Slavery and Human Progress* (New York: Oxford University Press, 1984), p. 89.

35. Baron, *Social and Religious History of the Jews*, IV, 196.

36. Werner Sombart, *The Jews and Modern Capitalism*, tr. M. Epstein (Glencoe, IL: Free Press, 1951), p. 175.

37. *Ibid.,* p. 13.

38. *Ibid.,* p. 171.

39. Uriah Z.Engelman, *The Rise of the Jews in the Western World* (New York: Behrman's Book House, 1944), p. 45.

40. arvin Lowenthal, *The Jews of Germany* (New York: Longmans, Green & Co., 1936), pp. 157–58.

41. Weinryb, *Jews of Poland*, pp. 38–55.

42. *Ibid.,* p. 46.

43. Salo Baron, *The Russian Jews under Tsar and Soviets* (New York: Macmillan, 1964), p. 9.

44. See Louis Greenberg, *The Jews in Russia* (New Haven, CT: Yale University Press, 1944, 1951); Michael Stanislawski, *Tsar Nicholas I and the Jews* (Philadelphia, PA: Jewish Publication Society, 1983) and Ismar Elbogen, *A Century of Jewish Life* (Philadelphia, PA: Jewish Publication Society, 1944), pp. 355–407.

45. For a description of Jewish poverty in Kiev, See Leo Errera, *The Russian Jews: Extermination or Emancipation*, tr. Bella Lowy (Westport, CT: Greenwood Press, 1975, 1994), pp. 29–30.

46. Weber and Kempter, *Report of the Commissioners of Immigration upon the Causes which Incite Immigration to the U.S.* (Washington, DC: GPO, 1892), pp. 34ff.

47. Leo Errera, *The Russian Jews*, pp. 115–16.

48. Weber, *General Economic History,* tr. Frank Knight (New York: Greenberg Publ., 1937), p. 359. See also Jacob Katz, *Tradition and Crisis: Jewish Society at the End of the Middle Ages* (Glencoe, IL: Free Press, 1960).

49. *The Chronicles of Rabbi Joseph ben Joshua ben Meir,* tr. C.H.F. Bialloblotzky (London: Oriental Trns. Fund Publications, 1836), p. 430. James Baldwin, Cornel West, and Henry Louis Gates offer varying points of view on the wisdom of reciting Jewish history. The former believed that such information merely increased black rage at Jews who, seemingly, ignored their current plight. Baldwin, "Negroes Are Anti-Semitic Because They're Anti-White, " p. 37 in Paul Berman (ed.) *Blacks and Jews: Alliances and Arguments* (New York: Delacorte Press, 1994). West, on the other hand, opened his own essay in this collection ("On Black-Jewish Relations", pp. 144–46) with a rendition of pogroms and expulsions suffered by Jews. And Gates urged the two minorities not to engage in

"this hateful sport of victimology." ("The Uses of Anti-Semitism with Memoirs of an Anti-Anti-Semite," p. 220.)

Notes to Chapter 4

1. Already in the fourteenth century, price was linked to lightness of color. William Phillips, *Slavery from Roman Times to the Early Transatlantic Trade* (St. Paul: University of Minnesota Press, 1985), pp. 106, 154–55.
2. *Ibid.*, pp. 103 and 60.
3. Accoding to Ralph Austen, more than 3.3 million Africans were uprooted between 900 and 1400 A.D., chiefly by Arabs. "The Trans-Saharan Slave Trade: A Tentative Census" in *The Uncommon Market: Essays in the Economic History of the Alantic Slave Trade*, ed. Henry Gemery and Jans Hogendorn (New York: Academic Press, 1979), p. 66. For the impact of sugar, see Phillips, *Slavery from Roman Times*, pp. 93–97.
4. Lee Anne Durham Seminario, *The History of the Blacks, the Jews, and the Moors in Spain* (Madrid: Coleccion Plaza Mayor Scholar, 1975),pp. 11–17.
5. *Ibid.*, pp. 19–21. See also John Blake, *Europeans in West Africa 1450–1560* (London: Hakluyt Society, 1942); C.R. Boxer, *The Portuguese Seaborne Empire 1415–1825* (New York: Knopf, 1969); and A.H. de Oliveira Marques, *History of Portugal* (New York: Columbia University Press, 1972).
6. Curtin, "Major Trends" in *The Slave Economies: Historical andTheoretical Perspectives*, Eugene Genovese (ed.) (New York: Wiley and Sons, 1973), I, p. 76.
7. See W.Walton Claridge, *A History of the Gold Coast and Ashanti* (London: Frank Cass, 1964) I, 34–39 and Winfield Collins, *The Domestic Slave Trade of the Southern States* (New York: Broadway Pub., 1904), p. 2. On the brutality of the Portuguese trade in Angola and Guinea , see also C.R. Boxer, *The Golden Age of Brazil* (Berkeley: University of California Press, 1962), pp. 4–7, 24–26, and 153–55.
8. Donnan, *Documents Illustrative of the Slave Trade* , I, p. 15.
9. Phillips, *American Negro Slavery*, pp. 17–18; Donnan, *Documents Illustrative of the Slave Trade*, I, pp. 14–15.
10. Donnan, *Documents Illustrative of the Slave Trade*, I, 14–16, 104–7, 343–46.
11. According to Hubert Aimes, much of the trade in the eighteenth century was in the hands of *Real Compania Mercantil de la Habana*. The top era of imports was 1816–20 when nearly 25,000 were brought over. Aimes, *A History of Slavery in Cuba 1511 to 1608* (New York: Putnam's, 1907), pp. 29–54.
12. For these early settlements, see Solomon Katz, *The Jews in the Visigothic and Frankish Kingdoms of Spain and Gaul* (Cambridge, MA: Medieval Academy of New York, 1937; Kraus Reprint, 1970) and Eliyahu Ashtor, *The Jews of Muslim Spain* (Philadelphia, PA: Jewish Publication Society, 1973–84).
13. For a general history of Jews in Spain, see Heinrich Graetz, *History of the Jews* (Philadelphia, PA: Jewish Publication Society , 1896), IV, pp. 143–55, 166–73, 231–38, 274–76, 353–54, 387–89; Abraham Neuman, *The Jews in Spain* (Philadelphia, PA: Jewish Publication Society), 1942; Seminario, *History of Blacks, Jews and Moors in Spain*, pp. 35–72; and Elmer Brendiner, *The Rise and Fall of Paradise* (New York: Putnam's, 1983).
14. Cecil Roth, *The Spanish Inqusition* (New York: Norton, 1964), pp. 20–22 and John Longhurst, *The Age of Torquemada* (Lawrence, KA: Coronado Press, 1964), pp. 31–44.
15. Roth, *Spanish Inqustion*, p. 27.

16. *Ibid.*, p. 32.
17. *Ibid.*, pp. 94–101.
18. *Ibid.*, p. 123.
19. Neuman lists two pages of jobs filled by Jews in Spain from diplomats and furriers to sailors, tailors, locksmiths, vinters, cambists, farmers, jewelers and horse traders. *Jews of Spain* , I, pp. 166–67.
20. According to a contemporary observer, Andres Bernaldez, there were 35,000 families in Castile, another 6,000 in Aragon, totalling more than 200,000 persons in all. According to Isidore Loeb, 50,000 may have undergone baptism; 165,000 emigrated, of whom 20,000 perished in transit. "Le Nombre de Juifs de Castille et d'Espagnol," *Revued es Etudes Juives* (1887), XIV, p. 182. Many returned in rags to face the dangers of the inquisition rather than continue a life of exile. Longhurst, *Age of Torquemada*, pp. 129–37. See also Valeriu Marcu, *The Expulsion of the Jews from Spain* (New York: Viking, 1935) and Jacob Minkin, *Abarbanel and the Expulsion of the Jews from Spain* (New York: Behrman's, 1938).
21. On the fate of exiles in Portugal, Flanders, and Italy, see Mair Jose Bernardete, *Hispanic Culture and the Character of the Sephardic Jews* (New York: Sepher-Hermon Press, 1982), pp. 32–43; Gerber, *Jews of Spain*, pp. 132–44 and 182–86; and Paloma Diaz Mas, *Sephardim: The Jews from Spain*, tr. G.Zucker (Chicago: University of Chicago Press, 1992), pp. 35–71.
22. Seymour Liebman describes how Jews would hang chili peppers on crucifixes or strike crosses with boards in the privacy of their homes. *The Jews in New Spain* (Coral Gables, FL: University of Miami Press, 1970), pp. 52–53.
23. Seymour Liebman, *The Inquisitors and the Jews in the New World* (Coral Gables, FL: University of Miami Press, 1974), pp. 22–39. See also Liebman, *New World Jewry, 1493–1825* (New York: Ktav, 1982) and *Jews and the Inqusition of Mexico: The Great Auto da Fe of 1649* (Lawrence, KA: Coronado Press, 1974).
24. Liebman, *Jews in New Spain*, pp. 135–36.
25. Rabbi Bertram W. Korn Papers (hereafter referred to as Korn Papers), American Jewish Archives, Hebrew Union College, Cincinnati, Ms. Collection no. 99, "Slavery, Jewish Participation in, 1450–1860," Box 31, Folder 1.
26. The church prepared a manual of Jewish practices to assist authorities in their hunt for Judaizers. Longhurst, *Age of Torquemada*, pp. 85–91.
27. Cecil Roth, *A History of the Marranos* (Philadelphia, PA: Jewish Publication Society, 1932, Harper Torch, 1966), pp. 277–83.
28. Liebman, *Jews in New Spain*, pp. 305–33.
29. Frederick Bowser, *The African Slave in Colonial Peru 1524–1650* (Palo Alto, CA: Stanford University Press, 1974), pp. 58–59.
30. Elkan Nathan Adler, "The Inquisition in Peru," *PAJHS* (1904), XII, pp. 5–38. Arnold Wiznitzer says of Judaizers in Mexico, their history was a sad one. The omnipresent Inquisition was their pitiless and deadly enemy. "Crypto-Jews in Mexico during the Seventeenth Century," *PAJHS*, LI , 222–268.
31. Cardozo de Bethencourt, "Notes on the Spanish and Portuguese Jews in the U.S., Guiana, and the Dutch and British West Indies during the 17th and 18th centuries," *PAJHS*, XXIX, p. 23.
32. Liebman, *Jews in New Spain*, p. 288.
33. Ira lerner, *Mexican Jewry in the Land of the Aztecs* (Mexico: B.Costa-Amic, 1973), pp. 84–85 and 123. See also Henry Lea, *History of the Inquisition in the Spanish Dependencies* (New York: Macmillan, 1922) and Alfonso Toro, *Los Judios en la Nueva Espana* (Mexico: Publicaciones del AGN, 1932).
34. Judith Laikin Elkin, *The Jews of the Latin American Republics* (Chapel Hill: University of North Carolina Press, 1980), pp. 30–50. Jacob Lestchinsky esti-

mates that fewer than 4,000 Jews came to South America between 1840 and 1880. By way of contrast more than 10,000 went to Palestine and 200,000 to the U.S.

35. Faur, *In the Shadow of History: Jews and Conversos at the Dawn of Modernity* (Albany: State University of New York Press, 1992), pp. 43–52.
36. Longhurst, *Age of Torquemada*, p. 48.
37. *Ibid.*, p. 47.
38. Graetz, *History of the Jews*, IV, p. 308.
39. Kamen, *The Spanish Inquisition* (New York: NAL, 1965), pp. 21–22.
40. Baer, *A History of the Jews in Christian Spain*, tr. Louis Schoffman (Philadelphia, PA: Jewish Publication Society, 1966), II, p. 278.
41. Liebman, *The Inquisitors and the Jews in the New World*, pp. 213–18.
42. Roth, *History of the Marranos*, pp. 168–90.
43. *Ibid.*, p. 194.
44. Netanyahu argues that the Marranos not only converted but lost their faith in God. *The Marranos of Spain* (New York: American Academy for Jewish Research, 1966), pp. 117, 132–34.
45. Davis, *Slavery and Human Progress*, p. 96.
46. Liebman, *The Inquistors and the Jews in the New World*, pp. 100–30.
47. *Ibid.*, p. 203.
48. Elkin, *The Jews of the Latin American Republics*, p. 20. Jane Gerber suggests the loss of identity came much sooner, as early as the first generation of children born to the Marranos. "Steeped in the Christian way of life," she writes, "this generation became increasingly detached from the beliefs and traditions of their parents as the fifteenth century (sic)progressed." *Jews of Spain*, p. 122.
49. Liebman, *The Inquisitors and the Jews in the New World*, pp. 140–41.
50. *Ibid.*, pp. 213–18.
51. C.R. Boxer, *The Dutch in Brazil, 1624–1654* (New York: Archon Books, 1973), p. 209.
52. *Ibid.* p. 101. Dr. Laurenco de Mendoca protested to the crown over the practice of misidentifying Portuguese as Jews.
53. Merrill, "The Role of Sephardic Jews in the British Caribbean Area during the 17th century," *Caribbean Studies*, IV, no. 3, pp. 32–49. See also Egon Wolff and Frieda Wolff, *Judeus Judaizantes e seus escravos* (Rio de Janeiro: Erca Editorial e Grafica, 1987), pp. 24–31.
54. Arnold Wiznitzer, *Jews in Colonial Brazil* (New York: Columbia University Press, 1960), pp. 3–5.
55. For a discussion of Jewish involvement in the three-roller mill system of Brazil, see J.H. Galloway, *The Sugar Cane Industry: An Historical Geography from Its Origins to 1914* (Cambridge: Cambridge University Press, 1989), pp. 70–77. See also F.W. Knight, "Caribbean Sugar Industry and Slavery," *Latin American Research Review* XVIII (1983), pp. 219–29.
56. C.R.Boxer, *Race Relations in the Portuguese Colonial Empire, 1415–1825* (Oxford: Clarendon Press, 1963), p. 16.
57. Wiznitzer, *Jews in Colonial Brazil*, p. 10. See also Herbert Klein, *African Slavery in Latin America and the Caribbean* (Oxford: Oxford University Press, 1986), pp. 38–43.
58. Wiznitzer, *Jews in Colonial Brazil*, pp. 12–18.
59. Liebman, *The Inquisitors and the Jews* , p. 170. See also J.Lucio D'Azevedo, *Historia does Christaos Novos Portugueses* (Lisbon: Libraria Classica Editora de A.M. Teixeira, 1921), pp. 232–78. See also Jose Goncalves Salvador , *Os Cristaos-Novos Povoamento e Conquista do Solo Brasilerio (1530–1680)* (Sao Paulo: Universidade de Sao Paulo and Libraria Pioneira Editora, 1976) and

Salvador, *Os Cristaos-Novos: Em Minas Gerais durante O Circlo do Ouro (1695–1755)* (Livraria Editora Sao Bernando do campo, 1992).

60. Liebman, *The Inquisitors and the Jews*, p. 159.

61. *Ibid.*, p. 137. Boxer points out that for a long time, to the end of the Dutch War, the task of raiding the interior of Brazil in search of additional slaves fell mainly to mulattoes from Sao Paulo. *Golden Age of Brazil*, pp. 14–15. In separate lectures, the distinguished professor from King's College noted the different status of of mixed bloods (*Mamelucos, Mulattoes, Mestizos,* and *Cabozlos*) in Brazil. *Race Relations in the Portuguese Colonial Empire*, p. 86.

62. Freyre's source is none other than Houston Stewart Chamberlain. Freyre, *The Masters and the Slaves: A Study in the Development of Brazilian Civilization,* tr. Samuel Putnam (New York: Knopf, 1946), p. 232. In the wake of the Holocaust, Freyre scored "Hebrew plutocrats" for comingling their blood with "the best of Portugal's nobility." *Ibid.*, p. 235.

63. Letter of Amzalak to Korn, April 9, 1970, Korn Files, American Jewish Archives, File 31, Folder 2.

64. Letter of Bessa, April 9, 1974, Korn Files, American Jewish Archives, File 31, Folder 6.

65. Letter of Bresa to Korn, July 26, 1974, AJA, Korn Files, File 31, Folder 6.

66. Letter of Ettinghause to Korn, March 20, 1970, AJA, Korn Files, File 31, Folder 6.

67. Letter of Roditi to Korn, Jan. 8, 1971, AJA, Korn Files, File 31, Folder 2.

68. Letter of Vansina to Korn, November 29, 1971, AJA, Korn Files, File 31, Folder 6. See also letter of Seymour Liebman to Korn, February 27, 1970, 31–6 and letter from C.Wyffles, Archives Generals Brussels, May 19, 1970, 31–4.

69. Slavers in London, Amsterdam, Antwerp, AJA, Korn Files, 31–6, and undated typed manuscript 31–3. See lists of Jewish shippers from Guinea/Loango 1600–1643 in Frederic Mauro," Le Portugal et L'Atlantique que 12e Siecle 1570–1670," *Ecole Practique des Hautes Etudes* (6e section Centre de Recherches Historique, 1960), X, pp. 158–61.

70. C.R. Boxer, *The Portuguese Seaborne Empire*

71. Boxer, *Dutch in Brazil,* p. 102. Boxer points out that when Juan IV chartered the Brazil Company *(Companhia Geral para o estado do Brazil)* in 1648, many of its investors were New Christians in Lisbon. In accordance with the proposal of Padre Antonio Vieira, they were given immunity from the Inquistion in exchange for their pledges. The company enjoyed a monopoly on wine, flour, olive oil, and codfish , but as Boxer points out, not slaves. *Dutch in Brazil*, p. 212.

72. Liebman, *The Inquisitions and the Jews*, p. 144; Merrill, "The Role of Sephardic Jews," p. 37; Boxer, *Dutch in Brazil,* p. 227.

73. Wiznitzer, *Jews in Colonial Brazil*, p. 129.

74. Herbert Bloom, "A Study of Brazilian Jewish History 1623–1654 Based Chiefly upon the Findings of the Late Samuel Oppenheim," *PAJHS* (1934) XXXIII, p. 75.

75. *Ibid.*, pp. 52–57 and 69–75. Calvinists in Recife were not much better, complaining about Jews converting slaves and keeping women as concubines. Boxer, *Dutch in Brazil*, p. 123.

76. Boxer, *Dutch in Brazil*, p. 164.

77. Arnold Wiznitzer, "The Jews in the Sugar Industry of Colonial Brazil," *Jewish Social Studies,* (July, 1956), XVIII, pp. 194–95.

78. Hermann Waetjen, *O Dominio Colonial no Brasil Hollandes* (Sao Paulo, 1938), 334–335.

79. Bloom, "A Study of Brazilian Jewish History," pp. 80–81 and Wiznitzer, "The Jews in the Sugar Industry," pp. 189–98. It is equally anomalous to identify

directors of the Brazil Company with Jews. Ships of this line flew a flag embla-
zoned on one side with the royal arms of Portugal and a representation of Our
Lady of the Immaculate Conception and two Latin inscriptions. Boxer, *Dutch
in Brazil*, p. 209.
80. Wiznitzer, "Jews in the Sugar Industry," p. 196.
81. Marcus, *The Colonial American Jew 1492–1776* (Detroit, MI: Wayne State
University Press, 1970), I, pp. 73–75, 220. Galloway says substantially the same
thing, devoting one paragraph to Jews who participated in the sugar industry.
Most, he concluded were advisers or technicians. *The Sugar Cane Industry*, p.
79. Boxer makes no mention of Jews and the sugar industry in Pernambuco,
where many resided, in his *Golden Age of Brazil 1695–1750* (Berkeley: University of California Press, 1962), pp. 24–27 and 302–4.
82. Bloom, A Study of Brazilian Jewish History," pp. 93–100.
83. Anita Novinsky, "Jewish Roots of Brazil," in *The Jewish Presence in Latin
America*, Judith Laikin Elkin and Gilbert Merkx (eds.) (Boston: Allen & Unwin,
1987), pp. 39–40. On the panic felt by Jews and New Christians see also Arnold
Witznitzer, "The Exodus from Brazil and Arrival in New Amsterdam of the
Jewish Pilgrim Fathers, 1654," in *The Jewish Experience in America*, ed.
Abraham Karp (New York: Ktav, 1969), I, p. 150.
84. Robert Toplin, *The Abolition of Slavery in Brazil* (New York: Atheneum, 1972),
pp. 4–5,9, 11–14, 33. See also Toplin, *Slavery and Race Relations in Latin
America* (Westport, CT: Greenwood Press, 1974).
85. Perre Verger, *Trade Relations between the Bight of Benin and Bahia from the
Seventeenth to the Nineteenth Century* (Ibadan: Ibadan University Press, 1976),
pp. 43–55.
86. Drescher, "The Role of Jews in the Transatlantic Slave Trade, " *Immigrants and
Jews* (London: Frank Cass, 1993), XII, p. 119.

Notes to Chapter 5

1. *The Secret Relationship between Blacks and Jews*, p. 19.
2. Cornelis Goslinga, *The Dutch in the Caribbean and on the Wild Coast, 1580–
1680* (Gainesville: University of Florida Press, 1971), pp. 341–42.
3. *Ibid.*, pp. 91–92.
4. Boxer, *Dutch in Brazil*, p. 11.
5. Goslinga, *The Dutch in the Caribbean*, p. 97.
6. Boxer, *Dutch in Brazil*, p. 10.
7. Wiznitzer, *Jews in Colonial Brazil*, p. 44.
8. Marcus, *The Colonial American Jew*, I, p. 273.
9. Roth, *History of the Marranos*, pp. 236–39.
10. *The Secret Relationship*. p. 22.
11. Bloom, "A Study of Brazilian Jewish History," *PAJHS*, XXIII, pp. 49–50.
12. *Ibid.*, p. 50. See also H.K. Brugmans and A. Frank, *Geschiedenis den Joden in
Nederland* (Amsterdam, 1940), p. 567.
13. Seymour Drescher, "The Role of Jews in the Transatlantic Slave Trade," p. 120.
14. Bloom, "A Study of Brazilian Jewish History," p. 49. As Cornelis Goslinga puts
it, after 1640 the DWIC declined from a mighty war instrument into an ordinary smuggling and slave-trading organization. Goslinga, *The Dutch in the
Caribbean*, p. 105. See also Peter Emmer, "History of Dutch Slave Trade,"
Journal of Economic History XXXII (September 1972), pp. 728–29.
15. *Ibid.*, p. 106.
16. *Ibid.*, pp. 146–72.
17. Donnan, *Documents*, I, pp. 136–41.

18. Johannes Postma, *The Dutch in the Atlantic Slave Trade 1600–1815* (Cambridge: Cambridge Univesity Press, 1990), pp. 377ff. The vessels averaged 300 slaves, with an 80 percent survival rate. The names included Jan Solomons, David Salomi, Beekman, Daniel Berg, Arie Parre, Simon Maas, Samuel Engelsman, and Joshua Doos. See also Dr. W.S.Unger, "Bijdragen Tot de Geschiedenis van de Nederlande Slavenhandel," report on Middleburg Commerce Co., 1732–1808, pp. 91–94, *Economisch Historisch daarboek* (Martinus Nijhoff, 1961), pp. 91–94.

19. Goslinga, *The Dutch in the Caribbean*, p. 424.

20. Boxer, *Dutch in Brazil*, pp. 10–11.

21. *Secret Relationship*, p. 36–48.

22. See P.A. Hilfman, "Some Further Notes on the History of the Jews in Surinam," *PAJHS* (1907), XVI pp. 7–22; Samuel Oppenheim, "An Early Jewish Colony in Western Guiana 1658–1666: And Its Relation to the Jews in Surinam, Cayenne and Tobago," *PAJHS* (1907), XVI, pp. 95–186; Oppenheim, "An Early Jewish Colony in Western Guiana: Supplemental Data," *PAJHS* (1909), XVII, pp. 53–70; and Cardozo de Bethencourt, "Notes on the Spanish and Portuguese Jews in the United States, Guiana and the Dutch and British West Indies during the Seventeenth and Eighteenth Centuries, *PAJHS* (1925), XXIX, pp. 7–38. See also Swierenga, *The Forerunners*, p. 33.

23. Herbert Bloom, "The Dutch Archives, with Special Reference to American Jewish History," *PAJHS* (1931), XXXII, p. 11.

24. The estimated value for slaves imported between February 21 and 23 was 127,632 florins. 39 Jews purchased 136 slaves at 32,160 florins. The following month, 10 Jews paid 10,400 florins of the total of 38,605 florins for slaves, again slightly over one-fourth. Bloom, "The Dutch Archives, With Special Reference to AmericanJewish History," *PAJHS* (1931), XXXII, p. 12.

25. Merrill,"The Role of Sephardic Jews in the British Caribbean," pp. 40–42.

26. Oppenheim, "An Early Jewish colony in Western Guiana," p. 57. This was later reversed. See L.C.Barbosa, "Manumission in Brazil and Surinam: The Role of Dutch Hegemony and Decline in the Capitalist World-Economy," *Ethnic and Racial Studies* X (July 1987), pp. 349–65.

27. Merrill, "The Role of Sephardic Jews in the British Caribbean," p. 39.

28. Letter from Koen to Korn, Amsterdam, March 17, 1970, Korn Papers, AJA, 31/22. See also Summary of Documents, City Archives of Amsterdam, Notarial Archives 643, Folder 304. There is reference to David Nassy receiving 114 Negroes for delivery to Cayenne. Nortarial Archives, 1309, fol.40–43, September 35, 1659. A more typical entry complained of the wormy, hot condition aboard ships bound for the Angola Coast in December 1636. Considering the risks of the Inquisition, it may be questioned how valid it is to identify any of those trading with New Spain as Jews.

29. Goslinga contends the DWIC realized that only healthy slaves were worth good money. *Ibid.*, p. 350. In the New World, it was a different story, as Goslinga relates "the future for every slave was pretty grim."

30. Isaac and Suzanne Emmanuel, *A History of the Jews of the Netherland Antilles* (Cincinnati, OH: American Jewish Archives, 1970),I, p. 79.

31. Goslinga, *The Dutch in the Caribbean*, p. 369.

32. As one example, of 702 slaves liberated in Curaçao between 1856 and 1863, 191 or 27 percent came from Jewish masters. Emmanuels, *History of Jews of Netherland Antilles*, II, p. 80.

33. A peace settlement arranged by Salomon de la Parra in May 1761 did not last very long. Within a decade, militia were building a line of forts along the

Commoimber River to the sea. Dr.B. Felsenthal and Professor Richard Gottheil, "Chronological Skech of the History of theJews in Surinam," *PAJHS* (1896), IV, pp. 2–5.

34. In April 1994, when Jews around the world were observing a memorial for Holocaust victims, Wellesley's Tony Martin delighted the audience at Howard University with tales of how one black rebel in Surinam had flayed and beheaded a Jewish slave owner, then used the skull to bowl. *Washington Jewish Week*, April 28, 1994, p. 6.
35. Hilfman,"Some Further Notes onthe History of the Jews in Surinam, "pp. 10–12; and Marcus, *The Colonial American Jew*, I, pp. 150–54.
36. Marcus, *The Colonial American Jew*, I, pp. 159–61.
37. Klein, *African Slavery in Latin America and the Caribbean* (Oxford: Oxford University Press, 1986), p. 133.
38. Marcus, *The Colonial American Jew*, I, p. 180.
39. *The Secret Relationship between Blacks and Jews*, p. 66.
40. Mills, "Half Truths and History: The Debate over Jews and the Slave Trade," reprinted in *The Guardian Weekly*, October 31, 1993, pp. 18–19.
41. Emmanuels, *History of Jews of the Netherland Antilles*, pp. 74–75 and Goslinga, *The Dutch in the Caribbean*, p. 105.
42. Marcus, *Colonial American Jew*, I, p. 175.
43. Donnan, *Documents*, III, p. 415.
44. Marcus, *Colonial American Jew*, I,p. 178.
45. Emmanuels, *Jews of the Netherland Antilles*, I, pp. 133–34, 144–45.
46. Swierenga, *The Forerunners*, p. 36.
47. Emmanuels, *Jews of the Netherland Antilles*, I, pp. 74–77.
48. *Ibid.*, pp. 75–76. The Emmanuels list a number of slave traders in the seventeenth century who had contacts with Amsterdam, including David Israel, Abraham Querido, Abraham Cohen, N. Deliaan, Jan deLion, Isaac Nunez, Moseh Curiel, Francisco Lopez Henriquez, Manuel de Pina, David Senior, and Philippe Henriquez, all of whose Sephardic names suggest Portuguese ancestry.
49. Fortune, *Merchants and Jews*, p. 157.
50. Marcus, *Colonial American Jews*, I, p. 181.
51. Emmanuels, *Jews of the Netherland Antilles*, I, p. 78.
52. Goslinga, *The Dutch in the Caribbean*, p. 480.
53. Marcus, *Colonial American Jew*, I, p. 186.
54. *Ibid.*, p. 181 and Emmanuels, *Jews of the Netherland Antilles*, I, pp. 14–45.
55. The Emmanuels demonstrate how Jews were insulted and overtaxed in 1727–1745 to underwrite building of a sailors' hospital. *Jews of the Netherland Antilles*, pp. 133–34.
56. Goslinga, *Dutch in the Caribbean*, pp. 351–54.
57. Merrill, "Role of Sephardic Jews in the British Caribbean," p. 49.
58. Letter from Professor Emmer to Korn, September 25, 1973, Korn Files, AJA, 31/2.
59. Untitled typed manuscript, Korn Files, AJA, 31–3, p. 161. There is no mention of Jewish involvement in correspondence from Brandenburg, Donnan, *Documents*, I, p. 103.
60. The principal Swedish fort in Africa, Stockholms Slott, was captured by the Dutch and Danes in 1657 and its governor Philipe von Krusentierna made prisoner. The only other names of prominence mentioned in the Swedish trade are those of Louis de Geer of Liege and Henry Carloff, neither of them Jews. See Jacques Macau, *La Guinee Danoise* (Aix-en-Provence: Institut d'Histoire des Pays d'Outre Mer, 1971), pp. 5–6 and Donnan, *Documents*, I, p. 77.

61. Macau, *La Guinée Danoise*, p. 3.
62. *Ibid.*, pp. 5–8. See also Georg Norregaard, *Danish Settlements in West Africa 1658–1850* (Boston: Boston University Press, 1966).
63. John Knox, *A Historical Account of St.Thomas W.I.* (New York: Scribners, 1852), p. 47.
64. Thorkild Hansen's *Slavernes Kyst: Tegninger af Birte Lund* (Copenhagen: Gyldendal, 1967). For a description of Danish slaving vessels, see Hansen, *Slavernes Skibe* (Gyldendal, 1967), pp. 11–22.
65. Most of the islands south of Puerto Rico were virtually uninhabited following decades of warfare among the British, Dutch, French, and Spanish. Apparently no one feared the Danes who claimed St. Thomas in 1671 and St. John in 1684 and purchased St. Croix in 1733. See U.S. Bureau of Statistics, *The Danish West Indies 1621–1901* (Washington, D.C., 1902), pp. 2768–69; Spectator (pseud.) *Our West Indian Islands* (Copenhagen: C.A. Reitzel, 1862); and James Parton, *The Danish Islands* (Boston: Fields, Osgood and Co., 1869.)
66. Macau, *La Guinée Danoise*, p. 34.
67. *Ibid.*, p. 1. The prominent sugar and cotton planters on St. Thomas, where there were 3,500 slaves, included the Beverhout, Charles, Runnels, Badger, deWint, and Zytsema families. Knox, *Historical Account of St.Thomas* , pp. 68–75.
68. Knox says there were 22 families on St.Thomas in 1803, p. 163.
69. See Pool, *Portraits Etched in Stone*, p. 8.
70. Julian Margolinsky, librarian of the Jewish Community of Copenhagen, described Henriques as a very rich merchant and shipowner who was an important member of the Danish West Indies and Guinea Comopany. So, apparently, were his two sons, Joshua and Isaac. See letter of Margolinsky to Korn, August 1, 1971, Korn Files, AJA, 31–3. Professor Emmer also commented on the importance of the Henriques family which continued to exercise leadership in the small Jewish community in Denmark down to the Nazi occupation of that country. Letter of Emmer to Korn, October 23, 1973. Korn Files, AJA, 31–2. See also Samuel Tolkowsky, *They Took to the Sea* (New York: T. Yoseloff, 1964) and *Gluckstadt im Wandel der Zeiten* (Gluckstadt: J.J.Augustin, 1963–68).
71. Untitled manuscript, Korn Files, AJA, 31–3, p. 419.
72. See the numerous references to Danes in Wilks, *Forests of Gold: Essays on the Akan and the Kingdom of Asante* (Athens: Ohio University Press, 1993), pp. 97, 308–9, 340–41, 343, 348–49.
73. Neville Hall notes incidents of Jewish brutality toward slaves (p. 99), as well as anti-Semitism on St.Croix (p. 104) in *Slave Society in the Danish West Indies* (Baltimore, MD: Johns Hopkins University Press, 1992).
74. Drescher,"The Role of Jews in the Transatlantic Slave Trade," p. 121.

Notes to Chapter 6

1. In 1627 Cardinal Richelieu created the *Compagnie des Îles Occidentales,* later the *Compagnie des Isles de l'Amerique.* Colbert's own Compagnie des Indies Occidentales was dissolved in 1674. His interpretation of mercantilism differed radically from that of the English because Colbert realized the virtual impossibility of filling the colonies with transplanted Europeans. In despatches dated 1666–67, he encouraged intermarriage with Indians, the creation of one law, one master, "one people, one blood. " See Jerah Johnson, "Colonial New Orleans: A Fragment of the Eighteenth Century French Ethos, " in *Creole New Orleans: Race and Americanization* , Arnold Hirsch and Joseph Logsdon (eds.) (Baton Rouge: Louisiana State Press, pp. 16–24). See also Arthur Hertzberg,

The French Enlightenment and the Jews (New York: Columbia University Press and Jewish Publication Society of America, 1968), pp. 22–25; William Eccles, *Canada under Louis XIV 1663–1701* (Toronto, 1969); Ines Murat, *Colbert* (Paris: Fayard, 1983); Charles Cole, *Colbert and a Century of French Mercantilism* (New York: Columbia University Press, 1939); Andrew Trout, *Jean-Baptiste Colbert* (Boston: Twayne, 1978); and Stewart Mims, *Colbert's West India Policy* (New Haven, CT: Yale University Press, 1912).

2. In 1670–72, 9,000 Africans were brought to the West Indies by these French companies. See Clarence Mumford, *The Black Ordeal of Slavery and Slave Trading in the French West Indies, 1625–1715* (Lewiston, NY: Edwin Mellen Press, 1991), I, p. 161.

3. Mumford, *Black Ordeal of Slavery*, I, x, and Donnan, *Documents*, I, p. 95.

4. Robert Stein, *The French Sugar Business in the Eighteenth Century* (Baton Rouge: Louisiana State University Press, 1988), pp. 20–23.

5. Stein notes the sugar islands were deemed so important to France that the mother country was willing to surrender all of Canada merely to retain Guadeloupe at the end of the Seven Years War in 1763. *The French Sugar Business*, p. x.

6. Donnan, *Documents*, I, pp. 95–99 and Mumford, *Black Ordeal of Slavery*, I, pp. 156–60.

7. Gary Abraham, *Max Weber and the Jewish Question: A Study of the Social Outlook of His Sociology* (Urbana: University of Illinois Press, 1992), p. 210. See also Julius Guttman, review for *Archiv for Socialwissenschaft und Socialpolitik* , 1913.

8. Marcus, *The Colonial American Jew*, I, p. 229.

9. See Heinrich Graetz, *History of the Jews*, IV, pp. 56, 102–7; and V, pp. 341–44; Hertzberg, *The French Enlightenment and the Jews* , pp. 14–24, and 33; Georges Cirot, "Les Juifs de Bordeaux, leur situation morale et sociale de 1550 a la Revolution," *Revue d'historique de Bordeaux*, XXXII (1939), pp. 15–21, 60–66; Zosa Szajkowski, "Trade Relations of Marranos in France with the Iberian Peninsula in the Sixteenth and Seventeenth Centuries," *Jewish Quarterly Review* I (1959–60), pp. 69–78; and report of Dr. Clement Lanier, *Le National Magazine* (Port au Prince, Sept. 19, 1954), p. 1 in Korn Files, AJA, 31–3.

10. J. Rennard, "Documents: Juifs et Protestants aux Antilles au xviie siècle," *Revue d'historique des Missions* (Paris, September 1933), dixième année, p. 456.

11. For a brief introduction to the early history of the islands, see Germaine Finifter, *Nous venons des Antilles* (Paris: Syros, 1993), pp. 15–17. France's problems with the slave trade in the nineteenth century are outlined in Francoise Thesee, *Les Ibos de l'Amelie:destinée d'un cargaison de traite clandestine à la Martinique que 1822–1838* (Paris: Editions Caribéees, 1986).

12. J. Petitjean-Roget, "Les Juifs à la Martinique sous l'ancien Régime," *Revue d'historique des Colonies* (Paris, 1956), XLIII, p. 154. According to Rennard, Da Costa was a merchant, not a planter. The first actual planting of cane in the French sugar islands should be credited to Daniel Trezel, a Dutchman, in 1640. Rennard, "Documents: Juifs et Protestants," p. 458. Nevertheless, the *Secret Relationship* stresses the Jewish role in sugar on Martinique, p. 78.

13. Gerard Lafleur, *Les protestants aux Antilles françaises du Vert sous l'ancien Regime* (Basse-Terre: Societé d'historique de la Guadeloupe, 1988).

14. Rennard, "Documents: Juifs et Protestants," p. 437.

15. The French Jewish scholar Abraham Cahen attributes such success to policies of the governor-generals and intenants, noting that Gentile merchants and Jesuit priests remained hostile to Jews. Cahen, "Les Juifs de la Martinique au xviie siècle," *Revue des Études Juives* (Paris, 1881), II, p. 95–96.

16. Accoding to Zvi Locker, Cap Haitien was the "center par excellence of the colonies," constituting an "unexplored link" in the migrations of Jews from Brazil to North America. Locker, "Toponymies juives en Haïti," *la Revue France-Haitienne* (October 1977), no. 35, pp. 92–93. Locker also laments the failure of research on the Jewish quarter in "Un Cimetière juif au Cap-Haïtien," *Revue des Études juives* (July-December, 1977), CXXXVI, nos. 3–4, pp. 425–27. See also Max Wischnitzer, "The Historical Background of the Settlement of Jewish Refugees in Santo Domingo," *Jewish Social Archives* (Jan. 1942).

17. Marcus, *Colonial American Jew,* I, p. 88 and Renard, "Documents: Juifs et Protestants," p. 437.

18. "Having been informed that Jews who settled at Martinique and the othe r islands inhabited by my subjects have contributed very considerable sums to the cultivation of the land and that they continue to strengthen their settlement, I have issued this letter to inform you that my intention is that you cooperate so that they may enjoy the same privliges as the other inhabitants of the said islands of my possession and that you allow them complete freedom of conscience, nevertheless taking necessary precautions to prevent the execise of their religion which might cause some scandal to Catholics." Petitjean-Roget, "Les Juifs à la Martinique," p. 146 and Cahen, "Les Juifs de la Martinique," II, p. 99.

19. Hertzberg, *French Enlightenment and the Jews*, p. 24.

20. Rennard, "Documents: Juifs et Protestants," p. 438.

21. Petitjean-Roget, "Les Juifs a la Martinique," p. 141.

22. *Ibid.*, pp. 149–50.

23. So were many subalterns. See Rennard, "Documents: Juifs et Protestants," pp. 440–41.

24. *Ibid.*, pp. 444–47.

25. Rennard, "Documents: Juifs et Protestants," pp. 449–54 and Petitjean-Roget, "Les Juifs à la Martinique," p. 151.

26. " His majesty, not wishing to endure the bad example that Jews residing in the French islands of America give to his subjects by the exercise of their religion nor to permit their residence any longer, mandates and orders said Jews to leave the vicinity of said islands one month after the publication of this order." *Archives Nationales Colonies, Ordres du Roi,* 24 September 1863, in Petitjean-Roget, "Les Juifs à la Martinique," p. 151.

27. Rennard, "Documents: Juifs et Protestants," pp. 459–60.

28. Louis Sala-Molins, *Code noir ou le calvaire de Canaan* (Presses universitaires de France, 1988), pp. 55–56. For a discussion of the abolitionist movement in France led by Condorcet and Abbé Gregoire see also Sala-Molins' *Les Misères des Lumières sous la Raison, l'outrage* (Paris: Editions Robert Laffont, 1992).

29. *Ibid.*, p. 458.

30. Korn notes the West Indies Company recommended keeping Jews out of Louisiana in 1716 because they were politically unreliable and economically too aggressive. Korn Papers, untitled manuscript AJA, 31–5.

31. Query of Moreau de Saint-Méry, advocate of Paris, cited in Report of Dr. Clement Lanier, *Le National Magazine*. Korn Papers, AJA, 31–3, p. 2.

32. Cahen mentions multiple denunciations on Santo Domingo, Martinique, and Guiana. "Les Juifs de la Martinique," p. 113.

33. Petitjean-Roget, "Les Juifs a la Martinique," p. 152.

34. Ab. Cahen, "Les Juifs dans les Colonies Françaises au xviiie siècle," *Revue des Études Juives* (Paris, 1882), IV, pp. 236–47.

35. Marcus, *Colonial American Jew,* I, p. 91.

36. Ab. Cahen, "Les Juifs dans les Colonies françaises au xviiie siècle," *Revue des Études Juives*, part 6, V, p. 75.

37. *Ibid.*, p. 76.

38. From a memoir produced by Jews of Bordeaux, April 1776. *Ibid.*, pp. 85–86.

39. *Ibid.*, pp. 7–77.

40. Statements of Ministers d'Estaing and Magon, noted in Archives Nationales, C9A127 Fo. 1., Jan. 8, 1766. From report of Marie Antoinette Menier to Korn, June 9, 1972, Korn Files, AJA, 31–6.

41. Cahen, "Les Juifs dans les Colonies françaises, " part 6, V, pp. 68–70.

42. *Ibid.*, pp. 72–73.

43. *Ibid.*, pp. 87–88. Jews petitioned Lt. General Henri-Leonard Bertin, head of police, Comte de Nolivos, governor-general of the islands, Etienne Louis Ferron, commanding general on Santo Domingo, and Antoine Raymond Sartine of the Ministry of Marine.

44. *Ibid.*, pp. 78–79, 90–92.

45. *Ibid.*, p. 81.

46. *Ibid.*, p. 90.

47. Drescher, "The Role of Jews in the Transatlantic Slave Trade, " p. 122.

48. Hertzberg, *The French Enlightenment and the Jews*, pp. 86–88. According to Hertzberg, there were sixty multi-millionaires in Bordeaux, only five or six of whom were Jews.

49. Stein, *The French Slave Trade in the Eighteenth Century*, p. 159.

50. Ab. Cahen, "Les Juifs dans les Colonies françaises au xviiie siècle, " *Revue des Études juives* (Paris, 1882), III, pp. 132–33 and Petitjean-Roget, "Les Juifs à la Martinique, " p. 155. He was actually the second scion sent—Samuel having died of malignant fever that same year.

51. *Ibid.*, p. 157. On the activities of the Gradis family during the colonial wars, see also Hertzberg, *French Enlightenment and the Jews*, pp. 88–89.

52. Max Kohler, "Jewish Activity in American Colonial Commerce, " *PAJHS* (1902), X, p. 60.

53. Letter from Rene Le Gardeur to Korn, June 24, 1971, Korn Papers, AJA, Gradis File, 31–2. Marie-Antoinette Menier had an equally fruitless search through the Archives Nationales. Letter to Korn, July 11, 1972, *loc. cit.*, 31–2.

54. According to Gradis, each cargo should consist of men, women, and children in equal numbers. Memorandum of Abraham Gradis, May 21, 1748, Korn Papers, AJA, 9–10.

55. Cahen, "Les Juifs dans les Colonies françaises, " III, 132.

56. Stein, *The French Slave Trade in the Eighteenth Century*, p. 232.

57. Letter from DeBien to Korn, May 12, 1971, Korn Papers, AJA, 31–2. There is no reference to either Gradis or Mendes families or any Jew, for that matter, in Dale Tomich's important study, *Slavery in the Circuit of Sugar: Martinique and the World Economy 1830–1848* (Baltimore, MD: Johns Hopkins Press, 1990).

58. See "Denombrement des Juifs demeurant en Îsle de la Martinique, 1693." The ten-page handwritten document lists free Jews, age, family, and Negroes. Ministère des Colonies, papers Publiquest des Colonies, Martinique in Korn Papers, AJA, 31–6. See also Max Wischnitzer, "The Historical Background of the Settlement of Jewish Refugees in Santo Domingo."

59. Her correspondence indicates the bulk of these were willed to Isaac Mendes by Fayette Brounschwieg in a will in 1778. Letter of Menier to Korn, August 31, 1972. Korn Papers, AJA, 31–2.

60. Marcus, *Colonial American Jew*, I, pp. 91–92.

61. G. Debien, J. Houdaille, R. Masso, and R. Richard (eds.) *Les origines des esclaves des Antilles* (*Extraits Bulletin de l'Institut français d'Afrique noire*, 1961–67), Bulletin XXVI, Series B, pp. 602–75; XXVII, 1965, pp. 320–69; and XXVI (1964), pp. 194–97.

62. *Ibid.* p. 89–91. See also Mumford, *Black Ordeal of Slavery*, II, pp. 505–27.

63. Marcus, *Colonial American Jew,* Î, p. 87. Jews did not play a major role in the refining or distribution of sugar back in Europe. A single refinery of the ten in Bordeaux belonged to the Gradis family. Hertzberg, *French Enlightenment and the Jews*, p. 90. Prominent in such activities were a Swedish immigrant to Bordeaux named Dohrmann, Jean Othod Dede of Hamburg, the Orleans Company of Veuve Ravot and Demadieres, the family of Rene Beguyer along the Loire River, the Sabatiers of Montpelier, and the Toulouse merchant Jean Baptiste Fontanilhe. Stein, *The French Sugar Business*, pp. 123–30, and 150–161.

64. Hertzberg, *French Enlightenment and Jews*, p. 79–82.

65. Cahen, "Les Juifs dans les Colonies françaises," V, p. 81.

Notes to Chapter 7

1. Eric Williams, "The Golden Age of the Slave System in Britain," *Journal of Negro History* (January , 1940), XXV, p. 66.

2. Donnan, *Documents*, II pp. 169–72.

3. *Ibid.*, II, pp. 126–28.

4. *Ibid.*, II, pp. 655–66. For a list of 72 Liverpool merchants trading to Africa in 1750, see also *An Historical Account of the Liverpool-African Slave Trade* (Liverpool: A. Bowker, 1884), pp. 118–19.

5. Richard Sheridan, *Sugar and Slavery: An Economic History of the British West Indies 1623–1775* (Baltimore, MD: Johns Hopkins University Press, 1973), pp. 81–91.

6. J.R. Ward, *British West Indian Slavery 1750–1834* (Oxford: Clarendon Press, 1988), pp. 99–100.

7. Williams, "The Golden Age of the Slave System in Britain," pp. 69–78.

8. Sheridan offers a complete list: Bannister, Hammond & Manning; Beckford & James, Singsby Bethell; Bourryau, Turner & Luard; Rowland & Samuel Frye; Stephen & Rose Fuller; Sir Alexander Grant; Hibbert, Purrier & Horton; Alexander Houston & Co; Lascelles & Maxwell; Long, Drake & Long; Maitland & Boddingtons; Morse & Smith; Mure, Son & Atkinson; Arnold Nesbitt & Co; Richard & Richard Oliver; Sir Samuel Pennant; Serocold & Jackson; Samuel Touchet & Co; Trecothick, Apthorp & Thomlinson; Truman, Douglas & Neave; Nicholas Tuite; Samuel Turner & Son; Warner & Johnson; and William Whitaker. Sheridan, *Sugar and Slavery,* p. 299.

9. Lowell Ragatz, *The Fall of the Planter Class in the British Caribbean 1763–1833* (New York: Octagon, 1963), pp. 93–98.

10. Sheridan, *Sugar and Slavery*, p. 60. Sheridan lists more than 100 politically active businessmen from the Indies, none of them Jews.

11. Letter of Richardson to Korn, January 17, 1974, Korn Papers, AJA, 31–2. In fact, W.E. Minchinton identifies Bristol's leading slavers as Nathaniel Wraxall from the firm of Inglis, Pickering and Wraxall, John Lloyd of Inglis, Lloyd and Hall, John Powell of Powell, Hopton and Co., Isaac Hobhouse, Robert Smyth, John Crofts, Charles Gwynne, Henry Bright, Thomas Easton & Co., Henry Weare & Co., and Joseph Daltera, Devonsheir and Reeve. "The Slave Trade of Bristol and the British Mainland Colonies in North America 1699–1770," in Anstey and Hair, *Liverpool, the African Slave Trade and Abolition*, pp. 31–59.

12. Letter of Temkin to Korn, August 9, 1971, Korn Papers, AJA, 31–2. The most complete study of Bristol's involvement is David Richardson's three-volume *Bristol, Africa and the Eighteenth Century Slave Trade to America* (Gloucester: A. Sutton, 1986–1991).

13. *Historical Account of the Liverpool-African Slave Trade*, p. 15.

14. *Ibid.*, II, pp. 496–98 and 642–49. Donnan reports that 878 Liverpool slave ships transported 303,737 slaves between 1783 and 1793. *Ibid.*, II, p. 625. No Jew is listed among the masters of 41 ships which brought nearly 5,000 slaves to Antigua between 1698 and 1707. See also *Historical Account of the Liverpool-African Slave Trade*, pp. 120ff.

15. Drake, "The Liverpool-African Voyage, c.1790–1807: Commercial Problems," in *Liverpool, The African Slave Trade and Abolition*, pp. 127–28.

16. Donnan, *Documents*, II, p. 168.

17. South Seas Company Minutes, Add.Mss 25497–25498, Department of Mss., South Seas Trading Co. Papers, in Korn Papers, AJA, 32–1.

18. Lists of Governors and Company of Great Britain trading to the South Seas and Parts of America, December 25, 1714, Korn Papers, AJA, 32–1. Korn notes most were listed as merchants, jobbers, and brokers.

19. London Jewish merchants on index cards, Korn Papers, AJA, 32–1. Korn notes most were listed as merchants, jobbers, and brokers.

20. Roth, *History of Marranos*, pp. 252–67.

21. Marcus, *Colonial American Jew*, I, p. 390; Harold Pollins, *Economic History of the Jews in England* (Rutherford, NJ: Farleigh Dickinson Press, 1982), p. 87; and William Fishman, "The Jews of London's East End," lecture Youngstown State University, April 25, 1994.

22. Malcolm Stern,"New Light on the Jewish Settlement of Savannah," in Abraham Karp, *The Jewish Experience in America*, p. 70.

23. Pollins, *Economic History of the Jews in England*, p. 43.

24. *Ibid.*, pp. 45–46 and 63–68.

25. Todd Endelman, *The Jews of Georgia England 1714–1830* (Philadelphia, PA: Jewish Publication Society, 1979), p. 31.

26. Pollins, *Economic History of the Jews in England*, pp. 103–19.

27. *Ibid.*, pp. 91 and 108.

28. Endelman, *Jews of Georgian England*, p. 31. See also Endelman's *Radical Asssimilation in English Jewish History 1656–1945* (Bloomington: Indiana University Press, 1990).

29. Fishman, lecture, April 28, 1994.

30. Endelman, *Jews of Georgian England,* pp. 86–117.

31. Marcus, *Colonial American Jews*,I, 28–29.

32. Seymour Drescher, *Capitalism and Antislavery* (Oxford: Oxford University Press, 1987), p. 187. See also Jacob Katz, *From Prejudice to Destruction: Anti-Semitism 1700–1933* (Cambridge: Harvard University Press, 1980), pp. 30–33.

33. Petition of Three Jews, July 24, 1661, no. 140, *Calendar of State Papers, Colonial Series, American and the West Indies,* ed. K.G. Davies (HMSO, 1969) V, 166–68, p. 49.

34. *Ibid.*, no. 948 to Francis Lord Willoughby, March 1665, p. 284; no. 949 to Sir Thomas Modyford of Jamaica, March 1, 1665, p. 284; no. 1657 in 1667, p. 530; and $1,895, December 23, 1668, p. 635.

35. Pollins, *Economic History of the Jews in England*, pp. 44–45.

36. *The Secret Relationship between Blacks and Jews,* p. 56.

37. *Ibid.*, pp. 73–79.

38. Lousada may be the only Jew listed among the likes of George Paplay, Alexander Harvie and Zachary Bayly. Sheridan, *Sugar and Slavery*, pp. 367 and 294. Al-

though he discusses the Sepharic Jews in two pages, much of what Sheridan writes is debatable. He paints a gloomy picture of Jewish money lenders and traders with "international connections," but adds they played no role in owner-ship or management of plantations, p. 367.

39. Notes on Jamaica slave traders, from Kingston *Journal* and *Royal Gazette* , Korn Papers, AJA, 31–6.
40. Steven Fortune, *Merchants and Jews: The Struggle for British West Indian Commerce 1650–1750* (Gainesville: University of Florida Press, 1984), p. 160.
41. *Ibid.*,p. 161.
42. *Ibid.*, pp. 161–62.
43. Royal African Invoice Books, T.70/937-T. 70/959, Reports from the Islands. Korn Papers, AJA, 32–1.
44. Notes on Accounts of Slave Compensation Claims, March 1838. Awards from 1835–36. *British Sessional Papers 1837–1838*, vol. XLVIII , in Korn Papers, AJA, 31–6.
45. Royal Africa Company Invoice Books, Public Record Office, London, T.70, vol.940, pp. 60–61, in Korn Papers, AJA, 32–1.
46. T.70/940, pp. 124–27.
47. T.70/941, p. 36.
48. T.70/941, pp. 124–27.
49. T.70/942, p. 133.
50. T.70/949, p. 10.
51. T.70/951, p. 19.
52. T.70/954, p. 42.
53. Notes on British Sessional papers from 1837–38, Korn Papers, AJA, 31–6.
54. Marcus, *Colonial American Jew,* I, p. 113 and Bethencourt, "Notes on the Spanish and Portuguese Jews in the US," *PAJHS*, XXIX, p. 13.
55. Jerome Handler and Frederick Lange, *Plantation Slavery in Barbados: An Archaeological and Historical Investigation* (Cambridge: Harvard University Press, 1978), p. 21. See also Galloway, *The Sugar Industry,* pp. 80–83.
56. Donnan, *Documents*, II, pp. 25–27.
57. Seymour Liebman, *New WorldJewy 1493–1825* (New York: Ktav, 1982), p. 176.
58. Handler and Lange, *Plantation Slavery in Barbados*, p. 17.
59. *Ibid.*,pp. 180–81.
60. Merrill, "The Role of Sephardic Jews in the British Caribbean Area," pp. 44–45.
61. Handler and Lange, *Plantation Slavery in Barbados,* p. 41.
62. Marcus, *Colonial American Jew,* I, p. 120.
63. Dr. Cyrus Adler, "Jews in the American Plantations between 1600–1700," *PAJHS* (1893), I, pp. 105–6.
64. Undated manuscript titled "Barbadian Jewish Wills, 1676–1740," Korn Papers, AJA, 2–12.
65. Winthrop Jordan, *White over Black: American Attitudes toward the Negro 1550–1812* (Chapel Hill: University of North Carolina Press, 1968), p. 65.
66. *Calendar of State Papers*, V, no. 1657, p. 530.
67. Fortune, *Merchants and Jews*, p. 156.
68. Daniel Davis, "Notes of the History of the Jews in Barbados," *PAJHS* (1909), XVIII, p. 144.
69. Marcus, *Colonial American Jew,* I, p. 114. Pollins says the sugar trade was restricted and nonplanters like Jews did not participate. *Economic History of Jews in England*, pp. 50–51.
70. Merrill, "The Role of Sephardic Jews in the British Caribbean Area," p. 45.

71. Davis, "Notes on the History of Jews in Barbados, " p. 144.
72. Handler and Lange, *Plantation Slavery in Barbados*, pp. 180–81.
73. This happened in 1698 when Lopez Depass was forced to kneel before the Assembly. Fortune, *Jews and Merchants*, p. 156.
74. Merrill, "The Role of Sephardic Jews in the British Caribbean Area," p. 47.
75. *Jamaica Gazette*, May 4, 1771, in Korn Papers, AJA, 11–13.
76. Jay Coughtry, *The Notorious Triangle: Rhode Island and the African Slave Trade 1700–1807* (Philadelphia, PA: Temple University Press, 1981), p. 192.
77. *Calendar of State Papers*, V, no. 348 , July 14, 1738, p. 164.
78. Marcus, *Colonial American Jew*, I, pp. 110–11.
79. Korn cites 14 references in the *Jamaica Daily Telegraph* of 1900. Korn Papers, AJA, 11–13.
80. Merrill, "The Role of Sephardic Jews in the British Caibbean," p. 47.
81. Ward, *British West Indian Slavery*, p. 12.
82. B.W. Higman, *Slave Population and Economy in Jamaica, 1807–1834* (Cambridge: Cambridge University Press, 1976), pp. 23, 27, 69, 94–95, 188, 196 , 200, 237; and Ward, *British West Indian Slavery*, pp. 30, 51, 54, 92–94.
83. Based on Accounts of Slave Compensation claims, British Sessional Papers 1837–38. Korn Papers, AJA, 31–6 and Higman, *Slave Population and Economy in Jamaica*, p. 16.
84. Merrill,"The Role of Sephardic Jews in the British Caribbean," p. 47.
85. Marcus, *Colonial American Jew*, I, p. 102.
86. *Calendar of State Papers*, V, no. 348, July 14, 1738, p. 164.
87. *Ibid.*, p. 164.
88. Ward indicates that mortality ranged between 3 and 50 percent on transatlantic passages. Ward, *British West Indian Slavery*, pp. 129–40.
89. Marcus, *Colonial American Jew*, I, p. 118.
90. *Ibid.*, pp. 115–19.

Notes to Chapter 8

1. There is some dispute whether the ship was called the *Ste. Catherine* or the *St. Charles*. Official British records for the port favor the latter. Passengers aboard the French vessel were unable to pay the 2,500 gold guilders (treble the normal fare) demanded by their captain Jacques de la Motte until assistance was provided by the Amsterdam Jewish community. David and Tamar Pool, *An Old Faith in the New World: Portrait of Shearith Israel* (New York: Columbia University Press, 1955), pp. 8–12.
2. See Jose Faur, *In the Shadow of History: Jews and Conversos at the Dawn of Modernity* (Albany, NY: SUNY Press, 1994).
3. In fact, Barsimson was an unemployed manual laborer. Samuel Oppenheim,"More about Jacob Barsimson, the First Jewish Settler in New York," pp. 37–50 in Karp, *The Jewish Experience in America*, I.
4. Marcus, *Colonial American Jew*, I, pp. 388–89.
5. *Ibid.*, p. 255.
6. "Slavery," *Encyclopedia Judaica*, xiv.
7. Rosenwaike, "An Estimate and Analysis of the Jewish Population of the United States in 1790," *PAJHS* (Sept. 1960–June 1961), L, pp. 23–25. There is also a discrepancy between Rosenwaike and the author of the *Encyclopedia Judaica* article for 1820. Karp estimates that there were 4,000 Jews in the general population of 4,000,000, again 0.1 percent. Rosenwaike lists 2,700, not too far off Mordecai Noah's figure of 3,000 in 1818.

8. *Secret Relationship*, p. 89.

9. "Slavery," p. 1590.

10. *Ibid.*, p. 1587.

11. Marcus, *Early American Jewry: The Jews of Pennsylvania and the South 1655–1790* (Philadelphia, PA: Jewish Publication Society), II, p. 390. Macus makes the point clearly in *The Colonial America n Jew*, I, 284, that the Jew with substantial capital definitely was in the minority.

12. Marcus, *Colonial American Jew*, III, 1331.

13. *Ibid.* I, p. 229.

14. Anita Lebeson, *Pilgrim People: A History of the Jews in America from 1492 to 1974* (New York: Minerva Press, 1975), pp. 59–61. Richard Morris claims "the Jews were fighting the battle of other minority groups, for if they obtained liberties, so would Lutherans and Papists." "Civil Liberties and the Jewish Tradition in Early America," in Karp, *The Jewish Experience in America*, p. 410.

15. Jews in Amsterdam also sent an eloquent epistle to the directors of the Dutch West Indies Company stressing the loyalty of Jews in Brazil and the hopelessness of their options in a world dominated by the bigoted Spanish and Portuguese. Pools, *An Old Faith in the New World,* pp. 16–17; Wiznitzer, "The Exodus from Brazil, " in *The Jewish Experience in America*, pp. 19–36 and Michael Kamen, *Colonial New York: A History* (New York: Scribner's, 1975), pp. 60–61.

16. By 1657 Jews won the right to own land and Asher Levy, a fur trader to Albany, was permitted to patrol Wall Street. See Leon Huhner, "Asser Levy, A Noted Jewish Burgher of New Amsterdam," pp. 51–65, in Karp, *The Jewish Experience in America.*

17. For a description of the DWIC monopoly on this trade between Angola and New York, see Edgar McManus, *A History of Negro Slavery in New York* (Syracuse, NY: Syracuse University Press, 1966), pp. 2–11.

18. Marcus, *Colonial American Jew*,I, 235–38.

19. Morris, "Civil Liberties and the Jewish Tradition in Early America," pp. 413–15. See also J.H. Hollander, "Naturalization of Jews in the American Colonies under the Act of 1740," *PAJHS* (1897), V, 130–148.

20. Marcus, *Colonial American Jew*, III, p. 113 and Pools, *An Old Faith in the New World*, pp. 33–36.

21. *Secret Relationship.* p. 97.

22. Marcus, *Colonial American Jew*, III, p. 1178.

23. Hershkowitz, "Asser Levy and the Inventories of Early New York Jews," *AJHQ* (Autumn 1990) LXXX, p. 25.

24. *Ibid.*, p. 11.

25. Leon Hühner, "Daniel Gomez, a Pioneer Merchant of Early New York, " in *The Jewish Experience in America*, pp. 175–93. Gomez is more renowned as the man who opened the fur trade with Indians decades before an employee, John Jacob Astor, took over his outpost at Newburgh. Stephen Birmingham, *The Grandees: America's Sephardic Elite* (New York: Harper and Row, 1971), pp. 88–99.

26. Leo Hershkowitz, "Wills of Early New York Jews 1743-1744, " *AJHQ* (1966–67), LVI, pp. 62–122. For a more complete study, see Hershkowitz, *Wills of Early New York Jews 1704–1799* (New York: American Jewish Historical Society, 1967).

27. Nathan Kaganoff, *AJHQ* (1976), LXVI, and Birmingham, *The Grandees*, pp. 146–57.

28. Kohler, "Phases of Jewish Life in New York before 1800," *PAJHS* (1894), II, p. 84.

29. There were exceptions. Isaac Pinheiro had 21 . Simja de Torres also imported three slaves on two separate occasions (March 1728 and July 1742). Hershkowitz, *Wills of Early New York Jews*, p. 79.

30. Moses Michael and Manuel Myers provide for the emancipation of their slaves. Hershkowitz, *Wills of Early New York Jews*, pp. 60 and 208.

31. These are the only actual figures confirmed by David de Sola Pool in *Portraits Etched in Stone: Early Jewish Settlers 1682–1831* (New York: Columbia University Press, 1952), pp. 189–91, 197–201, 238–40, 272–74, and 329–31.

32. Herskowitz, "Asser Levy and Inventories of Early New York Jews," pp. 11 and 32–33 and Pools, *Old Faith in the New World*, p. 471. The seatholders of Shearith Israel in 1834 included five auctioneers; four brokers; three clothiers, druggists and inspectors; two marshals, police, tobacconists, copper store owners, liquor dealers, attorneys and watchmakers; and one each revenue officer, dry goods mechant, dyer, fancy store keeper, dealer in hardware, importer, lithographer, mercer, realtor, coal yard owner, boardinghouse keeper, master in chancery, counselor at law, editor, physician, professor of language, exchange broker, lottery offcial, manufacturer of blacking, pencils, quills, reflectors, and umbrellas. *Ibid.*, p. 472.

33. *Ibid.*, pp. 24 and 27.

34. *Ibid.*, p. 27.

35. John Spears, *The American Slave-Trade: An Account of Its Origin, Growth and Suppression* (New York: Scribner's, 1900), pp. 8–9.

36. References are to Isaak Asher in 1683, Arthur Levy in 1692, and Jacob Franks and Samuel Israel in 1761. McKee, *Labor in Colonial New York 1664–1776* (Pt. Washington, NY: Ira Friedman, 1935), pp. 128–34.

37. Kaganoff, p. 36. Had Salomon been the coldhearted slaver suggested by *Secret Relationship*, how explain the paean offered by Howard Fast to this "Son of Liberty, who gave without stint and without putting shame in the hearts of those who asked"? *Haym Salomon: Son of Liberty* (New York: Julian Messner, 1941), p. 242. There is no mention of slavery in this book or Charles Russell's *Haym Salomon and the Revolution* (New York: Cosmopolitan Book Co., 1930).

38. Edmund O'Callaghan, "Census of Slaves" in *The Documentary History of the State of New York* (Albany, NY: Weed Parsons & Co., 1850), III, pp. 843–68.

39. McManus, *Slavery in New York*, pp. 26–39, 45–46, 69.

40. The hysteria began when a fire broke out in the fort where Lt. Gov. Clarke was residing. Before sanity was restored, 154 blacks were prosecuted. Four whites, including two women, were hanged as co-conspirators. McKee, *Labor in New York*, pp. 156–65.

41. James Lydon,"New York and the Slave Trade 1700 to 1774," *William and Mary Quarterly* (April 1978), XXXV, p. 381.

42. Donnan, *Documents*, III, p. 470.

43. Donnan's arithmetic comes up with a larger figure of 707 ships with 4,897 slaves. *Ibid.*, III, 462–510. Lydon has the figure for 1715–1764 at 4,398.

44. *Documentary History of the State of New York* (Albany, NY: 1850), I, pp. 395 ff.

45. Bertram Korn, "Jews and Negro Slavery in the Old South," in *Jews in the South*, Leonard Dinnerstein and Mary Palsson (eds.) (Baton Rouge: Louisiana State University Press, 1973), p. 95.

46. Hershkowitz, "Asser Levy and the Inventories of Early New York Jews, "p. 29.

47. Ira Rosenwaike, "The Jewish Population of the United States as Estimated from the Census of 1820, " *AJHQ* (December 1963), III, pp. 150–78.

48. Leo Hirsch, "The Negro and New York 1783 to 1865," *Journal of Negro History* (October 1931), XVI, pp. 382–473.

49. Henry S. Cooley, *A Study of Slavery in New Jersey* (Baltimore, MD: Johns Hopkins University Press, 1896), p. 31.

50. *Ibid.*, p. 11.

51. A.D.Mellick, *Story of an Old Farm or Life in New Jersey in the 18th Century* (Somerville, NJ, 1889), pp. 220–28.

52. Abraham Rosenbach, "Notes on the First Settlement of Jews in Pennsylvania, 1655–1703," *PAJHS* (1897), V, pp. 191–95.

53. Rosenwaike lists only Simeon Hart, Joseph Shannon, Aaron Gomez, Uriah Hendricks, and Solomon Isaacks in his "Jewish Population in the US fromthe Census of 1820," p. 137.

54. Benjamin Franklin maintained that Samuel Keimer, his employer at the *Pennsylvania Gazette*, was the first Jew in the colony. Franklin's only evidence that Keimer was a Jew was his long beard and sabbath observance. Henry Morais, *The Jews of Philadelphia: Their History from the Earliest Settlers to the Present Time* (Philadelphia, PA: Levtype Co., 1894), pp. 10–11.

55. Marcus, *Colonial American Jew*, I, 321–25.

56. See Hyman Resenbach, *The Jews in Philadelphia to 1800* (Philadelphia, PA: E.Stern & Co., 1883).

57. Edwin Wolf and Maxwell Whiteman, *The History of the Jews of Philadelphia from Colonial Times to the Age of Jackson* (Philadelphia, PA: Jewish Publication Society, 1957), pp. 98–113.

58. Herbert Friedenwald, "Some Newspaper Ads of the 18th century," in *Jewish Experience in America*, pp. 229–39. See also Samuel Oppenheim, "Jewish Owners of Ships Registered at the Port of Philadelphia, 1730–1775," *PAJHS* (1918), XXVI, pp. 235–36. One of the most acive was Joseph Marks who outfitted eight fifty-ton ships between 1743 and 1751.

59. Charles Blockson, *African Americans in Pennsylvania: A History and Guide* (Baltimore, MD: Black Classic Press, 1994), p. 10.

60. Edward Turner, *The Negro in Pennsylvania: Slavery—Servitude—Freedom 1639–1861* (New York: Negro Universities Press reprint, 1969), pp. 5–12.

61. *Secret Relationship between Blacks and Jews*, p. 93.

62. See Franks, David. Correspondence Business Matters, 1761–64, Small Collection, AJA.

63. Darold Wax, "Quaker Merchants and the Slave Trade in Colonial America," *Pennsylvania Magazine of History* (1962) LXXXVI, pp. 143–59.

64. Monsanto, Manuel Jacob, Documents File, AJA.

65. Wolf and Whiteman, *History of Jews of Philadelphia*, p. 24. On Franks, see p. 168.

66. Korn in Dinnerstein and Palsson, *Jews in the South*, p. 95. Rosenwaike counts 32 Jewish heads of households. "An Estimate and Analysis of theJewish Population of the United States in 1790," *PAJHS* (September 1960–June 1961), L, p. 39. There is some confusion in Stern's figures for he later lists 4 families with 4 slaves. Stern,"Some Additions and "Corrections in Rosenwaike's 'An Estimate and Analysis of the Jewish Population of the United States in 1790'," *PAJHS* (March 1964), LIII, p. 286.

67. Rosenwaike, "The Jewish Population of the US in 1820," p. 150. The Nation of Islam claims Rosenwaike admits to 23 Jews with 27 slaves in 1830 in *Edge of Greatness*, p. 124.

68. Wolf and Whiteman, *History of Jews of Philadelphia*, pp. 190–92.

69. Morris Schappes, "The Jews and American Slavery," *Jewish Life* (May 1954), pp. 15–19 and Schappes, "Anti-Semitism and Reaction 1795–1800," *Jewish Experience in America*, p. 362.

70. Turner, *The Negro in Pennsyvlania,* pp. 40 and 57.
71. Blockson, *African Americans in Pennsylvania,* p. 10.

Notes to Chapter 9

1. Lorenzo Greene, *The Negro in Colonial New England 1620–1776* (New York: Columbia University Press, 1942), pp.25–26. Jay Coughtry estimates that rum exports to Africa amounted to between 150,000 and 230,000 gallons each year. *The Notorious Triangle: Rhode Island and the African Slave Trade, 1700–1807* (Philadelphia, PA: Temple University Press, 1981), p. 16.
2. At the end of the seventeenth century Baxter denounced slavers as "the common enemies of mankind." Mrs. Benn authored the antislavery novel *Oroonoko* in 1678. Twenty years later, Sewalls wrote the pamphlet "The Selling of Joseph." Crooke, an actor, denounced slavery in Liverpool. See Oliver Ransford, *The Slave Trade* (1971), pp. 173–90.
3. Greene notes that even philanthropists like the Brown brothers who founded Rhode Island College, later Brown University, owned some. *The Negro in Colonial New England,* pp. 57–60.
4. Donnan, *Documents, New England and the Middle Colonies,* III, p. 16.
5. Weeden, "The Early African Slave-Trade in New England," *American Antiquarian Society* (1887), V, p. 107.
6. Greene, *The Negro in Colonial New England,* pp. 16–34.
7. *Ibid.,* p. 50.
8. Franklin and Moss, *From Slavery to Freedom,* p. 62.
9. Greene, *The Negro in Colonial New England,* pp. 29–31.
10. Bernard Steiner, *History of Slavery in Connecticut* (Baltimore, MD: Johns Hopkins University Press, 1893), pp. 20–21.
11. Greene, *The Negro in Colonial New England,* pp. 350–59.
12. Donnan, *Documents,* III,pp. 4, 31, and 108.
13. *Ibid.,* p. 27.
14. *Ibid.,* p. 16.
15. Ezra Stiles reported that there were 8 to 10 Jews in New Haven, with 6 to 8 slaves, in 1772. Morris Jastrow, "References to Jews in the Diary of Ezra Stiles," *Jewish Experience in America,* p. 171.
16. Marcus, *Early American Jewry,* II, p. 387. Solomon Franco, a Dutch Jew, made a stopover in Boston in 1649. More than a century later, in 1772, Judah Monis served as instructor of Hebrew at Harvard. Harry Smith and J.Hugo Tatsch, *Moses Michael Hays: Merchant-Citizen-Freemason* (Boston, 1937), p. 12.
17. Joseph Lebowich,"The Jews in Boston till 1875," *PAJHS* (1904), XIII, pp. 101–4.
18. Rosenwaike, "Estimate of Jewish Population in US in 1790," p. 34.
19. Korn, *Jews in the South.*
20. *Secret Relationship between Blacks and Jews,"*pp. 50–75 and 99–102.
21. Marcus, *Colonial American Jew,* I, p. 314.
22. Max Kohler, "The Jews in Newport," *PAJHS* (1898), VI, p. 63.
23. Jastrow, "References to Jews in Stiles Diary," p. 147.
24. See List of Taxpayers Newport, 1775, Newport, Rhode Island Folder, Miscellaneous File, AJA.
25. Marcus, *Colonial American Jew,* I, 318–20.
26. Greene, *The Negro in Colonial New England,* p. 99 and Rosenswaike, "Estimate of Jewish Population in 1790, " pp. 25–26.
27. Rosenwaike, "Jewish Pouplation of US in 1820," p. 141.

28. Max Kohler, "The Jews in Newport," *PAJHS* (1898), VI, pp. 69–70; Leon Huhner, "The Jews of Newport: Address on the Unveiling of Memorial Tablet and Synagogue at Newport," September 7, 1908; and Morris Gulstein, *The Story of the Jews of Newport* (New York: Block, 1936).

29. Donnan, *Documents*, III, p. 108.

30. According to Donnan, none arrived from Africa between 1698 and 1707, 20–30 from Barbados in 1708. *Ibid*, pp. 109–10.

31. Stanely Chyet, *Lopez of Newport: Colonial American Merchant Prince* (Detroit, MI: Wayne State University Press, 1970), p. 67.

32. Greene, *The Negro in Colonial New England*, p. 93.

33. Coughtry says it would have taken 78 voyages to the West Indies with normal cargoes of tobacco,rum, etc. to equal three slaving junkets. *Triangular Trade*, p. 20.

34. *Ibid.*, p. 25.

35. *Ibid.*, pp. 25–26.

36. Donnan, *Documents*, III, pp. 125–27.

37. *Ibid.*, p. 117.

38. *Ibid.*, p. 121.

39. *Ibid.*, p. 139.

40. Spears, *American Slave Trade*, pp. 21–90.

41. Coughtry, *Triangular Trade*, pp. 81 and 92.

42. *Ibid.*, pp. 167–70 and 189–91.

43. Sterry, from Providence, outfitted half of the ships after 1794. *Ibid.*, pp. 203–13.

44. According to Coughtry, it was customary for 3–6 men to pool their resources. *Ibid.*, pp. 45–46.

45. *Ibid.*, pp. 47–49.

46. *Secret Relationship.* pp. 232–33. The hasty identification of D'Wolf as a Jew may derive from the fact that he came to Rhode Island in 1744 from Guadelupe. Nation of Islam scholars must assume that all West Indian refugees at that time were Jews or Marranos.

47. Symposium on Jews in Slave Trade, Hebrew Union College, May 18, 1995.

48. A rough family history of the aristocratic D'Wolfs is recorded in M.A. DeWolf Howe's *Bristol, Rhode Island: A Town Biography* (Cambridge, MA: Harvard University Press), p. 92.

49. *Secret Relationship*, pp. 262–67. In fact, Lopez owed a great deal of money to Bristol merchant Henry Cruger and, writes Sydney James, "neither man could afford to halt trade." Adds Professor James, "there was no occasion for making scapegoats of the Newport Jews." *Colonial Rhode Island: A History* (New York: Scribners, 1975), p. 336.

50. Of £1,800 collected in Newport in 1775, Lopez paid 32£, 9S, and 10D, almost twice the 18£, 16S, 6D paid by the next highest taxpayer George Rome. Newport, Rhode Island Folder, List of All Taxpayers 1775, AJA, Miscellaneous File.

51. Marcus, *Colonial American Jew,* III, p. 1290.

52. Lopez Papers, Ms. Collection 231, AJA, 1–5, no. 169.

53. Memorandum Book, Lopez Papers, Ms. Collection 231, AJA, 2–6; Account Books for 1763–70, 2–7; and Invoice Sailor's Book for 1767, 2–8.

54. Jastrow, "Refrences to Jews in the Diary of Ezra Stiles," pp. 152–54.

55. B.M. Bigelow, "Aaron Lopez, Colonial Merchant of Newport," *New England Quarterly* IV, pp. 757–76.

56. Chyet, "Aaron Lopez: A Study in Buenafama," *Jewish Experience in America*, pp. 194–208.

57. Lopez Papers, 1754–1783, Ms. Collection 231, AJA, General Correspondence, Business Documents. Letter Book of Aaron Lopez 1781–82, Box 1.

58. The quote within a quote is from Jacques Savary des Bruslons in the *Universal Dictionary of Trade and Commerce*, tr. and ed., Malachy Postlethwayt (London: John and Paul Khapton 1751), I, p. 924 and was cited by Chyet in *Jewish Experience in America*, p. 199.

59. Hamilton, *The Roman Way to Western Civilization* (New York: Mentor, 1957), p. 107, cited in Chyet, "Aaron Lopez," *PAJHS* (1962–63), LII, p. 300.

60. Marcus, *Colonial American Jew*, III, pp. 1288–90.

61. Ledger Books, Lopez Papers, Ms. Collection 231, AJA, 3–6.

62. Donnan cites correspondence with his solicitor William Stead, June 22, 1764, and the London merchants of Kender, Mason and Co., January 12, 1770, *Documents*, III, p. 245. See also "Lopez, Aaron, Letter Books, Shipping Papers, Account Books, " AJA, Box 269.

63. A proposal to supply Clarke with a new double-deck brigantine fell through in February 1772. Lopez Papers, Ms. Collection 231, Business and Correspondence File, 1–8, February 6, 1772.

64. Lopez Papers, Ms. Collection 231, Memo Book 1769, Box 2, p. 128.

65. Aaron Lopez File, Log of Ship *Sally* and Ship *Cleopatra*, Nathaneil Briggs master 1767–1783, Korn Papers, AJA, 31–6, pp. 4–7.

66. Donnan, *Documents*, III, p. 212.

67. Letter, July 15, 1773, from coast of Africa containing two bills of lading for 40 and 65 slaves. Lopez Papers, AJA, Ms. Collection 231, Correspondence with Christian Merchants, 1–9. See also correspondence between Lopez and Rivera in this period. Donnan, *Documents*, III, pp. 245–76.

68. Chyet, *Lopez of Newport: Colonial American Merchant Prince* (Detroit, MI: Wayne State University Press, 1970), p. 73.

69. "I found the Negroes nothing to what I expected," wrote Pereira on November 1 and November 29, 1767. Donnan, *Documents*, III, pp. 225–27.

70. Lopez Collection, AJA, Business Letters, 1767–1783, 2–5, November 20, 1771. See also folder 2–6, 1766, p. 57.

71. Lopez Collection, AJA, Account Book 1763–1770, 2–7, November 13, 1767.

72. Lopez Collection, AJA, Ledger Book 1767–71, Ms. Collection 231, 3–1, p. 292.

73. On psalters, see Lopez Collection, AJAl, Ms. collection 231, Book 1767, 3–2. On snuff and sassafrass, Ledger book 176 7–71, 3–1, p. 292. On cotton, 1769–74, 3–2. On kosher cheeses, Memo Book 1769–72, 3–1.

74. Lopez Papers, AJA, Ms. 231, May 18, 1773, 3–3. For additional bills of lading involving shipments of soap, indigo, corn, pitch, candles, rum, oil, hemp see also Lopez Collection, AJA, Boxes 269–73.

75. Coughtry, *Triangular Trade*, p. 18.

76. Stephen Birmingham, *The Grandees: America's Sephardic Elite* (New York: Harper & Row, 1971), p. 103.

Notes to Chapter 10

1. *Secret Relationship*, pp. 123–25.

2. Spears, *The American Slave-Trade*, p. 4.

3. *Ibid.*, pp. 6–9.

4. John Boles, *Black Southerners 1619–1869* (Lexington: University of Kentucky, 1983), pp. 12–16.

5. Donnan, *Documents*, IV, pp. 175–80.

6. *Ibid.*, pp. 182–87.
7. *Ibid.* , pp. 108–9. Donnan cites Bristol mechants Jas. Hilhouse, Jno. Parkin, Graffin Prankard, John Norman, george Whitehead, Isaac Knight, James Jeanes, Ro. Addison, John Scandrett, John Scandrett Jr. , Chas. Scandrett, Chr. Shuter, P. Day, John Price, John Rich, John Vechell, James Day, Noblet Ruddock, Phill Harris, Isaac Holchouse, Wm. Challoner. London merchants include: Chris. Smyth, Phill. Perry, John Hyde, Sam Hyde, Ed. Randolph, Henry Dee, Robt. Willimott, Jona. Scarth, Micajah Perry, John Maynard, Wm. Hunt, Humphrey Bell, Smuel Haswell, Arthur Dee, and W. Quare. Liverpool merchants include James Gibbon, John Pemberton, Samuel Ogden, James Halsall, George Norton, Wm. Marsden, Henry Stratford, Edward Trafford, Thom. Speers, John Pemberton Jr. , James Perceivall, Wm. Tatlock, Jos. Clegg, Dan Danvers, Samuel Anejier, Tho. Cockshutt, John ScarbrickMay, Edward Ratehouse, Richard Norris, Josia Poole, Wm. Webster, John Seacombe, Tho. Tillingham, Bryan Blundell, Richard Gililary, Robt. Hornby, Wm. Rolling, Jno. Goodwin, Wm. Hornwall, and Tho. Kendrick. p. 113.
8. *Ibid.* , pp. 188–254.
9. Between 1727 and 1769, 714 vessels carrying 45, 440 slaves docked in Virginia's ports. For the activities of Jacob and Joel seeWalter Minchington, Celia King, and Peter Waite (eds.) *Virginia Slave Trade Statistics 1698–1775* (Richmond: Virginia State Library 1984), pp. 63, 65, 113, 121, 117, 209.
10. U. B. Phillips, *Life and Labor in the Old South* (New York: Grosset and Dunlap, 1929), pp. 14–41.
11. *Ibid.* , pp. 220, 232.
12. *Ibid.* , pp. 238–49.
13. *Ibid.* , pp. 232–38.
14. Donnan, *Documents*, IV, p. 49.
15. Phillips, *Life and Labor inthe Old South*, p. 229.
16. *Ibid.* , pp. 249–51.
17. Stampp, *Peculiar Institution*, pp. 52, 65, 68, 70, 73, 269, 279, 326.
18. *Ibid.* , pp. 36, 52, 204–5, 230.
19. Ronald Lewis, *Coal, Iron and Slaves: Industrial Slavery in Maryland and Virginia, 1715–1865* (Westport, Conn.: Greenwood Press, 1979), pp. 13, 21, 23, 25, 29, 31. Hughes was the foremost manufacturer of heavy weapons.
20. Heth came to Frederick County in the 1760s andheld between 100 and 200 hands. Wooldridge had as many as 200 before 1841. Thomplins owned 150 in the Dover Coal Mines in the 1850s. *Ibid.* , pp. 64–71.
21. *Ibid.* , pp. 4 and 7.
22. Richard Wade, *Slavery in the Cities: The South 1820–1860* (New York: Oxford University Press, 1964), pp. 33–35.
23. Ira Rosenswaike, *On the Edge of Greatness: A Portrait of American Jewry in the Early National Period* (Cincinnati, OH: American Jewish Archives, 1985), p. 70.
24. Phillips, *Life and Labor in the Old South*, p. 196.
25. Michael Tadman, *Speculators and Slaves: Masters, Traders and Slaves in the Old South* (Madison: University of Wisconsin Press, 1989), pp. 61 and 196–98. See also Stampp, *Peculiar Institution*, p. 261 and Owens, *The Ruling Race*, p. 277. An appreciation of the blase attitudes of these slave traders may be obtained from reviewing family documents of the Omohumdros and Tompkins slavers in the Virginia Historical Society, Richmond . See Slave Markets, Files 286, 499 and 548.
26. Bancroft, *Slave Trading in the Old South*, p. 97.

27. Korn, *Jews in the South*, Dinnerstein and Palsson (eds.), pp. 111–113. Louis Ginsberg strongly denies that Jews were highly active in the "Negro trade, " and insists, "Without exception every one of thse men were recent arrivals in America and in the South and were small merchants trying to make a living. " *History of the Jews of Petersburg 1789–1950* (Richmond, VA: Williams Printing Co. , 1954), p. 43.

28. Monroe Billington, *The American South: A Brief History* (New York: Scribner's, 1971), p. 93.

29. When Union forces occupied Alexandria in 1861, the facility was converted into a military prison. See Janice Artemel and Jeff parker, "Alexandria Slave Pen Archaeology: Public Profits from Private Efforts, " *Fairfax Chronicles Newsletter*, Fairfax County Virginia (Feb.-April, 1985), pp. 1–4.

30. Ethan Allan Andrews, *Slavery and The Domestic Slave Trade in the United States* (Boston, MA: Light and Stearns, 1836), pp. 135–43. See also Wendall Stephenson, *Isaac Franklin, Slave trader and Planter of the Old South* (Gloucester, MA: P. Smith, 1938).

31. Donald Sweig suggests Armfield kept families together when they left Virginia in order to head off conflicts with abolitionists. Once the slaves were purchased by traders out of public sight in Mississippi, the family units were broken up. "Reassessing the Human Dimension of the Interstate Slave Trade, " *Prologue: The Journal of the National Archives* (Spring 1980), XII, p. 16.

32. Stampp, *Peculiar Institution*, p. 261. See also Winfield Collins, *Domestic Slave Trade of the Southern States*, pp. 96–99 and Tadman, *Speculators and Slaves*, pp. 64–82.

33. Klephart, a veteran of the war of 1812, was notorious for his ill treatment of slaves. In 1858, he sold the business to Charles Price and John Cook of Washington, DC who reconstituted themselves as Price, Birch and Co. See F.L. Brockett, *The Lodge of Washington: A History of the Alexandria Washington Lodge 1783–1876* (Alexandria, VA: G. H. Ramey, 1899) and Janice Artemel, Elizabeth Cromwell, and Jeff Parker, *The Alexandria Slave Pen: The Archaeology of Urban Captivity* (Washington, DC: Engineering Science, 1987).

34. There is no exact count. Sweig maintains Franklin and Armfield shipped between 300 and 1,500 a year for 10 years. The number aboad 28 ships was 3,600. "Reassessing the Human Dimension of Interstate Slave Trade, " pp. 6–8.

35. Artemel and Parker, "Alexandria Slave Pen Archaeology, " p. 1.

36. Phillips, *Life and Labor in the Old South*, p. 194.

37. Korn, "Jews and Negro Slavery in the Old South, 1789–1865, " *PAJHS* (1960–61), L, pp. 152–53.

38. See Censer, "Planters and the Southern Community: A Review Essay, " *Virginia Magazine of History and Biography* (October 1986), XCIV, pp. 387–408. Jews are absent from the selected papers of Edgar Thompson. *Plantation Societies, Race Relations and the South: The Regiimentation of Populations* (Durham, N.C.: Duke University Press, 1975). See also Bertram Wyatt-Brown, *Southern Honor: Ethics and Behavior in the Old South* (New York: Oxford 1982); James Oakes, *The Ruling Race: A History of American Slaveholders* (New York, 1982), and J. William Harris, *Plain Folks and Gentry in a Slave Society*.

39. Leon Huhner, "The Jews of Virginia from the Earliest Time to the Close of the Eighteenth Century, " *PAJHS* (1911), XX, pp. 85–87.

40. Davis, *Problem of Slavery in Western Culture*, p. 101.

41. Louis Ginsberg, *Chapters on the Jews of Virginia 1658–1900* (Richmond, VA: Cavalier Press, 1969, pp. 1–3.

42. Huhner, "Jews of Virginia, " pp. 88–99.

43. Marcus, *Early American Jewry,* II, p. 188. Louis Ginsberg claims that cantor Benjamin Pereira came to Richmond in 1748. *Chapters on the Jews of Virginia,* p. 6.

44. Marcus, *Early American Jewry,* III, p. 215.

45. The list included Samuel Alexander, Moses Cardozo, Jacob Cohen, Myer Cohen, Joseph Darmstadt, Myer Derkheim, Marcus Elkan, Isaiah Isaacs and Jesse Stoball, isaac Judah, Isaac Mordecai, Joseph Modrecai, and Reuben Norvell, Moses Myers, Joseph Myers and Benjamin Wolfe by 1787; Lyon Hart, Gershom Judah, Manuel Judah, Baruch Judah, Isaac Michaels, Jacob Mordecai in 1791; Aaron Cardozo, David Isaacs, Benjamin Myers, Zalman Rehine in 1792; Isaac Levy, Abraham Myers, Benjamin Solomon in 1793; Jacob Abrahams, Joseph de Palacios, Philip Russell in 1794; Israel Cohen 1798; Michael Myers, Solomon Marks, Joseph Max, Raphael Solomon, Samuel Myers by 1800. Richmond Virgina file. Misc. File AJA. Listing of Jews in Richmond, city personal and land books 1784–1784 and 1800 compiled by Rabbi Malcolm Stern.

46. Jacob Ezekiel, "The Jews of Richmond, " *PAJHS* (1896), IV, pp. 21–22. The temple lists 49, including 15 women in 1834, p. 23.

47. Marcus, *Early American Jewry,* II, p. 188.

48. See list of Virginia Tax payers 1782–87 compiled by Augusta Fothergill and John M. Naugle, Richmond, 1940, related to Korn in letter from Stern 2-2-61. Korn Papers, AJA, Ms. Coll. 99. These include 5 owned by Joseph Abrahams, 23 by Mordecai Abrahams, 5 by Solomon Abrahams, 5 by Isaiah Isaacs, 1 by Enoch Lyon, and 6 by Michael Marx.

49. Rosenwaike, "Jewish Population of the US in 1820, " pp. 150–78. The largest number were held by Jacob Mordecai on his Henrico country farm.

50. Wade, *Slavery in the Cities,* pp. 325–27.

51. Rosenwaike, *Edge of Greatness,* pp. 132–33.

52. There were also two unattached women and five men without professions. Herbert Ezekiel and Gaston Lichtenstein, *The History of the Jews of Richmond from 1769 to 1917* (Richmond, VA: by the author, 1917), pp. 142–145.

53. There are another 14 men without jobs listed. *Ibid.* , pp. 145–46.

54. Michelbacher apparently had no formal training in a seminary when he arrived in 1846 and disdained the title of rabbi. Reform Judaism leader Isaac Mayer Wise abominated this man who organized a women's study group and introduced confirmation to the rituals of Richmond. Allan Creeger writes, "Whether an ordained rabbi or not, Reverend Michelbacher was Congregation Beth Ahabah's religious spokesman and leader for over 20 years. " "Maximilian J. Michelbacher (1810–1897): His Times and His Legacy, " *Generations: Journal of Congregation of Beth Ahabah* (April 1933), V, pp. 1–7.

55. Rosenwaike, "Jewish Population of the US in 1790, " p. 161.

56. Korn, *Jews in the South,* p. 97.

57. *Ibid.* , p. 98.

58. See references to slaves Jenny and Mary Anderson in wills of Joseph Tobias, July 23, 1798, and Jacob Cohen, October 31, 1823. Dcouments Pertaining to the Jews of Richmond, 1792–1910, Ms. Collection 491, AJA.

59. Emma Mordecai rewarded Sarrah Norris in 1867. Korn, *Jews in the South,* p. 97.

60. See October 10, 1838 will of Samuel Myers detailing disposition of five slaves, Noah, Peter, Jack, Fanny and Jane. Richmond Wills, AJA, Ms. Collection 491.

61. Marcus, *Early American Jews,* II, pp. 182–83.

62. Korn, *Jews in the South,* p. 101.

63. Berman, *Richmond's Jewry 1769–1976 : Shabbat in Schokoe* (Jewish Federation of Richmond and University Press of Virginia, 1979), p. 168.

64. *Ibid.*, p. 168.
65. Korn, *Jews in the South*, p. 129. As examples, Korn cites Judah Touro and Lazarus Straus from Talbottom, Georgia. See also Leon Hühner, *Life of Judah Touro* (Philadelphia, Pa.: Jewish Publication Society, 1946), p. 69.
66. Berman, *Richmond's Jewry 1769-1976: Shabbat in Schokoe* (Jewish Federation of Richmond and University Press of Virginia, 1979), p. 163.
67. Clayton Hall, *Naratives of Early Maryland 1633-1684* (New York: Scribner's, 1910), p. 112.
68. Lumbrozo's fascinating story is recounted in a number of sources. See Matthew Andrews, *History of Maryland: Province and State* (Hatboro, Pa.: Tradition Press, 1965), pp. 95–96; A. D. Glushakov, *Maryland Bicentennial Jewish Book* (Baltimore, MD: Jewish Voice Printing, 1975), pp. 20–21; Isaac Fein, *The Making of An American Jewish Community: The History of Baltimore Jewry from 1773 to 1920* (Philadelphia, Pa.: Jewish Publication Society, 1971), pp. 7–8; and Eric Goldstein, "Traders and Transports: The Jews of Colonial Maryland, " (Baltimore, MD: Jewish Historical Society of Maryland, 1993), pp. 8–13.
69. E. Milton Altfeld, *The Jew's Struggle for Religious and Civil Liberty in Maryland* (Baltimore, MD: M. Curlander, 1924), p. 9.
70. The list of "rebels" responsible fo the transformation in Maryland's status included tobacco magnates John Coode, Kenylm Cheseldyne, Nehemiah Blakiston, henry Jowles, Ninian Beale, and John Adison. Robert Brugger, *Maryland: A Middle Temperament 1634-1980* (Baltimore, MD: Johns Hopkins and Maryland Historical Society, 1988), p. 39.
71. J. H. Hollander, "The Civil Status of the Jews in Maryland, 1634-1776, " *PAJHS* (1894), II, pp. 37–41.
72. Edward Eitches, "Maryland's 'Jews Bill'" *AJHQ* (1970–71), LX, pp. 258–79.
73. W. Wayne Smith, "Politics and Democracy in Maryland 1800–1854, " in *Maryland: A History 1632-1974*, Richard Walsh and William Fox (eds.) (Baltimore: Maryland Historical Society, 1974), pp. 258–59. See also Andrews, *History of Maryland*, pp. 450–51 and Altfeld, *Jew's Struggle for Religious and Civil Liberty in Maryland*.
74. Goldstein, "Traders and Transports," p. 16.
75. The Baltimore community trumpets itself as the first permanent Jewish settlement in Maryland. See *And So They Came: The Jewish Experience of Settlement in Maryland 1656-1929* (Baltimore, MD: Jewish Historical Society of Maryland, 1987); *Fertile Ground: Two Hundred Years of Jewish Life in Baltimore* (Baltimore: Jewish Historical Society of Maryland, 1992); and Rose Greenberg, T*he Chronicle of Baltimore Hebrew Congregation 1830-1975* (1975). Goldstein disputes these claims and makes a good case for earlier settlements at Annapolis and Fredericktown. "Traders and Transports," pp. 3, 18–26.
76. For discussion of these convicts and their crimes, see Goldstein, "Traders and Transports, " pp. 27–36. Goldstein cites a complete list from Peter Coldham's *Bonded Passengers to America 1718-1725* (Baltimore, MD 1983) on pp. 58–65.
77. Rosenwaike, "Jewish Population of the US in 1790," pp. 29–30 and 34.
78. Donnan, *Documents*, IV, pp. 17, 18.
79. *Ibid.*, p. 48.
80. Randall Miller, "Slaves and Southern Catholicism," in *Masters and Slaves in the House of the Lord: Race and Religion in the American South 1740-1870*, John Boles (ed.) (Lexington: University Press of Kentucky, 1988), pp. 129–30.
81. Brugger, *Maryland*, p. 145.
82. *Ibid.*, p. 254.

83. *Ibid.* , pp. 134, 141, 145, and 198.
84. Brugger, *Maryland,* p. 252.
85. Donald Wright, *African Americans in the Early Republic, 1789–1831* (Arlington Hts. : Harlan Davidson, 1993), pp. 28–29.
86. Ralph Clayton, *Slavery, Slaveholding and the Free Black Population of Antebellum Baltimore* (Bowie, MD: Heritage Books, 1993), pp. 29–34.
87. Isaac Fein, *The Making of an American Jewish Community*, p. 18; and Isidor Blum, *The Jews of Baltimore* (Baltimore, MD: Baltimore Historical Review Publ. Co. , 1910), p. 8.
88. *Ibid.* , pp. 260 and 315.
89. Rosenwaike, "Jewish Poulaltion of US in 1820, " pp. 150–178.
90. Wade, *Slavery in the Cities,* pp. 325–27.
91. Rosenwaike, *Edge of Greatness*, p. 112. See also Table 2: Jewish Heads of Households in Baltimore Censuses of 1820 and 1830. Korn Papers, AJA, mss. 99, Box 32, folder 1.
92. Ralph Clayton, *Black Baltimore 1820–1870* (Bowie, MD : Heritage Books, 1987), pp. 57–75.
93. Clayton, *Slavery, Slaveholding and The Free Black Population of Baltimore,* pp. 6–9.
94. Morris Schappes, *A Documentary History of the Jews in the United States 1654–1875* (New York: Schocken, 1950, 1971), pp. 408–418.
95. *Ibid.* , pp. 418–28.
96. *Sinai* (October, 1856), I, no. 9, pp. 258–59.
97. *Sinai* (December, 1856), no. 11, ppl. 353–9; July 1857, II, no. 6, 599–601; Agusut 1862, VII, no. 7, pp. 183–192. See also "War with Amalek, " Korn Papers, AJA, 32–3.
98. "Dr. Raphael's rede uber das Verhaltniss der Bibel zum Sklaveninstitute, "*Sinai* (February, 1861), VI, no. 1, p. 2–22.
99. "Noch ein Wort uber Dr. Raphael's Prosklaverei-Rede, " *Sinai* (March, 1861), VI, no. 2, pp. 45–50 and 60–61.
100. Einhorn likened his adversary to a *Gassenbube* (street Arab). *Sinai* (June 1861), VI, pp. 135–42.
101. *Sinai* (July, 1861), VI, 169–73.
102. Fein, *Making of an American Jewish Community,* pp. 96–97. See also Bertram Korn (ed.) "The Jews of the Union, " *American Jewish Archives* (November 1961), XIII, pp. 131–230 and Kaufmann Kohler (ed.) *David Einhorn Memorial Volume* (New York, 1911).

Notes to Chapter 11

1. Elizabeth Donnan, "The Slave Trade into South Carolina before the Revolution," *American Historical Review* (July 1928), XXXIII, pp. 80–85.
2. Daniel C. Littlefield, "The Slave Trade to Colonial South Carolina: A Profile," *South Carolina Historical Magazine* (April 1990), XCI, p. 69.
3. Daniel Littlefield, *Rice and Slaves: Ethnicity and the Slave Trade in Colonial South Carolina* (Baton Rouge: Louisiana State University Press, 1981), pp. 98–109. In 1699 South Carolina produced 2,000 barrels of rice. Thirty years later the figure rose to 48,155 barrels. By 1839, the Palmetto State produced 75 percent of all the rice in the United States. Larry Koger, *Black Slaveowners and Free Black Masters in South Carolina, 1790–1860* (Jefferson, NC: McFarland Press, 1985), p. 102.
4. For a discussion of the alleged immunity to malaria for people susceptible to sickle cell anemia, see Boles, *Black Southeners*, pp. 96–105.

5. W.Robert Higgins, "Charles Town Merchants and Factors Dealing in the External Negro Trade, 1735–1775," *South Carolina Historical Magazine* (October 1964), LXV, p. 205. Higgins notes that only 11 cargoes entered other ports in the forty years under examination, while 1,108 came to Charleston.

6. Said Rosen,"To understand Charleston, you must see it as part of the Caribbean world. A map shows Charleston as part of the Caribbean world. Slavery came from Barbados. It was more a part of the Caribbean and London world than New England." Interview, August 14, 1993.

7. Robert N. Rosen, *A Short History of Charleston* (Charleston, SC: Peninsula Press, 1982), p. 67.

8. Ship Registers in the South Carolina Archives, intro. R.Nicholas Olsberg (South Carolina Historical Society, 1973), South Carolina Room, Charleston City Library. See pp. 207, 231, 233, 241, 247, 253.

9. From Donnan, *Documents*, IV, pp. 278–80, 296–97, 301, 310–11, 314, 338, 365, 372, 375–76, 378, 380, 381, 386, 411–13, 428–29, 438, 442, 453–54, 467, 474, 475, 477, 490, 504, 508–9, 513–5, 521–22. Discrepancies exist numbers listed by Donnan on p. 807. My figures, based on actual cargoes previously listed are somewhat lower than Donnan. As an example she lists 4,865 for 1772. Totalling each individual cargo comes to little more than 3,717.The difference may come from estimates based on Laurents' record books and other uncited source material.

10. Higgins, "Charles Town Merchants and Factors," p. 210.

11. Hagy, *This Happy Land: The Jews of Colonial and Antebellum Charleston* (Tuscaloosa: University of Alabama Press, 1993), p. 186.

12. See Ships Clearances and Entries into the Port of Charleston, South Carolina Historical Society, Thomas J. Tobias Papers, 11–417.

13. Littlefield, "Slave Trade into South Carolina," p. 77. South Carolina Treasury records for 1735–1775 are substantially higher with 1,092 ships and 70,887 slaves.

14. Tobias Papers, S.C. Historical Society, 11/418/5.

15. Higgins,"Charles Town Merchants and Factors,"p. 207.

16. Donnan, *Documents*, IV, pp. 278–80, 296–97.

17. *Ibid.*, pp. 268–72.

18. *Ibid.*, pp. 310–11, 314, 338, 365, 372, 375–76, 378, 386, 411–13, 428–99, 438, 442, 453–54, 467.

19. Rachel Klein, *Unification of a Slave State: The Rise of the Planter Class in the South Carolina Back Country , 1760–1808* (Chapel Hill: Universitry of North Carolina Pess, 1990), pp. 20–34.

20. Rosen, *Short History of Charleston*, p. 95. Laurens has been the focus of a major study undertaken by the University of South Carolina. See *The Papers of Henry Laurens*, vols. 1–10, Philip Hamer, David Chestnutt, and George Rogers (eds.) (Columbia: University of South Carolina Press, 1968–1985).

21. Donnan, *Documents*, IV, pp. 301–473 passim; and "The Slave Trade into South Carolina," p. 819.

22. Alphabetic Index to Secretary of State, South Carolina State Historical Library, Columbia, South Carolina. Recorded Insturments, Miscellaneous Records, Main Series, Bills of Sale volumes 1773–1843, reel 1, pp. 2379–81.

23. Rosen, *Short History of Charleston*, p. 25.

24. Carol Bleser (ed.) *The Hammonds of Redcliffe* (New York: Oxford University Press, 1981) and *Secret and Sacred: The Diaries of James Hammond* (Chapel Hill: University of North Carolina Press, 1990).

25. Stampp, *Peculiar Institution*, pp. 35, 40, 42, 66, 230, 238, 240, 276, 247, 286, 291, 298.

26. Phillips, *Life and Labor in the Old South*, p. 233.
27. Rosen, *Short History of Charleston*, pp. 86 and 123. For a list of early rice planters (e.g., John Yeamans, James Colleton, Nathaniel Johnson, Seth Sothell) see Peter Wood, *Black Majority: Negroes in Colonial South Carolina from 1670 through the Stono Rebellion* (New York: Knopf, 1974), p. 46.
28. Alphabetic Index, Bills of Sale, pp. 1228–1325.
29. *Ibid.*, p. 168.
30. *Ibid.*, p. 3482. See also entries for James Doughty, p. 1089; William Doughty with 53 in 1819, pp. 1089–90, W.J. Bennett with 105 between 1833 and 1855, p. 293; also records of John and William Ravanel, pp. 3535–40; and Sophia LaRouche, pp. 2373–74).
31. *Ibid.*, pp. 4319–21.
32. *Ibid.*, pp. 1850–56.
33. *Ibid.*, pp. 1096–1101.
34. *Ibid.*, p. 2856.
35. Hagy, *This Happy Land*, p. 94. Marcus allows that individual Jews owned farms and plantations in the Carolinas, but stresses that "agriculture was not a Jewish vocation." *Early American Jewry*, II, p. 245.
36. Alphabetic Index, Bills of Sale, p. 215.
37. *Ibid.*, p. 788.
38. *Ibid.*, p. 789.
39. *Ibid.*, pp. 790–91.
40. *Ibid.*, p. 793.
41. *Ibid.*, p. 900.
42. *Ibid.*, p. 2026.
43. *Ibid.*, p. 2589.
44. *Ibid.*, p. 2984.
45. *Ibid.*, pp. 3120–21.
46. *Ibid.*, p. 2983.
47. *Ibid.*, pp. 2435–37.
48. *Ibid.*, pp. 1695–96.
49. *Ibid.*, pp. 4336–37.
50. Hagy, *This Happy Land*, p. 94.
51. Alphabetical Index, Bills of Sale, p. 3225.
52. Lindo Family Papers, Misc. Papers, South Carolina Historical Society, 30–34.
53. Barnett Elzas, *The Jews of South Carolina: From the Earliest Times to the Present Day* (Philadelphia, PA: J.B.Lippincott, 1905), p. 54.
54. *Ibid.*, p. 61.
55. Bill of sale from John Gordon, tavern keeper, for boys Peter and Frank.Lindo, Moses, Documents File, AJA, December 1, 1756.
56. Leon Huhner, "The Jews of South Carolina from the Earliest Settlement to the End of the American Revolution, " *PAJHS* (1904), XII, p. 39.
57. Ibid., pp. 41–42 and Elzas, *Jews of South Carolina*, pp. 17,18.
58. Huhner, "Jews of South Carolina," p. 40.
59. Elzas, *Jews of South Carolina*, p. 25.
60. See Harry Golden's praise of Pinckney as "quite a man" who influenced Madison to insert the clause dropping religious tests in the U.S. Constitution. *Our Southern Landsmen*, pp. 232–33.
61. Huhner, "Jews of South Carolina," pp. 42–43.
62. Elzas, *Jews of South Carolina*, p. 26.
63. *Ibid.* pp. 277–80.

64. Marcus, *Colonial American Jew*, I, p. 347.
65. Hagy, *This Happy Land*, pp. 14–16.
66. In 1760 Da Costa and his Gentile parnter Thomas Farr purchased 200 slaves out of 3,573 slaves imported to Charleston, less than 6 percent of the total for the year. Marcus, *Early American Jew*, I, p. 321.
67. Hagy, *This Happy Land*, pp. 19. Despite Harry Golden's panegyrics, Jews played virtually no role in the early development of this state, pp. 6–97. By way of contrast, there was very little appeal in the more sparsely settled region of North Carolina. In 1860 there were 331,000 slaves in the state, an average of 9.6 slaves per owner, most of whom were Methodists, Baptists and Presbyterians. See John Bassett, *Slavery in the State of North Carolina* (Baltimore, MD: Johns Hopkins University Press, 1899), pp. 47 and 78. The leading slave traders in North Carolina were E.W. Ferguson, Obadiah Fields, William Long, J.S. Totten and H. Badgett, D.S. Reid and the firm of Tyre Glen and Isaac Jarrett. Glen sent more than 800 to Alabama between 1824 and 1847. Michael Tadman, *Speculators and Slaves: Masters, Traders and Slaves in the Old South* (Madison: University of Wisconsin Press, 1989), pp. 198–99.There were perhaps 11 Jews in North Carolina at the time of the American Revolution, few landholders. The U.S. census lists only one Jew in the entire region in 1790. Isaac Harby, writing for the *North American Review* suggests there may have been no more than 400 in 1826. In 1808, the General Assembly attempted to expel a member who was Jewish. Jacob Marcus rightly concluded there was really no organized Jewish community in North Carolina till the second half of the nineteenth century. See Leon Hühner, "The Jews of North Carolina Prior to 1800," *PAJHS* (1925), XXIX, pp. 137–48.
68. Hagy, *This Happy Land* , p. 93.
69. *Ibid.*, p. 91.
70. *Ibid.*, pp. 99–100.
71. *Ibid.*, pp. 103–4.
72. *Ibid.*, p. 91. Valentine, brother-in-law of Asser Levy, dealt primarily in indigo, flour and sugar. He was the first Jew to own land in Carolina, in 1699.
73. Rosenswaike, *Edge of Greatness*, pp. 113–15.
74. *Ibid.*, pp. 113–15. See also Rosen, *Short History of Charleston*, p. 70.
75. Hagy, *This Happy Land*, p. 93.
76. See *A Key to Uncle Tom's Cabin* (Boston: J.P. Jewett, 1853).
77. Interview with Breibart, Charleston, August 9, 1993.
78. Korn, *Jews in the South*, pp. 105–13.
79. *Ibid.*,p. 111.
80. *Ibid.*, pp. 107–8.
81. Bancroft, *Slave Trading in the Old South*, pp. 175–76.
82. *Ibid.*, pp. 189–90.
83. Tadman, *Speculators and Slaves*, pp. 192–95 and 253–71.
84. Based on City of Charleston, Tax Assessor: Assessment Books 1860 CC19. Columbia SC State Library,
85. *Ibid.*
86. Notes on Jacob Levin, Korn Papers, AJA, 32–1.
87. Bancroft, *Slave Trading in the Old South*, p. 239.
88. *Ibid.*, p. 239.
89. John Hammon Moore, *Columbia and Richland County: A South Carolina Community 1740–1990* (Columbia: University of South Carolina Press, 1993), pp. 119–20.
90. *Ibid.*, pp. 120–36.

91. See Helen Kohn Hennig, *The Tree of Life: 50 Years of Congregational Life at the Tree of Life Synagogue. Columbia SC*, 1984, pp. 3–4.
92. Moore, *Columbia and Richland County*, p. 188. Tadman cites nine prominent Richland county slavers. Levin's name is not on the list. *Speculators and Slaves*, pp. 23–71.
93. Interview with Rubin, Columbia, August 21, 1993.
94. Rosen Interview, August 14, 1993.
95. Rubin Interview, August 21, 1993.
96. Moore, Columbia and Richland County, pp. 84–85.

Notes to Chapter 12

1. Leon Hühner disputes that, saying it was not founded for criminals but for needy, respectable people. "The Jews of Georgia in Colonial Times," *PAJHS* (1902), X, p. 65. Rabbi Saul Rubin argues that Parliament debated on what to do with people released from prisons with no place to go. *Third to None: The Saga of Savannah Jewry 1733–1983* (Savannah, GA: Congregation Mickve Israel, 1983), pp. 1–16.
2. This was not be the last time Britain would attempt this sort of thing. Australia was founded by a similar forced transfer of population in nineteenth century. See Robert Glenn, "Slavery in Georgia 1733–1793," senior thesis, Princeton University, April 1972, pp. 1–2.
3. Interview with Attorney Warren Swartz, Savannah, August 17, 1993.
4. Donnan, *Documents*, IV, pp. 587–89.
5. Julia Floyd Smith, *Slavery and Rice Culture in Low Country Georgia 1750–1860* (Knoxville: University of Tennessee Press, 1985), p. 95.
6. Donnan, *Documents*, IV, pp. 592–93.
7. *Ibid.*, p. 500.
8. Ralph Betts Flanders, *Plantation Slavery in Georgia* (Chapel Hill: University of North Carolina Press, 1933), p. 21.
9. Donnan, *Documents*, IV, pp. 590–93.
10. *Ibid.*, pp. 612–25, 633.
11. *Ibid.*, pp. 620–21.
12. See Records of U.S. Customs Service, Slave Manifests of Customs Houses: Savannah 1801–1860, RG 36.4, National Archives , Washington, D.C. The papers for King and Jones can be found in Box 13 (1854–55), August-December folder. Those of Johnston, haversham, Sheftall and Cohen are in Box 1 (1820). Similarly blended records exist for Philadellphia (1790–1840), New Orleans (1819–52, 1860–61), and Mobile (1822–60).
13. Betty Wood, *Slavery in Colonial Georgia 1730–1775* (Athens: University of Georgia Press, 1984), p. 130.
14. Smith, *Slavery and Rice Culture in Low Country Georgia,* p. 108.
15. Land grants averaged 300–600 acres. Glenn, "Slavery in Georgia," pp. 58–61.
16. Smith, *Slavery and Rice Culture in Low Country Georgia,* p. 108. See also Stampp, *The Peculiar Institution*, pp. 173, 234, 283.
17. Smith, *Slavery and Rice Culture,* pp. 219–26.
18. J.Carlyle Sitterson, *Sugar Country: The Cane Sugar Industry in the South 1758–1950* (Lexington: University of Kentucky Press, 1953), pp. 31–33 and 76–77.
19. Between 1790 and 1810, the number of slaves in Georgia increased from 29,264 to 105, 218. Flanders, *Plantation Slavery in Georgia,* p. 56.
20. *Ibid.*, pp. 87–109, 112–19, and 280–88.
21. Mohr cites the slaving activity of Howell Cobb, James Potter, James Postell, Thomas Butler King, Samuel and Rufus Varnedoe, Charles Jones, none of them

Jews. *On the Threshold of Freedom: Masters and Slaves in Civil War Georgia* (Athens: University of Georgia Press, 1986), pp. 108–14.

22. Jeremiah Evarts Diary, Collection 240, Georgia Historical Society, Savannah, p. 17.
23. *Ibid.*, pp. 18–21.
24. See vol. I, section I of Slave Bills of Sale Project, African-American Family History Association, Atlanta March 1986, pp. 3–6, 53–6597, and vol. II, section 1, p. 2.
25. Slave Owners , Warren County 1798, Georgia Historical Archives, Atlanta, Drawer 32, Box 20.
26. Slave Grantors/Grantees, Jones County, 1791–1864, Georgia Historical Archives, Atlanta, Drawer 154, Box 62.
27. Slave Importers to Columbia County 1817–1838, Georgia Historical Archives, Atlanta, Drawer 48, Box 80.
28. Importation of Slaves, Franklin County 1818–31, Georgia Historical Archives, Atlanta, Drawer 200, Box 12.
29. Slave Register, Morgan County 1818–24, Georgia Historical Archives, Atlanta, Drawer 41, Box 8.
30. Court of Ordinary Slave Record, Pulaski County 1818–1865, Georgia Historical Archives, Atlanta, Drawer 38, Box 46.
31. Smith, *Slavery and Rice Culture*, p. 99.
32. Phillips, *Life and Labor in the Old South*, p. 200.
33. Bancroft, *Slave Trading in the Old South*, p. 248.
34. Phillips, *Life and Labor in the Old South*, p. 200.
35. Joseph Karl Menn, "The Large Slaveholders of the Deep South 1860," University of Texas Dissertation, 1964, p. 215.
36. Bancroft, *Slave Trading in the Old South*, pp. 245–48 and Flanders, *Plantation Slavery in Georgia*, pp. 186–87.
37. Korn, *Jews in the South*, pp. 107–12.
38. Stephen Hertzberg, "Southern Jews and Their Encounter with Blacks: Atlanta 1850–1917," *Atlanta Historical Journal* (Fall, 1979), XXIII , pp. 8–9.
39. *Ibid.*, pp. 8–9 . See also Levin Cohen Papers, American Jewish Archives, Sept.28, 1862, p. 2 and Nov. 12, 1862, p. 4.
40. Hertzberg, "Southern Jews and Their Encounter with Blacks," p. 8.
41. Marcus, *Colonial American Jew,* I, pp. 356–57.
42. Hühner, "Jews of Georgia in Colonial Times," pp. 79–80.
43. For a complete listing see Levi Sheftall Diary, 1733–1808, X-1414-1 Sheftall Papers, from the Keith Read Manuscripts Collection, University of Georgia Libraries, in Georgia Historical Society, Savannah.
44. "The Jews in Early Georgia, typed ms. by Horace Folsom, 1-14-33, pp. 1–2 in Hughes-Folsom papers, no. 406, Box 4, Folder 67 Georgia Historical Society, Savannah.
45. See "The First Native Georgian," by John Boifeuillet, Minis Colonial Papers 1768–1793, Collection 568, bound volume of primary documents (originals presented to Georgia Historical Society by J. Florance Minis 1925, no. 11.
46. See Folsom, typed ms. 2-9-33, "From the Tagus to the Savannah" p. 3, in Floyd Papers, 1308 Box.36, Folder 439 Georgia Historical Society. Nunez offspring Daniel became harbor master in Savannah in 1784 and Moses a linguist to Indians in 1778.See also article on Dr. Marcos Fernan Nunez, *Bulletin of Geogia Medical Society* (July 31, 1962), vol. 2, pp. 8–10.
47. Interview with Attorney Warren Swartz, Savannah, August 17, 1993.
48. Webb Garrison, *Oglethorpe's Folly: The Birth of Georgia* (Lakemont, GA: Cople House Books, 1982), pp. 84–85 and 106. See also Rubin, *Third to None*, p. 11.

49. This was not true. Garrison, *Oglethorpe's Folly*, p. 85. Diaries of German minister Boltzius relate, "There are here some Jews who in eating, in the celebration of the Sabbath, etc. do not follow the Jewish customs. Pp. 197–99, Boltzius Diaries, vol.1 in M.H. and D.B.Floyd Papers no. 1308 Box 36 Folder 439, Georgia Historical Society, Savannah. See also letter from S. Quincy to Henry Newman in London, July 4, 1735 from Savannah: "You desire in one of your letters to know whether the Jews amongst us seem inclined to imbrace (*sic*) Christianity. We have here two sorts of Jews, Protuguese and Germans. The first having professed Christianity in Portugal or the Brazils are more lax in their way, and dispense with a great many of their Jewish Rites, and two young men, the sons of a Jew Doctor, sometimes come to Church, and for these reasons are thought by some people to be inclined to be Christians but I cannot find that they really are so, only that their education; in those countries wherethey were obliged to appear Christians, make them less rigid and stiff in their way. The German Jews, who are thought the better sort of them, are a great deal more strict in their way, and rigid observations of their laws."Original Papers, Correspondence, Trustees, General Oglethorpe and Others, 1734–1735 Floyd Papers 1308 Box 36 Folder 439, pp. 207–9, Georgia Historical Society, Savannah.
50. Levi Sheftall records an entry in his diary for July 17,1787—"Joseph Veazor came to live here but he remained only a very short time and went away."
51. Jews in Georgia, Box 1157, Item 10. Article from *Zeitung des Jundenthums*, 1844. Georgia historical Society, Savannah. See also Rubin, *Third to None*, p. 18.
52. Wood, *Slavery in Colonial Georgia*, pp. 160–63 and 250; Rubin, *Third to None*, pp. 81–88 and Boifeuillet, "The First Native Georgian," Minis Papers 1768–93, Collection 568, Georgia Historical Society.
53. *Georgia Gazette*, March 21, 1770, p. 3 and January 18, 1781, p. 1. in Floyd Papers 1308, Box 36, Folder 439, Georgia Historical Society.
54. Marcus, *Colonial American Jew*, III, pp. 1241–42. Lucena's son John married a gentile in London and died a Catholic after serving as Consul General in Portugal. *Ibid.*, p. 326.
55. Sheftall was described in a royal proclamation published in the *Georgia Gazette* of July 6, 1780 as "a great rebel." Chairman of the rebel parochial committee, he was captured and put on a prison ship to the West Indies. His son Sheftall Sheftall was appointed by the War Board in Philadelphia to continue supplying General Moultrie and the inhabitants of Charleston. in October 1782 Mordecai Sheftall was subsequently exchanged under a flag of truce. See Edmund Abrahams, "Some Notes on the Early History of the Shfetalls of Georgia," *PAJHS* (1909), XVII,pp. 167–86.)

    File X1414-01 in the Georgia Historical Society contains a number of documents telling of sale of slaves by Sheftall family between 1791 and 1822—usually 1 or 2. Folder 3, Folder 14 July 9,1822 See also Levi Sheftall Receipt book, 1777–1810. Folder 17 contains hundreds of documents, however, that typify business dealings in rice, nails, grindstones, indigo, paper, rum, salmon, sugar and chocolate.
56. Henry Aaron Alexander, "Notes on the Alexander Family of South Carolina and Georgia , 1651–1954," 142 pg. pamphlet published by same, 1954, Atlanta Jewish Community Archives, pp. 19–33, 51, 56.
57. Korn, *Jews in the South*, pp. 91–92.
58. One acted as executor after receiving an education. Marcus, *Early American Jewry*, p. 334.
59. Sheftall Papers, Marion Abrams Levy collection, Georgia Historical Society, Savannah, X1414-02, no. 6.

60. Kole, *The Minis Family of Georgia*, p. 36.
61. Rabbi Rubin notes that his salary went from $ 5 in 1842 to $25 in 1854. *Third to None*, p. 117.
62. Raphael Moses Papers, File 86-002, Atlanta Jewish Community Archives, pp. 60–61.
63. The estimate comes from Rabbi Isaac Leeser's *Occident* , July 6, 1859, XVII, pp. 88–89.
64. Ella Mitchell, *History of Washington County* (Atlanta: Cherokee Publ., 1924, 1973), pp. 133–39.
65. Dinnerstein, "Atlanta in the Progressive Era: A Dreyfus Affair in Ga. 170–198," p. 182. Straus took his family to New York where he established Macy's department store.
66. See eight-page typed memo on Jews of Atlanta for Rabbi David Marx by Aaron Haas, c.1900, "Early History of Atlanta Jewish 1845–87." Atlanta Jewish Community Archives. See also "Notes on the Alexander Family of South Carolina and Georgia," by Henry Aaron Alexander, p. 30.
67. Kole, *The Minis Family of Georgia*, pp. 13–15.
68. *Ibid.*, pp. 22–89, passim.
69. *Ibid.*, p. 54.
70. *Ibid.*, p. 71.
71. Rosenwaike, "The Jewish Population of the US in 1820,"p. 53.
72. Stephen Hertzberg, *Strangers within the Gate City: The Jews of Atlanta, 1845–1915* (Philadelphia, PA, Jewish Publication Society, 1978), p. 22.
73. Interview with Rubin, Savannah, August 17, 1993.
74. *Ibid.*
75. Interview with Law, Savannah, August 17, 1993.
76. Interview with Greene, Savannah, August 18, 1993.
77. *Ibid.*

Notes to Chapter 13

1. Clement Eaton, *The Civilization of the Old South*, ed. Albert Kirwan (Lexington: University of Kentucky Press, 1968), p. 78.
2. Just as in Georgia and Australia, Louisiana's patricians gloss over the origins of their society. Of the first settlers, Charles Dufour writes: "France was purged of its human dregs and worst derelicts, as prisons, detention houses and hospitals were eptied and denizens of the streets were rounded up and shipped to Louisiana." "The People of New Orleans," in *The Past as Prelude: New Orleans 1718–1968,* Hodding Carter (ed.) (New Orleans: Pelican Publ. House, 1968), pp. 24–25.
3. Roger Shugg, *Origins of Class Struggle in Louisiana: A Social History of White Farmers and Laborers During Slavery and After 1840–1875* (Baton Rouge: Louisiana State University Press, 1939), pp. 39–41.
4. See Gwendolyn Hall, *Africans in Colonial Louisiana: The Development of Afro-Creole Culture in the Eighteenth Century* (Baton Rouge: Louisiana State University Press, 1992), pp. 58 and 130.
5. Donnan, *Documents*, IV, pp. 636–38, 640, 649. See also Marcel Giraud, *A History of French Louisiana: The Reign of Louis XIV 1698–1715* , vol. I, tr. Joseph Lambert (Baton Rouge: Louisiana State University Press, 1974), pp. 180–81 and *Years of transitiion 1715–1717*, vol. II, tr. Brian Pearce (Baton Rouge: Louisiana State University Press, 1993), pp. 28–30 and 129–31.
6. Hall, *Africans in Colonial Louisiana*, pp. 100–10.

7. *Ibid.*, p. 137.
8. *Ibid.*, pp. 150–52.
9. *Ibid.*, pp. 278–80.
10. Sitterson, *Sugar Country*, pp. 3–5.
11. Eaton, *Civilization of the Old South*, pp. 88–98.
12. Sitterson, *Sugar Country*, pp. 68–70.
13. Phillips, *Life and Labor in the Old South*, p. 244.
14. Sitterson, *Sugar Country*, p. 86.
15. Phillips, *Life and Labor*, pp. 242–43 and Stampp, *Peculiar Institution*, pp. 42–43, 50, 186, 354.
16. Menn, *Large Slaveholders of the Deep South*, p. 233.
17. Phillips, *Life and Labor in the Old South*, p. 166.
18. *Inventory of the Church and Synagogue Archives of Louisiana: Louisiana Historical Records Survey*, Works Projects Administration (Baton Rouge: Louisiana State University Department of Archives, 1941), p. 1.
19. Bertram Korn, *The Early Jews of New Orleans* (Waltham, MA: American Jewish Historical Society, 1969, pp. 3–7 and 23–26. See also Leo Shpall, *The Jews in Louisiana* (New Orleans: Steeg Publishing, 1936) and *History of the Jews of Louisiana* (New Orleans: Jewish Historical Publishing Co. of Louisiana, 1903.)
20. Liliane Crete, *Daily Life in Louisiana 1815–1830*, tr. Patrick Gregory (Baton Rouge: Louisiana State University Press, 1978), pp. 153–55. O'Reilly based his decrees upon laws from Castille dating to the time of Alfonso deSabio (1252–1284). See Jack Holmes, "A Spanish Province, 1779–1798," in Richard McLemore (ed.) *A History of Mississippi* (Hattiesburg: University Press of Mississippi, 1973), I, p. 161.
21. *Secret Relationship*, pp. 273–75.
22. Korn, *Early Jews of New Orleans*, pp. 10–17, 35–38.
23. *Ibid.* p. 62.
24. *Ibid.* pp. 48–65. There are only three large transactions included in Natchez and New Orleans notary records. Benjamin bartered 12 slaves for 3,280 pounds of indigo in 1785. Manuel purchased 123 for 3,780 pesos in 1787. That same year, Manuel and Jacob paid 9300 Mexican pesos for 31 slaves. *Ibid.*, p. 62. See also file on Manuel Monsanto, AJA, Miscellaneous Collection #99, for 12 slave contracts sold between 1787 and 1789) and Korn papers, Monsanto Family Documents, 19–5 through 20–4.
25. Korn, *Early Jews of New Orleans*, pp. 40–45.
26. Lafitte was raised by his grandmother and attributed his ingeniuty and intuition to this lady. *Ibid.*, pp. 98–99.
27. *Ibid.*, p. 67.
28. *Ibid.* , p. 212.
29. *Ibid.*, p. 214.
30. When he died in 1839, his wife wanted a crucifix placed in his coffin. *Ibid.*, pp. 199–203.
31. *Ibid.*, pp. 144–53.
32. *Ibid.*, p. 119.
33. Kohler, "Judah Benjamin: Statesman and Jurist, " *PAJHS* (1904), XII, p. 63,
34. Korn, "Jews and Negro Slavery in the Old South, 1789–1865," *PAJHS* (Sept.1960–June 1961), p. 191.
35. Kohler, "Judah Benjamin," p. 84.
36. Eli Evans, *Judah P. Benjamin: The Jewish Confederate* (New York: Free Press, 1988), p. 29.
37. Kohler, "Judah Benjamin," p. 82. There is some question whether such meeting every took place, as Benjamin did not become a senator until 1853.

38. Evans, *Judah P. Benjamin*, p. 92.
39. *Ibid.*, pp. 134–35.
40. Kohler, "Judah Benjamin," p. 83. Simon Neiman fantasizes a deathbed scene with extreme unction being administered in *Judah Benjamin* (Indianapolis, IN: Bobbs-Merrill, 1963), pp. 219–20.
41. Evans, *Judah P. Benjamin: the Jewish Confederate*, p. 29. See also Evans, *The Provincials: A Personal History of Jews in the South* (New York: Free Press, 1988.) Oddly, Robert Meade's *Judah P. Benjamin, Confederate Statesman* (New York: Oxford, 1943), offers very little insight into Benjamin's Jewishness other than a brief family background, pp. 12–13.
42. *Ibid.*, p. 403.
43. Korn, "Jews and Negro Slavery in the Old South,"pp. 91–92 and New Orleans, Jews, Korn Papers, AJA, 311–3.
44. Elliott Ashkenazi, *The Business of Jews in Louisiana 1840–1875* (Tuscaloosa: University of Alabama Press, 1989), pp. 81–82.
45. Korn, *Early Jews of New Orleans*, p. 174.
46. *Ibid.*, p. 163. Korn says, "He (Jacobs) came as close as any New Orleans Jew to specializing in this business." Jacobs acquired a notorious reputation for trying to pass of Kentucky-bred slaves as coming from Virginia. Crete, *Daily Life in Louisiana*, p. 154.
47. Korn, *Early Jews of New Orleans*, pp. 105–9.
48. Sitterson, *Sugar Country*, pp. 185–200. Jews are also absent from Sitterson's list of overseers, p. 55.
49. Crete, *Daily Life in Louisiana*, p. 153.
50. Irving Sloan, *The Jews in America 1621–1970: A Chronology and Fact Book* (Dobbs Ferry, NY: Oceana Publications, 1971), pp. 77–83.
51. Korn, *Early Jews of New Orleans*, pp. 88–89 and Huhner, *Life of Judah Touro* (Philadelphia, PA: Jewish Publication Society, 1946), p. 69. A contrary view is offered by Morris Schappes in *Jewish Life* (April 1947), pp. 21–24, who says there is no evidence Touro was opposed to slavery. Schappes attributes a proslavery sermon by Parson Clapp used after Touro's death to the Jewish philanthropist.
52. Korn, *Early Jews of New Orleans*, pp. 88–89. Stephen Birmingham offers a totally different picture of Touro, suggesting that he was a timid loner who was not particularly intelligent. His aversion to trading in slaves stemmed from a reluctance to trade in anything. Birmingham claims there is no evidence short of the reference to a "F.W.C." (free woman of color) to support the notion that Touro intended a legacy for Ellen Wilson. Most important, he declares that upon coming to New Orleans, Touro rented a pew at Christ Church and became an Episcopalian. *The Grandees*, pp. 129–45.
53. Kohn's granddaughter became a Catholic. Korn, *Early Jews of New Orleans*, pp. 119–27.
54. *Ibid.*, pp. 127–35.
55. Ashkenazi, *Business of Jews in Louisiana*, pp. 109–18.
56. *Occident*, July 6, 1859, XVI, pp. 88–89.
57. Korn, *Early Jews of New Orleans*, pp. 176–86.
58. Ashkenazi, *Business of Jews in Louisiana*, pp. 2, 13, 15, 21.
59. Korn, *Early Jews of New Orleans*, p. 158.
60. *A Directory and a Census*, introduction by Charles L. Thompson, (New Orleans: The Pelican Gallery, Livre au Conseil de Commune, August 1805). Hartman's Historical Series No.48. Slavery, Jewish Participation in, 1450–1860, Korn's Notes, Korn Papers, AJA, 31–6.
61. Korn, *Early Jews of New Orleans*, pp. 92–94.

62. Department of Commerce. Fourth Census 1820. Population of Louisiana Parish of Orleans. Parish of Plaquemine.

63. 1830 Census, Orleans Parish. New Orleans Public Library.

64. Korn's Notes, Korn Papers, AJA, 32–1. WPA historians estimate the number of Jewish families in New Orleans in 1843 at 125. There were only 7,500 Jews in all of Louisiana in 1877. *Inventory of the Church and Synagogue Archives of Louisiana*, p. 16.

65. Rosenwaike, *Edge of Greatness*, p. 118.

66. Slaves of Jewish masters in New Orleans, Louisiana Historical Society Library, September 28, 1960 p. 3, Korn Papers, AJA, 32–1.

67. Warren Howard, *American Slavers and the Federal Law 1837–1862* (Berkeley: University of California Press, 1963), pp. 253–54.

68. Carter Woodson, *Free Negro Heads of Families in the United States in 1830*, (Washington, DC: Association for Study of Negro Life and History, 1925) p. xxxv.

69. Twenty-five owned ten or more slaves. Carter Woodson, *Free Negro Owners of Slaves in the United States in 1830* (Washington, DC: 1925), pp. 9–15.

70. Carter Woodson, *Free Negro Heads of Families in the United States in 1830* p. xxxv. H.E. Sterkx estimates the combined wealth of free blacks (in real property and slaves) in Natchitoches, St.Landry, Pointe Coupee, and Plaquinines Parishes by 1860 at more than $2,000,000. *The Free Negro in Ante-Bellum Louisiana* (Rutherford, NJ: Farleigh Dickinson Press, 1972), pp. 234–38.

71. Wade, *Slave Trading in the Old South*, p. 205.

72. Oakes, *The Ruling Race*, p. 49.

73. Crete, *Daily Life in Louisiana*, p. 78.

74. *Ibid.*, p. 90.

75. Korn, *Early Jews of New Orleans*, pp. 88–89.

76. Blake Touchstone, "Planters and Slave Religion in the Deep South," in Boles, *Masters and Slaves in the House of the Lord*, p. 113.

Notes to Chapter 14

1. Samuel Morison, Henry Steele Commager, and William E. Leuchtenburg, *The Growth of the American Republic* (New York: Oxford University Press, 1969), p. 468.

2. Melvin Copeland, *The Cotton Manufacturing Industry of the United States* (Cambridge, MA: Harvard University Press, 1923), p. 6. See also Gavin Wright, *The Political Economy of the Cotton South: Households, Markets and Wealth in the Nineteenth Century* (New York: Norton, 1978), pp. 35–36.

3. Davis, *Cotton Kingdom in Alabama*, pp. 12–19.

4. Gary McDonough (ed.) *The Florida Negro: A Federal Writers' Project Legacy* (Jackson: University Press of Mississippi, 1993), pp. 5–7.

5. The council at Pensacola included James McPherson, John Suart, Robert Mackinen, James Bruce, William Struthers, Jacob Blackwell, Francis Morcier, and Robert Cook. Among the British governors in this period were George Johnstone (a Scotsman), John Eliot, Peter Chester, and Elias Dumford. See Byrle Kynerd, "British West Florida," in *A History of Mississippi,* ed. Richard McLemore (Hattiesburg: University Press of Mississippi, 1973), I, pp. 137–38. See also Robert Gold, *Borderland Empires in Transition: The Triple-Nation Transfer of Florida* (Carbondale: Southern Illinois University Press, 1969.)

6. Julia Floyd Smith, *Slavery and Plantation Growth in Antebellum Florida 1821–1860* (Gainesville: University of Florida Press, 1973), p. 32.

7. *Ibid.*, pp. 28–52. See also Stampp, *Peculiar Institution*, pp. 66, 107, 135; Sitterson, *Sugar Country,* pp. 8–9, 37–38; Robert Hall, "Black and White Christians in Florida, 1822–1861," in Boles, *Masters and Slaves in the House of the Lord,* pp. 81–98; and U.P. Phillips and J.D. Glunt, *Forida Plantation Records from the Papers of George Noble Jones* (St. Louis: Missouri Historical Society, 1923).

8. Smith, *Slavery and Plantation Growth in Florida,* p. 32. For the activities of a lesser Florida slaveholder, see Abraham Cabell Papers, 1824–34, Mss. 2C11116, Virginia Historical Society, Richmond.

9. Lucille Griffith, *Alabama: A Documentary History to 1900* (Tuscaloosa: University of Alabama Press, 1968), pp. 150–53. For the early history of the state, see Willis Brewer, *Alabama: Her History, Resources, War Record, and Public Men from 1540 to 1872* (Spartanburg, SC: Reprint Co. Publishers, 1975 reprint of 1872 edition), pp. 19–38.

10. Phillips, *Life and Labor in the Old South,* pp. 274–84 ; Stampp, *Peculiar Institution*, pp. 37, 45, 50, 66, 80, 108, 114; and Davis, *Cotton Kingdom in Alabama,* pp. 49–72.

11. Griffith, *Alabama,* p. 158.

12. Davis, *Cotton Kingdom in Alabama*, pp. 49–58 and 60–62.

13. William Scarborough, "Heartland of the Cotton Kingdom," in *History of Mississippi,* p. 321.

14. *Ibid.*, pp. 325–27.

15. *Ibid.*, p. 351.

16. Charles Sydnor, *Slavery in Mississippi* (Goucester, MA: Peter Smith, 1965), pp. 192–96. See also Stampp, *Peculiar Institution*, pp. 39, 40, 80, 104, 137, 166, 169, 295, 298; Phillips, *Life and Labor in the Old South*, pp. 284–90; and Edith Wyatt Moore, "Early Jewish Settlers in the Natchez County," unpublished ms., Korn Papers, AJA, 23/3, p.9.

17. Scarbough, *History of Mississippi,* pp. 344–48.There are discrepancies between Scarborough's figures (based on official U.S. census reports) and those of Karl Menn. The latter has Duncan with 858 slaves, Brandon with 58 and Robinson with 550 in 1860. *Large Slaveholders of the Deep South*, p. 233. Scarborough does concede that official reports may have inconsistencies. "Heartland of the Cotton Kingdom," p. 343.

18. Adams County tax records for 1833 list the firm of Samuel Wakefield as the biggest slave broker with sales amounting to $18,270. By 1859, the firm of Blackwell, Murphy, and Ferguson had the highest number of sales. Sydnor, *Slavery in Missippi,* pp. 152–57.

19. Leon Hühner, "David Yulee: Florida's First Senator," *PAJHS* (1917), XVII, pp. 3–4.

20. Moore, "Early Jewish Settlers in the Natchez Country," Korn Papers, 23-3.

21. Pillar, "Religious and Cultural Life," *History of Mississippi,* p. 392.

22. See Mrs. Julius Kerman, "Story of Temple B'nai Israel, Natchez, Mississipi" (October 1955), unpublished ms. in Korn Papers, AJA, 23-3, pp. 1–2. See also documents listing births and deaths in pre-Civil War Natchez, *loc.cit* . The Moses family counted five members, those of the Hyams, Montz and Jacobs four each.

23. Pillar, "Religion and Cultural Life, 1817–1860," *History of Mississippi,* pp. 393.

24. "Mississippi," *Encyclopedia Judaica* , XII, pp. 154–56.

25. Korn, *The Jews of Mobile, Alabama 1762–1841* (Cincinnati, OH: Hebrew Union Press, 1970), p. 15.

26. In 1881, there were 3,086 citizens in Birmingham, only 30 of whom were Jews. Mark Elovitz, *A Century of Jewish Life in Dixie: The Birmingham Experience*

(Tuscaloosa: University of Alabama Press, 1974), p. 5.

27. Alfred Moses, "The History of the Jews of Montgomery," *PAJHS* (1905), XIII, pp. 83–88.

28. Harriett Amos, *Cotton City: Urban Development in Antebellum Mobile* (Tuscaloosa:University of Alabama Press, 1985),pp. 87–89.

29. Korn, *Jews in the South*, pp. 107–8.

30. Korn, *Jews of Mobile*, pp. 38–41.

31. *Ibid.*, p. 23.

32. Davis, *Cotton Kingdom in Alabama*, pp. 75–76.

33. Kate Pickard related how the Friedmans helped Peter Still obtain his freedom in *The Kidnapped and the Ransomed: Narative of Peter and Vina Still after 40 Years of Slavery* (New York: Miller, Orton and Mulligan, 1856). The book was subsequently edited by Maxwell Whiteman and reissued by Jewish Publication Society of America in 1970. See also Robert Weisbord and Arthur Stein, *Bittersweet Encounter: The Afro-American and the American Jew* (Westport, CT: Negro Universities Press, 1970), p. 22.

34. See Henry Alan Green, *Jewish Life in Florida: A Documentary Exhibition from 1763 to the Present,* 1991.

35. Sellers, *Slavery in Alabama*, pp. 386–87.

36. Oakes, *The Ruling Race*, p. 48.

37. Moses, "History of Jews of Montgomery," pp. 83–88.

38. Orville Taylor, *Negro Slavery in Arkansas* (Durham, NC: Duke University Press, 1958), pp. 5–7, 25, 48.

39. *Ibid.*, p. 100.

40. *Ibid.*, pp. 54–86 and 123–28.

41. Ira Sanders and Elijah Palnick, The Centennial History of Congregation Bnai Israel (Little Rock, 1966).

42. As late as 1967 there were only 3,000 Jews out of 1.8 million people in Arkansas. *Encyclopedia Judaica*, III, pp. 458–59.

43. Mordecai Podet, *Pioneer Jews of Waco* (1986, no publisher listed), p. 14.

44. R. Henry Cohen, "Settlement of the Jews in Texas," *PAJHS* (1894), II, pp. 139–43. After 1877, Galveston would outstrip all other communities with 1,000 Jews. Elaine Maas, *The Jews of Houston* (New York: AMS Press, 1983), p. 34.

45. Maas, *Jews of Houston*, p. 29.

46. The main adversaries were Calhoun, Houston, William Hart Benton, Abel Upshur, John Quincy Adams, and William Channing. Frederick Merk, *Slavery and the Annexation of Texas* (New York: Knopf, 1972).

47. Randolph Campbell, *An Empire for Slavery: The Peculiar Institution in Texas, 1821–1865* (Baton Rouge: Lousina State University Press, 1989), pp. 52–53.

48. Helena Frenkil Schlam, "The Early Jews of Houston," MA Thesis (Ohio State University, 1971) and Maas, *Jews of Houston*, pp. 28–29.

49. See Elizabeth Silverthorne's magnificent volume, *Plantation Life in Texas* (College Station: Texas A. & M. Press, 1986), pp. 12–18.

50. Campbell, *An Empire for Slavery*, pp. 190–95 and 274–76.

51. Olmsted, *A Journey in the Seaboard States in the Years 1853–54* (New York: Putnam's, 1914), pp. 129 and 250.

52. Olmsted, *A Journey Through Texas* (New York: Burt Franklin, 1969 reprint of 1860 edition), p. 329.

53. Trexler, *Slavery in Missouri*, pp. 45–48.

54. William Foley, *The Genesis of Missouri: From Wilderness Outpost to Statehood* (Columbia: University of Missouri Press, 1989), p. 293. Foley, Professor of history at Central Missouri State, makes no reference to Jews in this impor-

tant study. He does, however, allude to the arrival of Jews and the development of a synagogue in St. Louis in a more comprehensive three volume work. See Foley, *A History of Missouri* (Columbia: University of Missouri Press, 1971), Vol.II, pp. 314–15.

55. *Ibid.,* pp. 122–24.

56. R.Douglas Hurt, *Agriculture and Slavery in Missouri's Little Dixie* (Columbia: University of Missouri, 1992), pp. 230–36. Harrison Trexler lists Jabez Smith of Jackson County as the biggest slaver with 165. *Slavery in Missouri 1804–1865* (Baltimore, MD: Johns Hopkins University Press, 1914), p. 13.

57. Charles Mooney, *Slavery in Tennessee* (Bloomington: Indiana University Press, 1957), pp. 158–74. See also the diaries of Harrod Clopton Anderson, Samuel Henderson, and Robert Cartmell, pp. 147–78.

58. *bid.,* pp. 49–51. See also Stampp, *Peculiar Institution*, pp. 67, 122, 265.

59. Monroe Lee Billington, *The American South: A Brief History* (New York: Scribners' Sons, 1971), p. 93. See also Mooney, *Slavery in Tennessee*, pp. 46–48.

60. Mooney, *Slavery in Tennessee*, pp. 40–45.

61. *Historical Records Survey Tennessee: Inventory of Church and Synagogue Archives of Tennessee*: (Nashville: Tennessee Historical Records Survey, Works Projects Administration, 1941), pp. 3–8. See also "Tennessee," *Encyclopedia Judaica,* XV; F.S. Frank, *Five Famillies and Eight Young Men: Nashville and Her Jewry, 1850–1861* (1962); and S. Shankman, *Baron Hirsch Congregation: From Ur to Memphis* (1957).

62. Eaton describes the business deallings of Ashland, Clay's plantation outside Lexington. *Civilization of Old South,* pp. 25–39.

63. Ivan McDougle, *Slavery in Kentucky, 1792–1865* (Westport, CT: Negro Universities Press, 1970 reprint of 1918 original), p. 21.

64. J.Winston Coleman, *Slavery Times in Kentucky* (Chapel Hill: University of North Carolina Press, 1940), p. 166.

65. *Ibid.,* p. 147.

66. *Ibid.,* pp. 164–66.

67. Marion Lucas, *A History of Blacks in Kentucky: From Slavery to Segregation, 1760–1891* (Frankfort: Kentucky Historical Society, 1992), I, pp. 90–92.

68. Coleman, *Slavery Times in Kentucky,* pp. 155–63. Mary Todd grew up on Main Street in Lexington, just yards away from the main auction block . A gentile neighbor, Fielding Turner, owned more slaves than anyone in town. In 1837, Turner's wife, a socialite from Boston, pitched a young black boy off the second floor of their mansion, crippling the youth. Mary Todd was horrified by the Turners' behavior and like her husband, who had been revolted by witnessing the sale of a slave in New Orleans and a subsquent visit to the Speed plantation, the future Mrs. Lincoln became an ardent abolitionist. William Townshend, *Lincoln and The Bluegrass Kentucky* (Lexington: University of Kentucky, 1955), pp. 72–74.

69. Lewis Dembitz mentions Nathanael Hart, Isaiah Marks, and a Mr. Salomon. "Jewish Beginnings in Kentucky," *PAJHS* (1893), I, p. 99. Others, like Bernard and Michael Gratz, Joseph Simon, and the Richmond firm of Cohen and Isaacs claimed large areas to the Mammoth Caves as early as 1781. See "Kentucky" *Encyclopedia Judaica,* X, p. 910; I.T. Namani, "Louisville Lore," *JewishFrontie,* XXII (April 1944, pp. 8–13) and L.Collins, *History of Kentucky* (1966).

70. Dembitz, "Jewish Beginnings in Kentucky," p. 100.

71. Rosenwaike, *Edge of Greatness,* p. 135.

72. Stampp, *Peculiar Institution,* pp. 64–65.

73. According to Olmsted, Jews were running competitors out of business by trading with blacks. *Journey in Seabord Slave States,* II, p. 70.

74. Olmsted, *The Cotton Kingdom: A Traveller's Observations on Cotton and Slavery in the American Slave States* (New York: Mason Brothers, 1861), pp. 510–63.

Notes to Chapter 15

1. See Isaac Bernheim, *History of the Settlement of Jews in Paducah and the Lower Ohio Valley* (Paducah, 1912). Library of Congress Microfilm 494721.

2. Anita Lebeson, *Pilgrim People: A History of the Jews in America from 1492 to 1974* (New York: Minerva Press, 1950, 1975), pp. 289–95 and Schappes, *Documentary History of Jews in the U. S.,* pp. 472–75.

3. Between 1834 and 1844, cotton was selling in New Yorkk at 17 1/2 cents a pound. During the depression that followed, the price plummeted to 5 1/2 cents. By 1860 it was back to 12 cents. Flanders, *Plantation Slavery in Georgia,* pp. 191–93.

4. Evans, *Judah Benjamin,* pp. 208–10.

5. For a copy of the Grants' complaint on file in the Ravenna, Ohio courthouse, see Korn "The Jews of the Union,," *American Jewish Archives,* pp. 208–9. Contrast Grant's behavior with that of General Robert E. Lee. Between 1861 and 1864, Lee indicated that Jewish soldiers should be permitted to observe their holidays and intervened in September 1864 to suspend the execution of Private Isaac Arnold, an eighteen-year-old immigrant accused of desertion. Creeger, "Maximilian Michelbacher," pp. 3–4.

6. *Secret Relationship,* pp. 161–68.

7. Rosenwaike, *Edge of Greatness,* p. 66.

8. *Ibid.*

9. Wade, *Slavery in the Cities,* p. 243.

10. *Ibid.,* pp. 325–27.

11. Stampp, *Peculiar Institution,* pp. 60–67.

12. Wade, *Slavery in the Cities,* p. 95.

13. *Ibid.,* p. 195.

14. *Ibid.,* p. 110.

15. Phillips, *Life and Labor in the Old South,* p. 414.

16. Wade, *Slavery in the Cities,* p. 55.

17. *Ibid.,* pp. 125–45.

18. *Ibid.,* pp. 228–38. There is some debate whether Vesey actually planned an uprising or whether it was mere talk. Larry Kroger has contended that the plot was real. (*Black Slaveowners and Free Black Masters in South Carolina 1790–1860* [Jefferson, NC:; Mcfarland, 1985], pp. 160–85).

19. Wade, *Slavery in the Cities,* pp. 180–91. Stampp describes operations of slave patrols. *Peculiar Institution,* pp. 206–14.

20. Letter from Falk to Korn, October 31, 1960, Korn Papers, AJA, 31–3.

21. Korn, *Jews in the South,* pp. 102–3.

22. Stampp, *Peculiar Institution,* p. 214.

23. Korn, "Jews and Negro Slavery," pp. 163–64.

24. Interview with Rosen, Charleston, August 15, 1993.

25. See Alphabetical Index, Soouth Carolina Department of Archives and History, Columbia, pp. 27978–80.

26. Discussion with Sasportas, Charleston, August 12, 1993.

27. MacKay, *Life and Liberty in America* (London: Smith, Elder and Co., 1859), I, p. 322. These are virtually the same charges outlined by Olmsted in *A Journey*

in the Seaboard Slave States, II, p. 70. See also Sir Charles Lyell, *Second Visit to the United States* (London: Charles Murrray, 1849).

28. Rosenwaike, "Jewish Population of the US in 1790," p. 165.
29. Harry Golden, *Our Southern Landsmen* (New York: Putnam's, 1974), p. 147.
30. Rudolph Glanz, *The Jew in the Old American Follkore* (New York: Waldron Press, 1969), p. 130.
31. *Ibid*, pp. 12 and 130.
32. Leslie Bethell, *The Abolition of the Brazilian Slave Trade: Britain, Brazil and the Slave Trade Question 1807–1869* (Cambridge: Cambridge University Press, 1970), pp. 5 and 39.
33. Pierre Verger, *Trade Relations between the Bight of Benin and Bahia from the Seventeenth to Nineteenth Centuries* (Ibadan: Ibadan University Press, 1976), pp. 353–91, 432, and 479–89.
34. Robert Toplin, *The Abolition of Slavery in Brazil* (New York: Atheneum, 1972), pp. 117, 131–44. See also Toplin, S*lavery and Race Relations in Latin America* (Westport, CT: Greenwood, 1974); Bethell, *The Abolition of the Brazilian Slave Trade*, pp. 311, 328, 343; Mary Williams, "The Treatment of Negro Slaves in the Brazilian Empire: A Comparison with the United States of America," *Journal of Negro History* (July 1930), pp. 315–55; ;and J. K. Eads, "The Negro in Brazil' *Journal of Negro History* (Oct. 1936), XXI, 365–75.
35. Spears, *The American Slave Trade*, pp. 140–47. It was reported that the *Brillante,* a ship commanded by an Englishman named Homans made ten voyages, carrying 5,000 Africans to Cuba.
36. DuBois, *The Suppression of the African Slave Trade to the United States of America 1638–1870* (Baton Rouge: Louisiana State University Press, 1969 reprint of 1896 ms.), pp. 288–98.
37. Eaton, *Civilzation of Old South*, p. 114, and Silverthorne, *Plantation Life in Texas*, pp. 191–92.
38. Warren Howard, *American Slaves and the Federal Law 1837–1862* (Berkeley: University of California Press, 1963), p. 37 and p. 255.
39. *Ibid.*, p. 49.
40. Spears, *The American Slave Trade*, pp. 199–207.
41. *The Wanderer Case: Speech of H. R. Jackson of Atlanta, November 13, 1891* (Atlanta, GA: Young Men's Library Association), p. 55.
42. Douglas Levilen, *The Case of the Slaver Echo* (Weed, Parsons & Co. 1859), pp. 51, 64–65.
43. Harriett *Amos, Cotton City: Urban Development in Antebellum Mobile* (Tuscaloosa: University of Alabama Press, 1995), p. 87.
44. Howard, *American Slavers and Federal Law*, pp. 49–51.
45. Spears, *American Slave Trade*, p. 229. Howard lists 98 criminal prosecutions under the slave trade statutes between 1837 and 1862 with Weinberg/Wenburg listed once (*American Slavers and Federal Law*, pp. 224–35). Curiously, there is no record of prosecution against Weinberg in the dockets of the U.S. District Court for the Southern District of New York (vol. 1, inventory 115), the U. S. Circuit Court (vol. 1, entries 67, 68), or the Court of Admiralty for the State of New York (vols. 13–14, 1855–58.)
46. In Huntsville, Tallahassee, and Scottsville, Griffith named Patton-Donegan, Barent DuBoise, Heckerson and Burnham, Thomas Barnett and William Marks, the Bell factory, and Scott Company. Griffith, *Alabama: A Documentary History to 1900* (Tuscaloosa: University of Alabama Press, 1968), pp. 191–92.
47. The names include J. F. Ross, Rives, and Mather, Franklin Robinson, Jere Austill, McGehee and Scott, Walter Lucas, Charles Thomas, Manuel White, James Crawford, Malone and Foote, Hartwell Davis, Boykin and McRae, Joseph Wil-

son, John Bowie, and Alexander Pope who earned $67,000 in profits in 1843. Charles Davis, *The Cotton Kingdom in Alabama* (Philadelphia, PA: Porcupine Press, 1974), pp. 142–68.

48. Moore cites the following cotton industrialists and financiers: Benjamin Gullttt, Richard Gladney, R. C. Beckett and Dr. John Tindall of Aberdeen, T. G. Atwood in Kosciusko, Samuel Griswold in Griswoldville, Daniel Pratt in Prattville, Robertson, Osgood and Wills at Natchez, and James Wesson, Daniel Booker, Richard Ector, and John Nance. *The Emergence of the Cotton Kingdom in the Old Southwest: Mississippi 1770–1860* (Baton Rouge: Louisiana State University Press, 1988), pp. 216–24.

49. Woodman, *King Cotton and His Retainers: Financing and Marketing the Cotton Crop of the South 1800–1925* (Charleston: University of South Carolina Press, 1990), p. 98.

50. *Ibid.*, pp. 98–125.

51. *Ibid.*, p. 304. Jack Lichtenstein offers no reference to Jews in his study, *Field to Fabric: The Story of American Cotton Growers* (Lubbock: Texas Tech, 1990).

52. Paul McGouldrick indicated that in 1861 eleven Massachusetts companies held assets of between $800,000 and $2,000,000. *New England Textiles in the Nineteenth Century: Profits and Investments* (Cambridge, MA: Harvard University Press, 1968), pp. 4–5 and 73–120.

53. Caroline Ware, *The Early New England Cotton Manufacture* (New York: Russell and Russell, 1966 reprint of 1931 volume), pp. 19 and 122–30.

54. *Ibid.*, pp. 60–78.

55. McGouldrick, *New England Textiles*, pp. 23–25.

56. Olmsted, *Journey in Seaboard Slave States*, II, p. 184.

57. Eugene Genovese, *The Political Economy of Slavery : Studies in the Economy and Society of the Slave South* (New York: Pantheon, 1961), pp. 164–67 and 180–208.

58. Stephen Birmingham, *Our Crowd* (New York: Harper & Row, 1967), p. 31.

59. Pools, *Old Faith in New World*, p. 483.

60. Birmingham, *Our Crowd*, pp. 24–32 and 58–62.

61. Ross Muir, *Over the Long Term* (New York: J. and W. Seligman, 1964.)

62. Historically, Jews faced discrimination in the field of banking. Leon Poliakov chronicles some of their misadventures in *English Jewish Bankers and the Holy See from the Thirteenth to the Seventeenth Century* (London: Routledge and Kegan Paul, 1977). Unfortunatley there is only one poorly written study of anti-Semitism in American banking—Chaim Lipschitz' *Discrmination in Banking* (New York: 1970).

63. See Michael Jensen, *The Financiers: The World of the Great Wall Street Investment Banking Houses* (New York: Weybright and Talley, 1976) and Judith Ehrlich and Barry Rehfeld, *The New Crowd: The Changing of the Jewish Guard on Wall Street* (Boston: Little, Brown & Co., 1981).

64. Jeffrey Gurock, *When Harlem Was Jewish 1870–1930* (New York: Columbia University Press, 1979), p. 6. See also Ronald Sanders, *The Downtown Jews:Portraits of an Immigrant Generation* (New York: Harper and Row, 1969.)

65. Henry Lanier, *A Century of Banking in New York : 1822–1922* (New York: Gillis Press, 1922), pp. 82–83.

66. *Ibid.*, pp. 99–142.

67. "Wealth and Biography of the Wealthy Citizens of New York City" (New York *Sun*, 1845) pp. 3, 12, 13, 27.

68. Of 279 persons who worked for the Manhattan Company over fifty years, none were Jewish. Gregory Hunter, *The Manhattan Company: Managing a Multi-Unit Corporation in New York 1799–1842* (New York: Garland Press, 1985),

pp. 295–318. See also J. S. Gibbons, *The Banks of New York, Their Dealings, The Clearing Hoouse and the Panic of 1857* (New York: Appleton, 1859).

69. See *New York Mercantile Register 1848–49* (T. Morehead, 1848) and *The New York Merchants Directory 1869* (J. Harford and Co., 1869).

70. The top banks, capitalized at $3–10 millions were the American Exchange, Bank of America, Bank of Commerce, Center, Bank of New York, Fourth National, Merchants, and Metropolitan. *United States Register/Blue Book for 1875* (Philadelphia, PA, December 1874.)

71. Most of these were associated with the West Side Bank, Solomon Loeb's Bank of North America, the German-American Bank, the German Exchange, the Irving Bank, Ninth National People's Bank, or Importers and Traders. *Blue Book for 1874*, pp. 143–70.

72. *Ibid.*, pp. 155–61.

73. Ibid., pp. 167–76.

74. Nathan Ausubel, *Pictorial History of the Jewish People* (New York: Crown, 1965), p. 280.

75. Treasury Secretary Salmon Chase had reported difficulties in selling these bonds. J. George Fredman and Louis Falk, *Jews in American Wars* (Washington, DC: Jewish War Veterans of America, 1954), p. 53. See also Birmingham, *Our Crowd*, pp. 71–74.

76. Korn angrily dismisses the rebel sermon of Michelbacher reported in the June 19, 1986 *Jewish Record* as "partisan rigmarol dictated by some stump speaker. There is no evidence Michelbacher ever studied rabbinics." He could, Korn noted sarcastically, just as easily have written a work on astronomy.

77. Korn Papers, 32–1.

78. Korn Papers, 31–3.s.

79. See letters in Cincinnati newspapers from several Jews condemning his position on Dred Scott. "Wise, Isaac Mayer," Miscellaneous file, American Jewish Archive. Wise would later urge Jews to vote for Grant as President. Hasia Diner, *A Time for Gathering: The Second Migration 1820–1860* (Baltimore, MD: Johns Hopkins Press, 1992), pp. 156–57.

80. Typed manuscript, Korn Papers, 32–2.

81. *Occident*, XVIII, no. 33, p. 197, Nov. 8, 1860.

82. Shappes, "Anti-Semitism and Reaction 1795–1800,"*Jewish Experience in America*, p. 362.

83. Schappes, "Jews and American Slavery," p. 19.

84. Schappes, "Ernestine L. Rose: Her Address on the Anniversary of West Indian Emancipation," *Journal of Negro History* (1949), XXXIV, p. 350.

85. Schappes, "Jews in Lincoln's Third Party,1854–1860," *Jewish Life* (October 1948), pp. 13–16.

86. Moses Rischlin, "The Jews and the Liberal Tradition in America," *PAJHS* (1961–62), LI, pp. 4–29.

87. Weisbord and Stein, *Bittersweet Encounter,* p. 24.

88. Lebeson, *Pilgrim People*, p. 260.

89. Whiteman, *Kidnapped and Ransomed*, pp. 58–60.

90. *Ibid.*, pp. 50–52.

91. Korn, "The Jews of the Union," *American Jewish Archives*, p. 137.

92. Typed manuscript, Korn Papers, 32–2.

93. Letter of Weil to his brother Josiah, Montgomery, May 16, 1861, Miscellaneous Collection 99, American Jewish Archives.

94. Mordecai, Alfred File, June 2, 1861, Correspondence File, 99, American Jewish Archives.

95. See Daniel Conway, *Autobiography, Memories, and Experiences* (Boston and

New York: Casseli, 1904) I, pp. 313–14. See also Clement Eaton, *Freedom of Thought in the Old South* (Durham, NC: Duke Univesity Press, 1940).

96. Leonard Dinnerstein, *Uneasy at Home: Anti-Semitism and the American Jewish Experience* (New York: Columbia University Press, 1987), p. 87.

97. Secretary of Interior, Statistics on Churches, Statistics of the United States, Eighth Census, 1860 (Washington: GPO, 1866), p. 499. By way of contrast there were 153 Methodist churches in Georgia alone.

98. Oakes, *The Ruling Race*, pp. 96–122.

99. Blasingame, *Plantation Life and Community*, pp. 60–104 and Hughes, *Black Odyssey*, pp. 173–177. See also the degrading slave catechism in Leslie Fishel and Benjamin Quarles, *The Negro American: A Documentary History* (Glenview, IL.: Scott Foresman, 1967), p. 114.

100. Touchstone, "Planters and Slave Religion in the Deep South," in Boles, *Masters and Slaves*, p. 107.

101. Oakes, *The Ruling Race*, p. 96.

102. Touchstone, "Planters and Slave Religion," pp. 100–101. See Diner, *A Time for Gathering*, pp. 156–60 for strife in the mainline Protestant churches.

103. Blasingame, *Plantation Life and Community*, p. 81.

104. Only a few priests or bishops challenged the institution of slavery. Kenneth Zanca, *American Catholics and Slavery: 1789–1866, An Anthology of Primary Documents* (Lanham, MD.: University Press of America, 1994), pp. 171–254.

105. Stanley Campbell, *The Slave Catchers: Enforcement of the Fugitive Slave Law 1850–1860* (Chapel Hill: University of North Carolina Press, 1970), p. 56.

106. Samuel Joseph May, *Some Recollections of Our Antislavery Conflict* (Boston: Fields, Osgood & Co., 1861), pp. 329–32, 365.

107. Statistics on Churches, 8th Census, p. 501.

108. Typed ms., Korn Papers, 32–2, p. 19.

109. *Ibid.*, p. 2. Dinnerstein offers virtually the same opinion, writing, "Because there were no pogroms,no tax-supported churches (after colonial times) and no statewide legal restrictions on most economic and social activities, possibly erronenous conclusions have been reached about the position of Jews in Southern society. It seems that a number of writers have equated equal opportunity with social approval." Dinnerstein, *Uneasy at Home*, p. 77.

110. Myron Berman, *Richmond's Jewry 1769–1976* (Charlottesville: University Press of Virginia, 1979), p. 163.

111. Carolyn Lipson-Walker, "Shalom Y'all: The Folklore and Culture of Southern Jews," Ph. D. dissertation, University of Indiana, 1986, pp. 49–51. See also John Dollard, *Caste and Class in a Southern Town* (New York: Doubleday Anchor, 1945).

112. Golden, *Our Southern Landsmen*, p. 107.

113. Korn, *Jews in the South*, pp. 136–37.

114. Stephen Hertzberg, "Southern Jews and Their Encounter with Blacks: Atlanta 1850–1915," *Atlanta Historical Journal* (Fall 1979), XXIII, p. 8.

115. Korn, *Jews in the South*, p. 155.

116. Stampp, *Peculiar Institution*, pp. 385–86.

117. Eli Evans, *The Provincials: A Personal History of Jews in the South* (New York: Atheneum, 1973), p. 40.

118. *Ibid.*, p. 42.

119. *Secret Relationship*, p. 182.

120. James Oakes, *The Ruling Race: A History of American Slaveholders* (New York: Alfred A. Knopf, 1982), p. 46. Booker T. Washington also mentions Indians

slaveholders in Georgia, Alabama and the Western states, *The Story of the Negro*, pp. 131 and 141.

121. Dubois lists mainly Spanish and French ships in this illegal activity. *The Suppression of the African Slave Trade to the United States of America 1638–1870* (Baton Rouge: Louisiana State University Press, 1969 reprint of 1896 ms.), pp. 288–98.

122. Pierre Verger, *Trade Relations between the Bight of Benin and Bahia from the Seventeenth to the Nineteenth Century* (Ibadan, Nigeria: Ibadan University Press, 1976), pp. 355–91, 432, and 489.

123. Instead, Dubois cites such fire-eaters as Howell Cobb of Georgia, H. S. Foote of Mississippi, R. A. Pryor of Louisiana, L. W. Spratt of South Carolina, and J. B. Clay of Kentucky. Dubois, *Suppression of Slave Trade*, pp. 168–76.

124. Korn, *Jews in the South*, p. 93.

125. Michael Tadman, *Speculators and Slaves: Masters, Traders, and Slaves in the Old South* (Madison: University of Wisconsin Press, 1989) p. 232.

126. Menn, "The Large Slaveholders of the Deep South 1860," Ph. D. Dissertation, University of Texas (Austin, 1964), pp. 182–83.

127. *Ibid.*, p. 175.

128. *Ibid.*, pp. 236–41.

129. *Ibid.*, pp. 244–56.

130. Korn, *Jews in the South*, p. 133.

Notes to Chapter 16

1. Theodor Gaster, *Thespis: Ritual, Myth and Drama in the Ancient Near East* (New York: Harper Torch, 1951, 1961), pp. 23–25.

2. Anthony Storr, *Human Destructiveness* (New York: Basic Books, 1972, p. 86. See also Rollo May, *Power and Innocence: A Search for the Sources of Violence* (New York: W. W. Norton, 1972), pp. 165–179; Erich Fromm, *Anatomy of Human Destructiveness* (New York: Holt, Rinehart and Winston, 1973); Irenaus Eibl-Eibesfeldt, *Love and Hate: The Natural History of Behavior Patterns*, tr. Geoffrey Strachan (New York: Holt, Rinehart and Winston, 1971), pp. 99–102; Konrad Lorenz, *On Aggression*, tr. Marjorie Wilson (New York: Harcourt, Brace and World, 1963); Denis Madden and John Lion, eds. *Rage, Hate, Assault and Other Forms of Violence* (New York: Spectrum Publications, Halsted Press, 1976).

3. Cheikh Anta Diop, *Civilization or Barbarism: An Authentic Anthropology*, tr. Yaa-Lengi Mema Ngemi, ed. Harold Salemson and Marjolijn de Jager (Brooklyn, NY: Lawrence Hill Books, 1991), pp. 65 and 102.

4. There are no negative references to Jews in the writings of Moses Nwulia, *Britain and Slavery in East Africa* (Washington, DC: Three Continents Press, 1975), Claude Meillaussoux, *The Anthropology of Slavery*, or Harvey Sindima, *Africa's Agenda: The Legacy of Liberalism and Colonialism in the Crisis of African Values* (Westport, CT: Greenwood Press, 1995). Each of these scholars highlights the role of Arab slavers. As Sindima writes (p. 4), "long before the European slave trade, Arabs sold Africans into slavery in the Middle East and beyond."

5. David Northrup of Boston College concedes that Equiano's work should be recognized as a polemic, written more than three decades after the African was uprooted from his home as a youth. "The Ideological Context of Slavery in Southeast Nigeria in the Nineteenth Century," in *The Ideology of Slavery in Africa*, Paul Lovejoy (ed.) (London: Sage Pubs., 1981).

6. John Newton, once a slaver to Sierre Leone, later an abolitionist rector of St. Mary, Woolnoth, wrote in the eighteenth century, "The state of slavery among these wild barbarous people [the Sherbros] as we esteem them, is much milder than in our colonies. " *The Journal of a Slave Trader,* Bernard Martin and Mark Spurrell (eds.) (London: Epworth Press, 1962), p. 107. More recently, Babatunde Agiri of the University of Lagos stressed the integration, kinship and cheerful attiudes of African slaves. "Slavery in Yoruba Society in the Nineteenth Century," *Ideology of Slavery in Africa,* pp. 127–29. Robert Smith has also suggested that with the exception of a few who might be used for human sacrifice, "all slaves, even the humblest, seem otherwise to havfe been well-treated. " *Kingdoms of the Yoruba* (Madison: University of Wisconsin Press, 1969, 1988), p. 96. See also Spears, *American Slave-Trade,* p. 47.

7. Citing Gustav Nachtigal and David Livingstone as his sources, Patrick Manning notes the extent of brtuality in the East African slave trade where African chieftains were ruthless in pursuing runaways. *Slavery and African Life: Occidental, Oriental and African Slave Trades* (Cambridge: Cambridge University Press, 1990), pp. 112–18. H. Ling Roth of the British Museum and Anthropological Institute tells of the sacrifice of "bad men" with defects and adds that slaves who survived worked twelve hours "under the lash" for four ounces of boiled yam or plantain. *Great Benin: Its Customs, Art and Horrors* (New York: Barnes and Noble, 1968), pp. 103–5.

8. Manning points out cowries do not grow in the Atlantic. *Slavery and African Life,* p. 99.

9. Duignan and Gann, *The United States and Africa: A History* (Hoover Institute and Cambridge University Press, 1984), p. 6. See also A. Norman Klein, "The Two Asantes: Competing Interpretations of 'Slavery' in Akan-Asante Culture and Society," pp. 149–68, in Lovejoy, *The Ideology of Slavery in Africa.*

10. Manning, *Slavery and African Life,* pp. 34–35.

11. Bennett, *Before the Mayflower,* pp. 31–32.

12. C. B. Wadstrom, *Observations on the Slave Trade, 1787–1788* (London, 1789).

13. *Ibid.,* p. 36.

14. Nehemia Levtzion comments on the extensive slave trade out of Timbuktu (pp. 75–91) and across the Sahara (pp. 174–78) in *Ancient Ghana and Mali* (New York: Africana Publications, 1973).

15. Michael Crowder, *The Story of Nigeria* (London: Faber and Faber, 1962, 1978), pp. 54–55.

16. James Walvin reports that in the 1720s the rulers of Dahomey were anxious to obtain guns in exchange for slaves. *Black Ivory: A History of British Slavery* (Washington: Howard University Press, 1994), pp. 29–31.

17. Agiri concedes 1. 5 million slaves were sold by the Oyos between the seventeenth and nineteenth centuries. "Slavery in Yoruba Society in the Nineteenth Century," pp. 123–48.

18. Meillassoux, *The Anthropology of Slavery: The Womb of Iron and Gold ,* tr. Alide Dasnois (Chicago: University of Chicago, 1991), p. 76.

19. Phillips, *American Negro Slavery,* p. 45 and Spears, *The American Slave-Trade,* p. 55. Phillips says, "chiefs were eager to foster trade and cultivate good will, for it brought them pompous trappings, as well as useful goods." p. 34.

20. Donnan, *Documents,* I, p. 32.

21. Donnan, Documents, I, pp. 35–36.

22. *Ibid.,* pp. 384–85.

23. Verger, *Trade Relations between the Bight of Benin and Bahia,* pp. 139–46. Subsequent kings of Dahomey sent several trade embassies from Lagos to Brazil between 1750 and 1811, pp. 218–37.

24. Newton, *Journal of of a Slave Trader*, pp. 15, 19, 23, 25, 67.
25. Crowder, *Story of Nigeria*, pp. 54–55.
26. From report of Robert Craigie, papers Relating to Engagements entered into by King Pepple and the Chiefs of Bonny with Her Majesty's Naval Officers on the Subject of the Suppression of the Slave Trade 1848 in *Through African Eyes: Cultures in Change* (New York: Praeger, 1971), p. 345.
27. *Plain Dealer* , July 27, 1995, p. 3B.
28. Duignan and Gann, *United States and Africa*, p. 41. See also A. G. Hopkins, *An Economic History of West Africa* (New York: Columbia University, 1973), pp. 23–7.
29. Genovese, *Roll, Jordan Roll, The World the Slaves Made* (New York: Pantheon Books, 1974), p. 408.
30. Klein, *African Slavery in Latin America and the Caribbean*, p. 237.
31. Greene, *The Negro in Colonial New England*, pp. 305–8.
32. *Ibid.,* p. 311.
33. As early as 1670, blacks were barred from securing contracts with white indentured servants but couldacquire porperty "in persons of their own color. " Carter Woodson, *Free Negro Heads of Families in the United States in 1830* (Washington, DC: Association for Study of Negro Life and History, 1925), p. xxxii.
34. Genovese argues that the total number was never large, though it has yet to be tabulated properly. *Roll, Jordan, Roll*, pp. 406–8. The contention is suported by John Russell of Whitman College who has written of the purchase and good treatment of 1, 2, or 3 slaves including many relatives. "Colored Freemen as Slave owners in Virginia," *Journal of Negro History* (June 1916),I, pp. 233–42.
35. Smith, *Slavery and Rice in Georgia*, p. 195.
36. *Ibid.,* p. 196.
37. James Johnston, *Race Relations in Virginia and Miscegenation in the South, 1776–1860* (Amherst: University of Massachusetts Press, 1970), p. 69.
38. Moore, *Emergence of the Cotton Kingdom in the Old Southwest*, pp. 256–62.
39. Genovese, *Roll, Jordan, Roll*, p. 408.
40. Smith, *Slavery and Rice Culture in Georgia*, p. 197.
41. Cited in Phillips, *American Negro Slavery*, pp. 435–36.
42. Citing Horace Fitchett's *Traditions of the Free Negro in Charleston*, Genovese argues this was just an intermediate caste. *Roll, Jordan, Roll*, p. 749.
43. Koger, *Black Slaveowners and Free Black Masters*, pp. 167 and 110.
44. *Ibid.,* pp. 174–78.
45. *Ibid.,* pp. 104–8.
46. *Ibid.,* pp. 86–93.
47. Menn, *Large Slaveholders in the Deep South*, pp. 208–10.
48. Rosen, *History of Charleston,* p. 75.
49. Youngstown *Vindicator*, October 10, 1994, p. B4.
50. Allan Austin, African Muslims in Antebellum America (New York: Garland, 1974), pp. 29–36 and Mattias Gardell, "The Sun of Islam Will Rise in the West," in *Muslim Communities in Norh America*, ed. Yvonne Haddad and Jane Smith (Albany: SUNY Press, 1994), p. 31.
51. Harvey Sindima, *Africa's Agenda: the Legacy of Liberalism and Colonialism in the Crisis of African Values* (Westport, CT: Greenwood Press, 1995), p. 10.
52. Francis Robinson, *Atlas of the Islamic World since 1500* (Facts on File, 1982), p. 175.
53. Molefi Asante, *Afrocentricity* (Trenton, NJ: Africa World Press, 1988, 1992), pp. 2–5.
54. In the ninth century, Wahab ibn Munabbih related how Ham, the son of Noah, had been a handsome white man till God "changed his color and the color of

his descendants in response to his father's curse. " See Bernard Lewis, *Islam from the Prophet to the Capture of Constantinople* (New York: Harper Torch 1974), II, 210. For other interpretations of the curse of Ham, see Akbar Muhammad, "The Image of Africans in Arabic Literature," *Slaves and Slavery in Muslim Africa*, John Willis (ed.) (London: F. Cass, 1985), I, pp. 47–75 and Ephraim Isaac, "Genesis, Judaism and the Sons of Ham," *loc. cit.*, pp. 75–91.

55. According to one Arabic saying, three things interrupted prayer—a donkey, a dog, and a mawla. To be called "the son of a black woman" was the ultimate insult. The prophet Muhammad himself was said to have commented of the Ethiopian-Zanj, "when he is hungry he steals, when he is sated, he fornicates. " Although that hadith may be spurious, the prophet was also quoted as warning against "bringing black into your pedigree" for the Zanji is "a distorted creature." See Bernard Lewis, *Race and Color in Islam* (New York: Harper Torch, 1970), pp. 19, 91–92, and William John Sersen, "Stereotypes and Attitudes towards Slaves in Arabic Proverbs: A Preliminary View," *Slaves and Slavery in Muslim Africa*, pp. 92–105.

56. The geographer Ibn al-Faqih constrasted the "murky, malodorus, depraved" blacks with fairer people and attributed their color to remaining too long in the womb. The tenth century historian al-Masudi, quoting Galen, listed traits found in blacks alone: "frizzy hair, thin eyebrows, broad nostrils, thick lips, pointed teeth, smelly skin, black eyes, furrowed hands and...and great merriment". Al-Masudi's contemporaries referred to the Zanj as "people distant from the standards of humanity" and possessing little understanding or intelligence. Said al-Andalusi, an eleventh-century Muslim judge from Toledo, faulted blacks for lacking self-control and steadiness of mind. A century later, Muhammad al-Idrisi, writing in his *Kitab Rujar*, took note of the Zanji's "furrowed feet, stinking sweat" and "lack of knowledge and defective minds. " The thirteenth-century Persian Nasir al-Din Tusi commented that the Zanj differed fromanimals only in that "their two hands are lifted above the ground" and "many have observed that the ape is more teachable and more intelligent than the Zanji." The fourteenth-century Tunisian chronicler Ibn Khaldun wrote: "the only people who accept slavery are the Negroes, owing to their low degree of humanity and their proximity to the animal stage. " And in a passage reminiscent of America's bigoted past, the eleventh-century Baghdad physician Ibn Butlan declared," If a Zanji were to fall from heaven to earth, he would beat time as he goes down. "Lewis, *Race and Color in Islam,* pp. 34–38, 99, and 209; and *Race and Slavery in the Middle East* (New York: Oxford University Press, 1990), pp. 46–52.

57. Lewis, *Islam from the Prophet Muhammad,* II, pp. 210–11.

58. Lewis, *Race and Color in Islam,* pp. 11–13.

59. On the enslavement of the Gambia, Yoruba, Yorko, Kurnu, Busa, Kutukuli and Bobo peoples, see John Willis, "Jihad and the Ideology of Enslavement," pp. 16–26, *Slaves and Slavery in Muslim Africa*. See also Mervyn Hiskett, "The Image of Slaves in Hausa Literature," *loc. cit.*, p. 123. See also James Johnston, "The Mohammedan Slave Trade," *Journal of Negro History*, XIII (October 1928), pp. 478–91.

60. Lester Brooks, *Great Civilizations of Ancient Africa* (New York: Four Winds Press, 1971), pp. 163–65.

61. Phillips, *American Negro Slavery*, p. 9.

62. John Laffin, *The Arabs as Master Slavers* (Englewood, NJ: SRS Publs., 1982), p. 9.

63. *Ibid.*, pp. 2–3.

64. Kwesi Otabil, *The Agonistic Imperative: The Rational Burden of Africa-Centeredness* (Bristol, IN: Wyndham Hall Press, 1994), p. 79. In his glossary,

C. Tsehloane Keto distinguishes between the Christian slave trade of the West and the Muslim in the north and east. *The Africa-Centered Perspective of History: An Introduction* (Laurel Springs, NJ: K.A. Publishers, 1991).

65. Moses Nwulia, Britain and Slavery in East Africa (Washington, DC: Three Continents Press, 1975), p. 64.

66. The economics of slavery are outlined in Patrick Manning, *Slavery and African Life* (Cambridge: Cambridge University Press, 1990), pp. 86–109, and Allan and Humphrey Fisher, *Slavery and Muslim Society in Africa* (Garden City, NY: Doubleday, 1971), pp. 121–28. See also Martin Klein, "Women and Slavery in Western Sudan," in *Women and Slavery in Africa*, Clair Robertson and Martin Klein (eds.) (Madison: University of Wisconsin Press, 1983), p. 67.

67. R. W. Beachey, *The Slave Trade of Eastern Africa* (London: Rex Collins, 1976), p. 184.

68. Farrant, *Tippu Tip and the East African Slave Trade* (London: Hamish Hamilton, 1975).

69. Allan and Humphrey Fisher, *Slavery and Muslim Society in Africa*, p. 33.

70. David and Charles Livingstone, *Narrative of an Expedition to the Zambesi and Its Tributaries, 1858–1864* (New York: Harper and Bros., 1866), pp. 481–83.

71. Walter Fairservis, *The Ancient Kingdoms of the Nile* (New York: Mentor, 1962), pp. 206–7.

72. See R. W. Beachey, *The Slave trade of Eastern Africa* (London: Rex Collins, 1976), pp. 169–74 and Fisher and Fisher, *Slavery and Muslim Society in Africa*, pp. 171–77.

73. Fisher and Fisher, *Slavery and Muslim Society in Africa*, pp. 91–98.

74. Beachey, *Slave Trade of Eastern Africa*, pp. 60–61.

75. Beachey, *The Slave Trade of Eastern Africa*, pp. 8–11, 17–23, 38–40, 89–92, 121–26. Jerome Dowd made the comparison between buying a slave and a horse and concluded "the sight was sickening." "Slavery and the Slave Trade in Africa," *Journal of Negro History*, II (January 1917), p. 18.

76. Laffin, *Arabs as Master Slavers*, pp. 21–30. See also Dr. Herinrich Brode, *Tippoo Tib: The Story of His Career in Central Africa*, tr. H. Havelock (London: Edward Arnold, 1907).

77. Frederick Cooper, *Plantation Slavery on the East Coast of Africa* (New Haven, CT: Yale University Press, 1977), pp. 33–38.

78. Laffin, *Arabs as Master Slavers*, p. 34. Beachey estimates that as many as 2 million blacks were taken in the nineteenth century alone. *Slave Trade of Eastern Africa*, p. 262.

79. Jonathan Derrick, *Africa's Slaves Today* (New York: Schocken Press, 1975), p. 32–63.

80. Jerusalem *Post*, January 20, 1976, p. 1.

81. Laffin, *Arabs as Master Slavers*, p. 18.

82. *Ibid.*, p. 56.

83. Andrea Rosenberg, "The Middle East Slave Trade," *Middle East Review* (Winter 1976/77), IX, pp. 58–62.

84. *Newsweek* (May 4, 1992), CXIX, pp. 32ff.

85. Laffin, *Arabs as Master Slavers*, p. 7.

86. *Ibid.*, p. 113.

87. A sampling of twentieth-century reports on slavery in the Middle East and Africa might include "Slavery in Africa," *Living Age*, CCCXVIII (September 22, 1923), p. 531; H. Rising, "Slavery Today: Status of Slavery in Abyssinia and Arabia," *Christian Century* XLIX (May 18, 1932), p. 643; G. Maxwell, "Slavery in Muhammadan Countries," *Contemporary Review* CLIV (July 1938), pp. 44–51; "J. L. Carver, "Slavery's Last Stronghold [Arabia], *U.N. World*, II

(June 7,1948), pp. 24–27; R. Alan, "Half a Million slaves in Arabia," *Reporter* XIV (April 19,1956), pp. 33–36; C. K. Yearley, Part Slave, Part Free: Arabia," *Commonweal* LXVIII (June 27, 1958), pp. 322–25; R. L. Tobin, "Slavery Still Plagues the Earth," *Saturday Review*, L (May 6, 1967), pp. 24ff; D. A. Offiong, "The Status of Slaves in Ingbo and Ibibio of Nigeria," *Phylon* XLVI (March,1985), pp. 49–57; and "Report on the Abolition in Mauretania," *U.N. Monthly Chronicle* XXII (March, 1985), p. 50.

Notes to Chapter 17

1. James Yaffe, *The American Jews* (New York: Random House, 1968), pp. 256–57.
2. Rosenwald supplied all but $600,000 of the first $4 million toward 10,000 such schools which proved to be "centers of community pride" in Texas, Louisiana, Mississippi, Arkansas, and Tennessee. T. W. Hantchett, "The Rosenwald Schools and Black Education in North Carolina," *North Carolina Historical Review* (October 1988), LXV, pp. 387–44. See also David L. Lewis, "Parallels and Divergences: Assimilationist Strategies of Afro-American and Jewish Elites from 1910 to the Early 1930s," in *Bridges and Boundaries*, pp. 17–35.
3. Dinnerstein, *Uneasy at Home*, p. 95.
4. N. Samuel Murrell, "What Ever Happened to the Black-Jewish Accord," Third Biennial Conference on Christianity and the Holocaust," Princeton/Rider College (March 7, 1994) See also the dismaying history of Stokely Carmichael and SNCC as recounted by Clayborne Carso, "Blacks and Jews in the Civil Rights Movement: The Case of SNCC," in *Bridges and Boundaries*, pp. 36–49.
5. Brenner, *Jews in America Today*, p. 227. Some militants like Leroi Jones dismissed Jewish volunteers as "artifacts" or "pictures on a wall. " See Harold Cruse, "Negroes and Jews—The Two Nationalisms and the Blocked Plurality," in *Bridges and Boundaries*, p. 124.
6. Freedom Seder Haggadah, compiled by Amy Ackerson, University of Maryland, Baltimore County, April 5, 1994, p. 19.
7. Forty-seven percent of whites surveyed and 66 percent of Hispanics maintained Jews wielded too much influence. Carolyn Settow and Renae Cohen, "New York Intergroup Relations Survey" (New York: American Jewish Committee, 1993).
8. Supposedly, there has been a decline over the past three decades. See "Highlights from an ADL Survey on Anti-Semitism and Prejudice in America," (New York: ADL, 1992).
9. *Time,* February, 28, 1994, p. 22. Eighty percent of African-Americans also believed whites had too much power and 26 percent thought Catholics had too much power.
10. Robert Schmuhl, "Past Accord and Present Dissonance," *Society*, XXXI (September-October, 1994), no. 6, p. 45.
11. Samuel Klausner, "The Religious 'Other' in Black/Jewish Relatiions," *Society, op. cit.,* p. 52.
12. Jacob Neusner, "Dissent from the Right," *Society*, p. 28. Harold Cruse also rejects the notion that Jews were the best friends of blacks as myth. "Negroes and Jews—the Two Nationalisms and the Blocked Plurality," in *Bridges and Boundaries,* p. 118.
13. Rieder, "Reflections on Crown Heights: Interpretive Dilemmas and Black-Jewish Conflict," in *Antisemitism in America Today,* Jerome Chanes (ed.) (New York: Carol Publ., 1995), p. 351.

14. Leon Wieseltier, "Taking Yes for an Answer," in *Blacks and Jews: Alliances and Arguments*, Paul Berman (ed.) (New York: Delacorte, 1994), p. 257.
15. Shelby Steele, "Breaking Our Bond of Shame," in Berman, *Blacks and Jews*, pp. 179–80.
16. D. Reddick, "Anti-Semitism among Negroes," *Negro Quarterly* I (Summer 1942) in *Bridges and Boundaries*, pp. 79–85.
17. Kenneth Clark, "Candor about Negro-Jewish Relations," *Commentary* (January 1946) in *Bridges and Boundaries*, pp. 91–98.
18. Paul Berman, "The Other and the Almost the Same," *Society* (Sept. /Oct. 1994), p. 5.
19. *Ibid.*, pp. 15 and 13. Berman ends his article optimistically, calling the collapse of communist totalitarianism in 1989–90 liberalism's greatest triumph.
20. Murray Friedman, *What Went Wrong? The Creation and Collapse of the Black Jewish Alliance* (New York: Free Press, 1995), pp. 344–45.
21. Cornel West,"On Black-Jewish Relatiions," in Berman, *Blacks and Jews*, pp. 150–51.
22. Henry L. Gates, "The Uses of Anti-Semitism," in Berman, *Blacks and Jews*, p. 222.
23. Gordon Allport, *The Nature of Prejudice* (New York: Addison-Wesley, 1954), pp. 221–30.
24. *Ibid.*, pp. 343–71.
25. Arnold Forster and Benjamin Epstein, *The New Anti-Semitism* (New York: McGraw-Hill, 1974), p. 178.
26. *Ibid.*, p. 177.
27. *Ibid.*, p. 51.
28. ABC News, December 1, 1996.
29. See Midge Decter's excellent article, "How the Rioters Won" in Theodore Rueter, *The Politics of Race: African-Americans and the Political System* (Armonk, NY: M. E. Sharpe, 1995), pp. 343–52.
30. Ginsberg, *Fatal Embrace*, p. 147, and West, "On Black-Jewish Relations," p. 150.
31. See Handlin, *Boston's Immigrants: A Study in Acculturation* (Cambridge, MA: Harvard University Press, 1959), pp. 132–33 and Nathan Glazer, "Negroes and Jews: The New Challenge to Pluralism," *Commentary* (Dec. 1964) reprinted in *Bridges and Boundaries: African Americans and American Jews*, Jack Salzman, Adina Back, and Gretchen Sorin (eds.) (New York: George Braziller, 1992), p. 100. Glazer claims that Jews never hated blacks as the Irish did. Jewish ethnocentrism was a defensive reaction toward all others. Robert Weisbord and Arthur Stein have noted,"On the whole their (Jewish) record was superior to some immigrant communities. "*Bittersweet Encounters*, pp. 25–26.
32. Taylor Branch analyzes the movement of Jews from Chicago neighborhoods in "Blacks and Jews: The Uncivil War," in *Bridges and Boundaries*, pp. 54–55. Benjamin Ginsberg suggests one reason is that Jews are more easilly intimidated than the Irish or Italians. *The Fatal Embrace: Jews and the State* (Chicago: University of Chicago Press, 1993), p. 154.
33. Baldwin, "Negroes Are Anti-Semitic Because They're Anti-White," p. 31. As a social worker in the inner city of Columbus, Ohio between 1962 and 1964, I witnessed the exploitation of tenants in slum dwelllings some of which were owned by Jewish landlords.
34. Friedman, *What Went Wrong*, pp. 214–15.
35. Baldwin, "Negroes Are Anti-Semitic Because They're Anti-White," p. 31.
36. Rieder, "Reflections on Crown Heights," p. 350. For an evaluation of the Hough riots in Cleveland, see Saul Friedman, "Riots, Violence, and Civil Rights," *National Review* (August, 1967).

37. Yaffe, *American Jews*, p. 264.

38. Forster and Epstein, *New Anti-Semitism*, p. 61.

39. Baldwin, "Negroes Are Anti-Semitic Because They're Anti-White," p. 39. Between 1964 and 1966, I was the only white probation officer in a federally funded Community Action for Youth program in Cleveland's Hough District. The man who hired me was black. My supervisor was black. All of my co-workers were black. So were the secretaries and head of research, community outreach staff, those who worked in the homemakers unit and scouting. At no time did I experience a feeling of resentment from my peers, clients or people in the community.

40. Forster and Epstein, *New Anti-Semitism*, p. 180. Ginsberg points out this was tactic proved very effective in Ocean Hill/Brownsville where Mayor John Lindsay and McGeorge Bundy of the Ford Foundation favored turning local control over to blacks. *Fatal Embrace*, p. 154.

41. Yaffe, *American Jews*, p. 263. See also Marcia Synnott, "Anti-Semitism and American Universities: Did Quotas Follow the Jews" in David Gerber (ed.) *Anti-Semitism in American History* (University of Illinois Press, 1987), pp. 233–71.

42. West,"On Black-Jewish Relations," p. 147.

43. Rieder, "Reflections on Crown Heights," p. 351.

44. Steven Cohen, *The Dimensions of Jewish Liberalism* (New York: American Jewish Committee, 1989).

45. Adolph Reed, "False Prophet: The Rise of Louis Farrakhan," in Rueter, *Politics of Race*, pp. 77–84.

46. Because blacks have been politically and economically impotent, Wilkinson denies the existence of an authentic and consistent anti-Semitism among blacks. "Anti-Semitism and African Americans," *Society*, p. 49.

47. For a general view of anti-Semitic canards in America , see Charles Glock and Rodney Stark, *Christian Beliefs and Anti-Semitism* (New York: Harper and Row, 1966), pp. 107–47.

48. Berman, "The Other and the Almost the Same," p. 10. Chancellor Williams regards the presence of millions of mulattoes and "jet-black" Muslims in Middle Eastern nations as an unforseen product of the expansive Arab slave trade. Blacks who occupied the lowest levels of American society could now identify with their kinsmen who were esteemed in Muslim society. *The Destructiion of Black Civilization*, p. 357.

49. Burundi, Chad, Congo, Dahomey, Equitorial Guinea, Gambia, Guinea, Guinea-Bissau, Mali, Mauretania, Mozambique, Niger, Nigeria, Rwanda, Sao Tome e Principe, Senegal, Somalia, Sudan, Tanzania, and Uganda (most of which were military dictatorships or one-party authoritarian regimes voted for the resolution. Most reversed themselves when the General Assembly rescinded the resolution in December 1991. Five African states should be mentioned for their consistency in opposing the Zionism=racism resolution. They included Ivory Coast, Malawi, Central African Republic, Liberia, and Swaziland. In recent dialogues with Michael Lerner, Cornel West opined that many blacks were disturbed by Zionism as expressed by "the Kahanes" and wondered whether a nation-state was the best way of achieving Jewish identity and security. See "A Conversation between Cornel West and Michael Lerner," in *Bridges and Boundaries*, pp. 143 and 148.

50. The Surahs of the Cow (2:42, 53, 65, 74, 89, 95, 102, 104, 109, 275), Imrams (3:55, 75, 79), Women (4:46, 55, 157, 160), Table (5:13, 51, 71, 82), Heights (7:168), Repentance (9:30), She who Pleaded (58:14–19), Day of Congrega-

tion (62:6), and Proof (98:7) all contain references that may interpreted against Jews in a spurious fashion.

51. See D. F. Green, ed. *Arab Theologians on Jews and Israel*, Fourth Conference of the Academy of Islamic Research, al-Azhar, Cairo (Geneva: Editions de l'Avenir, 1971) and *Islam and Revolution: Writings and Declarations of Imam Khomeini*, tr. Hamid Algar (London: Kegan Paul 1985). Those who still subscribe to the notion of a Semitic entente in the Middle East before the rise of modern Zionism should consult the following works: Dafna Alon, *Arab Racialism* (Jerusalem: Israel Economist, 1969); Bat Ye'or, *The Dhimmi: Jews and Christians under Islam*, tr. David Maisel, Paul Fenton, and David Littman (Rutherford, NJ: Farleigh Dickinson Press, 1985); Itzhak Ben Zvi, *The Exiled and the Redeemed* (Philadelphia, PA: Jewish Publicatiion Society, 1957); Andrei Chouraqui, *Between East and West: A History of the Jews of North Africa*, tr. Michael Bernet (New York: Atheneum 1973); Hayyim Cohen, *The Jews of the Middle East 1860–1972* (Jerusalem: Israel Universities Press, 1973); Renzo De Felice, *Jews in an Arab Land*, tr. Judith Roumani (Austin: University of Texas, 1985); Walter Fischel, *Jews in the Economic and Political Life of Medieval Islam* (New York: Ktav, 1969); Saul Friedman, *Without Future: The Plight of Syrian Jewry* (Westport, CT: Praeger, 1989); S. D. Goitein, *Jews and Arabs: Their Contacts through the Ages* (New York: Schocken, 1974); Davora and Menachem Hacohen, *One People: The Story of Eastern Jews* (New York: Funk and Wagnalls, 1969); Bernard Lewis, *The Jews of Islam* (Princeton, NJ: Princeton University Press, 1984) and *Semites and Anti-Semites* (New York: Norton, 1986); David Littman and Bat Ye'or, *Protected Peoples under Islam* (Geneva: Centre d'Information et de Documentation sur le Moyen-Orient, 1976); J. Mann, *The Jews in Egypt and Palestine during the Fatimid Caliphate* (Oxford: Oxford University Press, 1920); David Margoliouth, *The Relations between Arabs and Israelites prior to the Rise of Islam* (London: Oxford University Press, 1924); Albert Memmi, *Jews and Arabs*, tr. Eleanor Levieux (Chicago: O'Hara, 1975); Joan Peters, *From Time Immemorial* (New York: Harper and Row, 1984); Nissam Rejwan, *The Jews of Iraq: 3000 Years of History and Culture* (Boulder, CO: Westview Press, 1985); Cecil Roth, "Jews in the Arab World," *Near East Report: Myths and Facts*, Special Survey (August 1967), pp. 17–20; Maurice Roumani, *The Case of the Jews from Arab Countries: A Neglected Issue* (Tel Aviv: World Organization of Jews froom Arab Countries, 1977); Joseph Schechtman, *On Wings of Eagles: The Plight, Exodus, and Homecoming of Oriental Jews* (New York: T. Yoseloff, 1961); Aryeh Shmuelevitz, *The Jews of the Ottoman Empire in the Late Fifteenth and Sixteenth Centuries* (Leiden: Brill, 1984); Norman Stillman, *The Jews of Arab Lands: A History and Source Book* (Philadelphia, PA: Jewish Publication Society, 1979) and *The Jews of Arab Lands in Modern Times* (Philadelphia, PA: Jewish Publication Society, 1991); Arthur Tritton, *The Caliphs and Their Non-Muslim Subjects: A Critical Study of the Covenant of Umar* (London: F. Cass, 1970).

52. Forster and Epstein, *Cross Currents* (Garden City, NY: Doubleday, 1956), pp. 371–76.

54. Peter Goldman, *The Death and Life of Malcolm X* (University of Illinois, 1979), p. 14.

53. Forster and Epstein, *New Anti-Semitism*, p. 211.

55. Mattias, Gardell, "The Sun of Islam Will Rise in the West," *Muslim Communities in North America*, Yvonne Haddad and Jane Smith, (eds.) (Albany: SUNY Press, 1994), pp. 27–31.

56. *Ibid.*, p. 39.

57. Rieder, "Reflections on Crown Heights," pp. 356–67.
58. Friedman, *What Went Wrong*, p. 333.
59. Schmuhl, "Past Accord and Present Dissonance," pp. 42 and 44.
60. Gardell, "The Sun of Islam," p. 35.
61. *Ibid.*, p. 38.
62. *Ibid.*, p. 38.
63. Jeffrey Ross and Melanie Schneider point out that Holocaust deniers have no base on campus but black extremists often dominate fraternities and black student unions. "Such organizations have access to student programming funds and have the power to set an agenda through their choice of speakers. In this manner they provide the Farrakhans, Muhammads, Toures, and others with a national program." See Ross and Schneider, "Antisemitism on the Campus: Challenge and Response," p. 276 in Chanes, *Antisemitism in America Today*.
64. Gary Rubin, "How Should We Think about Black Antisemitism?" in Chanes, *Antisemitism in America Today*, p. 162.
65. Gates, "Uses of Anti-Semitism," p. 221.
66. Neusner, "Dissent from the Right," p. 31.
67. *Ibid.*, p. 29.
68. "Taking Offense, "*Newsweek*, CXVI (December 24, 1990), pp. 48–54.
69. Ozick, "Afterword 1993," in Berman, *Blacks and Jews*, p. 70.
70. Malcolm Hay, *The Roots of Christian Anti-Semitism* (New York: Freedom Library Reprint, 1981), p. 187.
71. Schmuhl, "Past Accord and Present Dissonance," p. 46.
72. Gates, "Uses of Anti-Semitism," p. 219.
73. Rubin, "How Should We Think about Black Antisemitism?" p. 154.
74. Manning, *Slavery and African Life*, p. 176.
75. *Ibid.*, p. 176.

Index

Africa, and slavery, 221–34, 311–316n; East Africa, 10–11, 230–32; West Africa, 47–49; North Africa, 48, 233; Sub-Saharan, 9, 47. *See also:* individual nations and American states.
Afrocentrism, 19, 20, 23, 221–22, 229, 311n.
Agaja, king of Dahomey, 224
Alabama, 188–89, 191–2, 207, 219, 303–309n
Algeria, 233
Allport, Gordon, 241–242
Amherst, Lord Jeffrey, 6–7, 257n
Amsterdam, 42
Angola, 9, 49, 130
Anna Pepple, king of Nigeria, 224
Anti-Defamation League, xi, 237, 240, 242, 252
Arabs: and slave trade, 9, 10, 11, 14, 17, 18, 47–48, 224, 227–234; and Israel, 247–252, 314–316n. *See also:* Islam.
Aristotle, 17
Arkansas, 193–194, 225
Asiento, 49, 89, 130
Atlanta, xii–xiii, 170–173

Babylonia, 24–25
Baldwin, James, 244–45, 266n
Balsdon, J.P.V.D., 27, 30, 263n.
Bancroft, Frederic, 13, 158, 159, 203, 218
Barnett, Maurice, 181–182
Barbados, 14, 95–100, 218
Baron, Salo, 39, 40, 45, 57
Beachey, R.W., 230
Benjamin, Judah, 33, 180–182, 210, 211, 216, 218, 300–301n
Benin, 217, 223, 229
Bennett, Lerone, 223, 260n
Berman, Myron, 137, 140, 216
Berman, Paul, 240–241, 246–247, 266n
Bethell, Leslie, 204–205

Beyan, Amos, 15
Bible: *See:* Canaan and Old Testament
Birmingham, Stephen, 59, 127, 301n
Blacks: scholarship on slavery 8–14; black slaveholders, 112, 185–186, 193, 225–227, 303n, 313n; folklore on Jews, 204; African kingdoms, 223–225; civil rights movement, 235–38; recent relations with Jews, 235–252, 316–330n. *See also:* Africa, Afrocentrism, Islam, European nations and American states
Bloom, Herbert, 60, 65
Boston, 117–118
Bournu, 230
Boxer, C.R., 57, 60, 270n.
Brackman, Harold, xi, 253
Brandeis, Louis, 235
Brazil: Portuguese control, 58–59; Dutch control, 60–61; illegal slave trade, 204–5; mentioned, 4, 10, 30, 33, 94, 218, 225, 269–270n.
Breasted, James Henry, 21–22
Breibart, Sol, xii
Brenner, Lenni, 5
Bristol, 91, 92, 94, 218
British: see Great Britain
Broussard, Sharon, 234

Cameroons, 228, 233
Canaan: curse of, 33, 39, 140–144, 228, 264n, 313n
Carver, George Washington, 237
Catholic Church: and slavery, 30–31, 36–37, 48–49. *See also:* Christianity
Cato, 28–29, 189
Chamberlain, Houston Stewart, 38
Charles II, 95, 99, 155
Charra, 224
Charleston, xii–xiii, 13, 33, 122, 145–160, 200, 202, 210, 218, 219, 226. *See also:* South Carolina